CANADA

TOP SIGHTS

THIS EDITION WRITTEN AND RESEARCHED BY

Korina Miller, Kate Armstrong, James Bainbridge,
Adam Karlin, John Lee, Carolyn McCarthy, Phillip Tang,
Ryan Ver Berkmoes and Benedict Walker

Contents

Plan Your Trip

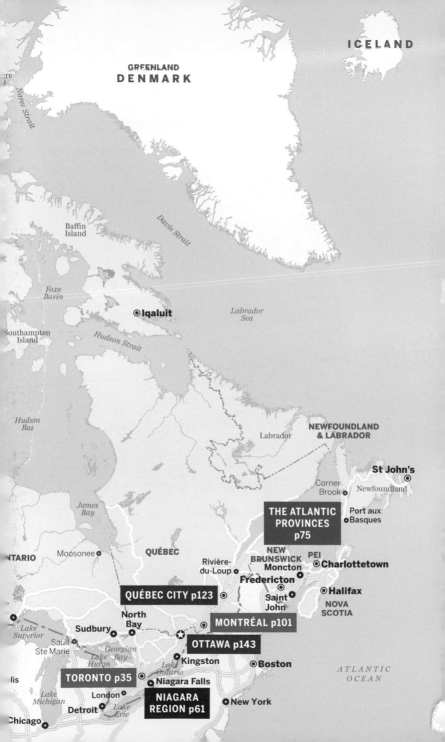

ICELAND

GREENLAND
DENMARK

Narés Strait

Davis Strait

Baffin
Island

*Foxe
Basin*

*Labrador
Sea*

Southampton
Island

◉Iqaluit

Hudson Strait

*Hudson
Bay*

Labrador

NEWFOUNDLAND
& LABRADOR

*James
Bay*

St John's ◉

Corner
Brook ◉

Newfoundland

Moosonee ◉

QUÉBEC

Port aux
◉Basques

ONTARIO

Rivière-
du-Loup ◉

NEW
BRUNSWICK
Moncton ◉

PEI

◉Charlottetown

Fredericton ◉

◉

Saint
John ◉

◉Halifax

NOVA
SCOTIA

North
Bay

◉

*Lake
Superior*

Sudbury ◉

⋆

Georgian
Bay

Sault
Ste Marie ◉

*Lake
Huron*

Kingston ◉

◉Boston

*ATLANTIC
OCEAN*

lis

*Lake
Ontario*

London ◉

◉Niagara Falls

◉

*Lake
Michigan*

Detroit ◉

*Lake
Erie*

◉New York

Chicago ◉

Welcome to Canada

Canada is more than its hulking-mountain, craggy-coast good looks: it also cooks extraordinary meals, rocks cool culture and unfurls wild, moose-spotting road trips.

The globe's second-biggest country has an endless variety of landscapes, from sky-high mountains and glinting glaciers to spectral rainforests and remote beaches, along with a big cast of local characters including grizzly bears, whales and moose. The terrain makes for a fantastic playground – whether it's snowboarding, surfing, kayaking, strolling Vancouver's Stanley Park or swimming off Prince Edward Island's pink-sand beaches.

Culturally, Canada is a mixed bag. You'll hear it in the wild-fiddling Celtic music, see it in the rainforest-cloaked Aboriginal villages on Haida Gwaii, and taste it in Vancouver's Asian dining scene.

Indeed, Canadian cuisine is another landscape to explore. If you grazed from west to east, you'd fill your plate with wild salmon, velvety scallops, and a bounty of cherries and peaches in British Columbia; poutine (golden fries topped with gravy and cheese curds) in Québec; and lobster with a dab of melted butter in the Atlantic provinces – all washed down with award-winning crisp whites and bold reds produced from the country's vine-striped valleys.

With all of this, you might be surprised to hear that Canada has world-class museums, too. Cultural hubs such as the new National Music Centre or Museum of Immigration at Pier 21 will leave you wowed, while the National Gallery of Canada gives you a taste of just how artistic these Canucks really are. It's true. Canada's got it all going on.

From sky-high mountains and glinting glaciers to spectral rainforests and remote beaches...

Icefields Parkway (p188), the Rockies
MICHAEL WHEATLEY / GETTY IMAGES ©

Toronto (p35)
D3SIGN / MOMENT RF / GETTY IMAGES ©

Plan Your Trip
Canada's Top 12

Toronto
A hyperactive stew of cultures and neighborhoods

Far and away Canada's largest city, as well as its most diverse – about half of its residents were born in another country – at every turn, Toronto (p35) strikes you with sheer urban awe. This fascinating metropolis mixes five-star fusion meals with peameal bacon sandwiches, designer shoes from Bloor-Yorkville with tattoos from Queen West, and then, for good measure, throws in rockin' band rooms, hockey mania, mod-art galleries and theater par excellence.

JUSTIN FOULKES / LONELY PLANET ©

PETE SEAWARD/LONELY PLANET ©

The Rockies

Sawtooth white-topped mountain wonderland

Straddling the British Columbia–Alberta border, the Rockies (p183) inspire both awe and action. Four national parks – Banff (pictured top), Yoho, Kootenay and Jasper – offer countless opportunities to delve into the wilderness with ribbons of hiking trails, rushing white water and powdery ski slopes. Or, for a more sedate way to experience the grandeur of luminous lakes, wildflower meadows and glistening glaciers, take the train (pictured above) and glide on by.

Vancouver

Harmonic convergence of city and nature

With skiable mountains on the outskirts, 11 beaches fringing the
core and Stanley Park's thick rainforest just blocks from the glass
skyscrapers downtown, Vancouver (p201) is a heady, bewitching
brew. Throw in Hollywood chic (many movies are filmed here), a
freewheeling counterculture and buzzing multicultural communities, and you have a city that keeps on landing atop worldwide 'best
places to live' lists. Above: Totem pole, Stanley Park (p204)

4

Vancouver Island

Beautiful buildings, fabulous food and superb scenery

C'mon, can a place really 'have it all'? Yes, if it's Vancouver Island (p229). Picture-postcard Victoria is the island's heart, beating with bohemian shops, bespoke coffee bars and a tea-soaked English past. Brooding Pacific Rim National Park Reserve sports the West Coast Trail, where a wind-bashed ocean meets a mist-shrouded wilderness, and surfers line up for Tofino's waves.

Right: Tofino (p234)

5

Montréal

Gallic elegance meets Canadian cool

Nowhere blends French-inspired joie de vivre and cosmopolitan culture quite like Montréal (p101), Canada's second-largest city and its cultural heart. An indie rock explosion, a flourishing arts scene, a medley of world-renowned boutique hotels, the Plateau's swank cache of eateries, and a cool Parisian vibe that pervades every *terrasse* (patio) in the Quartier Latin drive the playful scene. Monster festivals add a high note, and good times roll 24/7.

The Atlantic Provinces

Sandy shores with music on the breeze

At first glance, the Atlantic provinces (p75) appear as sweet as a
storybook, with paint-box-colored buildings and picture-perfect
lighthouses. But this is also the raw Canada, of fisherfolk braving
icy seas, of coal miners, moose and hockey. Celtic and Acadian
communities dot the landscape, and their upbeat-fiddlin' music
vibrates through local pubs. Slap on a bib for a lobster dinner and
keep your eyes on the coastline for breaching whales.

Québec City

Time to get lost in an atmospheric time capsule

Québec's capital (p123) is more than 400 years old, and its stone walls, glinting-spired cathedrals and jazz-soaked corner cafes suffuse it with romance, melancholy, eccentricity and intrigue on par with any European city. The best way to soak it up is to walk the Old Town's labyrinth of lanes and get lost amid the street performers and cozy inns, stopping every so often to refuel with a *café au lait* and flaky pastry.

Ottawa

Culture, architecture, art and ice-skating

There's no time to waste in Ottawa (p143), Canada's culture-rich capital. From the uber-mod, curved-walled Canadian Museum of History to the gothic-arched Canadian Museum of Nature and the glass-spired National Gallery of Canada, each attraction is an inspired architectural gesture with an intriguing exhibition space. In winter the Rideau Canal becomes the world's longest skating rink, where people swoosh by, pausing to purchase steaming hot chocolate and scrumptious slabs of fried dough known as beavertails.

ROAD TRIP RIP / 500PX ©

Haida Gwaii

Primeval forest and a resurgent indigenous community

Once known as the Queen Charlotte Islands, this dagger-shaped archipelago (p243) 80km off British Columbia's coast is a magical trip for those who make it. Colossal spruce and cedars cloak the wild, rain-sodden landscape. Bald eagles and bears roam the ancient forest. But the islands' real soul is the Haida people, best known for their war-canoe and totem-pole carvings. See the lot at Gwaii Haanas National Park Reserve, which combines lost villages, burial caves and hot springs with some of the continent's best kayaking.

STEFANO SALVETTI / GETTY IMAGES ©

DAWSON CITY GENERAL STORE LTD.

FRESH MEATS   GROCERIES & SUPPLIES   FRESH PRODUCE

MILES ERTMAN / GETTY IMAGES ©

The Yukon

Search for gold dust and epic adventures

The far-flung Yukon (p253) is home to Canada's tallest mountains, largest ice fields and sweetest end-of-the-road towns. It once drew thousands in the search for gold, but today, instead of miners after the shiny stuff, the region attracts artists, rugged individualists and outdoor enthusiasts. Give gold panning a go, try your hand at poker, hop in a canoe for an hour or a week, then sit back and marvel at the mesmerizing Northern Lights. Magic.

The Prairies

Solitude reigns in Canada's middle ground

Driving through the flatlands (p161) turns up uninterrupted fields of golden wheat that stretch to the horizon. When the wind blows, the wheat sways like waves on the ocean, punctuated by the occasional grain elevator rising up like a tall ship, and when big storms come they are visible on the skyline for kilometers.

Niagara Region

A world-renowned waterfall and a vineyard (or 10)

It may not be among the world's tallest waterfalls, but when those great bands of water arc over the precipice like liquid glass, roaring into the void below, Niagara Falls impresses big time. Nowhere in North America beats its thundering cascade, with more than a million bathtubs of water plummeting over the edge every second. Beyond it stretches a region (p61) speckled with vineyards and home to one of the country's best-preserved 19th-century towns.

Plan Your Trip
Need to Know

When to Go

- Dry climate
- Warm to hot summers, mild winters
- Summers – mild to warm (north & east) & warm to hot (south), cold winters
- Polar climate

Churchill
GO Sep–Nov

Banff
GO Jul–Sep

Vancouver
GO Jun–Aug

Montréal
GO Jun–Aug

Halifax
GO Jul–Sep

High Season (Jun–Aug)

○ Sunshine and warm weather prevail; far northern regions briefly thaw.

○ Accommodation prices peak (up 30% on average).

○ December through March is equally busy and expensive in ski resort towns.

Shoulder (May, Sep & Oct)

○ Crowds and prices drop off; attractions keep shorter hours.

○ Temperatures are cool but comfortable.

○ Fall foliage areas remain busy.

Low Season (Nov–Apr)

○ Places outside the big cities and ski resorts close.

○ Darkness and cold take over.

Currency
Canadian dollar ($)

Languages
English, French

Visas
Visitors from certain countries require a visa to enter Canada. Those who are exempt require an Electronic Travel Authorization, with the exception of Americans. This must be applied for prior to traveling and can be completed online; see www.cic.gc.ca/english/visit/eta-start.asp.

Money
ATMs widely available. Credit cards accepted in most hotels and restaurants.

Cell Phones
Local SIM cards can be used in unlocked GSM 850/1900 compatible phones. Other phones must be set to roaming.

Time
Canada spans six of the world's 24 time zones. The time difference from coast to coast is 4½ hours.

Daily Costs

Budget: Less than $100

- Dorm bed: $25–40
- Campsite: $25–35
- Self-catered meals: $8–12

Midrange: $100–250

- B&B or room in a midrange hotel: $80–180 ($100–250 in major cities)
- Meal in a good restaurant: from $20
- Rental car: $35–65 per day

Top End: More than $250

- Four-star hotel room: from $180 (from $250 in major cities)
- Three-course meal in a top restaurant: from $50 plus drinks
- Skiing day pass: $50–80

Useful Websites

Destination Canada (www.destination canada.com) Official tourism site.

Environment Canada Weather (www. weather.gc.ca) Forecasts for any town.

Lonely Planet (www.lonelyplanet.com/canada) Destination information, hotel bookings, traveler forum and more.

Government of Canada (www.gc.ca) National and regional information.

Opening Hours

These are high-season hours; hours generally decrease in the shoulder and low seasons.

Banks 10am–5pm Monday to Friday; some open 9am–noon Saturday

Bars 5pm–2am daily

Clubs 9pm–2am Wednesday to Saturday

Restaurants breakfast 8–11am, lunch 11:30am–2:30pm Monday to Friday, dinner 5–9:30pm daily; some open for brunch 8am–1pm Saturday and Sunday

Shops 10am–6pm Monday to Saturday, noon–5pm Sunday; some open to 8pm or 9pm Thursday and/or Friday

Supermarkets 9am–8pm; some open 24 hours

Arriving in Canada

Toronto Pearson International Airport Trains ($12) run downtown every 15 minutes from 5.30am to 1am; taxis cost around $60 (45 minutes).

Montréal Trudeau International Airport A 24-hour public bus ($10) runs downtown. Taxis cost a flat $40 (30 to 60 minutes).

Vancouver International Airport Trains ($7.50 to $9) run downtown every six to 20 minutes; taxis cost around $40 (30 minutes).

Land Border Crossings The Canadian Border Services Agency posts wait times (usually 30 minutes).

Getting Around

Car An extensive highway system links most towns. The Trans-Canada Hwy stretches from Newfoundland to Vancouver Island. Away from the population centers, distances can be deceivingly long and travel times slow due to single-lane highways.

Train Outside the Toronto–Montréal corridor, train travel is mostly for scenic journeys.

Ferry Public ferry systems operate extensively in British Columbia, Québec and the Atlantic provinces.

Air Regional and national carriers crisscross the country, and reach northern towns inaccessible by road.

For more on getting around, see p305 ➡

Plan Your Trip
Hot Spots for...

Adrenaline Activities

The wilderness here is not just about good looks. Locals have been jumping in head first – sometimes literally – for decades.

Seafood

With the Pacific, the Atlantic and plenty of lakes strung in between, seafood lovers are never far from a mouthwatering feast.

Cultural Museums

Canada's cultural legacy is served up in some fantastic museums filled with interactive exhibits.

Markets

Summer or winter, you'll find markets to meander. This is where you'll get an eyeful (and often a belly full) of Canadian culture, along with some fabulous deals.

Whistler (p198) If you want to ski or snowboard Canada's best, Whistler reigns supreme, with 37 lifts and over 200 runs.

Check into an excellent ski school for newbies on the slopes.

Tofino (p234) Little Tofino packs big adventure with its Pacific coast surfing, kayaking, hiking and storm watching.

Learn how to catch a wave on Tofino's spectacular local beaches.

Banff (p190) Queen of the Rockies, Banff has it all: skiing, hiking, rafting, horseback riding, mountain biking...phew!

Reach soaring heights with short jaunts even for beginner hikers.

PEI's Lobster (p92) Lobsters don't come fresher than this. Gear-up with your bib, pick and lobster fork and forget about getting butter in your hair.

Water Prince Corner Shop & Lobster Pound (p92) is the best place in town for lobster.

Vancouver Island's Bounty (p237) From mussels, clams and crabs to hickory-smoked salmon, local menus are peppered with fresh seafood.

Bistro 694 (p241) has a strong focus on using local ingredients.

Jasper's Lake Trout (p196) Being 1600km from the sea makes it an unlikely local, but the area's lake trout will keep any seafood cravings well satisfied.

Fiddle River Seafood Co (p197) creates inventive, fish dishes.

National Music Centre (p166) Live out your rock-and-roll fantasies at Calgary's newest and coolest museum. Full of entertaining history and fab hands-on exhibits.

Test your skill at the drums, electric guitar or in a sound-recording room.

Ukrainian Cultural Village (p168) Explore the cultures of early Ukrainian pioneers in an open-air museum.

Make your experience complete by enjoying authentic Ukrainian food.

Canadian Museum of Immigration at Pier 21 (p84) Brilliant exhibits about some of the million-plus immigrants who passed through Halifax between 1928 and 1971.

Listen to the audio testimonies for firsthand experiences. Bring tissues.

St Lawrence Market (p43) Butchers, bakers and pasta-makers fill Toronto's awesome 1845 market hall. Art and antiques, too.

Try the peameal bacon sandwiches at the Carousel Bakery (p43).

Granville Island Public Market (p206) Granville Island's highlight is the covered Public Market, a multisensory smorgasbord of fish, cheese, fruit and bakery treats.

Pick up picnic treats at Vanier Park or hit the international food court.

Marché Jean-Talon (p111) Farmers from the countryside bring their fruits, veggies, cheeses and sausages to Montréal's lively marketplace.

Visit the Marché des Saveurs for local cider and smoked meats.

Plan Your Trip
Local Life

BONCHAN / SHUTTERSTOCK ©

Activities

While the great Canadian outdoors is undeniably postcard pretty, the wilderness here has more than good looks, with activities ranging from hiking and kayaking to cycling and snowboarding. For the daring, there's ice-climbing and caving, and for those after something a little quieter, strap on some snowshoes or hop in a canoe.

Hockey is a national pastime and if you'd rather watch than play, Vancouver, Edmonton, Calgary, Toronto, Ottawa, Winnipeg and Montréal all have NHL (www.nhl.com) teams who skate tough and lose the odd tooth.

Shopping

Streets such as Robson in Vancouver and Yonge in Toronto are Canada's retail meccas, with plenty of high-end shops. For something more authentically Canadian beyond the typical maple syrup or vacuum-packed smoked salmon, check out aboriginal art shops and the many markets that highlight summer weekends and have work from local potters, jewelry makers and other artists. The nation's major museums often have fabulous gift shops with quality, locally inspired products.

Eating

Canadian cuisine is nothing if not eclectic, a casserole of food cultures blended together from centuries of immigration. Poutine (golden fries topped with gravy and cheese curds), Montréal-style bagels, salmon jerky and pierogi jostle for comfort-food attention. For something more refined, Montréal, Toronto and Vancouver have well-seasoned fine-dining scenes, while regions across the country have rediscovered the unique ingredients grown, foraged and produced on their doorsteps – bringing distinctive seafood, artisan cheeses and lip-smacking produce to menus.

DEYMOSHR / SHUTTERSTOCK ©

Tastemakers may not tout Canadian food the way they do, say, Italian or French fare, so let's just call the distinctive dishes and fresh, seasonal fruits and veggies our little secret. Ditto for the award-winning bold reds and crisp whites produced from the country's vine-striped valleys.

Drinking & Nightlife

Canadian nightlife is as varied as the landscape. Cities have packed pubs serving microbrews, cocktail bars for the well-heeled, clubs catering mainly to the young, and live-music bars for their parents. In small towns, you'll almost always find at least one pub, which is as much a meeting place as a drinking establishment. Cafes are everywhere, although espresso machines are used with varying success in far-flung locations.

★ Best Local Markets

St Lawrence Market (p43), Toronto

Marché Jean-Talon (p111), Montréal

Halifax Seaport Farmers Market (p85), Atlantic province

Marché du Vieux-Port (p135), Québec City

Granville Island Public Market (p206), Vancouver

Entertainment

Maybe it's the long, cold winters that drives teens into their basements to play music, but Canada has more local bands than you can shake a hockey stick at. Consequently, finding live music is not a challenge. Rock, folk and pop are the mainstays while clubs have a steady stream of local and international DJs. In major cities, you'll also find a smattering of opera, dance and drama.

From left: Poutine; Granville Island Public Market (p206)

Plan Your Trip
Month by Month

January

Ski season is in full swing. Toward the end of the month, cities begin winter carnivals to break the shackles of cold, dark days.

🍷 Ice Wine Festivals

British Columbia's Okanagan Valley (www.thewinefestivals.com) and Ontario's Niagara Peninsula (www.niagarawinofestival.com) celebrate their ice wines with good-time festivals.

February

🎎 Chinese New Year

Dragons dance, firecrackers burst and food sizzles. Vancouver hosts the biggest celebration (www.vancouver-chinatown.com), but Toronto, Calgary, Ottawa and Montréal also have festivities. The lunar calendar determines the date.

🎎 Québec City's Winter Carnival

Revelers watch ice-sculpture competitions, hurtle down snow slides, go ice fishing and cheer on their favorite paddlers in an insane canoe race on the St Lawrence River. It's the world's biggest winter fest (www.carnaval.qc.ca).

🍷 Vancouver Wine Festival

Vancouver uncorks 1700 wines from 200 vintners at this wine festival (www.vanwinefest.ca), a rite of spring for oenophiles.

March

Ski resorts still do brisk business, especially mid-month when kids typically have a week-long school break.

🍴 Sugar Shacks

Québec produces three-quarters of the world's maple syrup, and March is when trees get tapped. Head out to local sugar shacks, scoop up some snow, put it on a plate and have steaming syrup from a piping cauldron poured on.

Above: Canadian Tulip Festival

JOSEPH S L TAN MATT / SHUTTERSTOCK ©

April
🎿 World Ski & Snowboard Festival
Ski bums converge on Whistler for 10 days of adrenaline events, outdoor rock and hip-hop concerts, film screenings, dog parades and a whole lotta carousing (www.wssf.com).

☆ Hot Docs
Toronto hosts North America's largest documentary film festival (www.hotdocs.ca), which screens 170-plus docos from around the globe.

May
☉ Tiptoe Through the Tulips
After a long winter, Ottawa bursts with color – more than three million tulips of 200 types blanket the city for the Canadian Tulip Festival (www.tulipfestival.ca). Festivities include parades, regattas, car rallies, dances, concerts and fireworks.

★ Best Festivals
Montréal Jazz Festival, June

Québec City Winter Carnival, February

Pride Toronto, June–July

Dark Sky Festival, October

Festival Acadien, August

June
Take advantage of long, warm days to hike, paddle and soak up the great outdoors.

☆ Luminato
For 10 days in early June, big-name musicians, dancers, artists, writers, actors and filmmakers descend on Toronto for a celebration of creativity that reflects the city's diversity (www.luminatofestival.com). Many performances are free.

Above: Montréal Jazz Festival (p24)

☆ North by Northeast

Around 1000 emerging indie bands spill off the stages in Toronto's coolest clubs. Film screenings and comedy shows add to the mix. Over its 20-year history, NXNE (www.nxne.com) has become a must on the music-industry calendar.

☆ Montréal Jazz Festival

Two million music lovers descend on Montréal in late June, when the heart of downtown explodes with jazz and blues for 11 straight days (www.montrealjazzfest.com). Most concerts are outdoors and free.

🎎 Pride Toronto

Toronto's most flamboyant event (www.pridetoronto.com) celebrates all kinds of sexuality, climaxing with an out-of-the-closet Dyke March and the outrageous Pride Parade. Most events are free.

July

Weather is at its warmest, fresh produce and seafood fill plates, and festivals rock the nights away. Crowds are thick.

☆ Country Music in Cavendish

Some of the biggest names in country music come to Prince Edward Island for the Cavendish Beach Festival (www.cavendishbeachmusic.com). This is one of the largest outdoor music festivals in North America.

☉ Calgary Stampede

Raging bulls, chuckwagon racing and bad-ass, boot-wearing cowboys unite for the 'Greatest Outdoor Show on Earth.' A midway of rides and games makes it a family affair well beyond the usual rodeo event (www.calgarystampede.com).

August

☆ Festival Acadien

Acadians tune their fiddles and unleash their Franco-Canadian spirit for the Festival Acadien (www.festivalacadien.ca) in Caraquet, New Brunswick. It's the biggest event on the Acadian calendar, with singers, musicians and dancers letting loose for two weeks in early August.

☆ Edmonton Fringe Festival

Edmonton's Fringe Festival (www.fringe-theatreadventures.ca) is North America's largest fringe bash, staging some 1600 performances of wild, uncensored shows over 11 days in mid-August.

☉ Canadian National Exhibition

Akin to a state fair in the USA, 'The Ex' (www.theex.com) features more than 700 exhibitors, agricultural shows, lumberjack competitions, outdoor concerts and carnivalia at Toronto's Exhibition Place. The 18-day event runs through Labour Day and ends with a bang-up fireworks display.

September

✕ PEI Fall Flavours

This island-wide kitchen party merges toe-tapping traditional music with incredible seafood over the course of three weeks (www.fallflavours.ca).

☆ Toronto International Film Festival

Toronto's prestigious 10-day celebration (www.tiff.net) is a major cinematic event. Buy tickets well in advance.

October

🎎 Dark Sky Festival

In late October, Jasper's Dark Sky Festival (www.jasperdarksky.travel) fills two weeks with events celebrating space. Hear talks by astronauts and celebrities, listen to the symphony under the stars, see the aurora borealis reflected in a glacial lake and gaze through a telescope into the great beyond.

December

Get out the parka. Winter begins in earnest as snow falls, temperatures drop and ski resorts ramp up for the masses.

🎎 Niagara Festival of Lights

The Winter Festival of Lights (www.wfol.com) features three million twinkling bulbs and 125 animated displays brightening the town and the waterfall. Ice-skate on the 'rink at the brink' of the cascade.

Plan Your Trip
Get Inspired

Read

The Illegal (Lawrence Hill; 2015) A marathoner in a fictional land running from the law; takes on race and immigration.

Indian Horse (R Wagamese; 2012) An Ojibwe man in rehab recalls his life as a hockey star, touching on Ojibwe rituals and spirituality.

Dear Life (Alice Munro; 2012) Most recent collection of short stories by the 2013 Nobel Prize laureate.

Alias Grace (Margaret Atwood; 1996) A fictional drama set around the notorious real-life 1843 murders of a gentleman and his housekeeper.

Watch

Room (Lenny Abrahamson; 2015) Canadian-Irish film about a mother and son finally released after years of captivity.

Sleeping Giant (Andrew Cividino; 2015) Teens surviving summer in an isolated Ontario cottage community.

Bon Cop, Bad Cop (Eric Canuel; 2006) An Anglophone and Francophone join forces; one of Canada's top-grossing films.

C.R.A.Z.Y. (Jean-Marc Vallée; 2005) A gay teen growing up in a large Catholic family in 1970s Montréal does his best to fit in.

Listen

Arcade Fire *Neon Bible* (2006)

Tragically Hip *Fully Completely* (1992)

Neil Young *Massey Hall 1971* (2007)

The New Pornographers *Mass Romantic* (2000)

Drake *Hotline Bling* (2016)

Rush *Moving Pictures* (1981)

Great Big Sea *Road Rage* (2016)

Feist *The Reminder* (2007)

Bachman-Turner Overdrive *Bachman-Turner Overdrive II* (1973)

The Weeknd *Beauty Behind the Madness* (2015)

Stompin' Tom Connors *Ballad of Stompin' Tom* (2008)

Above: Indie rock band Arcade Fire

Plan Your Trip
Five-Day Itineraries

Wild West Coast

Sandwiched between sea and mountains, the West Coast will wow you with its beauty. Take in cultured Vancouver with its museums and parks before heading to Vancouver Island to explore picturesque Victoria and the wilds of Tofino.

Tofino (p234) Spend two days at Long Beach, visiting the Eagle Aerie Gallery and hopping a boat to Meares Island.

Vancouver (p202) Spend two days exploring the art gallery, Stanley Park and Granville Island's food market.
🚗 1 hr to Tsawwassen, then 🚢 2 hrs to Swartz Bay, then 🚗 30 mins to Victoria

Goldstream (p237) Hike through huge trees, with bald eagles overhead and the river rumbling past.
🚗 4 hrs to Tofino

Victoria (p236) Explore Chinatown, the Royal BC Museum and Craigdarroch Castle. Take a whale-watching tour from Fisherman's Wharf.
🚗 30 mins to Goldstream

4 JAIME KOWAL / GETTY IMAGES ©; 1 JULIEN HAUTCOEUR / SHUTTERSTOCK ©

Mountains & Prairies

Get in touch with your inner cowboy in surprisingly hip Calgary before crossing the prairies to the towering Rockies. Explore Banff and then drive one of the world's most stunning roads to Jasper, hopefully catching a glimpse of some wildlife en route.

Jasper (p194) Visit Maligne Lake and take a boat trip out to iconic Spirit Island.

Lake Louise (p186) Admire Lake Louise and hike to Lake Agnes for alpine tea. Take the gondola and watch for grizzly bears below. 🚗 3 hrs to Jasper

Banff Town (p190) Take in the Whyte Museum and then canoe down the Bow River, watching for elk and moose. 🚗 40 mins to Lake Louise

Calgary (p170) Visit the new National Music Centre, buy a Smithbilt cowboy hat and then take in Calgary's impressive restaurant scene. 🚗 1½ hrs to Banff Town

4 ZHUKOVA VALENTYNA / SHUTTERSTOCK ©; 1 JUSTIN FOULKES / LONELY PLANET ©

Plan Your Trip
10-Day Itinerary

City-Hopping

Urbanites will love taking in the world-class galleries, museums, arts scenes and nightlife of Canada's diverse cities. From buzzing Toronto to Québec City's old-world charm, with the vineyards of Niagara in between, you could easily stretch this itinerary out to a few weeks or more.

Ottawa (p143) Take in Ottawa's impressive museums, particularly the Canadian Museum of History and the National Gallery. And don't forget Parliament Hill. 🚗 2½ hrs to Montréal

Toronto (p36) Spend two days exploring Toronto's museums and galleries, taking a ride to the top of the CN Tower and browsing the markets. 🚗 1½ hrs to Niagara Falls

Niagara-on-the-Lake (p68) Soak up the atmosphere of this 19th-century town and enjoy its neighboring vineyards. 🚗 5½ hrs to Ottawa

Niagara Falls (p64) Take in the falls from different points, including tunnels and boats. Visit the Daredevil Exhibit. 🚗 30 mins to Niagara-on-the-Lake

Québec City (p124) Stroll the picturesque Old Town, visit the Musée de la Civilisation and cycle the city's scenic paths.

6

5

Montréal (p102) Explore Old Montréal and the Musée des Beaux-Arts. Take in the parks, the markets and some live music.

🚗 3 hrs to Québec City

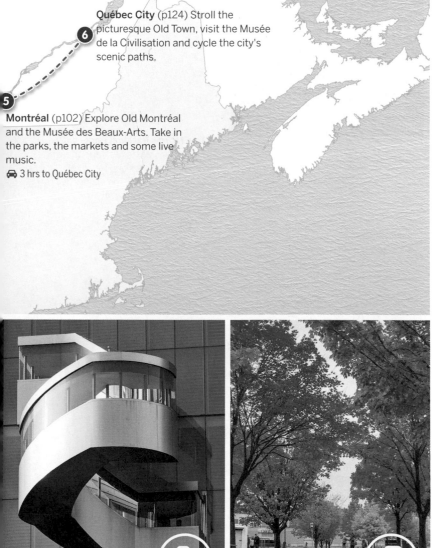

Plan Your Trip
Two-Week Itinerary

Atlantic Highlights

Wild, windswept and whale-riddled, a trip through the Atlantic provinces unfurls sea-and-cliff vistas, Viking vestiges and Celtic heritage. From foot-tapping music to buttery lobster feasts, this is satisfying traveling.

Charlottetown (p90) Explore beautiful Charlottetown and join a clam-digging tour to take in local culture and scenery. 🚗 35 mins to Cavendish

Gros Morne National Park (p80) Explore this World Heritage site with its fjord-like lakes and weird rock formations. Follow the Viking Trail to L'Anse aux Meadows. 🚗 11 hrs to St John's

Cavendish (p95) Visit the iconic Green Gables and take a walk on the red sand beach. 🚗 3 hrs to Fundy National Park

St John's (p96) After a long road trip across the wild land, relax in North America's oldest city and take a whale-watching trip.

Cape Breton (p82) Spend two days on Celtic-tinged Cape Breton. Visit the art studios along the Cabot Trail. ⚓ 6 hrs from North Sydney to Newfoundland

Halifax (p84) Spend two days enjoying the beer, markets and cosmopolitan life of Halifax. On day three, visit Peggy's Cove. 🚗 4½ hrs to Cape Breton

Fundy National Park (p92) Check out the world's highest tides, a colorful seashore and Cape Enrage. 🚗 3½ hrs to Halifax

Plan Your Trip
Family Travel

Choosing Your Destination

Deciding where to go with your kids in Canada can be a daunting decision. Mountains, prairies, beaches and easy-going cities are strewn across six time zones. Between wildlife sightings, cowboy encounters, hands-on pirate history, hunting for dinosaur fossils and ice-skating on mountain lakes, it's impossible to make a bad choice.

Outdoor Activities

Canada is all about open spaces, fresh air, rivers, lakes and mountains, snow, sand and wildlife.

Most Canadian cities are endowed with parks and promenades set up for even the tiniest of cyclists, while the Canadian National Parks system contains easy strolls as well as longer hiking trails. Horseback riding can be especially fun in cowboy country around Calgary.

Most lake areas offer canoe rentals perfect for family outings, and seafront regions are packed with kayak outfits. For a bigger adrenaline rush for older kids, try white-water rafting. On the coasts and the Bay of Fundy, whale-watching can be thrilling, and the small summer waves on the east and west coast are excellent for first-time surfing.

Skiing or snowboarding is an obvious family choice. Children under six often ski for free, and up to 18 receive discounts. There's also ice-skating, sledding and snowshoeing.

Museums & Monuments

Most large Canadian cities have science museums that specialize in hands-on activities, while at historic sites peppered across the country, costumed thespians get you right into the period, and often have demonstrations of everything from blacksmithing to cooking.

Above: Polar bears (p288)

MURIEL LASURE / SHUTTERSTOCK ©

Planning

Lonely Planet's *Travel with Children* offers a wealth of tips and tricks. The website Travel For Kids (www.travelforkids.com) is another good, general resource.

Note that children who are traveling to Canada without both parents need authorization from the nonaccompanying parent. Sometimes this is enforced and other times not; play it safe with a notarized letter.

Accommodations

Some properties offer 'kids stay free' promotions, while others (particularly B&Bs) may not accept children. Ask when booking.

Camping is huge in Canada. Some grounds offer exotic options like tipis or yurts, while others have swimming pools or minigolf. Cabins, which come with kitchens and other perks such as barbecues, are a great option. You can find full listings with each province's visitors guide online.

★ Best Destinations for Kids

Vancouver Island (p230)

The Rockies (p184)

Montréal (p102)

The Atlantic provinces (p76)

Toronto (p36)

Eating Out

Everywhere you turn in Canada you'll find fast food and fried fare. It's harder to find more wholesome options in small towns. Canadian foods your kids will love include poutine (French fries topped with brown gravy and cheese), fish-and-chips, Montréal-style bagels (wood-fired, dense and slightly sweet), pancakes or French toast with maple syrup, bear-claw doughnuts, butter tarts and Nanaimo bars (crumb crust topped with custard and chocolate).

Above: Kootenay Lake (p184) in the Rockies

TORONTO

CN Tower (p38)

Rogers Centre (p56)

Harbourfront Centre
(p42)

Toronto at a Glance...

Welcome to Toronto, the most multiculturally diverse city on the planet, where over 140 languages are spoken. It's estimated that over half of Toronto's residents were born outside Canada. When the weather is fine, Toronto is a blast: a vibrant, big-time city abuzz with activity. Some of the world's finest restaurants are found here, alongside happening bars, clubs and eclectic festivals. In winter, things get very cold. But come with patience and an open mind and you'll be too wrapped up in fun to notice the weather. This is a city that is waking up to its own greatness.

Two Days in Toronto

On day one, rocket-ride up the **CN Tower** (p38), lunch at **St Lawrence Market** (p43), window shop in **Bloor-Yorkville** (p50), then dine pan-Asian style at **Queen Mother Café** (p51). On day two, visit the **Royal Ontario Museum** (p45), **Casa Loma** (p47) or the **Art Gallery of Ontario** (p45), then catch the ferry to the **Toronto Islands** (p48) for an afternoon out from the urban bustle. Back in town, relax with a pint in the **Distillery District** (p42).

Four Days in Toronto

Begin day three with a double-decker sightseeing **tour** (p50), then see what's on at the **Harbourfront Centre** (p42). Make dinner Italian at **Trattoria Nervosa** (p52). Devote day four to exploring the **Museum of Contemporary Art_Toronto_Canada** (p47) and the surrounding design and arts precinct. Head to **High Park** (p48) for a picnic, or catch some baseball at the **Rogers Centre** (p56) or hockey at the **Air Canada Centre** (p57).

Bloor-Yorkville
The downtown home of Toronto's rich and famous. The Mink Mile is the place to go for high-end brand label shopping.

Downtown Yonge
Dundas Sq is the center of downtown, with nearby Eaton Centre mall, some historic theaters and Ryerson University.

Toronto erminal 🚉

Union Station 🚉

CN TOWER

Old York
Historic district extending east of Yonge St to the Don River, and from Queen St south to the waterfront esplanade.

Toronto Inner Harbour

Harbourfront
Packed with restaurants, theaters, galleries, stores, condominiums and parklands along Queens Quay.

Toronto Islands

Downtown Toronto North (p44)
Downtown Toronto South (p46)

Tourism Toronto
(p57)

Westin Harbour Castle

Air Canada
Centre (p57)

Harbour Square Park

Toronto Islands
Ferries (p58)

University of Toronto & The Annex
Canada's largest university has stately Victorian and Romanesque buildings, with The Annex neighbourhood nearby.

Chinatown & Baldwin Village
A dragon gate marks Chinatown's epicenter while Baldwin Village is a pretty strip of cheap eats and good vibes.

*Metro
Coach*

Financial District
Toronto's 'Wall St' and the nicest of the skyscrapers are here, plus Union Station – Canada's busiest transport hub.

*Toronto Pearson
International* ✈
(19km)

*Billy Bishop
Toronto City* ✈
Airport

Entertainment District & King Street West
Home to theaters, bars, clubs, design stores and some fine historic architecture.

*Lake
Ontario*

Ⓝ N 0 _____ 2 km
0 _____ 1 mile

Cherry Blossoms in High Park (p48)

Arriving in Toronto

Toronto Pearson International Airport Union Pearson Express (www.upexpress.com) trains link to Union Square ($12, 25 minutes, every 15 minutes 5:30am to 1am) or take a taxi ($60, 40 to 70 minutes).

Billy Bishop Toronto Airport A free shuttle bus (15 minutes, every 15 minutes, 5am to midnight Monday to Friday, reduced hours Saturday and Sunday) links Union Station to the mainland ferry terminal, from where there's a pedestrian path.

Where to Stay

Toronto has no shortage of accommodations, but it can get expensive, especially in summer when rooms sell quickly at up to double their regular rates. It's essential to book in advance for stays from mid-May to late September. Remember, 13% HST (harmonized sales tax) is almost always applied on top of the quoted rate. For more information on the best neighborhoods to stay, see p59.

CN Tower

This marvel of 1970s engineering – once the highest freestanding structure in the world – looks like a giant concrete hypodermic needle.

The CN Tower's function as a communications mast takes a backseat to its role as a beacon to tourists. Even if you don't feel its pull, you're bound to catch a glimpse of the tower at night, when the entire structure puts on a brilliant free light show year-round. The best street-level vantage of the tower is at the intersection of McCaul St and Queen St W, due north of the tower.

If you do decide to venture skyward, choose your day carefully. With clear weather, the views from the top are astounding, however if it's hazy, you won't see a thing. Queues for the elevator can be up to two hours long in each direction.

Great For...

☑ Don't Miss

The EdgeWalk, if you dare – a 20-minute outdoor walk around the unbounded perimeter of the main pod (356m).

History

The 1960s construction boom saw a surge in skyscrapers filling Toronto's skyline that dwarfed the city's transmissions towers.

ℹ Need to Know

Map p46; La Tour CN; ☎416-868-6937; www.cntower.ca; 301 Front St W; Tower Experience adult/child $35/25; ⊘9am-10:30pm; ⑤Union

✕ Take a Break

Take in views and a bite from **360°**, the obligatory revolving restaurant at the top. It's expensive, but the elevator price is waived for diners.

★ Top Tip

Buying tickets online saves 15%.

The solution was rather extreme: 1537 workers toiled 24 hours a day for five days a week for over three years. In 1975, when a helicopter placed the final piece of the antenna in place, the CN Tower became the tallest free standing structure in the world, a title it held until 2007. Built to withstand an earthquake of 8.5 on the Richter scale and winds of up to 420 km/h, it continues to provide some of the clearest reception in North America.

Tower Experiences

Daredevils are well catered for at the CN Tower. Hop in the highest glass-floor-paneled elevator in the world, installed in 2008 and rocketing 346m in 58 seconds. Join an Edgewalk Tour ($175), where you walk hands-free on a 1.5m-wide ledge around the top of the tower, attached by a harness that doesn't seem all that reassuring as you lean out over the city. Or, for an even loftier, though indoor, view, opt for the SkyPod (447m; an extra $12). Once you're up this high, you may not notice a huge difference to the regular view, but if you lean against the walls and stay very still, you can feel the sway of the tower. Not for the fainthearted.

Tower Statistics

The CN Tower:

- receives over 1.5 million people each year

- houses 16 TV and radio stations

- is designated one of the Seven Wonders of the Modern World

- is home to the world's highest wine cellar

- is struck by lightning an average of 75 times per year

Kensington Market

Diverse Dining

From Azerbaijan to Zimbabwe, and everywhere in between, nowhere is Toronto's multiculturalism more potent and thrilling than on the plates of its restaurants.

Great For...

☑ Don't Miss

Following vitamin-D starved locals to patio bars and restaurants when the sun peeks out. Try Hair of the Dog (p52) or Allen's (p53).

Eating here is a delight – you'll find everything from Korean walnut cakes to sweat-inducing Thai curries, New York steaks and good ol' Canuck pancakes with peameal bacon and maple syrup. Fusion food is hot: traditional Western recipes spiked with handfuls of zingy Eastern ingredients and cooked with pan-Asian flare. British influences also linger – hearty lunchtime pints and formal afternoon high teas are much-loved traditions.

Eating by Neighborhood

Executive diners file into classy restaurants in the Financial District and Old York, while eclectic, affordable eateries fill Baldwin Village, Kensington Market, Queen West, Ossington Ave and the Yonge St strip. More ethnically consistent are Little Italy, Greektown, Little India and Chinatown.

Old-School Diners

In a city where franchises are inescapable, and restaurants come and go, it's refreshing to know that some things never change. We've found some of Toronto's classic diners and cheap eats to take you back to the golden age of home cooking and vinyl booths:

Patrician Grill (☑416-366-4841; 219 King St E; meals $4-11; ☺7am-4pm Mon-Fri, 8am-2pm Sat; ⓢ King)

Avenue Open Kitchen (Map p46; ☑416-504-7131; 7 Camden St; sandwiches/burgers from $3/4.50; ☺7am-4pm Mon-Fri, 8am-3pm Sat; ⌂504)

Golden Diner (Map p44; ☑416-977-9898; 105 Carlton St; breakfast from $2.50; ☺6:30am-10pm; ⓢ College)

❶ Need to Know

Whenever possible, make a reservation – especially on weekends and for prime real estate on the patios.

✕ Take a Break

For people-watching 24/7, hit **Thompson Diner** (Map p46; ☑416-601-3533; www. thompsondiner.com; 550 Wellington St W; breakfast from $10, mains from $14; ☺24hr; ⌂504, 511).

★ Top Tip

Look out for good-value menus during the Summerlicious (www.toronto.ca/summerlicious) and Winterlicious (www.toronto.ca/winterlicious) food festivals, held in July and January respectively.

Gale's Snack Bar (539 Eastern Ave; meals $3-4; ☺10am-6pm Mon-Fri, noon-5pm Sat; ⌂501, 502, 503)

Senator Restaurant (Map p44; ☑416-364-7517; www.thesenator.com; 249 Victoria St; mains $8-18; ☺8am-2:30pm Sun & Mon, to 9pm Tue-Sat; ⓢ Dundas)

Vegetarian Havens

Meat- and/or dairy-free eating options in food-obsessed Toronto run the gamut from gourmet to passe. These are surefire hits:

Govinda's (Map p44; ☑888-218-1040; www. govindas.ca; 243 Avenue Rd; meal platters adult/child $10/5; ☺noon-3pm & 6-8pm Mon-Sat; ☑; ⓢ Rosedale)

Kupfert & Kim (Map p46; ☑416-504-2206; www.kupfertandkim.com; 140 Spadina Ave; mains $10-12; ☺7:30am-10pm Mon-Fri, 10:30am-10pm Sat & Sun; ❄☎☑🍴; ⓢ Osgoode, ⌂501)

Urban Herbivore (Map p44; ☑416-927-1231; www.herbivore.to; 64 Oxford St; mains $7-14; ☺9am-7pm; ☑; ⌂510)

◎ SIGHTS

Downtown Toronto is an easy-to-navigate grid, bounded by a hodgepodge of ethnic, bohemian and historic neighborhoods. Yonge St, the world's longest, dissects the city: any downtown street with an East or West designation refers to its position relative to Yonge. Most tourist sights hug the Harbourfront, Entertainment and Financial Districts at the southern end of downtown.

◎ Harbourfront

Harbourfront Centre   Landmark

(Map p46; ☑416-973-4000; www.harbourfront centre.com; York Quay, 235 Queens Quay W; ⊙box office 1-6pm Tue-Sat, show nights to 8pm; P ⊕; ☒509, 510) The 4-hectare not-for-profit Harbourfront Centre exists to educate and entertain Toronto's community through a variety of year-round events, including Sunday family events and free outdoor summer concerts in the Toronto Music Garden and on the Concert Stage. There's also a lakeside ice-skating rink where you can slice up the winter ice. Don't miss the free galleries, including the **Photo Passage** and the functioning **Craft Studio**. Arriving at **Ontario Square** from Queens Quay, head to **Canada Square** with its dawn redwood trees, peering across Lake Ontario.

Fort York National Historic Site   Historic Site

(Map p46; ☑416-392-6907; www.fortyork.ca; 250 Fort York Blvd; adult/child $9/4.25; ⊙10am-5pm Jun-Dec, to 4pm Mon-Fri Jan-May; P; ☒509, 511) Established by the British in 1793 to defend the then town of York, Fort York was almost entirely destroyed during the War of 1812 when a small band of Ojibwe warriors and British troops were unable to defeat their US attackers. A handful of the original log, stone and brick buildings have been restored. From May to September, men decked out in 19th-century British military uniforms carry out marches and drills, firing musket volleys into the sky.

Ripley's Aquarium of Canada   Aquarium

(Map p46; ☑647-351-3474; www.ripleysaquarium ofcanada.com; 288 Bremner Blvd; adult/child $30/20; ⊙9am-11pm; ☒Union) Toronto's newest attraction for young and old. Expect over 15,000 aquatic animals, 5.7 million liters of water in the combined tanks, as well as sleepovers, touch tanks and educational dive presentations. It opens 365 days a year but sometimes closes earlier than regular hours for special events. Peak hours are 11am to 4pm.

◎ Financial District

Hockey Hall of Fame   Museum

(Map p46; ☑416-360-7765; www.hhof.com; Brookfield Pl, 30 Yonge St; adult/child $18/12; ⊙9:30am-6pm Mon-Sat, 10am-6pm Sun; ☒Union) Inside an ornate rococo gray-stone Bank of Montréal building (c 1885), the Hockey Hall of Fame is a Canadian institution. Even those unfamiliar with the superfast ultraviolent sport are likely to be impressed by this, the largest collection of hockey memorabilia in the world. Check out the collection of *Texas Chainsaw Massacre*–esque goalkeeping masks or go head to head with the great Wayne Gretzky, virtual-reality style.

Cloud Gardens Conservatory   Gardens

(Map p46; Bay Adelaide Park; ☑416-392-7288; 14 Temperance St; ⊙10am-2:30pm Mon-Fri; ☒Queen) ✿**FREE** An unexpected sanctuary with its own waterfall, the steamy Cloud Gardens Conservatory is crowded with enormous jungle leaves, vines and palms Information plaques answer the question 'What Are Rainforests?' The greenhouse is a great place to warm up during winter, but avoid the area after dark – the adjacent park attracts some shady characters.

◎ Old York

Distillery District   Area

(☑416-364-1177; www.thedistillerydistrict.com; 9 Trinity St; ⊙10am-7pm Mon-Wed, to 8pm Thu-Sat, 11am-5pm Sun; ☒503, 504) Centered on the

Harbourfront Centre

1832 Gooderham and Worts distillery – once the British Empire's largest – the 5-hectare Distillery District is one of Toronto's best downtown attractions. Its Victorian industrial warehouses have been converted into soaring galleries, artists studios, design boutiques, cafes and eateries. On weekends, newlyweds pose before a backdrop of red brick and cobblestone, young families walk their dogs and the fashionable elite shop for art beneath charmingly decrepit gables and gantries. In summer, expect live jazz, activities, exhibitions and foodie events.

St Lawrence Market Market

(Map p46; ☑416-392-7129; www.stlawrence market.com; 92-95 Front St E; ☺8am-6pm Tue-Thu, to 7pm Fri, 5am-5pm Sat; P; ☐503, 504) Old York's sensational St Lawrence Market has been a neighborhood meeting place for over two centuries. The restored, high-trussed 1845 **South Market** houses more than 50 specialty food stalls: cheese vendors, fishmongers, butchers, bakers and pasta makers. The **Carousel Bakery** is famed for its peameal bacon sand-

wiches and **St Urbain** for its authentic Montréal-style bagels.

Inside the old council chambers upstairs, the **Market Gallery** (☑416-392-0572; www.toronto.ca/marketgallery; ☺10am-6pm Tue-Thu, to 7pm Fri, 9am-5pm Sat, 10am-4pm Sun) FREE has rotating displays of paintings, photographs, documents and historical relics.

◉ Entertainment District & King Street West

401 Richmond Gallery

(Map p46; www.401richmond.net; 401 Richmond St W; ☺9am-7pm Mon-Fri, to 6pm Sat; ☐510) FREE Inside an early 20th-century litho=grapher's warehouse, restored in 1994, this 18,500-sq-meter New York–style artist collective hums with the creative vibes of 130 diverse contemporary galleries showcasing works in almost any artistic medium you can think of. Grab a snack and a latte at the ground-floor cafe and enjoy it on the expansive roof garden: a little-known oasis in the summer.

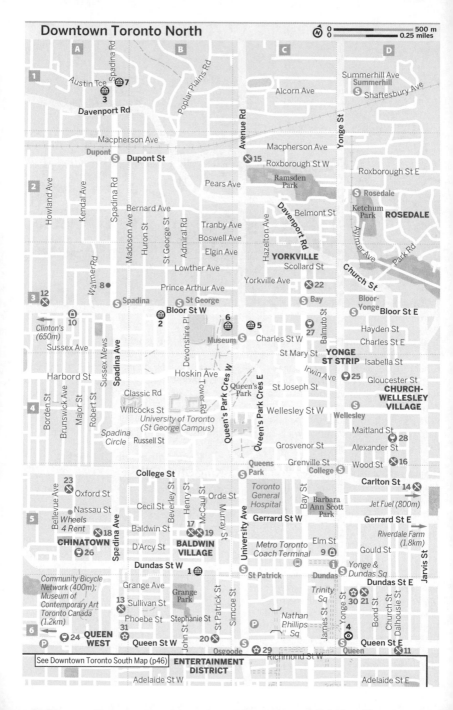

Downtown Toronto North

N 0   500 m
0   0.25 miles

See Downtown Toronto South Map (p46)

Downtown Toronto North

⊙ Downtown Yonge

Elgin & Winter Garden Theatre   Theater

(Map p44; ☑416-314-2871; www.heritagetrust.
on.ca/ewg; 189 Yonge St; tours adult/student
$12/10; Ⓢ Queen) This restored masterpiece
is the world's last operating Edwardian
double-decker theater. Celebrating its centennial in 2013, the Winter Garden was built
as the flagship for a vaudeville chain that
never really took off, while the downstairs
Elgin was converted into a movie house in
the 1920s. Fascinating tours run Thursdays
at 5pm and Saturdays at 11am; look for
shorter $5 lunchtime tours Wednesdays to
Fridays in July and August.

⊙ Chinatown & Baldwin Village

Art Gallery of Ontario   Gallery

(Map p44; AGO; ☑416-979-6648; www.ago.net;
317 Dundas St W; adult/under 18yr $19.50/11;
☺10:30am-5pm Tue & Thu, to 9pm Wed & Fri, to
5:30pm Sat & Sun; ⛟505) The AGO houses
art collections both excellent and extensive
(bring your stamina). Renovations of the
facade, designed by the great Frank Gehry
and completed in 2008, fail to impress at
street level: perhaps because of a drab
downtown location. Fortunately, everything

changes once you step inside. Highlights
of the permanent collection include rare
Québécois religious statuary, First Nations
and Inuit carvings, stunningly presented
works by Canadian greats, the Group of
Seven, the Henry Moore sculpture pavilion
and a restored Georgian house, the Grange.

There's a surcharge for special exhibits
but visits to the permanent collection on
Wednesday evenings are free. One-hour
tours leave from Walker Court daily at
11am, noon, 1pm and 3pm, and on Wednesdays at 7pm.

⊙ Bloor-Yorkville

Royal Ontario Museum   Museum

(Map p44; ROM; ☑416-586-8000; www.rom.
on.ca; 100 Queen's Park; adult/child $15/12;
☺10am-5:30pm Sat-Thu, to 8:30pm Fri; Ⓢ Museum) Celebrating its centennial in 2014, the
multidisciplinary ROM is Canada's biggest
natural history museum and one of the
largest museums in North America. You'll
either love or loathe the synergy between
the original heritage buildings at the main
entrance on Bloor St and the 2007 addition
of 'the Crystal,' which appears to pierce
the original structure and juts out into the
street like a massive shard.

Downtown Toronto South

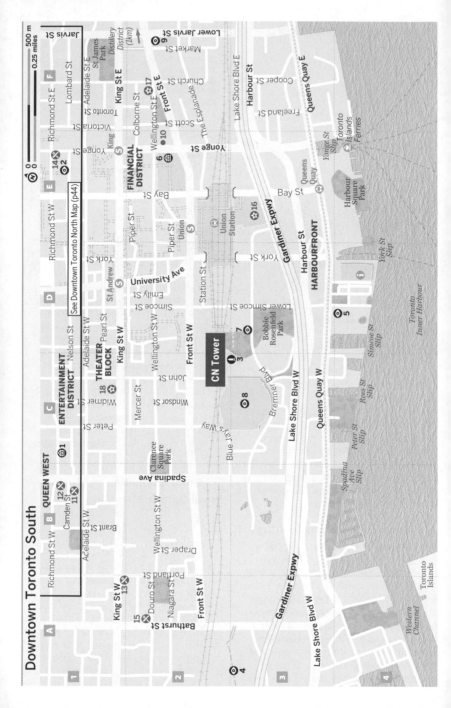

See Downtown Toronto North Map (p44)

Distillery District (1km)

St James Park

FINANCIAL DISTRICT

ENTERTAINMENT DISTRICT

THEATER BLOCK

QUEEN WEST

HARBOURFRONT

Union Station

CN Tower

Bobbie Rosenfeld Park

Clarence Square Park

Harbour Square Park

Toronto Islands Ferries

Toronto Inner Harbour

Toronto Islands

Western Channel

Gardiner Expwy

Lake Shore Blvd

Queens Quay

500 m
0.25 miles

Downtown Toronto South

Bata Shoe Museum   Museum

(Map p44; ☑416-979-7799; www.batashoe
museum.ca; 327 Bloor St W; adult/child $14/5,
5-8pm Thu suggested donation $5; ◷10am-5pm
Mon-Wed, Fri & Sat, to 8pm Thu, noon-5pm Sun;
ⓈSt George) It's important in life to be well
shod, a stance the Bata Shoe Museum
takes seriously. Impressively designed by
architect Raymond Moriyama to resemble
a stylized shoe box, the museum displays
10,000 'pedi-artifacts' from around the
globe. Peruse 19th-century French chestnut-
crushing clogs, Canadian aboriginal polar
boots or famous modern pairs worn by Elton John, Indira Gandhi and Pablo Picasso.
Come along for something truly different!

⊙ University of Toronto & the Annex

Casa Loma   Historic Building

(Map p44; ☑416-923-1171; www.casaloma.org;
1 Austin Tce; adult/child $18/10; ◷9:30am-5pm,
last entry 4pm; Ⓟ; ◻127, ⓈDupont) Toronto's
only castle may have never housed royalty,
but it certainly has grandeur, lording over
the Annex from a cliff that was once the
shoreline of the glacial Lake Iroquois, from
which Lake Ontario derived. A variety of
themed guided tours are available. If you're
in Toronto around Christmas, a visit is a
must. Check the website for details. To
reach the casa, climb the 27m **Baldwin
Steps** up the slope from Spadina Ave,
north of Davenport Rd.

Spadina Museum   Museum

(Map p44; ☑416-392-6910; www.toronto.
ca/museums; 285 Spadina Rd; tours adult/
child $8/5, grounds free; ◷noon-4pm
Tue-Sun; Ⓟ; ⓈDupont) Atop the Baldwin Steps, this gracious home and its
Victorian-Edwardian gardens were built
in 1866 as a country estate for financier
James Austin and his family. Donated
to the city in 1978, it became a museum
in 1984 and was recently painstakingly
transformed to evoke the heady age
of the roaring 1920s and '30s: highly
recommended.

⊙ Queen West & Trinity Bellwoods

Museum of Contemporary Art Toronto Canada   Museum

(www.museumofcontemporaryart.ca; Queen St
W; ◻501) In May 2017 MoCA will transform
into the Museum of Contemporary Art
Toronto Canada, across the road. At Queen
and Ossington, in the heart of West Queen
West's design and arts precinct, MoCA's
mandate had been to exhibit innovative
works by Canadian and international artists
that address themes of contemporary
relevance. The new, larger museum will create a digital archive of work and interpret
the modern world through art. Check the
website for hours and details.

 Toronto's Ice-Skating Scene

Locals love to skate. When the weather is freezing and the snow falling lightly, downtown Toronto's outdoor ice rinks come alive. The best-known rinks are at **Nathan Phillips Square** outside City Hall and at the **Harbourfront Centre** (p42). These artificial rinks are open daily (weather permitting) from 10am to 10pm mid-November to March. Admission is free; skate rental costs $10/5 per adult/child. Toronto Parks & Recreation (www.toronto.ca/parks) has info on other rinks around town, including those at **Kew Gardens** near Kew Beach and **Trinity Bellwoods Park** in West Toronto. If it's been *really* cold, you can skate on **Grenadier Pond** in High Park. Beginners might prefer the lesser-known **Ryerson Rink**, tucked away just north of Yonge-Dundas Sq at 25 Gould St – in summer the rink is a water feature.

Nathan Phillips Square
DAMION RAE PHOTOGRAPHY / 500PX ©

⊚ East End

Riverdale Farm   Museum
(☏416 392-6794; www.toronto.ca/riverdalefarm; 201 Winchester St; ☺9am-5pm; P👶; 🚃506) FREE On the former site of the Riverdale Zoo, where from 1888 to 1974 prairie wolves howled at night and spooked the Cabbagetown kids, Riverdale Farm is a rural oasis in the downtown. Now a working-farm museum, it has two barns, a summer wading pool and pens of feathered and furry friends. Kids follow the farmer around as they do their

daily chores, including milking the cows at 10:30am. There's a farmers market on Tuesdays (3pm to 7pm May to October).

⊚ The Beaches

Say the Beaches to locals and they picture the wealthy, professional neighborhood by the lake. To everyone else, it means the beaches themselves and the parklands along Lake Ontario. Of all the beaches, **Kew Beach** (☏416-392-8186; www.toronto. ca/parks/beaches; ☺dawn-dusk; 🚃501) is the most popular; its boardwalk runs east to **Balmy Beach** and west to **Woodbine Beach**.

Adjacent **Kew Gardens** has restrooms, snack bars, a skating rink, lawn bowls and tennis courts; at the western end there's an Olympic-size public swimming pool. For cyclists and in-line skaters, the **Martin Goodman Trail** leads past Ashbridge's Bay Park. Off Queen St E, with its restaurants, the sunken **Ivan Forrest Gardens** leads to Glen Stewart Ravine, a wilder patch of green running north to Kingston Rd.

⊚ Toronto Islands

Once upon a time there were no Toronto Islands, just an immense sandbar stretching 9km into the lake. On April 13, 1858, a hurricane blasted through the sandbar and Toronto's jewel-like islands were born – nearly two-dozen isles covering 240 hectares and home to close-knit, 800-strong communities on **Algonquin Island**, with an amusement park and kayaking, and **Ward's Island**, with a boardwalk and cafes. The islands are only accessible by ferry (15 minutes, adult/child $7.50/3.65). To get to the ferry docks from Union Station, take the 509 Harbourfront or the 510 Spadina streetcar south to the Bay and Queens Quay stop.

⊚ Greater Toronto Area (GTA)

High Park   Park
(www.toronto.ca/parks; 1873 Bloor St W; ☺dawn-dusk; P; S High Park, 🚃501, 506, 508) Toronto's favorite and best-known park is a wonderful place to unfurl a picnic blanket,

swim, play tennis, bike around, skate on the **Grenadier Pond** in the winter, or in the spring meander through the groves of cherry blossoms donated to the park by the Japanese ambassador in 1959. There's also a theatrical stage, a small children's zoo and Colborne Lodge, built in 1836 by the Howard family, who donated much of High Park to the city in 1873.

Bus 30B picks up at High Park subway station, then loops through the park, on weekends and holidays from mid-June to early September. Otherwise it's a 200m walk from the subway station to the north gates.

Scarborough Bluffs Park

(☑416-392-1111; www.toronto.ca; Scarborough; ⊙dawn-dusk; P; ⊟12, SVictoria Park) Atop this 14km stretch of glacial lakeshore cliffs, enjoy stunning views across Lake Ontario. Erosion has created cathedral spire formations, exposing evidence of five different glacial periods. Without wheels, getting to the bluffs can be a drag. Take the subway to Victoria Park, then bus 12 along Kingston Rd to Cathedral Bluffs Dr, east of the St Clair Ave E intersection.

McMichael Canadian Art Collection Gallery

(☑905-893-1121; www.mcmichael.com; 10365 Islington Ave, Kleinburg; adult/child $18/free; ⊙10am-5pm; P; ⊟13) Handcrafted wooden buildings (which include painter Tom Thomson's cabin, moved from its original location), set amid 40 hectares of conservation trails, contain works by Canada's best-known landscape painters, the Group of Seven, as well as First Nations, Inuit and other acclaimed Canadian artists. It's a 34km, 45-minute drive from Toronto: be sure to use a GPS. Tours are included with admission and parking is $5.

Sharon Temple Historic Building

(☑905-478-2389; www.sharontemple.ca; 18974 Leslie St, East Gwillimbury; adult/child $5/free; ⊙10am-4:30pm Thu-Sun May-Oct) A national historic site and one of the oldest museums in Canada, this quaint and fasci-

nating temple was built in 1832 by a Quaker sect called the Children of the Peace, to a unique architectural style. Lovingly restored in 2011, the simple museum tells the story of its founders and makes a wonderful day trip out of Toronto. It's about 55km north of downtown.

⊘ ACTIVITIES

Bike Share Toronto Cycling

(☑855-898-2378; www.bikesharetoronto.com; 1-/3-day passes $7/15) Bike Share Toronto is a service that allows unlimited 30-minute bike rides for one or three days. Collect and return a shared bicycle from any of over 200 docking stations dotted around the city – great for visitors. A $101 security deposit is frozen on your credit card on joining. Transit App lets you buy passes, locate stations and get ride codes to unlock bikes.

If you don't get a day pass, the first 30 minutes' rental is free. A second 30-minute block is $1.50, then $4 for the next, and $7 per each additional 30-minute period.

Community Bicycle Network Cycling

(CBN; ☑416-504-2918; www.communitybicycle network.org; 761 Queen St W; rental 1st day/weekend/week $25/35/65; ⊙noon-6pm Tue-Fri, 10am-6pm Sat; ⊟501) ⊘ Celebrating 20 years championing sustainable transportation, CBN offers rentals, repairs, workshops and events from a convenient Queen St W location.

Native Canadian Centre of Toronto Cultural

(Map p44; ☑416-964-9087; www.ncct.on.ca; 16 Spadina Rd; ⊙9am-8pm Mon-Thu, to 6pm Fri, 10am-4pm Sat; SSpadina) This community center hosts Thursday-night drum socials, seasonal powwows and elders' cultural events that promote harmony and conversation between tribal members and non–First Nations peoples. You can also sign up for workshops and craft classes, such as beading and dancing.

⊕ TOURS

Chariots of Fire — Bus

(Map p46; ☎905-877-0855; www.tourniagara falls.com; 33 Yonge St; day tours $77; ⑤King) Low-cost day tours from Toronto to Niagara Falls including a *Hornblower Niagara* boat ride and free time at Niagara-on-the-Lake. These guys are highly organized and comfortably present the best of the Falls, from Toronto, for those who only have a day to experience it all. Highly recommended.

City Sightseeing Toronto — Bus

(☎416-410-0536; www.citysightseeingtoronto. com; adult/child $38/20) Hop-on, hop-off sightseeing tours on an open-top double-decker London-style bus, around a 24-stop city loop. The route takes in most major sights with commentary and includes a free (seasonal) Lake Ontario cruise. Tickets are valid for 72 hours: good value if you plan to use the bus over three days and a great way to get oriented.

Heritage Toronto — Walking

(☎416-338-3886; www.heritagetoronto. org; 157 King St E; donations encouraged; ⊘Apr-Oct) A diverse offering of fascinating historical, cultural and nature walks, and bike and bus (TTC) tours, led by museum experts and neighborhood historical society members. Tours generally last one to three hours.

ROMWalks — Walking

(☎416-586-8000; www.rom.on.ca/en/whats-on/ romwalks; free-$10; ⊘Wed & Sun May-Sep) Well-informed volunteers from the Royal Ontario Museum (p45) lead one- to two-hour historical and architectural walking tours, including some of the city's lesser-known but most interesting buildings and neighborhoods. Most walks are free with appreciated tips, but some cost up to $10.

🛍 SHOPPING

When the weather's fine, explore **Kensington Market**, boho central, and the full length of **Queen St W**, with its smatterings

Kensington Market

JON BILOUS / SHUTTERSTOCK ©

of almost anything fashion, art and design you could imagine.

The Annex features a dwindling hodgepodge of art shops, bookstores and secondhand music, especially along Harbord St and on Markham St. **Bloor-Yorkville**, formerly 'Free Love' central in the 1960s, is now Toronto's most exclusive shopping district, where nothing is free.

Canadian and international design stores line King St E between Jarvis and Parliament Sts, in a trendy area known as the **Design Strip**. Nearby, the boutiques, galleries and craft studios fill the heritage-heavy **Distillery District**.

Craft Ontario Shop
Gifts & Souvenirs

(☑416-921-1721; www.craftontario.com; 1106 Queen St W; ⊙10am-6pm Mon-Wed & Sat, to 7pm Thu & Fri, noon-5pm Sun; 🚌501) Craft Ontario has been promoting artisans for over 70 years. Ceramics, jewelry, glasswork, prints and carvings make up most of the displays at this new Queen St W location, but you could also catch a special exhibition of Pangnirtung weaving or Cape Dorset graphics. Staff are knowledgeable about First Nations art.

Toronto Designers Market
Design

(☑416-570-8773; www.torontodesignersmarket. com; 1605 Queen St W; ⊙11am-6pm Wed-Sun; 🚌501) In the neglected far west of Queen, over 30 small designers have set up mini studio-storefronts within a cavernous space. It's a mixed bag, but there are plenty of fresh ideas in the pop-ups selling jewelry, clothes and gifts such as beard combs.

BMV
Books

(Map p44; Dundas Sq, 10 Edward St; ⊙10am-11pm Mon-Sat, noon-8pm Sun; ⑤Dundas) The biggest (and most popular) secondhand bookstore in Toronto, with a second outlet on **Bloor St** (Map p44; 471 Bloor St W; ⊙10am-11pm Mon-Wed, to midnight Thu-Sat, noon-9pm Sun; ⑤Spadina).

Where to Get Caffeinated

Too early for beer? Sidestep the coffee chains for some *real* barista action:

Rooster Coffee House (☑416-995-1530; www.roostercoffeehouse.com; 479 Broadview Ave; snacks $3-11; ⊙7am-8pm; 🚌504, 505)

Dark Horse Espresso (Map p44; ☑416-979-1200; www.darkhorseespresso.com; 215 Spadina Ave; coffees $3-6; ⊙7am-7pm Mon-Fri, 8am-7pm Sat & Sun; 🚌510)

B Espresso Bar (Map p44; ☑416-866-2111; www.bespressobar.com; 111 Queen St E; coffees $3-6; ⊙7:30am-5pm Mon-Fri; 🚌501)

Moonbean Coffee Company (Map p44; ☑416-595-0327; www.moonbeamcoffee. com; 30 St Andrews St; coffees $3-4.25; ⊙7am-9pm; 🚌510)

Jet Fuel (☑416-968-9982; www.jetfuel coffee.com; 519 Parliament St; coffees $3.25-5; ⊙6am-8pm; 🚌506)

Remarkable Bean (☑416-690-2420; 2242 Queen St E; snacks $3-10; ⊙7am-10pm; 🚌501)

ANASTASIA BELOUSOVA / 500PX ©

🍴 EATING

Queen Mother Café
Fusion $

(Map p44; ☑416-598-4719; www.queen mothercafe.ca; 208 Queen St W; mains $13-19; ⊙11:30am-1am Mon-Sat, to 11pm Sun; ⑤Osgoode) A Queen St institution, the Queen Mother is beloved for its cozy, dark wooden booths and excellent pan-Asian menu. Canadian comfort food is also on offer – try the Queen Mum burger. Check out the display of old stuff found in the walls the last

★ Top Five for Kids
CN Tower (p38)
Royal Ontario Museum (p45)
Ripley's Aquarium of Canada (p42)
Riverdale Farm (p48)
High Park (p48)

From left: High Park (p48); Riverdale Farm (p48); Ripley's Aquarium of Canada (p42)

time they renovated. The patio is hidden and one of the best in town.

Trattoria Nervosa
Italian $

(Map p44; ☎416-961-4642; www.eatnervosa. com; 75 Yorkville Ave; mains $16-29; ⊙11:30am-11pm Mon-Wed, to midnight Thu-Sat, noon-10pm Sun; ⊚; ⑤Bay) In the heart of the fancy-pants Yorkville area, this restaurant is an attitude-free Italian oasis. The patio is a good corner from which to people-watch Toronto's well-heeled while digging into simple, excellent pasta – the *mafalde al funghi* has incredibly deep mushroom flavors without being overly creamy.

Kekou Gelato House
Ice Cream $

(Map p44; ☎416-792-8858; www.kekou.ca; 13 Baldwin St; ⊙12:30-10:30pm Sun-Thu, to 11pm Fri & Sat; ☞; ⑤Osgoode) Whiskey, black sesame or oolong tea. No not cocktails, but excellent, Asian-inspired ice creams. The delicious flavors are not overly sweet or artificial, and the ginger and dark chocolate dairyfree is the punchiest vegan gelato in Toronto. On a villagey end of Baldwin, with another branch on Queen W near the corner with Spadina.

Hair of the Dog
Pub Food $$

(Map p44; ☎416-964-2708; www.hairofdogpub. com; 425 Church St; share plates $8-14, mains $13-25; ⊙11:30am-late Mon-Fri, 10:30am-late Sat & Sun; ⑤College) At its best in the warmer months when two levels of shaded patios spring to life with a mixed gay/straight crowd, this chilled puppy is delightfully less mainstream than its Village neighbors a few blocks north. Equally tempting as a drinking venue, the Dog serves great sharing plates and salads, too. No nonvegetarian can possibly resist the butter-chicken grilled cheese.

Country Style Hungarian Restaurant
Hungarian $$

(Map p44; ☎416-536-5966; 450 Bloor St W; schnitzels from $18; ⊙11am-10pm; ⑤Bathurst) This delightful Hungarian diner, with its checkered tablecloths and friendly family staff, hasn't changed a bit in at least a generation. The variety of enormous breaded schnitzels, cooked to crunchy perfection, are the best in town, and the cucumber salad is a treat. Hopefully they never change a thing. Note that menu prices *include* tax!

VALESTOCK / SHUTTERSTOCK ©

Richmond Station   International $$

(Map p46; ☎647-748-1444; www.richmond
station.ca; 1 Richmond St W; mains $21-28;
⏰11:30am-10:30pm Mon-Sat; Ⓢ Queen)
Reservations are strongly advised at
this busy and uncomplicated restaurant,
brainchild of celebrity *Top Chef Canada*
winner, Carl Heinrich. Dishes are 'ingre-
dient focused and technique driven.' Try
the excellent chunky lobster cocktail and
buttery mushroom fettuccine. The eclectic
menu is simple but gratifying, priced right
and complemented by a well-paired wine
list and daily chalkboard specials. Highly
recommended.

ND Sushi   Japanese $$

(Map p44; ☎416-551-6362; www.ndsushi
andgrill.com; 3 Baldwin St; mains $11-22;
⏰11:30am-3pm Mon-Fri & 5-10pm Mon-Sat;
🚋505, 506) From its pole position at the
beginning of Baldwin St, this unassuming
shokudō prepares favorite Japanese treats
like *gyoza*, tempura and mouthwatering
sashimi with authenticity. Its specialty is sushi, including a variety of not-so-traditional
Western *maki* rolls: the spicy rainbow roll is
divine. You could pay a whole lot more for
Japanese food of this caliber.

Lee   Asian $$

(Map p46; ☎416-504-7867; www.susur.com;
601 King St W; mains $15-45; ⏰5:30-10:30pm
Sun-Wed, to 11:30pm Thu-Sat; 🚋504, 508) Truly
a feast for the senses, dinner at acclaimed
cuisinier Susur Lee's self-titled flagship
restaurant is an experience best shared.
Slick servers assist in navigating the
artisan selection of East-meets-West Asian
delights: you really want to get the pairings
right. It's impossible to adequately convey
the wonderful dance of flavors, textures
and aromas one experiences in the signature Singaporean slaw, with...how many??
ingredients!

Allen's   Pub Food $$$

(☎416-463-3086; www.allens.to; 143 Danforth
Ave; mains $12-36; ⏰11:30am-2am; Ⓢ Broadview,
🚋504, 505) Featuring one of the city's nicest
patio dining areas (in warmer months),
Allen's is more than just a pub, although
it is a great place for lovers of Irish music
and dance. The seasonal menu has hearty,
sophisticated Irish fare: cuts of hormone- and

Gay & Lesbian Toronto

To say Toronto is LGBT-friendly is an understatement. That it embraces diversity more fully than most other centers of its size is closer to the mark. The city's LGBT **Pride Toronto** (www.pride toronto.com; ⊘Jun-Jul) is one of the largest in the world. On Parade day, the streets around Church and Wellesley swell with over a million people. At other times of the year, the Church St strip of the Village draws everyone from biker bears to lipstick lesbians to its modest smattering of sunny patios, pubs, cafes and restaurants.

For event listings, look up *Daily Xtra* (www.dailyxtra.com).

The fun multilevel gay club **Fly 2.0** (Map p44; ✏416-925-6222; www.flyyyz.com; 6 Gloucester St; cover $3-12; ⊘10:30pm-4am Sat; ⑤Wellesley), just outside the Village, off Yonge St, has the kind of monumental Saturdays thumping out electro dance that you might see on a TV drama. In fact it was the set for Club Babylon in Queer as Folk USA. It's still one of the best LGBT megaclubs in Toronto. Arrive early for cheaper cover.

Toronto's most well-known gay bar **Woody's/Sailor** (Map p44; ✏416-972-0887; www.woodystoronto.com; 465-7 Church St; ⊘noon-2am; ⑤Wellesley) is a sprawling complex with a grab bag of tricks, from drag shows, 'best ass' contests and billiards tables to nightly DJs. Sailor is a slick bar off to one side.

Pride parade
SHAWN GOLDBERG / SHUTTERSTOCK ©

additive-free beef (including one of Toronto's best burgers), lamb and veal, ale-battered halibut, and curries.

🍷 DRINKING & NIGHTLIFE

BarChef   Cocktail Bar
(Map p44; ✏416-868-4800; www.barchef toronto.com; 472 Queen St W; cocktails $15-45; ⊘6pm-1:30am Tue & Wed, to 2am Thu-Sat; ⑤Osgoode) Take a date here and there will never be awkward silence. You'll hear 'oohs' and 'aahs' from other tables in the intimate, near-darkness as cocktails emerge alongside a bonsai tree, or under a bell jar of vanilla and hickory-wood smoke. Beyond novelty, drinks show incredible, enticing complexity without overwhelming some unique flavors – truffle snow, chamomile syrup, cedar air, and soil!

Handlebar   Bar
(Map p44; ✏647-748-7433; 159 Augusta Ave; ⊘7pm-2am; 🚌505) A jolly little spot paying homage to the bicycle and its lovers, from owners with a fine pedigree. In a great spot south of Kensington Market, there's some wonderful retro styling and a nice mix of shiny happy punters. A calendar of quirky hip events makes it an easier bar to visit if you're traveling solo.

Mill Street Brewery   Brewery
(✏416-681-0338; www.millstreetbrewery. com; 55 Mill St, Bldg 63, Distillery District; ⊘11:30am-midnight; 🚌503, 504) With 13 specialty beers brewed on-site in the atmospheric Distillery District (p42), these guys are a leading light in local microbrewing. Order a sample platter so you can taste all the award-winning brews, including the Tankhouse Pale Ale, Stock Ale and Organic Lager. On a sunny afternoon, the courtyard is the place to be. Brewery-fare pairings include burgers and wraps.

One Eighty   Bar
(Map p44; ✏416-967-0000; www.the51stfloor. com; 51st fl, Manulife Centre, 55 Bloor St W; ⊘5pm-late Mon-Thu, noon-late Fri-Sun; ⑤Bay) Swanky and priced to match, the city's

highest licensed patio has arguably Toronto's best views outside the CN Tower. It's in the Manulife Centre building and, unlike the tower, there's no admission fee, though you'll be scoffed at if you don't drop some cash on a martini or a meal.

Clinton's   Bar

(www.clintons.ca; 693 Bloor St; ☺4pm-2am Mon-Fri, 11am-2am Sat & Sun; ⑤Christie) Weekly themed DJ nights, live music and comedy are all part of the lineup at iconic Clinton's, attracting a fun, arty crowd. There's a pub at the front serving decent food and a wicked dance hall at back: the 'Girl & Boy 90s Dance Party' on Fridays is kick-ass.

✪ ENTERTAINMENT

There's always something going on here, from hockey, art-house cinema and offbeat theater to jazz, opera, punk rock and hip-hop. In summer, free outdoor festivals and concerts are the norm, but Toronto's dance and live-music scene keeps grooving year-round.

For the latest club, alt-culture and live-music listings, check out *Now* (www.nowtoronto.com).

Horseshoe Tavern   Live Music

(Map p44; ☎416-598-4753; www.horseshoe tavern.com; 370 Queen St W; ☺noon-2am; ☐501, 510) Well past its 65th birthday, the legendary Horseshoe still plays a crucial role in the development of local indie rock. This place just oozes a history of good times and classic performances. Come for a beer and check it out.

Not so local, The Police played here on their first North American tour – Sting did an encore in his underwear and Bran Van 3000 made their long-awaited comeback.

Reservoir Lounge   Jazz

(Map p46; ☎416-955-0887; www.reservoir lounge.com; 52 Wellington St E; ☺7:30pm-2am Tue-Sat; ☐503, 504) Swing dancers, jazz singers and blues crooners call this cool candlelit basement lounge home, and it has hosted its fair share of musical greats over the years. Where else can you enjoy

VALESTOCK / SHUTTERSTOCK ©

Rogers Centre

a martini while dipping strawberries into chocolate fondue during the show?

Canadian Opera Company   Opera
(Map p44; ☑416-363-8231; www.coc.ca; Four Seasons Centre for the Performing Arts, 145 Queen St W; ⊘box office 11am-7pm Mon-Sat, to 3pm Sun; ⑤Osgoode) Canada's national opera company has been warbling its pipes for over 50 years. Tickets sell out fast; the Richard Bradshaw Amphitheatre (in the fabulous Four Seasons Centre) holds free concerts from September through June, usually at noon. Check the website for specific days.

Ed Mirvish Theatre   Theater
(Map p44; ☑416-872-1212; www.mirvish. com; 244 Victoria St; ⑤Dundas) Formerly the Canon, the Ed Mirvish Theatre was renamed in 2011 in honor of the late Ed Mirvish, Toronto's well-loved businessman, philanthropist and patron of the arts. One of four Mirvish theaters, the 1920s-era vaudeville hall is a hot ticket for musical extravaganzas.

TIFF Bell Lightbox   Cinema
(Map p46; www.tiff.net; cnr 350 King St W; ☐504) Home of the Toronto International Film Festival (TIFF), held over 10 days in September, this resplendent cinema complex is the hub of all the action when the festival is in town. Throughout the year, it's used primarily for TIFF Cinematheque, screening world cinema, independent films, directorial retrospectives and other special events. Try to see a film here if you can.

Toronto Blue Jays   Baseball
(☑416-341-1234; www.bluejays.com; ⊘Apr-Sep) Toronto's Major League Baseball team (an icon of Toronto and a source of pride) plays at the **Rogers Centre** (Map p46; ☑416-341-2770; www.rogerscentre.com; 1 Blue Jays Way; 1hr tours adult/child $16/10; ⑤Union). Buy tickets through Ticketmaster or at the Rogers Centre box office near Gate 9. Try for seats along the lower (pricier) level baselines where you have a better chance of catching a fly ball (or wearing one in the side of the head).

The Jays haven't won the World Series since 1993, but who knows, this could be their year.

Toronto Maple Leafs Ice Hockey
(☎416-815-5982; www.mapleleafs.com; ☯Oct-Apr) The 13-time Stanley Cup–winning Maple Leafs slap the puck around the **Air Canada Centre** (Map p46; ACC; ☎416-815-5500; www.theaircanadacentre.com; 40 Bay St; ⑤Union) in the National Hockey League (NHL). Every game sells out, but a limited number of same-day tickets go on sale through Ticketmaster at 10am and at the Air Canada Centre ticket window from 5pm.

ⓘ INFORMATION

INTERNET ACCESS

Free wi-fi is available at the airport, on downtown subway platforms, and in most larger restaurants and coffee shops; check out www.wirelesstoronto.ca for a list of free hot spots in the city.

TOURIST INFORMATION

Ontario Travel Information Centre (☎416-314-5899; www.ontariotravel.net; Union Station, 65 Front St W; ☯8am-8pm Mon-Sat, 10am-6pm Sun; ⑤Union) This large branch at the west side of Union Station has knowledgeable, multilingual staff and overflowing racks of brochures that cover every nook and cranny of Toronto.

Tourism Toronto (☎416-203-2500; www.see torontonow.com; 207 Queens Quay W; ☯8:30am-6pm Mon-Fri; ⑤Union) Contact one of the telephone agents; after hours use the automated touch-tone information menu.

ⓘ GETTING THERE & AWAY

AIR

Toronto is well-served by international and domestic flights. Most Canadian airlines and international carriers arrive at Canada's busiest airport, **Toronto Pearson International Airport** (YYZ; Lester B Pearson International Airport; ☎Terminal 3 416-776-5100, Terminals 1 & 2 416-247-7678; www.torontopearson.com; 6301 Silver Dart Dr, Mississauga), 27km northwest of downtown Toronto. Terminal assignments vary; be sure to check with your airline which one you'll be coming in to or leaving from.

On a small island just off the lakeshore, **Billy Bishop Toronto City Airport** (YTZ; ☎416-203-6942; www.torontoport.com) is the proud home of Porter airlines, with competitive fares to a wide range of destinations within eastern Canada and the USA. Air Canada also has services to Montréal from here. When planning your itinerary, be sure to keep your eyes on www.flyporter.com: seat sales are frequent and offer excellent value.

BUS

○ Long-distance buses operate from the art deco **Metro Toronto Coach Terminal** (☎416-393-4636; 610 Bay St; ⑤Dundas).

○ Greyhound Canada (www.greyhound.ca) has numerous routes from Toronto. Megabus has a smaller, and cheaper, selection of destinations. Advance tickets offer significant savings; online sales often close two hours before departure.

○ Union Station downtown serves as the bus and train depot for GO Transit (www.gotransit.com), the commuter service of the Greater Toronto Area (GTA).

CAR & MOTORCYCLE

○ Toronto is wrapped in a mesh of multilane highways, frequently crippled by congestion. The Gardiner Expwy runs west along the lakeshore into Queen Elizabeth Way (QEW) to Niagara Falls. At the city's western border Hwy 427 runs north to the airport. Hwy 401 is the main east–west arterial and is regularly jammed. On the eastern side of the city, the Don Valley Pkwy connects Hwy 401 to the Gardiner Expwy. Hwys 400 and 404 run north from Toronto. A GPS is strongly recommended.

○ All major car-rental agencies, such as **Avis** (☎800-230-4898; www.avis.ca) and **Enterprise** (☎800-261-7331; www.enterpriserentacar.ca), have desks at Pearson airport and offices downtown and throughout the city. Book in advance for the best rates. Cars sell out on busy summer weekends.

○ Smaller independent agencies offer lower rates, but may have fewer (and older) cars. **Wheels 4 Rent** (☎416-585-7782; www.wheels4rent.ca; 77 Nassau St; ☐510) rents compact cars from around $39 per day excluding taxes.

TRAIN

○ Grand **Union Station** (☏416-869-3000; www.viarail.com; 140 Bay St) downtown is Toronto's main rail hub.

○ VIA Rail plies the heavily trafficked Windsor–Montréal corridor and beyond.

○ Amtrak trains link Toronto's Union Station with Buffalo ($57, 4½ hours, daily) and New York City ($156, 13½ hours, daily).

ⓘ GETTING AROUND

BOAT

○ From April to September, **Toronto Islands Ferries** (☏416-392-8193; www.city.toronto.on.ca; Bay St; adult/child return $7.50/3.65; Ⓢ Union Station) runs every 15 to 30 minutes from 8am to 11pm.

○ From October to March, ferry services are slashed (to roughly hourly), only servicing Ward's Island, plus a couple per day to Hanlan's Point.

○ The journey (to either Ward's Island or Hanlan's Point) takes only 15 minutes, but queues can be long on weekends and holidays – show up early, or book online (https://secure.toronto.ca/FerryTicketOnline) to skip the purchase queue.

○ A few water taxis are also available from the terminal; they can take you anywhere for about $10 per person (pay onboard), and depart when full.

CAR & MOTORCYCLE

Parking in Toronto is expensive, usually $3 to $4 per half-hour. Private lots offer reduced rate parking before 7am and after 6pm. Traffic is horrendous amid ongoing construction. We don't recommend driving downtown. If you do, you must stop for streetcars – behind the rear doors, when the streetcar is collecting or ejecting passengers – and for pedestrians at crosswalks when signals are flashing. Look out for cyclists in your blind spots.

Hwy 407 (www.407etr.com), running east–west from Markham to Mississauga, is an electronic toll road and alternative to the congested 401. Cameras record your license plate and the time and distance traveled. Expect a bill in the mail (Canada, US or Zanzibar, they'll find you).

PUBLIC TRANSPORTATION

○ Subway lines operate regular service from around 6am (9am Sunday) to 1:30am daily. Stations are generally very safe and have Designated Waiting Areas (DWAs) monitored by security cameras.

○ Streetcars are notoriously slow during rush hours, stopping frequently.

○ You can buy and top-up smart card PRESTO (www.prestocard.ca) fare cards from credit-card-only machines at subway stations or also with cash from Union Station. Valid across the city.

TAXI

Metered fares start at $4, plus $1.75 per kilometer, depending on traffic.

Crown Taxi (☏416-240-0000; www.crowntaxi.com)

Diamond Taxicab (☏416-366-6868; www.diamondtaxi.ca)

Royal Taxi (☏416-777-9222; www.royaltaxi.ca).

Where to Stay

Toronto has top-notch luxury hotels, but midrange rooms can feel drab and dated. There are some great hostels and plenty of B&Bs to choose from. Book in advance: the best digs fill quickly in summer.

Neighborhood	Atmosphere
Harbourfront	Redeveloped lakeside with restaurants, galleries, shops and theaters. Ferries for Toronto Islands and parklands on your doorstep.
Financial District	Close to Union Station but largely under construction until 2018.
Entertainment District & King Street West	Home to theaters and preshow bars; quiet stretches with some of the city's best historic architecture.
Downtown Yonge	Home of the downtown core with plenty of midrange hotels.
Bloor-Yorkville	Rub elbows with Gucci and Prada and hang out with who's who in lovely neighborhood cafes.
Queen West & West Queen West	The hip hub of popular culture with no real sights but plenty happening and lots of places to eat, drink and be merry.

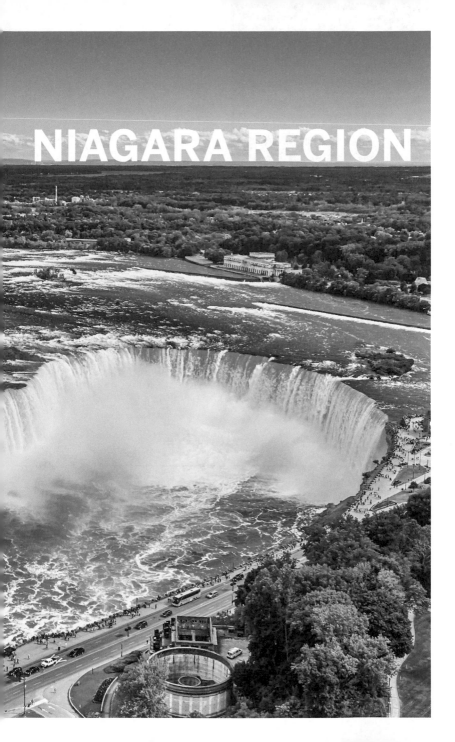

NIAGARA REGION

Niagara Region at a Glance...

Jutting east from Hamilton and forming a natural divide between Lake Erie and Lake Ontario, the Niagara Peninsula is a legitimate tourist hot spot. A steep limestone escarpment jags along the spine of the peninsula, generating a unique microclimate. Humid and often frost free, this is prime terrain for viticulture: a fact not lost on the award-winning wineries of Niagara-on-the-Lake. Many visitors, of course, come to the peninsula to see just one thing – the staggering Niagara Falls – but there is plenty more to explore; consider a several-day visit to fully experience the delights of the region.

One Day in the Niagara Region

Spend the day exploring **Niagara Falls**, (p64), starting early with a view of Horseshoe Falls from Table Rock. Don a plastic poncho and get up close with **Journey Behind the Falls** (p70), then feel the mist with **Hornblower Niagara Cruises** (p70). With your feet firmly back on the ground, check out the barrels at the **Daredevil Exhibit** (p70) and end with an interactive history lesson at **Niagara's Fury** (p70).

Three Days in the Niagara Region

Head out to **Niagara-on-the-lake** (p68) and explore its history museums and quaint store-lined 19th-century streets. Dine at the classy **Prince of Wales Hotel** (p69) and stay in one of the charming local B&Bs. The next day explore the many top-notch vineyards of the surrounding **Wine Country** (p66).

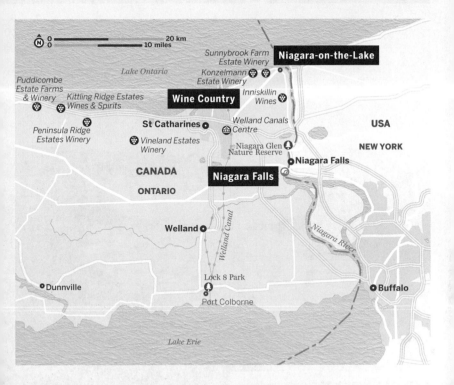

Arriving in the Niagara Region

Niagara Transportation Centre Greyhound Canada buses to Toronto ($19, two hours, five daily) and Buffalo, NY ($12, 1½ hours, six daily).

Niagara Airbus Door-to-door shared airport shuttle service to Toronto Pearson ($147, 1½ hours) or Buffalo International, NY ($95, 1½ hours).

Niagara Falls Train Station Weekend summer services to Toronto. Daily services to NYC ($151, 11½ hours).

Where to Stay

It isn't necessary to stay on the Niagara Peninsula if your goal is just to see the falls. There are usually more beds than heads in Niagara Falls, but the town is sometimes completely booked up. Prices spike sharply in summer, on weekends and during holidays. You might find you prefer waking in the town of Niagara-on-the-Lake more than next to the falls; when the local Shaw Festival (p69) is running, lodging is very tight, so plan ahead.

JAVEN / SHUTTERSTOCK ©

Visiting Niagara Falls

Join thousands of onlookers who delight in the spectacle of this magnificent, unstoppable flow of water every day.

Niagara Falls forms a natural rift between Ontario and New York State. On the US side, the American Falls and Bridal Veil Falls crash onto mammoth fallen rocks. On the Canadian side, the grander, more powerful Horseshoe Falls plunge into the cloudy Maid of the Mist Pool.

Height & Volume

Niagara is not the tallest of waterfalls – at just over 50m (165ft) it is actually quite short in the waterfall stakes – but in terms of sheer volume, there's nothing like it, with some 2830 cu meters (100,000 cu ft) of water plummeting downwards every second. By day or night, regardless of season, the falls never fail to awe. Even in winter, when the flow is partially hidden and the edges freeze solid, the watery extravaganza is undiminished.

Great For...

☑ **Don't Miss**

Taking a virtual plunge over the falls at IMAX Niagara (p70).

Niagara Falls (Bridal Veil Falls)

Niagara Reservation State Park

Niagara Falls (Horseshoe Falls)

USA / CANADA

Niagara River

❶ Need to Know

Arrive early to beat the crowds. Visiting the falls is free, but parking access around the falls and Clifton Hill is expensive and limited.

✕ Take a Break

Just a few blocks from the falls, Napoli Ristorante Pizzeria (p71) serves the best Italian in town, hands down.

★ Top Tip

The prime falls-watching spot is Table Rock, poised just meters from the drop of Horseshoe Falls.

Niagara Escarpment

The Niagara Escarpment, a 725km-long land formation that creates Niagara Falls, is a designated Unesco World Biosphere Reserve. Sweeping from eastern Wisconsin, through Ontario and ending in New York State, the escarpment is a combination of what was originally lime bed and ancient sea floor. The dolomitic limestone that makes up the land formation is more resistant than the land around it, which has eroded and left the bulge of limestone slithering around the Great Lakes.

Niagara Falls Daredevils

Surprisingly, more than a few people who have gone over Niagara Falls have actually lived to tell the tale. The first successful leap was in 1901, by a 63-year-old school-teacher named Annie Taylor, who did it in a skirt, no less. This promoted a rash of barrel-stunters that continued into the 1920s, including Bobby Leach, who survived the drop, but who met his untimely death after slipping on an orange peel and developing gangrene!

In 1984 Karl Soucek revived the tradition in a bright-red barrel. He made it, only to die six months later in another barrel stunt in Houston. Also during the 1980s two locals successfully took the plunge lying head to head in the same barrel.

A US citizen who tried to jet ski over the falls in 1995 might have made it – if his rocket-propelled parachute had opened. Another American, Kirk Jones, survived the trip over the falls unaided in 2003. After being charged by Canadian police with illegally performing a stunt, he joined the circus.

Only one accidental falls-faller has survived – a seven-year-old Tennessee boy fell out of a boat upstream in 1960 and survived the drop without even breaking a bone.

Konzelmann Estate Winery

JEAN B HEGUY / GETTY IMAGES ©

Wine Country

A visit to Niagara Wine Country makes an indulgent day trip or lazy weekend, with vineyards both old and new to explore.

The Niagara Peninsula adheres to the 43rd parallel: a similar latitude as Northern California and further south than France's Bordeaux. Here, the mineral-rich soils and a moderate microclimate are the perfect recipe for viticulture success.

Touring the vineyards by car is the best way to go. Regional tourist offices stock wine-route maps and brochures, which are also available at winery tasting rooms. Besides tastings, most places offer tours and dining. Parking is free at all vineyards.

Great For...

☑ Don't Miss

The weeklong Niagara Wine Festival (www.niagarawinefestival.com) in mid-September.

Top Wineries

Puddicombe Estate Farms & Winery (www.puddicombefarms.com; 1468 Hwy 8, Winona; tastings $0.50; ⊘9am-5pm daily May-Dec, 10am-4pm Mon-Fri Jan-Apr) Rustic farm specializing in fruit wines (try the peach or the iced apple).

Need to Know

The official Wine Route is signposted off the Queen Elizabeth Way, on rural highways and along backcountry roads. For more info, check out www.winesof ontario.ca.

✕ Take a Break

Fill your belly with pizza or meat pies at **Pie Plate** (☏905-468-9743; www.thepie plate.com; 41516 Niagara Stone Rd, Virgil; ⊙10am-6pm Tue-Sun).

★ Top Tip

Avoid being the designated driver and join a Crush on Niagara (www.crush tours.com) winery tour.

Sunnybrook Farm Estate Winery (www.sunny brookwine.com; 1425 Lakeshore Rd, Niagara-on-the-Lake; tastings $1-3; ⊙10am-6pm) Specializes in unique Niagara fruit and berry wines, and brews a mean 'hard' cider.

Inniskillin (www.inniskillin.com; 1499 Line 3, cnr Niagara Pkwy, Niagara-on-the-Lake; tastings $1-20, tours $5-15; ⊙9am-6pm, tours hourly May-Oct) The master of the ice-wine craft.

Kittling Ridge Winery (www.kittlingridge. com; 297 South Service Rd, Grimsby; tastings & tours free; ⊙10am-6pm Mon-Sat, 11am-5pm Sun) Friendly staff and award-winning ice- and late-harvest wines.

Peninsula Ridge Estates Winery (www.peninsula ridge.com; 5600 King St W, Beamsville; tours $5; ⊙10am-5pm) A lofty timber tasting room, a restaurant and a magical hilltop setting.

Vineland Estates Winery (www.vineland.com; 3620 Moyer Rd, Vineland; tours with tasting $12, with purchase $7; ⊙10am-6pm) The elder statesperson of Niagara viticulture; almost all the wines here are excellent.

Konzelmann Estate Winery (www.konzelmann. ca; 1096 Lakeshore Rd, Niagara-on-the-Lake; tours $5-15; ⊙10am-6pm, tours May-Sep) One of the oldest wineries in the region and the only one to take full advantage of the lakeside microclimate.

Niagara Region Ice Wine

Niagara's regional wineries burst onto the scene at Vinexpo 1991 in Bordeaux, France. In a blind taste test, judges awarded a coveted gold medal to an Ontario ice wine – international attendees' jaws hit the floor.

To make ice wine, a certain percentage of grapes are left on the vines after the regular harvest is over. If birds, storms and mildew don't get to them, the grapes grow ever-more sugary and concentrated. Winemakers wait patiently until December or January when three days of consistent, low temperature (-8°C/°18F) freeze the grapes entirely.

It takes 10 times the usual number of grapes to make just one bottle. This, combined with labor-intensive production and the high risk of crop failure, often drives the price above $50 per 375mL bottle.

Uniform detail, 41st regiment

STEVE RUSSELL / TORONTO STAR / GETTY IMAGES ©

Niagara-on-the-Lake

One of the best-preserved 19th-century towns in North America, affluent N-o-t-L boasts tree-lined streets and impeccably restored houses.

Great For...

☑ Don't Miss

A few blocks from Queen St, Queen's Royal Park is a sweet spot for a picnic beside the water.

Originally a neutral First Nations village, Niagara-on-the-Lake was founded by Loyalists from New York State after the American Revolution. It later became the first capital of the colony of Upper Canada. Today, lovely Queen St teems with shops of the ye-olde variety selling antiques, Brit-style souvenirs and homemade fudge, and with stampedes of tour-bus guests. Stay past 5pm, however, and you'll discover this is a *real* town, not just a fairy-tale ginger-bread lookalike.

Historical Sights

On the town's southeastern fringe, restored **Fort George** (☏905-468-6614; www.pc.gc.ca/fortgeorge; 51 Queens Pde; adult/child $11.70/5.80; ☺10am-5pm May-Oct, Sat & Sun only Apr & Nov; ℙ) dates from 1797. The fort saw some bloody battles during the War of

Morning parade at Fort George

JONATHAN NICHOLLS / GETTY IMAGES ©

Lake Ontario

Niagara-on-the-Lake

St Catharines

Lockport

Niagara Falls

USA / CANADA

❶ Need to Know

Chamber of Commerce Visitors Information Centre (☎905-468-1950; www.niagaraonthelake.com; 26 Queen St; ☺10am-7:30pm) Pick up maps and details on a self-guided walking tour.

✕ Take a Break

Make time to dine at the opulent **Prince of Wales Hotel** (☎905-468-3246; www.vintage-hotels.com; 6 Picton St).

★ Top Tip

Cycling is a great way to explore the region. Rent a bike from Zoom Leisure (www.zoomleisure.com).

1812, changing hands between British and US forces a couple of times. Ghost tours, skills demonstrations, retro tank displays and battle re-enactments occur throughout the summer.

For more military accoutrements, the **Lincoln & Welland Regimental Museum** (☎905-468-0888; www.lwmuseum.ca; cnr King & John Sts; adult/child $3/2; ☺10am-4pm Wed-Sun; ℗) boasts wonderfully aged displays of Canadian military regalia.

South of Simcoe Park, the **Niagara Historical Society Museum** (☎905-468-3912; www.niagarahistorical.museum; 43 Castlereagh St; adult/child $5/1; ☺10am-5pm; ℗) has a vast collection relating to the town's past, ranging from First Nations artifacts to Loyalist and War of 1812 collectibles (including the prized hat of Major General Sir Isaac Brock).

Shaw Festival

For more than 50 years, the theatrical **Shaw Festival** (☎905-468-2172; www.shawfest.com; 10 Queens Pde; ☺Apr-Oct, box office 10am-8pm) has lured global audiences, who haven't been shy about issuing praise. Performances run from April through October, including a variety of works from Victorian drama to contemporary plays, musicals and classics from Wilde, Woolf and Coward. Specialized seminars are held throughout the season, plus informal 'Lunchtime Conversations' on selected Saturdays.

Actors tread the boards in three venues around town – the Festival, Royal George and Court House Theaters. Rush seats go on sale at 9am on performance days (except for Saturdays). Students, under-30s and seniors receive discounts at some matinees; weekday matinees are the cheapest.

/ GETTY IMAGES ©

Niagara Falls

⦿ SIGHTS

IMAX Theatre & Daredevil Exhibit   Museum

(📞905-358-3611; www.imaxniagara.com; 6170 Fallsview Blvd; Daredevil Gallery adult/child $8/6.50, movie prices vary; ⊙9am-9pm) The best reason to come here is for the Daredevil Exhibit attached to IMAX Niagara (which screens blockbusters and films about the falls; combo tickets are available). Scratch your head in amazement at the battered collection of barrels and padded bubbles in which people have ridden over the falls (p65) – not all of them successfully. There's also a history of falls 'funambulism' (tightrope walking) here.

Niagara Glen Nature Reserve   Park

(📞905-371-0254; www.niagaraparks.com; Niagara Pkwy; ⊙dawn-dusk; 🅿) About 8km north of the falls is this exceptional reserve, where you can get a sense of what the area was like pre-Europeans. There are 4km of walking trails winding down into a gorge, past huge boulders, cold caves, wildflowers and woods. The Niagara Parks Commission offers **guided nature walks** daily during the summer season for a nominal fee. Bring something to drink – the water in the Niagara River is far from clean.

✪ ACTIVITIES

Hornblower Niagara Cruises   Boating

(www.niagaracruises.com; 5920 River Rd; adult/child $20/12.25; ⊙9am-7:45pm Jun-Aug, to 4:45pm Apr-May & Sep-Oct) Hornblower is the newer boat company in town, taking over from the age-old Maid of the Mist (which still runs on the American side of the falls). Hornblower's 700-person catamarans sail up close to **Bridal Veil Falls** (American Falls) and **Horseshoe Falls**, among other thundering cascades. You are supplied with flimsy raincoats but will still get doused (in a fun way).

Departures are every 15 minutes, weather permitting. Sunrise and evening fireworks cruises are being added to the schedule, so check for updates.

Journey Behind the Falls   Walking

(📞905-354-1551; www.niagarafallstourism.com; 6650 Niagara Pkwy; adult/child Apr-Dec $16.75/10.95, Jan-Mar $11.25/7.30; ⊙9am-10pm) From Table Rock Information Centre you can don a very unsexy plastic poncho and traverse rock-cut tunnels halfway down the cliff – as close as you can get to the falls without getting in a barrel. It's open year-round, but be prepared to queue. In winter, the lower deck is usually closed; hence the lower price.

Niagara's Fury   Simulator

(📞905-358-3268; 6650 Niagara Pkwy; adult/child $14.25/9.25; ⊙every 30min 10:30am-4pm) On the upper level of Table Rock, the falls' latest Universal Studios–style attraction takes you into an interactive 360-degree cinema-simulation of how the falls were created. Expect lots of high-tech tricks to suspend disbelief, including getting splashed, snow and a rapid drop in temperature. It feels aimed solely at kids.

White Water Walk   Walking

(📞905-374-1221; 4330 Niagara Pkwy; adult/child $12.25/8; ⊙9am-7:30pm) At the northern end of town, next to Whirlpool Bridge, the White Water Walk is another way to get up close and personal with the falls, this time via an elevator down to a 325m boardwalk suspended above the rampaging torrents, just downstream from the falls.

Whirlpool Aero Car   Cable Car

(Niagara Spanish Aero Car; 📞905-354-5711; 3850 Niagara Pkwy; adult/child $14.25/9.25; ⊙9am-8pm Mar-Nov) Dangling above the Niagara River, 4.5km north of Horseshoe Falls, the Whirlpool Aero Car was designed by Spanish engineer Leonardo Torres Quevedo and has been operating since 1916 (but don't worry – it's still in good shape). The gondola travels 550m between two outcrops above a deadly whirlpool cre-

Niagara Glen Nature Reserve

ated by the falls – count the logs and tires spinning in the eddies below. No wheelchair access.

✪ TOURS

Double Deck Tours   Bus
(📞905-374-7423; www.doubledecktours.com; cnr River Rd & Clifton Hill; tours adult/child from $80/52; ⏰11am Apr-Oct) Offers a deluxe four-hour tour on a red double-decker bus. The price includes admission to the Whirlpool Aero Car, Journey Behind the Falls and Hornblower Niagara Cruises.

✪ EATING

Flying Saucer   Fast Food $
(📞905-356-4453; www.flyingsaucerrestau-rant.com; 6768 Lundy's Lane; mains $8-27; ⏰6am-3am Sun-Thu, to 4am Fri & Sat) For extraterrestrial fast food, you can't go past this iconic diner on the Lundy's Lane motel strip. Famous $1.99 early-bird breakfasts are served from 6am to 10am

(eggs, fries and toast) with the purchase of a beverage. Heftier meals in the way of steaks, seafood, fajitas, burgers and hot dogs are also on board. Take-out is in the saucer to the left.

Napoli Ristorante
Pizzeria   Italian $$
(📞905-356-3345; www.napoliristorante.ca; 5545 Ferry St; mains $14-32; ⏰4-10:30pm) Head to Napoli for the best Italian in town, hands down. Delicious pizza, rich pasta, creamy risotto and veal parmigiana all feature on the familiar menu.

Taps on Queen
Brewhouse & Grill   International $$
(www.tapsbeer.com; 4680 Queen St; mains $9-14; ⏰noon-10pm Mon, Tue & Sun, to midnight Wed-Sat; 🖊) Does a mix of stuff, from shep-herd's pie to ancient grains curry (quinoa, couscous, adzuki beans, mung beans and veggies). All dishes are, naturally, best when paired with one of the brewery's tasty beers.

Crossing the Border

The Canadian side of Niagara Falls is considered by many to be the more spectacular. If you do wish to cross the border for a complete picture from the US side, you will need to arrange the normal visa requirements before arrival. You cannot obtain a tourist visa at any of the border crossings at the falls. US and Canadian citizens need to bring their passports, as usual.

AG Canadian $$$

(☏289-292-0005; www.agcuisine.com; 5195 Magdalen St; mains $18-36; ☺6-10:30pm Tue-Sun) Fine dining isn't something you find easily at the falls, which makes this fine restaurant at the **Sterling Inn & Spa** so refreshing. Service, decor, presentation and especially the quality of the food all rate highly. It has a seasonal menu featuring dishes like fennel pollen pickerel, roasted venison loin and crispy skinned trout, sourced locally.

ⓘ INFORMATION

Niagara Falls Tourism (☏905-356-6061; www.niagarafallstourism.com; 5400 Robinson St; ☺9am-5pm) On the Canadian side of the falls with information on the different neighborhoods and what's on. This office is located near the base of the Skylon Tower observation deck.

Niagara Parks Commission (☏905-371-0254; www.niagaraparks.com; ☺9am-11pm Jun-Aug) The falls' governing body, with information desks at Maid of the Mist Plaza and Table Rock Information Centre.

Ontario Travel Information (☏905-358-3221; www.ontariotravel.net; 5355 Stanley Ave; ☺8am-8pm) On the western outskirts of town; free tourist booklets containing maps and discount coupons.

ⓘ GETTING THERE & AWAY

Niagara Falls is well serviced by buses from both Canada and the US. Parking is a nightmare, so leave the car behind if possible.

BUS

Niagara Transportation Centre (☏905-357-2133; 4555 Erie Ave) In the old part of town; Greyhound Canada buses depart for Toronto ($19, 1½ to two hours, five daily) and Buffalo, NY ($12, one to 1½ hours, six daily). Go Transit also operates services from Toronto (via Burlington) by combination of rail and bus and, in recent years, direct rail services on weekends (June to September). Check with www.gotransit.com.

Niagara Airbus (☏905-374-8111; www.niagara airbus.com) Operates a door-to-door shared shuttle service between Niagara Falls and Toronto Pearson airport (one way/return $94/147, 1½ hours) or Buffalo Niagara International Airport, NY ($95/156, 1½ hours).

TRAIN

Rail services from **Niagara Falls Train Station** (☏888-842-7245; www.viarail.ca; 4267 Bridge St) to Toronto operate only as a weekend summer service operated by Go Transit. You can, however, get to New York City ($151, 11½ hours, daily).

ⓘ GETTING AROUND

CAR & MOTORCYCLE

Driving and parking around the center is an expensive headache. Park at the car park near the IMAX at the corner of Fallsview Blvd and Robinson St for just $5 for the whole day and walk, or follow the parking district signs and stash the car for the day (around $6 per 30 minutes, or $15 per day). The huge Rapidsview parking lot (also the WEGO depot) is 3km south of the falls off River Rd. See www.niagarafallstourism.com/plan/parking for all car-park locations.

PUBLIC TRANSPORTATION

○ Cranking up and down the steep 50m slope between the falls and Fallsview Blvd is a quaint **Incline Railway** (www.niagaraparks.com; 6635 Niagara Pkwy; one way $2.75, day passes $7). It saves you a 10- to 20-minute walk around, and is best taken uphill.

⊙ Formerly the seasonal Niagara Parks People Mover, **WEGO** (www.niagaraparks.com/wego; day passes adult/child $7.50/4.50) is an economical and efficient year-round transit system, geared for tourists. There are three lines: red, green and blue; between them, they've got all the major sights and accommodations covered.

Welland Canal Area

Built between 1914 and 1932, the historic Welland Canal, running from Lake Erie into Lake Ontario, functions as a shipping bypass around Niagara Falls. It's part of the St Lawrence Seaway, allowing shipping between the industrial heart of North America and the Atlantic Ocean, with eight locks along the 42km-long canal overcoming the difference of about 100m in the lakes' water levels.

Before it shifted east to Port Weller, the original Welland Canal opened into Lake Ontario at Lakeside Park in Port Dalhousie. This rustic harbor area is a blend of old and new, with a reconstructed wooden lock and an 1835 lighthouse alongside bars, restaurants and ice-cream parlors.

◎ SIGHTS

Lock 8 Park   Park
(Mellanby St; ⊘24hr) **Port Colborne**, where Lake Erie empties into the canal, contains the 420m Lock 8 – one of the longest in the world. South of Main St.

Welland Canals Centre   Museum
(☑905-984-8880; www.stcatharineslock3museum. ca; 1932 Welland Canals Pkwy; ⊘9am-5pm; P)
FREE For an up-to-date look at the canal, the Welland Canals Centre at Lock 3, just outside St Catharines, has a viewing platform close enough to almost let you touch the building-size ships as they wait for water levels to rise or fall. You can check the ships' schedules on the website and plan your visit accordingly.

Also here is the **St Catharines Museum** (adult/child/concession $4.20/2.50/4), with displays on town history and canal construction, plus a lacrosse hall of fame.

✖ EATING

The quiet, good-looking area around the canal has a canal-side boardwalk and shops and restaurants along West St, good for an afternoon stroll or evening meal.

ⓘ GETTING THERE & AWAY

You'll need your own transportation to get to the Welland Canal, passing interesting bridges along the way. The nearest town is St Catharines.

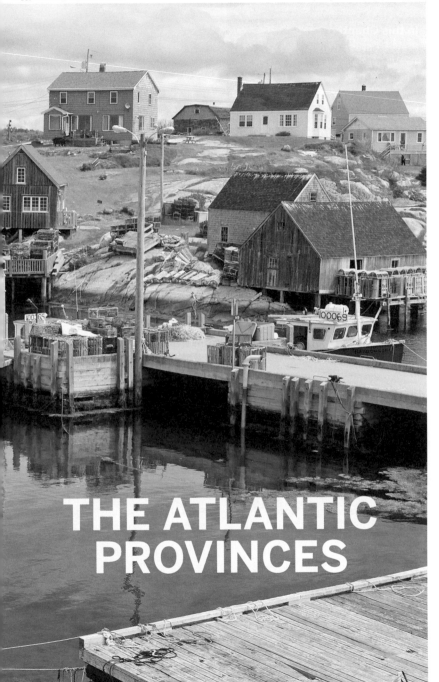

Peggy's Cove (p78), Nova Scotia

THE ATLANTIC
PROVINCES

The Atlantic Provinces at a Glance...

If the Atlantic provinces were a film, its protagonists would be rugged yet kind-hearted, burnt by the wind and at one with the sea. It would be shot against a backdrop of rolling green fields and high sea-cliffs; its soundtrack would feature fiddles, drums and evocative piano scores; and its plot would be a spirited romp around themes of history, community and family. Comprising a group of Canadian provinces – Nova Scotia, New Brunswick, Prince Edward Island, Newfoundland and Labrador – this region is an adventure waiting to happen.

Two Days in the Atlantic Provinces

Enjoy **Halifax** (p84) for a day, swinging down to snap a few photos at **Peggy's Cove** (p78) and feasting in the city's top restaurants – perhaps try **Bicycle Thief** (p87) for fine-dining Italian. Round out the day with a cocktail at **Lot Six** (p88). The following morning, head north to explore the **Cabot Trail** (p82), taking in amazing views and Acadian culture in **Chéticamp** (p83).

Four Days in the Atlantic Provinces

On day three, drive across the Confederation Bridge to Prince Edward Island (PEI) to visit Charlottetown's **Point Prim Lighthouse** (p91). Swing by **Cavendish** (p95) to meet Anne of Green Gables, and stop for seafood fresh from Malpeque Bay at **Carr's Oysters** (p95). Return to Halifax and hop a flight to hip **St John's** (p96), North America's oldest city and home to **Signal Hill** (p96) and the stunning **North Head Trail** (p97).

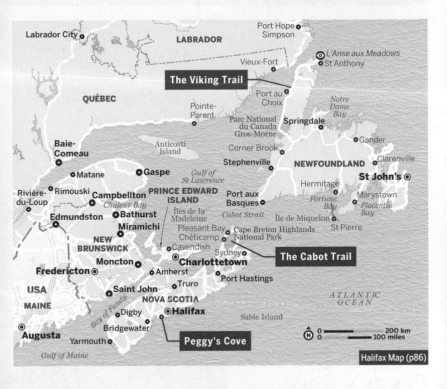

Halifax Map (p86)

Arriving in the Atlantic Provinces

Halifax Stanfield International Airport MetroX bus 320 runs frequently from 5:45am to 12:15am, or grab a taxi ($60, 30 minutes).

St John's International Airport Taxis to downtown (10 minutes) cost $25 plus $3 for each additional passenger.

Land Border Crossings The Canadian Border Services Agency posts updated wait times hourly; it's usually less than 30 minutes.

Where to Stay

In this part of the world, historic B&Bs rule the roost, ranging from boringly bland to ridiculously sublime. Road-trip lovers will be in motel heaven. Halifax has a wide range of accommodations, with an excellent selection of quality hostels and mid-priced hotels. Charlottetown's Old Town is a charming place to stay, while St John's has scores of good-value B&Bs. Remember to book in advance during Atlantic Canada's short-lived tourist season.

Peggy's Cove

This fishing village, with its rolling granite cove and perfect red-and-white lighthouse, exudes a dreamy seaside calm, even through the parading tour buses.

Great For...

☑ Don't Miss

Joining a free 45-minute walking tour from the tourist office, daily from mid-June through August.

Who Was Peggy?

The cove was first recorded as Pegg's Harbour in 1766. While many pragmatists claim this is simply a shortened version of Margaret (the harbor marks the eastern point of St Margaret's Bay), others prefer the more charming story of a young lass who was the sole survivor of a nearby shipwreck. Brought ashore, she was adopted and named Peggy. Her story spread and people came to see Peggy of the Cove – or Peggy's Cove.

Peggy's Point Lighthouse

The highlight of the cove is this picture-perfect **lighthouse** (185 Peggys Point Rd; ⊙9:30am-5:30pm May-Oct), which for many years was a working post office. Meander around the granite landscape that undulates much like the icy sea beyond.

Peggy's Point Lighthouse

ⓘ Need to Know

Peggy's Cove is 43km southwest of Halifax on Hwy 333. The **Visitor Information Centre** (VIC; ☎902-823-2253; 109 Peggy's Cove Rd; ☺9am-7pm May-Oct) has free parking.

✕ Take a Break

Cool off with a delicious homemade ice cream from **Dee Dee's** (www.deedees.ca; 110 Peggy's Cove Rd; cones from $3.50; ☺noon-6pm May-Sep).

★ Top Tip

Visit before 10am, after 6pm or in the off-season to avoid the crowds.

William E deGarthe Gallery & Monument

Finnish-born local artist William deGarthe (1907–83) sculpted the magnificent *Lasting Monument to Nova Scotian Fishermen* into a 30m granite outcropping behind his home. The sculpture depicts 32 fishermen, their wives and children, St Elmo with wings spread, and the legendary Peggy of her eponymous cove. The homestead is now a **gallery** (☎902-823-2256; 109 Peggy's Point Rd; $2; ☺gallery 9am-5pm May-Oct) showcasing 65 of deGarthe's other works.

Swissair 111 Memorial

This moving **memorial** (8250 Hwy 333) commemorates the 229 people who lost their lives on September 2, 1998, when Swissair Flight 111 plunged into the ocean 8km off the coast of Peggy's Cove, not long after taking off from New York's JFK airport, bound for Geneva, Switzerland.

Old Red Schoolhouse

Peggy's Cove's original one-room **schoolhouse** (☎902-823-2099; www.beales.ns.ca; 126 Peggy's Point Rd; suggested donation $10) was built in 1834. These days it's a performance venue where you can take in comedies and music performances through the high season. A few shows per season are serviced by shuttle vans that offer round-trips to Halifax hotels. Check the website for details.

What's Nearby

If you're looking for the same kind of vibe without the mass of visitors, albeit without the iconic lighthouse as well, cute-as-a-button **Lower Prospect** is 30km to the east via Terrence Bay.

GEORGE BURBA / SHUTTERSTOCK ©

The Viking Trail

The Viking Trail links Newfoundland's west coast to Southern Labrador, with two of the province's not-to-be-missed World Heritage—listed sites en route.

The Viking Trail follows the Northern Peninsula upward from the body of Newfoundland like an extended index finger. The region continues to gain in tourism, yet what's considered a crowd in Newfoundland might be considered a small gathering elsewhere.

Gros Morne National Park

A highlight of a visit to Newfoundland, this 1800-sq-km coastal **park** (709-458-2417; www.pc.gc.ca/grosmorne; per day adult/child/family $9.80/4.90/19.60) and Unesco World Heritage site features dramatic mountains, fjords, beaches, bogs and barren cliffs, and is popular for hiking, sea kayaking and sightseeing cruises. The bronze-colored Tablelands feature rock from deep within the earth's crust, supplying evidence for plate-tectonic theories. West of the Table-

Great For...

☑ Don't Miss

The stunning view of the Tablelands from a distance at the lookout above Norris Point.

Kayaks for hire along the Newfoundland coastline

❶ Need to Know

For the nitty-gritty, including where to see whales and stay along the trail, check out www.vikingtrail.org.

✖ Take a Break

In L'anse aux Meadows village, **Norseman Restaurant & Art Gallery** (☎709-623-2018; www.valhalla-lodge. com; Rte 436; mains $20-38; ⊙noon-9pm May-Sep) ranks among Newfoundland's best.

★ Top Tip

On the road, towns and amenities are few and far – make sure to fuel up when you can.

lands, dramatic volcanic sea stacks and caves mark the coast at Green Gardens.

Several small fishing villages dot the shoreline and provide amenities. Centrally located Rocky Harbour is the largest village and most popular place to stay.

Port Au Choix

These **ancient burial grounds** (☎709-861-3522; www.pc.gc.ca/portauchoix; Point Riche Rd; adult/child $3.90/1.90; ⊙9am-6pm Jun-Sep) of three different Aboriginal groups date back 5500 years. The modern visitors center tells of these groups' creative survival in the area and of one group's unexplained disappearance 3200 years ago.

L'Anse aux Meadows

Lying in a forlorn sweep of land, **L'Anse aux Meadows National Historic Site** (☎709-623-2608; www.pc.gc.ca/lanseauxmeadows; Rte 436; adult/child/family $11.70/5.80/29.40; ⊙9am-6pm Jun-Sep) is one of Newfoundland's most stirring attractions. Leif Eriksson and his Viking friends lived here circa AD 1000. Visitors can see the remains of their waterside settlement, now just vague outlines left in the spongy ground, plus three replica buildings inhabited by costumed docents.

Be sure to browse the interpretive center and take in the 3km trail that winds through the barren terrain and along the coast.

For more Viking action, also stop by **Norstead** (☎709-623-2828; www.norstead. com; Rte 436; adult/child/family $10/6.50/30; ⊙9:30am-5:30pm Jun-Sep), just beyond the turnoff to the national historic site. This recreated Viking village features costumed interpreters smelting, weaving and baking. There's also a large-scale replica of a Viking ship on hand.

VADIM PETROV / SHUTTERSTOCK ©

The Cabot Trail

Driving the Cabot Trail is Nova Scotia's most famous recreational activity, taking you along winding roads past jaw-dropping scenery.

Dotting the southeastern flank of the trail like Easter eggs, artists' workshops can be found from Englishtown to St Ann's Bay; drop in to a studio or two to meet an interesting mishmash of characters and to discover living remnants of Mi'kmaw and Acadian culture.

For the most breathtaking scenery, head to the island's northwestern shore where the trail slopes down to Pleasant Bay and Chéticamp. Keep your eyes on the circuitous road, as tempting as the views become; there are plenty of places to stop, look, and hike through a tapestry of terrain for vistas over the endless, icy ocean.

Great For...

☑ Don't Miss

Hopping on a whale-watching tour in Chéticamp or Pleasant Bay.

Cape Breton Highlands

This **national park** (☎902-224-2306; www.pc.gc.ca/capebreton; adult/child/vehicle & passengers $8/4/20) offers visitors some of

❶ Need to Know

You'll find tourist information centers in Cape Breton Highlands National Park and Chéticamp.

✕ Take a Break

Stop by the **Dancing Goat** (☏902-248-2727; www.facebook.com/DancingGoatCafe; 6289 Cabot Trail, Margaree Valley; items $5-13; ⏱8am-5pm Sat-Thu, to 8pm Fri; ☎), open year-round, for a hearty breakfast or huge sandwich.

★ Top Tip

The best way to enjoy the trail, with the freedom of starting and stopping as you choose, is by self-driving.

eastern Canada's most dramatic scenery. One-third of the Cabot Trail runs through the park. You'll find expanses of woodland, tundra and bog, and startling sea views. Established in 1936 and encompassing 20% of Cape Breton's landmass, it's the fancy feather in Nova Scotia's island cap.

There are two park entrances, one at Chéticamp and one at Ingonish Beach. Purchase an entry permit at either park entrance. A one-day pass is good until noon the next day. Wheelchair-accessible trails are indicated on the free park map available at either entrance.

Chéticamp

Chéticamp is Nova Scotia's most vibrant and thriving Acadian community, owing much of its cultural preservation to its geo-

graphical isolation; the road didn't make it this far until 1949. Upon entering the town from either direction you'll immediately feel like you've arrived in a little French village, although the landscape is decidedly reminiscent of the rugged Scottish highlands.

In the warmer months, there's always something going on, with plenty of opportunities to observe and experience Acadian culture, from interesting museums to sampling folk crafts (Chéticamp is famed for its hooked rugs) and toe-tapping live-music performances.

Pleasant Bay

Pleasant Bay is a carved-out bit of civilization hemmed in on all sides by wilderness. It's also an active fishing harbor known for its whale-watching tours and for its Tibetan monastery.

Halifax

Proud Halifax locals (known as Haligonians) have a great quality of life: sea breezes keep the air clean; leafy, manicured parks and gardens nestle between heritage buildings; there's a thriving arts, theater and culinary scene; and the numerous pubs, with their craft-brew culture and love for bands, quite simply, go off.

Not just a city for the young, Halifax' longevity ensures something of appeal for everyone. Stroll the historic waterfront, check out a museum or two, catch some live music and enjoy the best of what eastern Canada has to offer.

⊙ SIGHTS

Canadian Museum of Immigration at Pier 21   Museum

(☑902-425-7770; www.pier21.ca; 1055 Marginal Rd; adult/child $11/7; ◷9:30am-5:30pm May-Nov, reduced hours Dec-Apr) Pier 21 was to Canada what Ellis Island was to the USA. Between 1928 and 1971 over a million immigrants entered Canada through Pier 21. Their stories and the historical context that led them to abandon their homelands form the basis of this brilliant museum, the compelling permanent exhibits of which include the recently renovated *Pier 21 Story* and the new *Canadian Immigration Story*. The collection, featuring firsthand testimonies and artifacts, is complemented by visiting exhibitions along related themes.

Citadel Hill National Historic Site   Historic Site

(☑902-426-5080; www.pc.gc.ca/halifaxcitadel; 5425 Sackville St; adult/child $12/6; ◷9am-5pm) Canada's most visited national historic site, the huge and arguably spooky Citadel is a star-shaped fort atop Halifax' central hill. Construction began in 1749 with the founding of Halifax; this version of the Citadel is the fourth, built from 1818 to 1861. Guided tours explain the fort's shape and history. The grounds inside the fort are open year-round, with free admission when the exhibits are closed.

From November to May, while the grounds remain open, visitor experience services are limited.

Maritime Museum of the Atlantic   Museum

(☑902-424-7490; http://maritimemuseum.nova scotia.ca; 1675 Lower Water St; adult/child May-Oct $9.50/5, Nov-Apr $5/3; ◷9:30am-5pm May-Oct, reduced hours Nov-Apr) Part of this popular waterfront museum used to be a chandlery, where all the gear needed to outfit a vessel was sold. You can smell the charred ropes, cured to protect them from saltwater. There's a range of permanent exhibits including displays on the RMS *Titanic* and the Halifax Explosion. Outside at the dock you can explore the CSS *Acadia*, a retired hydrographic vessel from England.

Fairview Lawn Cemetery   Historic Site

(☑902-490-4883; 3720 Windsor St) When the RMS *Titanic* sank, the bodies not lost at sea were brought to Halifax. Among other sites, there are 19 graves at **Mt Olivet Catholic Cemetery** (7076 Mumford Rd) and 121 here at the Fairview Lawn Cemetery, including that of J Dawson, whose name was the basis for Leonardo DiCaprio's character in the film *Titanic*. Those with a keen eye will be able to locate the touching Celtic Cross and Unknown Child monuments.

St Paul's Church   Church

(☑902-429-2240; www.stpaulshalifax.org; 1749 Argyle St; ◷9am-4pm Mon-Sat, Mass 10am Sun) The oldest surviving building in Halifax is also the oldest protestant place of worship in Canada. Established in 1749 with the founding of Halifax, St Paul's Anglican Church once served parishioners from as far and wide as Newfoundland to Ontario. Drop in any time for a guided or self-directed tour of this fascinating building.

✪ ACTIVITIES

Cycling is a great way to see sites on the outskirts of Halifax. You can take bikes on the ferries to Dartmouth or cycle over the MacDonald Bridge. In summer, there's usually a few outfitters renting out bikes along the waterfront around Bishop's Landing (at the end of Bishop St).

I Heart Bikes   Cycling
(📞902-406-7774; www.iheartbikeshfx.com; 1507 Lower Water St; rentals per hour from $12) If you prefer two wheels to two legs, you'll heart these guys, too. Centrally located near the Halifax Waterfront, it's a great spot from where to pick up a chariot and start pedaling. Both rentals and cycling tours are available.

🅖 TOURS

Halifax Free Tours   Walking
(www.halifaxfreetours.wixsite.com/halifaxfree tours; ⏰10am & 3pm Jun-Sep) **FREE** You can't beat the price of these free 1½-hour walking tours of downtown Halifax, led by friendly, local guides. Send an email to reserve a spot and please remember to tip!

Local Tasting Tours   Food & Drink
(📞902-818-9055; www.localtastingtours.com; tours from $40) Eat your way around Halifax' burgeoning restaurant scene on these fun, foodie-themed tours, featuring up to six local restaurants per tour. A variety of itineraries are available.

🅐 SHOPPING

**Halifax Seaport
Farmers Market**   Market
(📞902-492-4043; www.halifaxfarmersmarket. com; 1209 Marginal Rd; ⏰10am-5pm Mon-Fri, 7am-3pm Sat, 9am-3pm Sun) Although it has operated in several locations since its inception in 1750, what's now known as the Halifax Seaport Farmers Market (in its present location since 2010) is North America's longest continuously operating market. With over 250 vendors from a province that prides itself on strong farm-to-table and maritime traditions, it's well worth a visit.

Historic Farmers Market   Market
(📞902-329-3276; www.historicfarmersmarket. ca; 1496 Lower Water St; ⏰7am-1pm Sat) If

🔜 **Sable
Island**

This ever-shifting, 44km-long spit of sand lies some 300km southeast of Halifax and has caused more than 350 documented shipwrecks. But what makes Sable Island most famous is that it's home to one of the world's only truly wild horse populations, as well as the planet's largest breeding colony of grey seals.

The first 60 ancestors of today's Sable Island horses were shipped to the island in 1760 when Acadians were being deported from Nova Scotia by the British. The Acadians were forced to abandon their livestock and it appears that Boston merchant-ship owner Thomas Hancock helped himself to their horses then put them to pasture on Sable Island to keep it low profile. The horses that survived became wild.

Seals, Sable Island
ALAINA LESLIE / SHUTTERSTOCK ©

you're in Halifax on a Saturday morning, pop by this grassroots, member-run, non-profit cooperative market, housed in a beautiful 1820s stone building.

Historic Properties   Shopping Centre
(www.historicproperties.ca; 1869 Upper Water St; ⏰store hours vary) The Historic Properties are a group of restored warehouse buildings on Upper Water St, built between 1800 and 1905, that have been converted into boutiques, restaurants and bars connected by waterfront boardwalks. The 1814 **Privateers Warehouse** was the former storehouse of government sanctioned pirates and is the area's oldest stone building.

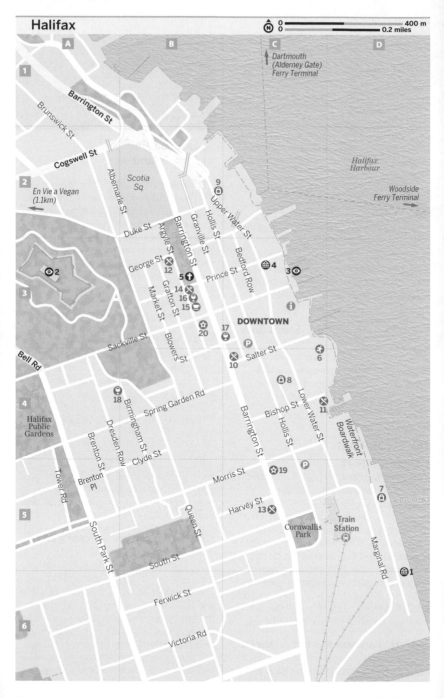

Halifax

Halifax

🍴 EATING

2 Doors Down   Canadian $$

(☏902-422-4224; www.go2doorsdown.com; 1533 Barrington St; mains $10-20; ☺11am-10pm) Reservations aren't accepted at this food-lovers haunt that tempts with a welcome array of staples such as burgers, curries, and fish-and-chips to more elevated offerings such as shrimp-and-snow-crab-stuffed shiitake caps and plenty of gluten-free goodness. The word is out about this cozy haunt, so be prepared for a short wait at busy times.

En Vie a Vegan   Vegetarian $$

(☏902-492-4077; www.enviehalifax.com; 5775 Charles St; mains $11-18; ☺11am-9pm Tue-Fri, 10am-9pm Sat & Sun; 🖊) Finally, a restaurant focused on sustainable, organic, locally sourced plant-based eating that has universal appeal. There's nothing bland or boring about what's on offer here. Most menu items, from the coconut shrimp to the double-bacon cheeseburger, feature the original name of their non-vegan counterpart; there's no animal products in any of the dishes, but the ruse is highly convincing.

Henry House   Pub Food $$

(☏902-423-5660; www.henryhouse.ca; 1222 Barrington St; mains $11-24; ☺11:30am-midnight) Jazz and classical music lilt above the din of respectably dressed diners chatting by the open fire in this handsome 1834 iron-stone serving upscale pub fare. When the gorgeous yet unpretentious Drawing Room upstairs is open (6pm to midnight Friday and Saturday) you'll be able to dazzle your date with your extensive knowledge of the fine house whiskeys and smoked cocktails.

Bicycle Thief   Italian $$$

(☏902-425-7993; www.bicyclethief.ca; 1475 Lower Water St; mains lunch $10-26, dinner $20-39; ☺11.30am-late Mon-Fri, 5:30pm-late Sat) Named for the classic 1948 Italian film, this shabby-chic waterfront restaurant has won similar critical acclaim by local foodies – and with good reason. Start with regional oysters or polenta with wild mushroom ragout, then continue with dishes such as pistachio-honey roasted salmon or pancetta-wrapped pork tenderloin. The wine and cocktail list is several pages longer than the food menu.

Five Fishermen   Seafood $$$

(☏902-422-4421; www.fivefishermen.com; 1740 Argyle St; mains $29-39; ☺noon-10pm Mon-Fri, 5-10pm Sat & Sun) This fabulous restaurant housed in what was once the John Snow funeral home that interred many of Halifax' 150 *Titanic* victims doesn't have to rely on this macabre and quirky fact to put bums on seats: thankfully, the seafood sells itself. Expect elevated oceanic delicacies with lamb and steak thrown in for good measure.

Atlantic Music

If Atlantic Canada were a bowl of chowder, music would be the hearty broth in which everything floats. This playlist will get you in the mood for highland hills, long stretches of Atlantic coastline and perhaps a stop for some step-dancing on the way:

Guysborough Train Stan Rogers
The Silver Spear Natalie MacMaster
These Roads David Gunning
Rant and Roar Great Big Sea
Walk With Me Pogey
Maple Sugar Don Messer
Sail Away to the Sea The Once

Press Gang Restaurant & Oyster Bar
Seafood $$$

(☎902-423-8816; www.thepressgang.ca; 5218 Prince St; single oysters $3.25, mains $36-40; ⊘5-10pm Sun-Wed, to midnight Thu-Sat) Order any number and combination of Nova Scotia and PEI oysters raw or baked – if you're a fan of the briny bivalves, you've found nirvana. Otherwise, choose from a short but impressive menu of delicious appetizers and mains and soak up the atmosphere of this slick and stylish outfit. Dress to impress.

🍸 DRINKING & NIGHTLIFE

Economy Shoe Shop Cafe Bar
Cafe

(☎902-423-8845; www.economyshoeshop.ca; 1663 Argyle St; ⊘11:30am-midnight Mon-Thu, to 2am Fri-Sun) This has been the 'it' place to drink and people-watch in Halifax for well over a decade. On weekend nights, actors and journalists figure heavily in the crush. It's a pleasant place for afternoon drinks and the kitchen dishes out tapas until last call at 1:45am.

Lot Six
Cocktail Bar

(☎902-428-7428; www.lotsix.ca; 1685 Argyle St; ⊘4pm-2am) This slick bar and restaurant

has a fabulous glass atrium that delivers extra atmosphere points, whatever the season. Score a cushy seat at the counter if you're flying solo or an extra-cute two-person booth if you're angling for *amour*.

Middle Spoon
Cocktail Bar

(☎902-407-4002; www.themiddlespoon.ca; 1559 Barrington St; ⊘4-11pm Mon-Sat) What could be better than a place that serves only beer, wine, creative cocktails and decadent desserts? How about one with a super secret? (Should we even be writing this?) It has a speakeasy-inspired lounge downstairs that serves even better cocktails. Get the password by clicking on the >: symbol on the website and don't tell anyone we told you...

Tom's Little Havana
Bar

(☎902-423-8667; www.tomslittlehavana.wix.com/cafe; 1540 Birmingham St; 11:30am-2am) Craft beers, game nights, Scotch nights and a daily happy hour (5pm to 8pm) make Tom's feel like an extension of the living room at your best mate's place. There's a warm and friendly vibe here, which gets even warmer as the night wears on.

🌟 ENTERTAINMENT

Bearly's House of Blues & Ribs
Live Music

(☎902-423-2526; www.bearlys.ca; 1269 Barrington St; ⊘5pm-midnight) The best blues musicians in Atlantic Canada play here at incredibly low cover charges. Wednesday karaoke nights draw a crowd and some fine singers.

Neptune Theatre
Theater

(☎902-429-7070; www.neptunetheatre.com; 1593 Argyle St) This downtown theater presents musicals and well-known plays on its main stage (from $35) and edgier stuff in the studio (from $15).

Seahorse Tavern
Live Music

(☎902-423-7200; www.theseahorsetavern.ca; 1665 Argyle St) This joint hosts the events that attract the crowds who are actually cool (and not just faux-cool). Punk, indie,

Halifax waterfront

metal, funk, Motown, soul...and monthly themed dance parties. Check the website for what's on and when.

Shakespeare by the Sea   Theater
(✆902-422-0295; www.shakespearebythesea.ca; Point Pleasant Park; ⊙Jun-Sep) Performances of the Bard's works at the Cambridge Battery, an old fortification in the middle of Point Pleasant Park. Another reason to love Halifax! Check the website for a map and details.

ℹ️ INFORMATION

Tourism Nova Scotia (✆800-565-0000, 902-425-5781; www.novascotia.com) Operates visitor information centers in Halifax and other locations within Nova Scotia province, plus a free booking service for accommodations, which is useful when rooms are scarce in midsummer. It publishes the *Doers & Dreamers Guide,* which lists places to stay, attractions and tour operators.

Visitor Information Centre (VIC; ✆902-424-4248; www.novascotia.com; 1655 Lower Water St; ⊙9am-5pm) On the Halifax Waterfront, this official province-run plaza is a great place to start your wanderings of downtown Halifax; staff will load you up with maps and friendly advice. There is also an official VIC welcome center at the **airport** (✆902-873-1223; www.novascotia. com; Halifax International Airport; ⊙9am-9pm).

ℹ️ GETTING THERE & AWAY

AIR

Halifax Stanfield International Airport (YHZ; ✆902-873-4422; www.hiaa.ca; 1 Bell Blvd) is 32km northeast of town on Hwy 102 toward Truro.

BUS

The only province-wide (and beyond) bus company is **Maritime Bus** (✆800-575-1807; www.maritimebus.com), which services the main highways from Kentville to Halifax and up to Truro.

Advance Shuttle (✆877-886-3322; www.advanceshuttle.ca) Offers slow-going shuttle services from Halifax airport and downtown hotels to Prince Edward Island (from $69).

Cloud Nine Shuttle (✆902-742-3992; www.thecloudnineshuttle.com) Can drop you at points

Victoria Park, Charlottetown

along the South Shore as far as Yarmouth. Fares start at $75 and the journey takes about 3½ hours.

TRAIN

One of the few examples of monumental Canadian train station architecture left in the Atlantic provinces is found at 1161 Hollis St. VIA Rail (www.viarail.ca) operates an overnight service to Montréal (from $134, 21 hours, daily except Tuesday).

ℹ️ GETTING AROUND

CAR & MOTORCYCLE

Outside the downtown core, you can usually find free on-street parking for up to two hours. Halifax' parking meters are enforced from 8am to 6pm Monday to Friday.

All the major national car-rental chains are represented at the airport and in downtown Halifax. Some will let you pick up in town and drop off at the airport free of charge.

PUBLIC TRANSPORTATION

Halifax Transit (902-480-8000; www.halifax.ca/transit; single ride $2.50-3.50) runs the city bus system and the ferries to Dartmouth. Maps and schedules are available at the ferry terminals and at the information booth in Scotia Sq mall.

Bus 7 cuts through downtown and North End Halifax via Robie St and Gottingen St, passing both of Halifax' hostels. Bus 1 travels along Spring Garden Rd, Barrington St and the south part of Gottingen St before crossing the bridge to Dartmouth.

Charlottetown

It was here in 1864 that the Confederation Conference set in motion a series of events that led to the birth of the nation of Canada, and strolling through the compact capital is like walking through a beautifully preserved local history museum.

Charming Charlottetown also boasts a burgeoning restaurant scene that capitalizes on the island's abundant seafood and fresh produce, as well as its wealth of talented graduates from the Culinary Institute of Canada. Add a lively cultural scene and you have a capital city oozing small-town feel and appeal.

⊙ SIGHTS

Point Prim Lighthouse   Lighthouse

(☑902-659-2768; www.pointprimlighthouse.com; 2147 Point Prim Rd, Belfast; adult/child $3.50/2; ☺10am-6pm Jul & Aug, 10am-6pm Wed-Sun Jun & Sep) Purchased from the Provincial Government for $1, the not-for-profit Point Prim Lighthouse Society maintains this gorgeous historic lighthouse, the oldest on PEI. Inside is a wonderful museum that shows what life must have been like for the lightkeepers. From the top, enjoy fabulous views and a real sense of history and wonder.

Victoria Park   Park

(www.city.charlottetown.pe.ca/victoriapark.php) Dedicated in 1873, Charlottetown's most popular and beautiful waterfront green space has 16 hectares of loveliness for you to enjoy on a fine day.

Sir Andrew MacPhail
Homestead   Historic Site

(☑902-651-2789; www.macphailhomestead.ca; 271 MacPhail Park Rd, Vernon Bridge; ☺10am-5pm Wed-Sun Jul-Sep) Check the website for the off-season hours of this wonderful 1850s house, birthplace of Sir Andrew MacPhail, local author, physician and soldier. The homestead is now a museum celebrating his life, and its beautiful grounds, with nursery, vegetable garden and woods, open every day from 9am to 5pm. In summer, drop into the tearoom for refreshments!

COWS Creamery   Factory

(☑902-566-5558; www.cowscreamery.ca; 397 Capital Dr; ☺10am-6pm) **FREE** Who doesn't love a self-guided, buttery, *fromagerie* and ice-creamery tour that spits you out in the mecca retail store that is this PEI institution's award-winning dairy heaven, hmm? OK, the lactose intolerant among us, but otherwise...'I scream, you scream, we all scream for...'

⊕ ACTIVITIES

Happy Clammers   Fishing

(☑866-887-3238; www.experiencepei.ca/happy-clammers; Rte 1, Pinette; adult/child

📖 History of the Acadians

When the French first settled the area around the Minas Basin, they called the region Arcadia, a Greek and Roman term for 'pastoral paradise.' This became Acadia and, by the 18th century, the Acadians felt more connection with the land here than with the distant Loire Valley they'd come from.

To the English, however, they would always be French, with whom rivalry and suspicion was constant. Considering it an affront to their Catholic faith, the Acadians refused to take an oath of allegiance to the English king after the Treaty of Utrecht granted Nova Scotia to the British. When hard-line lieutenant governor Charles Lawrence was appointed in 1754, he became fed up with the Acadians and ordered their deportation. The English burned many villages and forced some 14,000 Acadians onto ships.

Many Acadians headed for Louisiana and New Orleans; others went to various Maritime points, New England, Martinique in the Caribbean, Santo Domingo in the Dominican Republic, or back to Europe. Not once were they greeted warmly or with open arms. Some hid out and remained in Acadia. In later years many of the deported people returned, but found their lands occupied. In Nova Scotia, Acadians resettled the Chéticamp area on Cape Breton Island and the French Shore north of Yarmouth.

$100/25, minimum 4 people; ☺Mon-Sat Jul-Oct, times vary with tides) Many folks come out this way to dig razor, soft shell, bar and quahog clams. Once you've filled your buckets, go home to Gilbert and Goldie's house to steam up your catch and dine on other treats cooked up by this charming local family.

Bay of Fundy

The tides of New Brunswick's Bay of Fundy are the highest in the world. A Mi'kmaw legend explains the tide as the effect of a whale's thrashing tail sending the water forever sloshing back and forth. A more prosaic explanation is in the length, depth and gradual funnel shape of the bay itself.

The contrasts between the high and ebb tide are most pronounced at the eastern end of the bay and around the Minas Basin, with tides of 10m to 15m twice daily 12½ hours apart. The highest tide ever recorded anywhere was 16.6m, the height of a four-story building, at Burncoat Head near Noel, Nova Scotia.

Experience the tides at **Fundy National Park** (www.pc.gc.ca/fundy; daily permit adult/child/family $7.80/3.90/19.60; ◷May-Oct) and explore the irregularly eroded sandstone cliffs and the wide beach at low tide. The park is delightfully wooded and lush and features an extensive network of impressive hiking trails.

At the northern end of the bay, **Cape Enrage** (www.capenrage.ca; off Rte 905; adult/child $6/5; ◷10am-5pm mid-May–Oct, to 8pm Jul & Aug) has a dramatic 150-year-old clifftop light station, with its lighthouse, former lighthouse-keeper's house (now a restaurant) and a small gallery. The more adventurous can try on-site rappelling ($90 per person for two hours) or zip-lining ($45 per person for three runs).

🍴 TOURS

Confederation Players Walking Tours   Walking
(☎800-565-0278; www.confederationcentre. com; 6 Prince St; adult/child $15/8; ◷daily Jul-Aug) There is no better way to tour Charlottetown. Playing the fathers and ladies of Confederation, actors garbed in 19th-century dress educate and entertain through the town's historic streets. Tours leave from Founders' Hall, with a variety of themes and itineraries to choose from.

🍴 EATING

Point Prim Chowder House   Seafood $
(☎902-659-2187; www.chowderhousepei.com; 2150 Point Prim Rd, Belfast; mains $8-25; ◷11am-7pm Jun-Oct) For an atmospheric, authentic, sea-salty good time, check out the Chowder House, with its seasonal beachfront patio and seafood and chowder selection (yes, that's a *range* of chowders!) worth getting giddy over. Phone ahead for hours in the off-season.

Claddagh Oyster House   Seafood $$
(☎902-892-6992; www.claddaghoysterhouse. com; 131 Sydney St; mains $13-32; ◷5-9pm) Locals herald the Claddagh as one of the best seafood restaurants in Charlottetown. Trust 'em! The Irish-inspired Galway Bay Delight features a coating of fresh cream and seasonings over scallops and shrimp that have been sautéed with mushrooms and onions, then flambéed with Irish Mist liqueur.

Water Prince Corner Shop & Lobster Pound   Seafood $$
(☎902-368-3212; www.waterprincelobster.ca; 141 Water St; mains $12-36; ◷9:30am-8pm) When locals want seafood they head to this inconspicuous, sea-blue eatery near the wharf. It is deservedly famous for its scallop burgers, but it's also the best place in town for fresh lobster. You'll probably have to line up for a seat, otherwise order take-out lobster, which gets you a significant discount.

Brickhouse Kitchen & Bar   Canadian $$
(☎902-566-4620; www.brickhousepei.com; 125 Sydney St; mains $16-36; ◷11am-10pm) The chic ambience of this heritage brick building is matched by creative dishes inspired by island culture and made with

Confederation Players

local ingredients. Try the lobster poutine, seafood bouillabaisse, Thai curry chicken or just a good PEI beef burger. Don't leave without enjoying a cocktail or dessert in the upstairs lounge.

Pilot House   Canadian $$$

(✆902-894-4800; http://thepilothouse.ca; 70 Grafton St; mains $24-39; ⊙11am-10pm Mon-Sat) The oversized wood beams and brick columns of the historic Roger's Hardware building provide a bold setting for fine dining or light pub fare. A loyal clientele tucks into lobster-stuffed chicken, vegetarian pizza or seafood torte. Lunch specials start at $10.

🍷 DRINKING & NIGHTLIFE

Gahan House   Pub

(✆902-626-2337; http://charlottetown.gahan.ca; 126 Sydney St; ⊙11am-midnight) Within these homey, historic walls the pub owners brew PEI homegrown ales. Sir John A's Honey Wheat Ale is well worth introducing to your insides, as is the medium- to full-bodied Sydney Street Stout. The food here is also great – enjoy with friends old and new.

Hopyard   Bar

(✆902-367-2599; 131 Kent St; ⊙11am-midnight) Beer, food and vinyl: that's the promise of these newcomers to the burgeoning Charlottetown bar scene...and the locals are loving it!

Merchantman   Bar

(✆902-892-9150; www.merchantman.ca; 23 Queen St; ⊙11am-9pm) Merchantman wears many hats; it's a bar, it's a restaurant, it's a takeout. In summer months, the patio tables are a great place to soak up the sun and enjoy a drink while you work up your appetite for fresh PEI oysters, seafood or all manner of upscale pub grub.

★ ENTERTAINMENT

Confederation Centre of the Arts   Theater

(%902-566-1267; www.confederationcentre.com; 145 Richmond St) This modern complex's large theater and outdoor amphitheater host concerts, comedic performances and elaborate musicals. *Anne of Green Gables – The Musical* has been entertaining audiences here as part of the Charlottetown Festival since 1964, making it Canada's longest-running musical. You'll enjoy it, and your friends will never have to know.

Baba's Lounge
Live Music

(☎902-892-7377; 81 University Ave; ⊘noon-midnight) Located above Cedar's Eatery, this welcoming, intimate venue hosts great local bands playing their own tunes. Occasionally there are poetry readings.

Benevolent Irish Society
Live Music

(☎902-963-3156; 582 North River Rd; $10; ⊘8pm Fri) On the north side of town, this is a great place to catch a ceilidh. Come early, as seating is limited.

ℹ INFORMATION

The provincial tourist board maintains an excellent website of all things PEI at www.tourismpei.com.

ℹ GETTING THERE & AWAY

Charlottetown Airport (YYG; ☎902-566-7997; www.flypei.com; 250 Maple Hills Ave) is 8km north of the city center. A taxi to the center costs $12, plus $3.50 for each additional person.

ℹ GETTING AROUND

Rental cars, available from a variety of providers with city and airport depots, are the preferred method of transportation. During summer cars are in short supply, so be sure to book ahead.

Limited public transportation is provided by **Trius Transit** (T3 Transit; ☎902-566-9962; www.triustransit.ca), but walking or renting a bike are both great ways to get around this compact city.

> *It's the seafood that attracts the lion's share of culinary fans*

Mussels

JOE RAEDLE / GETTY IMAGES ©

Cavendish

Anyone familiar with *Anne of Green Gables* might have lofty ideas of finding Cavendish as a quaint village bedecked in flowers and country charm. While the Anne and Lucy Maud Montgomery sites are right out of the imagination-inspiring book pages, Cavendish itself is a mishmash of attractions with no particular town center.

◉ SIGHTS

Green Gables
Heritage Place   Historic Site

(☏902-672-7874; www.pc.gc.ca/greengables; 8619 Hwy 6; adult/child $8/4; ◷10am-5pm Mon-Sat) Cavendish is the hometown of Lucy Maud Montgomery (1874–1942), author of *Anne of Green Gables*. Here she is simply known as Lucy Maud or LM. Owned by her grandfather's cousins, the now-famous House of Green Gables and its Victorian surrounds inspired the setting for her fictional tale. A variety of combination tickets and packages are available.

In 1937 the house became part of the national park and it's now administered as a national heritage site, celebrating Lucy Maud and Anne with exhibits and audio visual displays.

Lucy Maud Montgomery's
Cavendish Homestead Historic Site

(☏902-963-2231; www.peisland.com/lmm; 8523 Cavendish Rd; adult/child $3/1; ◷9am-5pm) This is considered hallowed ground to Anne fans worldwide. Raised by her grandparents, Lucy Maud lived in this house from 1876 to 1911 and it is here that she wrote *Anne of Green Gables*. You'll find the old foundation of the house, many interpretive panels about Lucy Maud, a small on-site museum and a bookshop.

Cavendish Beach   Beach

(www.cavendishbeachpei.com) Beautiful Cavendish Beach gets crowded during summer months, but with perfect sand and a warm(ish) ocean in front, you won't really care.

📖🍴 Anne of Green Gables

If you haven't read the 1908 novel, this is the place to do it – not just to enjoy it, but to try and understand all the hype. The story revolves around Anne Shirley, a spirited 11-year-old orphan with red pigtails and a creative wit, who was mistakenly sent from Nova Scotia to Prince Edward Island. The aging Cuthberts (who were brother and sister) were expecting a strapping boy to help them with farm chores. In the end, Anne's strength of character wins over everyone in her path.

To really get a feel for the *Anne of Green Gables* scenery, get out and walk the green creek-crossed woods that the author, Lucy Maud Montgomery, knew like the back of her hand. The best way is to start at the Lucy Maud Montgomery's Cavendish Homestead, then walk the 1.1km return trail to the Green Gables Heritage Place through the 'Haunted Wood.'

In this way you arrive to a magical view from below the house rather than via a big parking lot and modern entrance. Once you're at the House of Green Gables you can enjoy the site plus many other surrounding trails, including 'Lover's Lane,' before hoofing it back to the Homestead.

✖ EATING

Carr's Oysters   Seafood $$

(☏902-886-3355; www.carrspei.ca; 32 Campbellton Rd, Stanley Bridge; mains $14-32; ◷10am-7pm) Dine on oysters straight from Malpeque Bay, or lobster, mussels and seafood you've never even heard of, like quahogs from Carr's own saltwater tanks. There is also plenty of fish on offer from salmon to trout. The setting over the bay is sociable and bright, and there's also an on-site market selling fresh and smoked sea critters.

Pearl Eatery
Canadian $$$

(☎902-963-2111; www.pearleatery.com; 7792 Cavendish Rd, North Rustico; brunch $8-12, mains $22-32; ☉from 4:30pm daily, 10am-2pm Sun) This shingled house just outside Cavendish is surrounded by flowers and is an absolutely lovely place to eat. There are plenty of unusual and seasonally changing options like ice-wine-infused chicken liver pâté on a Gouda brioche for starters and locally inspired mains, such as delicious butter-poached scallops.

ⓘ INFORMATION

Anne fans will want to chat with the friendly staff at the **Cavendish Visitor Information Centre** (☎902-963-7830; cnr Rte 6 & Hwy 13; ☉9am-5pm) who really know their stuff about all things PEI.

St John's

North America's oldest city sits on the steep slopes of a snug and sheltered harbor. With jelly-bean-colored row houses lining the hilly streets, the city begs comparisons to San Francisco – though in miniature. It too is home to artists, musicians, cutting-edge eateries, inflated real estate and young, smartphone-using denizens. Yet the vibe of Newfoundland's largest city and capital remains refreshingly small-town.

◎ SIGHTS

Rooms
Museum

(☎709-757-8000; www.therooms.ca; 9 Bonaventure Ave; adult/child $7.50/4, 6-9pm Wed free; ☉10am-5pm Mon, Tue & Thu-Sat, to 9pm Wed, noon-5pm Sun) Not many museums offer the chance to see a giant squid, hear avant-garde sound sculptures and peruse ancient weaponry all under one roof. But that's the Rooms, the province's all-in-one historical museum, art gallery and archives. The building itself, a massive stone-and-glass complex, is impressive to look at, with views that lord it over the city. Has an on-site cafe and excellent restaurant.

Signal Hill National Historic Site
Historic Site

(☎709-772-5367; www.pc.gc.ca/signalhill; ☉grounds 24hr) The city's most famous landmark is worth it for the glorious view alone, though there's much more to see. The tiny castle atop the hill is **Cabot Tower** (☉8:30am-5pm Apr-Nov) FREE, built in 1900 to honor both John Cabot's arrival in 1497 and Queen Victoria's Diamond Jubilee. In midsummer, soldiers dressed as the 19th-century Royal Newfoundland Company perform a **tattoo** (www.rnchs.ca/tattoo; $10; ☉11am & 3pm Wed-Thu, Sat & Sun Jul & Aug) and fire cannons.

The **Signal Hill Visitor Centre** (adult/child $3.90/1.90; ☉10am-6pm May-Oct) features interactive displays on the site's history.

Johnson Geo Centre
Museum

(☎709-737-7880; www.geocentre.ca; 175 Signal Hill Rd; adult/child $12/6; ☉9:30am-5pm) Nowhere in the world can geo-history, going back to the birth of the earth, be accessed so easily as in Newfoundland, and the Geo Centre does a grand job of making snore-worthy geological information perk up with appeal via its underground, interactive displays. The center also has a fascinating exhibit on the *Titanic*.

Quidi Vidi
Historic Site

Over Signal Hill, away from town, is the tiny picturesque village of Quidi Vidi. Check out the 18th-century battery and the lakeside regatta museum, but make your first stop **Quidi Vidi Brewery** (☎709-738-4040; www.quidividibrewery.ca; 35 Barrows Rd; tasting or tour $10; ☉10am-4pm), which cooks up Newfoundland's most popular microbrews. Located in an old fish-processing plant on the small wharf, it's a scenic place to slake one's thirst.

Nearby you'll find the oldest cottage in North America, the 1750s-era **Mallard Cottage** (☎709-237-7314; www.mallardcottage.ca; 2 Barrows Rd; mains $19-35; ☉10am-2pm Wed-Sat, 5:30-9pm Tue-Sat, 10am-5pm Sun). At press time it was being converted into a restaurant serving Newfoundland comfort foods.

Quidi Vidi

Quidi Vidi is about 2km from the northeast edge of downtown.

🏃 ACTIVITIES

North Head Trail   Walking
An awesome way to return to downtown from Signal Hill is along the North Head Trail (1.7km) that connects Cabot Tower with the harborfront Battery neighborhood. The walk departs from the tower's parking lot and traces the cliffs, imparting tremendous sea views and sometimes whale spouts. Because much of the trail runs along the bluff's sheer edge, it isn't something to attempt in icy, foggy or dark conditions.

🎫 TOURS

St John's Haunted Hike   Walking
(www.hauntedhike.com; adult/child $10/5; ☺9:30pm Sun-Thu Jun-Sep) The black-caped Reverend Thomas Wyckham Jarvis Esq leads these super-popular explorations of the city's dark corners. He'll spook you with tales of headless captains, murderers and other ghosts. Departure is from the Anglican Cathedral's west entrance. On midsummer Fridays and Saturdays, the spine-tingling action moves to Signal Hill for a seated, indoor show of ghost stories (8pm, tickets $15).

Iceberg Quest   Boating
(☎709-722-1888; www.icebergquest.com; Pier 6; 2hr tour adult/child $65/28) Departs from St John's harbor and makes a run down to Cape Spear in search of icebergs in June and whales in July and August. There are multiple departures daily in a new 100-person boat.

🍴 EATING

Adelaide
Oyster House   International $
(☎709-722-7222; 334 Water St; small plates $8-17; ☺5-10pm) For a boisterous, busy happy hour it would be hard to do better than the Adelaide, a stylish sliver of a bar and restaurant in the thick of things. Its specialty is small plates – like fish tacos,

Kobe beef lettuce wraps topped with spicy kimchi, and, of course, fresh oysters from both coasts. With lovely cocktails. It's good for singles too.

Battery Cafe   Cafe $
(☑709-722-9167; 1 Duckworth St; snacks $3-9; ◷6:30am-6:30pm Mon-Fri, 7:30am-6:30pm Sat & Sun) This Aussie-run espresso bar and cafe brews the finest cup in town; there are also sandwiches and baked delights. With outdoor picnic-table seating in good weather.

Piatto   Pizza $
(☑709-726-0709; www.piattopizzeria.com; 377 Duckworth St; mains $12-19; ◷11:30am-10pm Mon-Thu, to 11pm Fri & Sat, to 9pm Sun) Offering a great night out without breaking the bank, cozy brick Piatto wood-fires pizza like nobody's business. Go trad or try a thin-crust pie topped with proscuitto, figs and balsamic. It's all good. There are nice fresh salads too, wine and Italian cocktails.

Merchant Tavern   Canadian $$$
(☑709-722-5050; http://themerchanttavern.ca; 291 Water St; mains $15-45; ◷11:30am-2pm & 5:30pm-midnight Tue-Thu, to 2am Fri, 10:30am-2am Sat, 10:30am-3pm Sun) An elegant tavern housed in a former bank building, Merchant shares its chef with Canadian top-tier restaurant Raymond's, but without the $400 price tag. Gorgeous seafood stews, grilled local lamb sausage and cod with smoked bacon near perfection. For happy endings, the salted caramel soft-serve is a must. Some seating faces the open-view kitchen – good for chatting with the cooks.

Chinched   Canadian $$$
(☑709-722-3100; www.chinchedbistro.com; 7 Queen St; mains $14-35; ◷5:30-9:30pm Mon-Sat) 🍴 Quality dishes without the white-tablecloth pretense – think octopus tacos or Newfoundland wild mushroom risotto served in a warm, dark-wood room. On an ever-changing menu, meat figures prominently – don't skip the charcuterie boards or homemade pickles. The young chefs' creativity extends to the singular desserts

(say, wild-nettle ice cream) and spirits (partridgeberry vodka) made in-house.

If you don't want to commit to a full meal, the bar menu lets you sample dishes for $6 to $10.

🍷 DRINKING & NIGHTLIFE

Duke of Duckworth   Pub
(www.dukeofduckworth.com; McMurdo's Lane, 325 Duckworth St; ◷noon-late; 🛜) 'The Duke,' as it's known, is an unpretentious English-style pub that represents all that's great about Newfoundland and Newfoundlanders. Stop in on a Friday night and you'll see a mix of blue-collar, white-collar, young and old, and perhaps even band members from Great Big Sea plunked down on the well-worn, red-velour bar stools.

Mochanopoly   Cafe
(☑709-576-3657; 204 Water St; per hour board games $2.50; ◷noon-midnight Mon-Thu, to 1am Fri & Sat, to 11pm Sun) Welcome to Newfoundland's first board-game cafe. Inspired by counterparts in South Korea, young brothers and game gurus Erich and Leon opened this welcoming branch with over 300 games, ranging from classics like Battleship to Pandemic and Exploding Kittens. It's usually packed after 7pm. It also serves small bites and coffee drinks. Kids under six can play free.

Yellow Belly Brewery   Pub
(☑709-757-3784; www.yellowbellybrewery.com; 288 Water St; ◷11:30am-2am Mon-Fri, to 3am Sat & Sun) Refreshing brews crafted on-site take front and center at this casual meeting spot, a brick behemoth dating back to 1725. Everyone's having a good time and there's decent pub grub to soak up the brews. For extra ambience descend to the underbelly – a dark basement bar with a speakeasy feel.

⭐ ENTERTAINMENT

Ship Pub   Live Music
(☑709-753-3870; 265 Duckworth St; ◷noon-late) Attitudes and ages are checked at

the door of this little pub, tucked down Solomon's Lane. You'll hear everything from jazz to indie, and even the odd poetry reading. Wednesday is folk-music night.

Resource Centre
for the Arts
Performing Arts

(☑709-753-4531; www.rca.nf.ca; 3 Victoria St) Sponsors indie theater, dance and film by Newfoundland artists, all of which plays downtown in the former longshoremen's union hall (aka LSPU Hall). Box office is on the website.

Rose & Thistle
Live Music

(☑709-579-6662; 208 Water St; ⊘9am-late) Pub where well-known local folk musicians strum.

INFORMATION

Quidi Vidi Visitors Centre (☑709-570-2038; tourism@stjohns.ca; 10 Maple View Pl, Quidi Vidi Village Plantation; ⊘11am-5pm Tue-Sun) An outpost of the St John's visitor center, with good information on local happenings. Open year-round.

Visitors Centre (☑709-576-8106; www.stjohns. ca; 348 Water St; ⊘10am-4:30pm May-early Oct) Excellent resource with free provincial and city roadmaps, and staff to answer questions and help with bookings.

GETTING THERE & AWAY

AIR

St John's International Airport (YYT; ☑709-758-8500; www.stjohnsairport.com; 100 World Pkwy; ☜) is 6km north of the city on Portugal Cove Rd (Rte 40). Air Canada offers a daily direct flight to and from London, WestJet goes direct to Dublin and Gatwick. United Airlines flies to the USA.

BUS

DRL (☑709-263-2171; www.drl-lr.com) sends one bus daily each way between St John's and Port

aux Basques ($126 cash only, 13½ hours) via the 905km-long Hwy 1, making 25 stops en route. It leaves at 7:30am from Memorial University's Student Centre, in CA Pippy Park.

CAR & MOTORCYCLE

All the major national car-rental chains have offices at the airport. Rent RVs and motorhomes from **Islander RV** (☑709-364-7368; www. islanderrv.com; Paddy's Pond, Exit 40, Trans Canada Hwy).

GETTING AROUND

TO/FROM THE AIRPORT

A government-set flat rate of $25 (plus $3 for each extra passenger) is charged by taxis to go from the airport to downtown hotels and B&Bs; **Citywide Taxi** (☑709-722-7777; www.citywide taxi.ca) provides the official service. For the trip from town to the airport, taxis run on meters and should cost a few dollars less.

BUS

The **Metrobus** (☑709-722-9400; www.metro bus.com; 25 Messenger Dr) system covers most of the city (fare $2.25). Maps and schedules are online and in the visitor center. The new 'trolley line' (it's actually a bus) loops around the main tourist sights, including Signal Hill. It costs $5/20 per person/family per day.

CAR & MOTORCYCLE

The city's one-way streets and unique intersections can be confounding. Thankfully, citizens are incredibly patient. The parking meters that line Water and Duckworth Sts cost $1.50 per hour. **Sonco Parking Garage** (☑709-754-1489; cnr Baird's Cove & Harbour Dr; ⊘6:30am-11pm) is central, but there are several others; most charge around $2 per hour.

TAXI

Except for the trip from the airport, all taxis operate on meters. A trip within town should cost around $8. **Jiffy Cabs** (☑709-722-2222; www. jiffycab.com) provides dependable service.

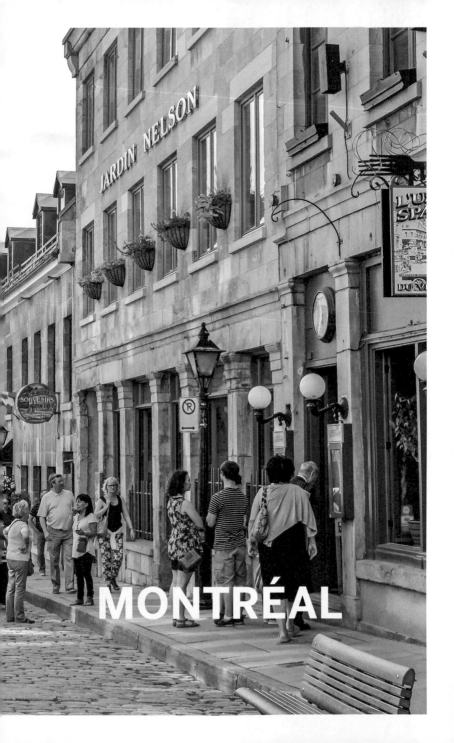

MONTRÉAL

Montréal at a Glance...

Montréal is a slice of old Europe in a pie of contemporary design. The architectural sweep of the city takes in photogenic 18th-century facades as well as 20th-century icons. The city is also at the forefront of Canada's cultural juggernaut, with a fascinating blend of festivals and celebrations. The Québécois love their summers and autumnal colors, but it is the winter that defines much of their lives – get set to join them on the slopes of local mountains via ski, snowboard or toboggan, or warm up and fill up in one of their irresistible patisseries, cozy English pubs, venerable Jewish delis or magnificent food markets.

One Day in Montréal

Beeline to the stunning **Basilique Notre-Dame** (p108), then explore the old town and stroll up **Place Jacques-Cartier** (p108) with its many buskers and artists. Visit the excellent **Musée d'Archéologie et d'Histoire Pointe-à-Callière** (p109), making sure to visit the archaeological crypt. Cap off the day with dinner at **Liverpool House** (p116) and a **Cirque du Soleil** (p119) show.

Two Days in Montréal

On day two, visit the **Musée des Beaux-Arts de Montréal** (p109), then head to **Marché Atwater** (p109) for croissants and local produce. Explore the **Canal de Lachine** (p115) either by bike with **My Bicyclette** (p113) or boat with **Le Petit Navire** (p113). In the evening catch some live music – perhaps go classical with the **Orchestre Symphonique de Montréal** (p119) or opt for a way-left-of-center gig at **Foufounes Électriques** (p119).

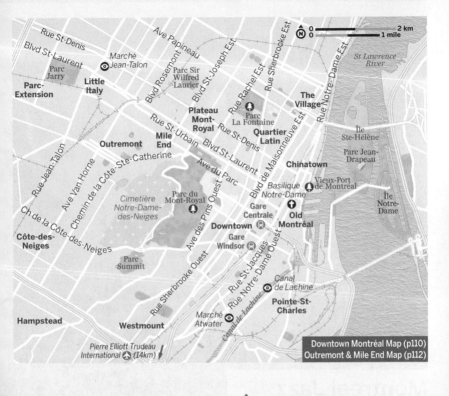

Arriving in Montréal

Pierre Elliott Trudeau International Airport Take a bus ($10, 45 minutes) or taxi ($40, 30 minutes) downtown.

Gare Centrale Trains pulling into Montréal arrive at this convenient downtown terminus, well serviced by local taxis.

Gare d'Autocars de Montréal Most long-distance buses arrive here in the Quartier Latin, with handy connections to the Berri-UQAM metro station.

Where to Stay

Montréal's accommodation scene is blessed with a tremendous variety of rooms and styles. Though rates aren't particularly cheap, they are reasonable by international standards – or even compared with Canadian cities such as Toronto or Vancouver. French- and Victorian-style inns and independent hotels cater to a variety of budgets.

See p121 for more information.

Montréal Jazz Festival

In a city that loves festivals, the Festival International de Jazz de Montréal is the mother of them all.

Although it is ranked as the world's largest jazz festival by Guinness World Records, this celebration of sound is no longer just about jazz, with hundreds of top-name performers bringing reggae, rock, blues, world music, Latin, Cajun, Dixieland and even pop to audiophiles from across the globe. Started as the pipe dream of a young local music producer, Alain Simard (since awarded the Knight of l'Ordre national du Québec), it's now the single biggest tourist event in Québec, attracting some two million visitors to more than 1000 concerts. Miles Davis, Herbie Hancock, Al Jarreau, Sonny Rollins, Wayne Shorter, Stevie Wonder, Diana Ross, Al Dimeola, James Cotton, Booker T Jones, Taj Mahal, Diana Krall, John Scofield, Jack DeJohnette and Sharon Jones are but

Great For...

☑ Don't Miss

Downloading the festival app for schedules, artist bios, tickets, and even a pocket photo booth.

a few of the giants who have graced the podiums over the years.

Local Talent

In the 1940s and '50s, Montréal was one of North America's most important venues for jazz music. It produced a number of major jazz musicians, such as pianist Oscar Peterson and trumpeter Maynard Ferguson. The scene went into decline in the late 1950s, but revived after the premiere of the jazz festival in 1980.

The city's other celebrated jazz pianist, Oliver Jones, was already in his fifties when he was discovered by the music world. Since the 1980s he has established himself as a major mainstream player with impressive technique and a hard-swinging style.

Singer and pianist Diana Krall has enjoyed mass appeal without sacrificing her bop and swing roots. In 1993 she launched her career on Montréal's Justin Time record label, and she remains a perennial local favorite during regular appearances at Montréal's jazz festival.

Originally from New York City, singer Ranee Lee is known for her virtuosity that spans silky ballads, swing standards and raw blues tunes. She has performed with many jazz notables and is a respected teacher on the McGill University music faculty.

The Scoop

Free festival programs can be found at kiosks around the Place des Arts. Some concerts are held indoors, others on outdoor stages; several downtown blocks are closed to traffic. The music starts around noon and lasts until late evening when the clubs take over.

Old Montréal Walking Tour

On the edge of the St Lawrence River, Old Montréal is the city's birthplace, composed of picturesque squares and grand old-world architecture.

Start Basilique Notre-Dame

Distance 2km

Duration 2 hours

3 Loop onto Rue Notre-Dame and down Rue St-Jean. On the corner of Rue de l'Hôpital, the **Lewis Building** has dragons and mischievous gargoyles on the facade. It was built for Cunard Shipping Lines, a steamship company founded in 1840.

2 Head along Rue St-Jacques, once known as Canada's Wall St. Stop at the grand **Royal Bank Tower**, Montréal's tallest building in 1928, to see its palatial interior.

✕ Take a Break
Refuel at Olive + Gourmando (p116) with hearty breakfasts and lunches

4 A few blocks further is **Place d'Youville**, one of Old Montréal's prettiest squares. Some of the first Europeans settled here in 1642. An obelisk commemorates the city's founding.

5 Nearby is the fascinating **Musée d'Archéologie et d'Histoire Pointe-à-Callière** (p109). Inside see the city's ancient foundations, or go to the top floor for fine views over the Old Port.

Rue St-Jacques

Rue Dollard

Rue Notre-Dame Ouest

Rue St-Alexis

Rue St-Jean

Rue de l'Hôpital

OLD MONTRÉAL

Rue du St-Sacrément

Rue St-Pierre

Rue Le Moyne

Rue St-Nicholas

Rue St-François-Xavier

Rue St-Paul Ouest

Pl d'Youville

Bassin Alexandra

Place-d'Armes

9 Turn right on Rue St-Sulpice and return to Place d'Armes. Note the **New York Life Building**, Montréal's first skyscraper (1888), eight stories tall.

Classic Photo
The ornate interior of Basilique Notre-Dame

Rue St-Jacques

FINISH
9

Pl d'Armes

START

Rue Notre-Dame Ouest

1

Blvd St-Laurent

Rue St-Sulpice

Rue de Brésoles

Rue St-Dizier

Rue le Royer

8

7

Rue St-Paul Ouest

6

Pl Royale

Rue de la Commune Ouest

5

1 Start with the city's most celebrated cathedral, the magnificent **Basilique Notre-Dame** (p108). Inside is a spectacularly carved pulpit and richly hued stained-glass windows relating key events from the city's founding.

8 Head up St-Dizier and turn left onto lovely **Cours Le Royer**, a tranquil pedestrian mall with fountains. On the north-side passageway is a stained-glass window of Jérôme Le Royer, one of Montréal's founders.

7 Walk down Rue St-Paul to see the 2006 bronze sculpture **Les Chuchoteuses** (the Whisperers), tucked in a corner near Rue St-Dizier. This was one of many projects to revitalize the old quarter.

6 Across the road is the 1836 **Old Customs House**. It's in front of Place Royale, the early settlement's marketplace in the 17th and 18th centuries.

Bassin King Edward

0   200 m
0   0.1 miles

◎ SIGHTS

◎ Old Montréal

Basilique Notre-Dame   Church
(Map p110; ☏514-842-2925; www.basiliquenddm.org; 110 Rue Notre-Dame Ouest; adult/child $5/4; ⏱8am-4:30pm Mon-Fri, to 4pm Sat, 12:30-4pm Sun) Montréal's famous landmark, Notre-Dame Basilica, is a visually pleasing if slightly gaudy symphony of carved wood, paintings, gilded sculptures and stained-glass windows. Built in 1829 on the site of an older and smaller church, it also sports a famous Casavant organ and the **Gros Bourdon**, said to be the biggest bell in North America.

Vieux-Port de Montréal   Park
(Map p110; 🚶) Montréal's Old Port has morphed into a park and fun zone paralleling the mighty St Lawrence River for 2.5km and punctuated by four grand *quais*. Locals and visitors alike come here for strolling, cycling and in-line skating. Cruise boats, ferries, jet boats and speedboats all depart for tours from various docks. In winter, you can cut a fine figure on an outdoor ice-skating rink.

Place Jacques-Cartier   Square
(Map p110; 🚶; Ⓜ Champ-de-Mars) FREE The liveliest spot in Old Montréal, this gently inclined square hums with performance artists, street musicians and the animated chatter from terrace restaurants lining its borders. A public market was set up here after a château burned down in 1803. At its top end stands the **Colonne Nelson**, a monument erected to Admiral Lord Nelson after his defeat of Napoleon's fleet at Trafalgar.

Place d'Armes   Historic Site
(Map p110; Ⓜ Place-d'Armes) This open square is framed by some of the finest buildings in Old Montréal, including its oldest bank, first skyscraper and Basilique Notre-Dame. The square's name references the bloody battles that took place here as religious settlers and Aboriginal tribes clashed over control of what would become Montréal. At its center stands the **Monument Maisonneuve**, dedicated to city founder Paul de Chomedey, *sieur* de Maisonneuve.

> *A symphony of carved wood, paintings, gilded sculptures and stained-glass windows*

Basilique Notre-Dame

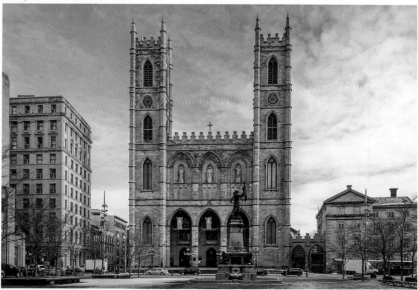

DIEGO GRANDI / SHUTTERSTOCK ©

Musée d'Archéologie et d'Histoire Pointe-à-Callière
Museum

(Map p110; Museum of Archaeology & History; ☑514-872-9150; www.pacmuseum.qc.ca; 350 Pl Royale; adult/child $20/8; ⊗10am-6pm Mon-Fri, 11am-6pm Sat & Sun; ⧉; Ⓜ Place-d'Armes) One of Montréal's most fascinating sites, this museum takes visitors on a historical journey through the centuries, beginning with the early days of Montréal. Visitors should start with *Yours Truly, Montréal,* an 18-minute multimedia show that covers the arrival of the Amerindians, the founding of Montréal and other key moments. Afterward, head to the **archaeological crypt** where you can explore the remains of the city's ancient sewage and river system, and the foundations of its first buildings and public square.

◎ Downtown

Musée des Beaux-Arts de Montréal
Museum

(Map p110; Museum of Fine Arts; www.mbam. qc.ca; 1380 Rue Sherbrooke Ouest; adult/under 13yr permanent collection $12/free, special exhibitions $20/12; ⊗10am-5pm, to 9pm Wed special exhibitions only; Ⓜ Guy-Concordia) A must for art lovers, the Museum of Fine Arts has amassed several millennia worth of paintings, sculpture, decorative arts, furniture, prints, drawings and photographs. European heavyweights include Rembrandt, Picasso and Monet, but the museum really shines when it comes to Canadian art. Highlights include works by Jean-Baptiste Roy-Audy and Paul Kane, landscapes by the Group of Seven and abstractions by Jean-Paul Riopelle. The temporary exhibits are often exceptional.

Marché Atwater
Market

(☑514-937-7754; www.marchespublics-mtl.com; 138 Ave Atwater; ⊗7am-6pm Mon-Wed, to 7pm Thu, to 8pm Fri, to 5pm Sat & Sun; ⧉; Ⓜ Atwater) 𝒫 Just off the Canal de Lachine (p115), this fantastic market has a mouthwatering assortment of fresh produce from local farms, excellent wines, crusty breads, fine cheeses and other delectable fare. The market's

Montréal Museums Pass

The Montréal Museums Pass allows free access to 39 museums for three days of your choice within a 21-day period ($75). For an extra $5, the pass comes with three consecutive days of free access to bus and metro. It's available from the city's tourist offices, or you can buy it online (www.museesmontreal.org).

specialty shops operate year-round, while outdoor stalls open from March to October. It's all housed in a 1933 brick hall, topped with a clock tower, and little bouts of live music pop off with pleasing regularity. The grassy banks overlooking the canal are great for a picnic.

Parc du Mont-Royal
Park

(☑514-843-8240; www.lemontroyal.qc.ca; ⧉) 𝒫 Montréalers are proud of their 'mountain,' the work of New York Central Park designer Frederick Law Olmsted. It's a sprawling, leafy playground that's perfect for cycling, jogging, horseback riding, picnicking and, in winter, cross-country skiing and tobogganing. In fine weather, enjoy panoramic views from the **Kondiaronk Lookout** near **Chalet du Mont-Royal**, a grand old stone villa that hosts big-band concerts in summer, or from the **Observatoire de l'Est**, a favorite rendezvous for lovebirds.

Musée McCord
Museum

(Map p110; McCord Museum of Canadian History; ☑514-398-7100; www.mccord-museum.qc.ca; 690 Rue Sherbrooke Ouest; adult/student/child $14/8/free, special exhibitions extra $5, after 5pm Wed free; ⊗10am-6pm Tue, Thu & Fri, to 9pm Wed, to 5pm Sat & Sun; Ⓜ McGill) With hardly an inch to spare in its cramped but welcoming galleries, the McCord Museum of Canadian History houses thousands of artifacts and documents illustrating Canada's social, cultural and archaeological history from the 18th century to the present day.

Downtown Montréal

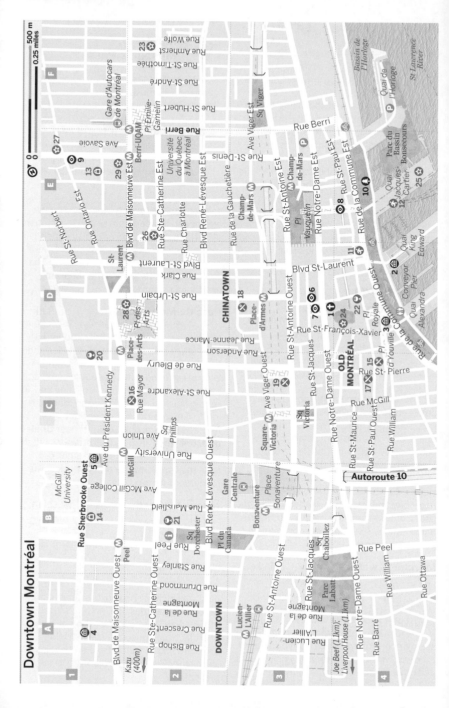

500 m
0.25 miles

McGill University

Kazu (400m)

Rue Sherbrooke Ouest

McGill University

DOWNTOWN

CHINATOWN

OLD MONTRÉAL

Joe Beef (1.1km);
Liverpool House (1.1km)

Autoroute 10

Université du Québec à Montréal

Gare d'Autocars de Montréal

Bassin de l'Horloge

St-Lawrence River

Parc du Bassin Bonsecours

Quai de l'Horloge

Downtown Montréal

◎ Plateau Mont-Royal

Avenue du Mont-Royal   Area

(Map p112; 📶 👪; Ⓜ Mont-Royal) Old-fashioned
five-and-dime stores rub shoulders with a
wide array of trendy cafes and fashion boutiques on Ave du Mont-Royal. The nightlife
here has surged to the point that it rivals
Blvd St-Laurent, with bars and nightclubs
ranging from the sedate to uproarious.
Intimate shops, secondhand stores and
ultramodern boutiques offer eye-catching
apparel.

Parc La Fontaine   Park

(cnr Rue Sherbrooke Est & Ave du Parc La Fontaine; ⊗6am-midnight; 📶 👪; Ⓜ Sherbrooke) ✔
At 34 hectares, this great verdant municipal
park is the city's third-largest, after Parc du
Mont-Royal (p109) and Parc Maisonneuve.
In the warmer months weary urbanites
flock to leafy La Fontaine to enjoy the walking and bicycle paths, the attractive ponds
and the general air of relaxation that pervades the park. There's also a chalet where
you can grab a bite or a drink, **Espace La
Fontaine** (📞514-280-2525; www.espacela
fontaine.com; 3933 Ave du Parc La Fontaine;
mains $10-16; ⊗11am-8pm Tue-Fri, from 10am
Sat, 10am-5pm Sun; 📶 👪; Ⓜ Sherbrooke).

◎ Quartier Latin & the Village

Rue St-Denis   Area

(Map p110; Ⓜ Berri-UQAM) The backbone of
Montréal's Francophone shopping district,
Rue St-Denis is lined with hat and garment
shops, uber-hip record stores and terrace
cafes designed to keep people from getting
any work done. Summer crowds flock to
the inviting bistros and bars on both sides
of the street.

◎ Little Italy, Mile End & Outremont

Marché Jean-Talon   Market

(📞514-937-7754; www.marchespublics-mtl.com;
7075 Ave Casgrain; ⊗7am-6pm Mon-Wed & Sat, to
8pm Thu & Fri, to 5pm Sun; 🅿 📶; Ⓜ Jean-Talon) ✔
The pride of Little Italy, this huge covered
market is Montréal's most diverse. Many
chefs buy ingredients for their menus
here or in the specialty food shops nearby.
Three long covered aisles are packed
with merchants selling fruit, vegetables,
flowers and baked goods, all flanked
by delis and cafe-restaurants with tiny
patios. Even in winter, the market is open
under big tents.

Outremont & Mile End

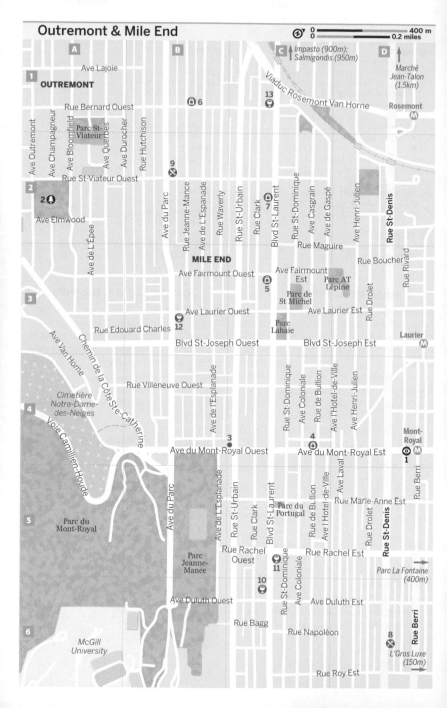

Outremont & Mile End

Parc Outremont   Park
(Map p112; cnr Ave Outremont & Rue St-Viateur; ⚑ 🚻; M Rosemont) One of Montréal's best-kept secrets, this small leafy green space is a great place for a bit of quiet time after exploring the neighborhood. Lovely Victorian homes ring the park, and benches provide a nice vantage point for viewing the small pond with fountain. This is a good spot to go with an ice cream from Le Bilboquet, two blocks northwest.

✪ ACTIVITIES

Ça Roule Montréal   Cycling
(Map p110; ☑514-866-0633; www.caroulemontreal.com; 27 Rue de la Commune Est, Old Port; bikes per hour/day from $8/30, in-line skates 1st/additional hour $9/4; ☺9am-7pm, reduced hours winter; M Place-d'Armes) Near the Old Port, Ça Roule Montréal has a wide selection of bicycles, in-line skates, spare parts and a good repair shop. Each rental includes a lock, helmet, patch kit and cycling map. You can rent children's bikes, tandems and bike trailers for pulling the little ones along while you pedal. Tours are also available.

Prices are for weekday rentals; weekend rentals cost slightly more.

My Bicyclette   Cycling
(☑514-317-6306; www.mybicyclette.com; 2985 Rue St-Patrick; bicycle per hour/day from $10/30; ☺9am-7pm Mon-Sat, to 6pm Sun; M Charlevoix) Located along the Canal de Lachine (p115; just across the bridge from the Atwater market, p109), this place rents bikes and

other gear during the warmer months. It also sponsors city bike tours, and the repair shop next door is a good place to go if your bike conks out on the canal path.

⊙ TOURS

Le Petit Navire   Boating
(Map p110; ☑514-602-1000; www.lepetitnavire.ca; Quai Jacques-Cartier; adult/child 45min tour $20/9, 2hr tour $26/19; ☺10am-7pm mid-May–mid-Oct; M Champ-de-Mars) Aside from rowing a boat yourself, this outfit offers the most ecologically friendly boat tours in Montréal. The silent, electric-powered *Le Petit Navire* takes passengers on 45-minute tours departing hourly around the Old Port area. Equally intriguing are the 1½-hour cruises up the Canal de Lachine (departing Friday, Saturday and Sunday at 11:30am from Quai Jacques-Cartier and 2pm from Marché Atwater).

Fitz & Follwell Walking, Cycling
(Map p112; ☑514-840-0739; www.fitzandfollwell.co; 115 Ave du Mont-Royal Ouest; tours from $79, bike hire per 4/8hr $20/30; ☺10am-7pm Tue-Fri, to 6pm Sat, to 5pm Sun; M Place-des-Arts, then bus 80) This recommended outfit offers a range of walking and cycling tours around Montréal. Tours have very much a local flavor, as young, knowledgeable guides take you on day and evening rides, stopping for a park picnic, visiting microbreweries, or exploring the leafy paths of Mont-Royal.

🛒 SHOPPING

Drawn & Quarterly — Books

(Map p112; 📞514-279-2224; http://211blog. drawnandquarterly.com; 211 Rue Bernard Ouest; ⊙10am-9pm; Ⓜ Outremont) The flagship store of this cult independent comic-book and graphic-novel publisher has become something of a local literary haven. Cool book launches take place here, and the quaint little shop sells all sorts of reading matter including children's books, vintage Tintin comics, recent fiction and art books.

Camellia Sinensis — Food & Drinks

(Map p110; www.camellia-sinensis.com; 351 Rue Émery; ⊙10am-6pm Mon-Wed, Sat & Sun, to 9pm Thu & Fri; Ⓜ Berri-UQAM) Right in front of the Cinéma Quartier Latin, this welcoming tea shop has more than 200 varieties of tea from China, Japan, India and elsewhere in Asia, plus quality teapots, tea accessories, books, and workshops such as pairing tea with chocolate. You can taste exotic teas and carefully selected desserts in the salon next door, which features brews from recent staff travels.

Monastiraki — Vintage

(Map p112; www.monastiraki.blogspot.ca; 5478 Blvd St-Laurent; ⊙noon-6pm Wed, to 8pm Thu & Fri, to 5pm Sat & Sun; Ⓜ Laurier) This unclassifiable store named after a flea-market neighborhood in Athens calls itself a 'hybrid curiosity shop/art space,' but that doesn't do justice to what illustrator Billy Mavreas sells: 1960s comic books, contemporary zines (homemade magazines), silkscreen posters, and myriad antique and collectible knickknacks, as well as recent works mainly by local graphic artists.

Cheap Thrills — Music

(Map p110; 📞514-844-8988; www.cheapthrills. ca; 2044 Rue Metcalfe; ⊙11am-6pm Mon-Wed & Sat, to 9pm Thu & Fri, noon-5pm Sun) It's easy to lose track of time as you browse through this big selection of used books and music (CDs and some vinyl), both with a mainstream and offbeat bent and sold at bargain prices.

Artpop — Arts & Crafts

(Map p112; 📞514-843-3443; 129 Ave du Mont-Royal Est; ⊙10am-8pm Mon-Wed, to

St-Viateur Bagel

9pm Thu & Fri, 10am-7pm Sat, from 11am Sun;
Ⓜ Mont-Royal) Though tiny in size, Artpop is
a real find when it comes to browsing for
unique Montréal-themed gift ideas. You'll
find graphic T-shirts, bags, pillowcases,
smartphone covers and prints with iconic
city signage (Farine Five Roses, the big
Orange Julep, Habitat 67 or the cross atop
Mont Royal).

Au Papier Japonais   Arts & Crafts
(Map p112; ☏ 514-276-6863; www.aupapierjapon
ais.com; 24 Ave Fairmount Ouest; ⊙10am-6pm
Mon-Sat, noon-4pm Sun; Ⓜ Laurier) You might
never guess how many guises Japanese
paper can come in until you visit this
gorgeous little shop, which stocks more
than 800 varieties. Origami kits and art
books make great gifts, as do the elegant
tea pots, pottery and Buddha boards
(where you can 'paint' ephemeral works
with water).

🍴 EATING
St-Viateur Bagel   Bakery $
(Map p112; ☏ 514-276-8044; www.stviateur-
bagel.com; 263 Rue St-Viateur Ouest; bagels
80¢; ⊙24hr; Ⓜ Place-des-Arts, then bus 80)
Currently the bagel favorite of Montréal,
St-Viateur Bagel was set up in 1957 and has
a reputation stretching across Canada and
beyond for its perfectly crusty, chewy and
slightly sweet creations. The secret to their
perfection seems to be boiling in honey
water followed by baking in the wood-fired
oven. Biting into a warm one straight out of
the oven is an absolute delight.

Kazu   Japanese $
(☏ 514-937-2333; www.kazumontreal.com; 1862
Rue Ste-Catherine Ouest; mains $10-17; ⊙noon-
3pm Sun, Mon & Wed-Fri, 5:30-9:30pm Wed-Mon;
Ⓜ Guy-Concordia) Kazuo Akutsu's frenetic
hole-in-the-wall in the Concordia Chinatown draws long lines of people waiting for
gyoza (dumplings), ramen noodle soup and
awesome creations such as the 48-hour
pork, attesting to its popularity. Be warned:
it gets cramped inside.

💬 Canal de Lachine

This canal was built in 1825 as a means
of bypassing the treacherous Lachine
Rapids on the St Lawrence River.
Today, it's a perfect marriage of urban
infrastructure and green civic planning:
a 14km-long cycling and pedestrian
pathway, with picnic areas and outdoor
spaces. Since the canal was reopened
for navigation in 2002, flotillas of
pleasure and sightseeing boats have
traveled its calm waters. Old warehouses
converted into luxury condos line the
canal near Atwater market.

It's well worth hiring a bike or in-line
skates and heading out along the canal
path, but try to avoid summer weekends,
when it's particularly crowded. For a
canal-side spin, you can hire bikes from
Ça Roule (p113) in Old Montréal or My Bicyclette (p113) near the Atwater market.
Kayaks and boats are also available at
nearby **H2O Adventures** (www.h2oadven-
tures.com). For a leisurely boat ride where
someone else does the work, take a ride
with *Le Petit Navire* (p113).

PAUL VANCE / SHUTTERSTOCK ©

Café Parvis   Bistro $$
(Map p110; ☏ 514-764-3589; www.cafeparvis.
com; 433 Rue Mayor; small plates $6-8; ⊙7am-
11pm Mon-Wed, to midnight Thu & Fri, 10am-mid-
night Sat, to 10pm Sun; ⊘; Ⓜ Place-des-Arts)
Hidden away on a quiet downtown lane,
Café Parvis is set with oversized windows,
hanging plants, old wooden floorboards
and vintage fixtures. Once part of the fur
district, this cleverly repurposed room

Montréal for Children

Montréal has many activities and sights for young visitors. Depending on the season, you can go boating, cycling and skating, or get some amusement park or skydiving thrills. On warm days, Parc du Mont-Royal (p109) is a great place for picnics and free-spirited outdoor activity, while in winter kids can try tobogganing, skiing, snowshoeing and ice skating.

World-renowned Cirque du Soleil (p119) combines dance, theater and circus in powerpacked summertime shows; it will thrill the kids, but is truly for all ages. At the Old Port (p108) you can hop into a paddleboat, go jet boating on the St Lawrence, or tootle along in a mini-train for a grand tour. Enjoy technological wonders, unusual games and an IMAX cinema at **Centre des Sciences de Montréal** (Map p110; www.montreal sciencecentre.com; King Edward Pier; adult/teen/child $15/13/8.50; ⊙9am-4pm Mon-Fri, 10am-5pm Sat & Sun; MPlace-d'Armes).

Mini-train at the Old Port
JOSEPH S L TAN MATT / SHUTTERSTOCK ©

serves up delicious pizzas in inventive combinations (such as smoked salmon, fennel and mascarpone, or roasted vegetables with Gruyère).

Olive + Gourmando   Cafe $$

(Map p110; ☑514-350-1083; www.oliveetgourmando .com; 351 Rue St-Paul Ouest; mains $10-17; ⊙8am-5pm Tue-Sat; ☑; MSquare-Victoria) Named after the owners' two cats, this bakery-cafe is legendary in town for its

hot panini, plump salads and flaky baked goods. Excellent choices include the melted goat's-cheese panini with caramelized onions, decadent mac 'n' cheese, and 'the Cubain' (a ham, roast pork and Gruyère sandwich).

Orange Rouge   Asian $$

(Map p110; ☑514-861-1116; www.orangerouge.ca; 106 de la Gauchetière Ouest; small plates $7-17; ⊙11:30am-2:30pm Tue-Fri & 5:30-10:30pm Tue-Sat; MPlace-d'Armes) Hidden down a narrow lane of Chinatown, Orange Rouge has a quaint, low-lit interior that's rather nondescript save for the bright open kitchen at one end and a neon-lit crab sculpture on the wall. Grab a seat at the bar or on one of the banquettes for a feast of Asian fusion.

L'Gros Luxe   Bistro $$

(☑514-447-2227; www.lgrosluxe.com; 3807 Rue St-André; small plates $5-10; ⊙5-11:30pm Mon-Fri, from 11am Sat & Sun; ☑; MSherbrooke) With its big windows, classy vintage decor and inexpensive comfort fare, L'Gros Luxe has obvious appeal. The small dining room is always packed with young Plateau residents who come for pork tacos, veggie burgers, and fish-and-chips. Plates are small, but nothing costs more than $10, and there's an extensive drinks menu.

L'Express   French $$

(Map p112; ☑514-845-5333; www.restaurant lexpress.com; 3927 Rue St-Denis; mains $22-28; ⊙8am-2am Mon-Fri, from 10am Sat & Sun; MSherbrooke) L'Express has all the hallmarks of a Parisian bistro – black-and-white checkered floor, art-deco globe lights, papered tables and mirrored walls. High-end bistro fare completes the picture with excellent dishes such as grilled salmon, bone marrow with sea salt, roast duck with salad and beef tartare. The waiters can advise on the extensive wine list. Reservations are essential.

Liverpool House   Québécois $$$

(☑514-313-6049; www.joebeef.ca; 2501 Rue Notre-Dame Ouest; mains $24-50; ⊙5-11pm Tue-Sat; ☑) The sister establishment (and neighbor) of Joe Beef, Liverpool House sets the standard so many Québec restaurants are racing for: an ambience that feels laid-back, like a friend's dinner party, where the food is sent from angels on high. Expect oysters, smoked trout, braised rabbit, lobster spaghetti and various other iterations of regional excellence.

Barroco
International $$$

(Map p110; ☏514-544-5800; www.barroco.ca; 312 Rue St-Paul Ouest; mains $28-41; ⊗6-10:30pm, to 11pm Fri & Sat; ⒨Square-Victoria) Small, cozy Barroco has stone walls, flickering candles and beautifully presented plates of roast duck, braised short ribs and grilled fish. The selection is small (just six or so mains and an equal number of appetizers), but you can't go wrong here – particularly if you opt for the outstanding seafood and chorizo paella.

Salmigondis
Québécois $$$

(www.salmigondis.ca; 6896 Rue St-Dominique; mains $25-43; ⊗11:30am-2pm Thu & Fri, 6-11pm Wed-Sat, 10am-3pm Sat & Sun, 5-10pm Sun; ☑; ⒨De Castelnau) Young waitstaff traverse an airy space and a back porch, bringing out plates topped with artful arrangements of *haute* Québécois cuisine: farm deer with arugula, arctic char ceviche and lobster risotto. The kitchen staff have carved a name for themselves in a competitive dining field; you'll see why the reputation is justified.

Joe Beef
Québécois $$$

(☏514-935-6504; www.joebeef.ca; 2491 Rue Notre-Dame Ouest; mains $29-52; ⊗6pm-late Tue-Sat; ⒨Lionel-Groulx) In the heart of the Little Burgundy neighborhood, Joe Beef remains a darling of food critics for its unfussy, market-fresh fare. The rustic, country-kitsch setting is a great spot to linger over fresh oysters, braised rabbit, roasted scallops with smoked onions and a changing selection of hearty Québécois dishes – all served with good humor and a welcome lack of pretension.

Toqué!
French $$$

(Map p110; ☏514-499-2084; www.restaurant-toque.com; 900 Pl Jean-Paul-Riopelle; mains $46-55; ⊗11:30am-1:45pm Tue-Fri, 5:30-10pm Tue-Thu, to 10:30pm Fri & Sat; ⒨Square-Victoria) Chef

Normand Laprise has earned rave reviews for his innovative recipes based on products sourced from local farms. The dining room has high ceilings with splashes of color, and a glass-enclosed wine cave with suspended bottles. The seven-course *menu dégustation* ($120) is the pinnacle of dining in Montréal.

Impasto
Italian $$$

(☏514-508-6508; www.impastomtl.ca; 48 Rue Dante; mains $29-36; ⊗11:30am-2pm Thu & Fri, 5-11pm Tue-Sat; ⒨De Castelnau) There's much buzz surrounding this Italian eatery – in no small part owing to the heavy-hitting foodies behind it: best-selling cookbook author Stefano Faita and celebrated chef Michele Forgione. Both have deep connections to Italian cooking, obvious in brilliant dishes such as braised beef cheeks with Savoy-style potatoes, arctic char with cauliflower puree and lentils, and housemade pastas like busiate with lobster.

🍷 DRINKING & NIGHTLIFE

Dominion Square Tavern
Taverna

(Map p110; ☏514-564-5056; www.dominiontavern.com; 1245 Rue Metcalfe; ⊗11:30am-midnight Mon-Fri, 4:30pm-midnight Sat & Sun; ⒨Peel) Once a down-and-out watering hole dating from the 1920s, this beautifully renovated tavern recalls a classic French bistro but with a long bar, English pub–style. Executive chef Éric Dupuis puts his own spin on pub grub, with mussels cooked with bacon, and smoked trout salad with curry dressing.

La Buvette Chez Simone
Wine Bar

(Map p112; ☏514-750-6577; www.buvettechez simone.com; 4869 Ave du Parc; ⊗4pm-3am; ⒨Laurier) An artsy-chic crowd of (mostly)

★ Top Five Outdoor Spots
Vieux-Port de Montréal (p108)
Parc du Mont-Royal (p109)
Parc La Fontaine (p111)
Canal de Lachine (p115)
Place Jacques-Cartier (p108)

Francophone bons vivants and professionals loves this cozy wine bar. The staff know their vino and the extensive list is complemented by a gourmet tapas menu. Weekends, the place is jammed from *cinc-à-sept* into the wee hours.

Whisky Café
Lounge

(Map p112; ☎514-278-2646; www.whiskycafe.com; 5800 Blvd St-Laurent; ☺5pm-1am Mon-Wed, to 3am Thu & Fri, 6pm-3am Sat, 7pm-1am Sun; Ⓜ Place-des-Arts, then bus 80) Cuban cigars and fine whiskeys are partners in crime at this classy 1930s-styled joint, hidden near the industrial sector of the Mile End. The well-ventilated cigar lounge is separated from the main bar, which stocks 150 Scotch whiskeys, plus wines, ports and tasting trios. Snacks range from duck rillettes to Belgian chocolates. Music is as sexy-smooth as the leather chairs.

Big in Japan
Cocktail Bar

(Map p112; ☎438-380-5658; 4175 Blvd St-Laurent; ☺5pm-3am; Ⓜ St-Laurent, then bus 55) Completely concealed from the street, Big in Japan always amazes first-timers. There you are walking along bustling St-Laurent, you find the unmarked door, walk down a rather unpromising corridor and emerge into a room lit with a thousand candles (or so it seems). The elegant but ethereal beauty seems to come through in the cocktails as well.

Barfly
Bar

(Map p112; ☎514-284-6665; www.facebook.com/BarflyMtl; 4062 Blvd St-Laurent; ☺4pm-2:30am; Ⓜ St-Laurent, then bus 55) Cheap, gritty, loud, fun and a little bit out of control – just the way we like our dive bars. Live bluegrass and rockabilly bands and bedraggled hipsters hold court alongside aging rockers at this St-Laurent hole-in-the-wall.

Bleury Bar à Vinyle
Bar

(Map p110; ☎514-439-2033; www.vinylebleury.ca; 2109 Rue de Bleury; ☺9pm-3am Tue, Wed, Fri & Sat, from 8pm Thu; Ⓜ Place-des-Arts) It's in a bit of a nightlife desert, but this cozy lounge-like space is well worth the trip if you're into music. A blend of DJs and live bands mixes things up, with a packed calendar of soul, funk, new-wave disco, world beats and house music. It draws a young, friendly crowd and the cocktails are first-rate.

L'Express (p116)

GUYLAIN DOYLE / GETTY IMAGES ©

Philémon
Club

(Map p110; ☑514-289-3777; www.philemonbar. com; 111 Rue St-Paul Ouest; ◷5pm-3am Mon-Wed, from 4pm Thu-Sat, from 6pm Sun; Ⓜ Place-d'Armes) A major stop for local scenesters rotating between watering holes in the old city, Philémon was carved out of stone, brick and wood with large windows looking out over Rue St-Paul. Twenty-somethings fill the space around a huge central bar sipping cocktails and nibbling on light fare (oysters, charcuterie plates, smoked-meat sandwiches), while a DJ spins house and hip-hop.

⊕ ENTERTAINMENT

Cirque du Soleil
Theater

(Map p110; www.cirquedusoleil.com; Quai Jacques-Cartier; Ⓜ Champ-de-Mars) Globally famous Cirque du Soleil, one of the city's most renowned exports, puts on a new production of acrobats and music in this marvelous tent complex roughly once every two years in summer. These shows rarely disappoint, so don't pass up a chance to see one on its home turf.

Orchestre Symphonique de Montréal
Classical Music

(Map p110; OSM; ☑514-840-7400; www.osm.ca; 1600 Rue St-Urbain, Maison Symphonique, Pl des Arts; Ⓜ Place-des-Arts) This internationally renowned orchestra plays to packed audiences in its Place des Arts base, the Maison Symphonique de Montréal, a venue with spectacular acoustics that was inaugurated in 2011. The OSM's Christmas performance of *The Nutcracker* is legendary.

Centaur Theatre
Theater

(Map p110; ☑514-288-3161; www.centaurtheatre. com; 453 Rue St-François-Xavier; Ⓜ Place-d'Armes) Montréal's chief English-language theater presents everything from Shakespearean classics to works by experimental Canadian playwrights. It occupies Montréal's former stock exchange (1903), a striking building with classical columns.

Le 4e Mur
Live Music

(Map p110; www.le4emur.com; 2021 Rue St-Denis; ◷5pm-3am, from 7pm Sun; Ⓜ Sherbrooke) This bar is located literally behind an unmarked door – look out for a big intimidating bouncer or the beautiful folks walking past him. Follow on, down into a basement bar where the cocktails are expertly mixed, live music pops off regularly, and burlesque is a regular fixture.

Foufounes Électriques
Live Music

(Map p110; ☑514-844-5539; www.foufounes electriques.com; 87 Rue Ste-Catherine Est; ◷3pm-3am; Ⓜ St-Laurent) A one-time bastion of the alternafreak, this cavernous quintessential punk venue still stages some wild music nights (featuring rockabilly, ska, metal), plus the odd one-off (a night of pro-wrestling or an indoor skateboarding contest). The graffiti-covered walls and industrial charm should tip you off that 'Electric Buttocks' isn't exactly a mainstream kinda place.

Théâtre St-Denis
Performing Arts

(Map p110; ☑514-849-4211; www.theatrestdenis. com; 1594 Rue St-Denis; ◷box office noon-6pm Mon-Sat; Ⓜ Berri-UQAM) This Montréal landmark and historic movie house hosts touring Broadway productions, rock concerts and various theatrical and musical performances. Its two halls (933 and 2218 seats) are equipped with the latest sound and lighting gizmos and figure prominently in the **Just for Laughs Festival** (www. hahaha.com; ◷Jul).

Cabaret Mado
Cabaret

(Map p110; ☑514-525-7566; www.mado.qc.ca; 1115 Rue Ste-Catherine Est; tickets $5-15; ◷4pm-3am Tue-Sun; Ⓜ Beaudry) Mado is a flamboyant celebrity who has been featured in *Fugues,* the gay entertainment mag. Her cabaret is a local institution, with drag shows featuring an assortment of hilariously sarcastic performers in eye-popping costumes. Shows take place Tuesday, Thursday and weekend nights; check the website for details.

ℹ INFORMATION

INTERNET ACCESS

Wi-fi is widely available throughout Montréal, at tourist offices, hotels, cafes and many restaurants. Except in a few high-end hotels, it's generally free of charge.

For a map of hundreds of places where you can get online for free in Montréal, see Île Sans Fil (www.ilesansfil.org).

MEDICAL SERVICES

If you're sick and need some advice, call Québec's provincial **Health Hotline** (📞811), which is staffed by nurses 24 hours a day.

For minor ailments, visit the **CLSC** (Centre Local de Services Communautaires; 📞514-934-0354; www.santemontreal.qc.ca; 1801 Blvd de Maisonneuve Ouest; ☺8am-8pm Mon-Fri; Ⓜ Guy-Concordia) clinic downtown.

TOURIST INFORMATION

Centre Infotouriste Montréal (📞514-844-5400, 800-230-0001; www.tourisme-montreal.org; 1255 Rue Peel; ☺8:30am-7pm; Ⓜ Peel) Provides maps, info about attractions, and booking services (hotels, car hire, tours).

ℹ GETTING THERE & AWAY

Most travelers arrive in Montréal by air. Located west of downtown, **Pierre Elliott Trudeau International Airport** (YUL; 📞800-465-1213, 514-394-7377; www.admtl.com) has frequent connections to cities in the US, Europe, the Caribbean, Latin America, Africa and the rest of Canada. It's easy to drive to Montréal from elsewhere in Canada or the US if you have the time, or take the train or intercity coach from cities such as Toronto or New York.

All the major international car-rental companies have branches at the airport, main train station and elsewhere around town. **Auto Plateau** (📞514-281-5000; www.autoplateau.com; 3585 Rue Berri; Ⓜ Sherbrooke) is a reputable local company.

Kangaride (📞855-526-4274; www.kangaride.com) is a reliable online ride-share agency. A sample fare is around $15 to Québec City.

ℹ GETTING AROUND

TO/FROM THE AIRPORT

Bus 747, the cheapest way to get into town, takes 45 to 60 minutes. Buses run round the clock, leaving from just outside the arrivals hall and dropping passengers downtown at the **Gare d'Autocars** (📞514-842-2281; www.gamtl.com; 1717 Rue Berri; Ⓜ Berri-UQAM) and the Berri-UQAM metro station, in the Quartier Latin. The $10 fare can be paid by Visa, MasterCard or cash at vending machines in the international arrivals area, or tickets may be bought on board (coins only, exact change). Your ticket gives you unlimited travel on Montréal's bus and metro network for 24 hours.

A taxi will take at least 20 minutes to get downtown from the airport ($40 fixed fare). Limousine services ($55 and up) are also available.

BICYCLE

The city's popular **Bixi** (📞514-789-2494; http://montreal.bixi.com; basic fees per 30min/1 day $3/5; ☺24hr mid-Apr–Oct) 🚲 bike-rental system has more than 450 stations, covering central and outlying areas. There is an extensive network of bike paths too.

PUBLIC TRANSPORTATION

The city's bus and metro (subway) operator is **STM** (Société de Transport de Montréal; 📞514-786-4636; www.stm.info). A single bus or metro ticket costs $3.25. Two-ride tickets ($6) are also available in metro stations.

Buses cover central parts of the island with well-marked routes. They run from 5am to 1am, with separate night services.

There are four metro lines; trains run from approximately 5am to midnight and until 1:30am on Friday and Saturday nights.

TAXI

Flag fall is a standard $3.45, plus another $1.70 per kilometer and 63¢ per minute spent waiting in traffic. Prices are posted on the windows inside taxis. Local operators include **Taxi Champlain** (📞514-273-1111; www.taxichamplain.qc.ca) and **Taxi Co-Op** (📞514-725-9885; www.taxi-coop.com).

Where to Stay

Hotels fill up fast in the summer, when warm weather and festivals galore bring hordes of tourists to Montréal, making reservations essential.

Neighborhood	Atmosphere
Old Montréal	Ultraconvenient for many sights, old-world charm, access to the Old Port. Crowded with tourists at peak times, few inexpensive rooms, hard to find parking.
Downtown	Convenient for public transportation and sights throughout the city. Can be congested, with few inexpensive options compared with other districts.
Plateau Mont-Royal	Home to the city's most charming B&Bs; atmospheric neighborhood with many parks. Removed from central Downtown and Old Montréal; few key sights.
Quartier Latin & the Village	Semiresidential area with bohemian charm, restaurants and cafes. Somewhat remote from central sights; has been the center of student protests.

QUÉBEC CITY

Québec City at a Glance...

Québec City is the soul of the province, with a fierce grip on French Canadian identity. One of North America's oldest and most magnificent settlements, its picturesque Old Town is a Unesco World Heritage site – a living museum of narrow cobblestone streets, 17th- and 18th-century houses, and soaring church spires. The city also goes to great lengths to entertain visitors. All summer, musicians, acrobats and actors in period costume take to the streets, while festivals fill the air with fireworks and song. In January and February, Québec's Winter Carnival is arguably the biggest and most colorful winter celebration around.

One Day in Québec City

Wander through the Old Town, taking a gander inside the historic **Le Château Frontenac** (p130) and following our **walking tour** (p128) to see the top sights. Visit the spectacular **Musée de la Civilisation** (p130) and then dine on local specialties at **Chez Boulay** (p136). Wrap up the day with a ghostly night tour at **La Citadelle** (p126) or a nightcap at **Le Sacrilège** (p138).

Two Days in Québec City

Begin the day at the absorbing **Musée National des Beaux-Arts du Québec** (p130). Pick up some picnic treats at **Le Croquembouche** (p135) and head to **Battlefields Park** (p131) to soak up some history. Return to the Old Town to burn off the croissants with a scenic trek around the **Fortifications** (p131). Finish the evening with live music at a local venue such as **Le Cercle** (p140) or **Les Yeux Bleus** (p140).

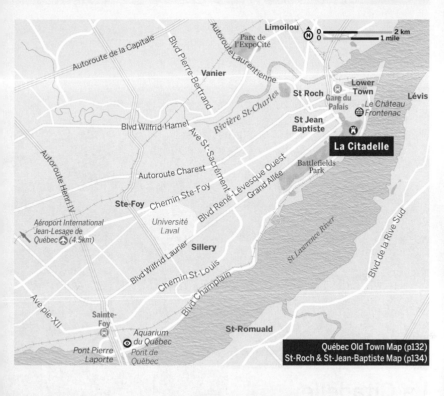

Québec Old Town Map (p132)
St-Roch & St-Jean-Baptiste Map (p134)

Arriving in Québec City

Aéroport International Jean-Lesage de Québec A taxi costs a flat fee of $34.25 into the city, or $15 if you're only going to the boroughs surrounding the airport.

Gare du Palais Conveniently located and served by daily VIA Rail trains from Montréal's Gare Centrale. There is also a major bus station adjacent to the train station, with regular bus service to Montréal.

Where to Stay

Québec City has some fantastic overnight options. The best choices are the small European-style hotels and Victorian B&Bs scattered around the Old Town. Make reservations well in advance. Many do not have elevators. A minimum two-night stay may be required in summer.

Beyond the Old Town, Beauport, Blvd Wilfrid-Hamel (Rte 138) and Blvd Laurier in Ste-Foy-Sillery all have stretches of motels.

La Citadelle

Towering above the St Lawrence River and covering 2.3 sq km, North America's largest fort was intended to defend against an American invasion that never came.

Great For...

☑ Don't Miss

Taking in the panoramic views from the northeastern ramparts.

History & Architecture

French forces started building a defensive structure here in the late 1750s, but the citadel we know today was built in the early to mid-1800s by the British, who feared two things: an American invasion of the colony and a possible revolt by the French-speaking population (that's why the cannons point not only at the river, but at Québec City itself).

By the time the citadel was completed, things were calming down. In 1871, the Treaty of Washington between the United States and the newly minted Dominion of Canada ended the threat of American invasion.

The giant fort, built atop the area's highest point, was designed to both intimidate and function as a stronghold; it was given

La Citadelle
Battlefields Park
(Parc des Champs
de Bataille)
Ave St-Denis
Grande Allée Est
Blvd Champlain
St Lawrence River

❶ Need to Know

Map p132; ☑418-694-2815; www.lacitadelle.
qc.ca; Côte de la Citadelle; adult/child $16/6;
⊘9am-5pm May-Oct, 10am-4pm Nov-Apr

✕ Take a Break

A cafe on the grounds serves up drinks,
snacks and, in the winter, hot chocolate.

★ Top Tip

Hour-long guided tours of the Citadelle are excellent. In summertime
don't miss the daily 10am changing of
the guard.

a complex system of controlled access and
the makings for a self-sufficient community inside. A polygonal star with a bastion
at each of the four corners, its shape was
inspired by the architecture of Vauban,
France's foremost military engineer in the
late 1600s.

Current Residents

La Citadelle now houses about 200 members of the Royal 22e Régiment. The Van-
doos, a nickname taken from the French
for 22 (vingt-deux), is the only entirely
French-speaking battalion in the Canadian
Forces. The second official residence of the
governor general (the Queen of England's
Canadian representative) has also been
located here since 1872.

The Noon-Day Gun

If you visit at noon, you may wonder if the
fort is under siege. Each day at 12pm, a
cannon is fired from the citadel, a tradition
that dates back to 1871 when the Royal
Canadian Artillery's garrison arrived. The
purpose was to allow city residents to
synchronize their watches. Some say it was
also a call to lunch while others argue it
was meant to mark Angelus, the noon-day
prayer.

Night Tour

Often referred to as the Ghost Tour, a tour
through La Citadelle in the evening gives
you a glimpse into the past. Led by a British
corporal from the 19th century and just
the light of his lantern, tours delve into the
dark recesses of the fort that are not open
during the day. Somewhat eerie stories add
to the already spooky mood. Night tours
take 90 minutes and run from late June to
the end of October.

Old Québec City Walking Tour

This historical walking tour encompasses a mix of well-known and lesser-known Vieux-Québec attractions. Set off early, before tour buses fill the streets.
Start Porte St-Louis
Distance 3km
Duration 1 to 2 hours

5 Descend **Côte de la Canoterie**, a longtime link between the Lower and Upper Towns. Hope Gate stood atop the *côte* until 1873 to keep the riffraff from entering the Upper Town. Turn right onto Rue St-Paul, the heart of Québec's antique district, then take a peek at Rue Sous-le-Cap, a former red-light district.

3 Left down Rue Cook is **Edifice Price**, one of Canada's first skyscrapers, built in 1929 for $1 million. Next door, admire the art deco lobby of Québec City's oldest hotel, the elegant 1870 Hotel Clarendon.

1 Begin at **Porte St-Louis**, an impressive gate first erected in 1693 (though this version dates from 1878). Follow Rue St-Louis to the corner of Rue du Corps-de-Garde, where a cannonball sits embedded in a tree (allegedly since 1759). Nearby, 47 Rue St-Louis is where French general Montcalm died, a day after being shot by the British during the destiny-changing Plains of Abraham Battle in September 1759.

Rue St-Paul
Côte de la Canoterie
Rue St-André
Rue des Remparts
Rue Hamel
Rue St-Flavier
Rue Ferland
Rue Charlevoix
Rue Garneau
Côte de la Fabrique
Rue de
OLD UPPER TOWN
Rue Cook
Rue des Jardins
Rue Ste-Anne
Rue Ste-Ursule
Rue St-Louis
Rue du Corps-de-Garde
Parc de l'Esplanade
Rue d'Auteuil
START
Ave St-Denis
Grande Allée Est
La Citadelle
Battlefields Park (Parc des Champs de Bataille)

4 A short jog along Rue des Jardins and Rue de Buade brings you face-to-face with the heavily restored Notre-Dame-de-Québec cathedral. Just to the left of the cathedral is the entrance to the **Québec Seminary**, founded in 1663; American officers were imprisoned here after their unsuccessful siege of Québec in 1775–76. Detour down pretty Rue Garneau, then descend to Rue des Remparts for fine views over Québec City's waterfront factory district.

Rue St-Paul
Rue Sous-le-Cap
Rue Hébert
Rue Dalhousie
Rue Sault-au-Matelot

4

LATIN QUARTIER

OLD PORT

Buade

PLACE
(FINISH) **ROYALE**

6

Classic Photo
Pose alongside historical figures such as Jacques Cartier and Samuel de Champlain at Fresque des Québécois.

6 Turn right and follow Rue Sault-au-Matelot to the 420-sq-meter trompe-l'oeil **Fresque des Québécois**, where you can pose for the requisite tourist pic.

✕ **Take a Break**
Request the *menu du jour* at historic Aux Anciens Canadiens (p138).

2 At 34 Rue St-Louis, a 1676 home houses the Québécois restaurant **Aux Anciens Canadiens** (p138). Its steeply slanted roof was typical of 17th-century French architecture. Follow Rue des Jardins to the Ursuline Convent and Museum, where generations of nuns educated both French and Aboriginal girls starting in 1641.

St Lawrence
River

Ⓝ 0
0
400 m
0.2 miles

◉ SIGHTS

Most of Québec City's sights are found within the compact cluster of Old Town walls, or just outside them, making this a dream destination for pedestrians.

Le Château
Frontenac   Historic Building

(Map p132; ☑418-692-3861; www.fairmont.com/frontenac-quebec; 1 Rue des Carrières) Reputedly the world's most photographed hotel, this audaciously elegant structure was built in 1893 by the Canadian Pacific Railway as part of its chain of luxury hotels. Its fabulous turrets, winding hallways and imposing wings graciously complement its dramatic location atop Cap Diamant, a cliff that swoops into the St Lawrence River. Over the years, it's lured a never-ending lineup of luminaries, including Alfred Hitchcock, who chose this setting for the opening scene of his 1953 mystery *I Confess*.

During WWII, Prime Minister MacKenzie King, Winston Churchill and Franklin Roosevelt planned D-Day here.

Musée de la Civilisation   Museum

(Map p132; Museum of Civilization; ☑418-643-2158; www.mcq.org; 85 Rue Dalhousie; adult/teen/child $16/5/free; ☺10am-5pm) This museum wows you even before you've clapped your eyes on the exhibitions. It is a fascinating mix of modern design that incorporates pre-existing buildings with contemporary architecture. The permanent exhibits, such as the one on the cultures of Québec's Aboriginals and the one titled *People of Québec: Then and Now* are unique and well worth seeing, and many include clever interactive elements. At any given moment there's an outstanding variety of rotating shows.

Musée National des
Beaux-Arts du Québec   Museum

(☑418-643-2150; www.mnbaq.org; Battlefields Park; adult/youth/child $18/5/free; ☺10am-5pm Tue-Sun Sep-May, 10am-6pm daily Jun-Aug, to 9pm Wed year-round) Carve out at least half a day to visit this excellent art museum, one of the province's best. Permanent exhibitions range from art in the early French colonies to Québec's abstract

Fortifications of Québec National Historic Site

NJENE / SHUTTERSTOCK ©

artists, with individual halls devoted entirely to 20th-century artistic giants such as Jean-Paul Lemieux and Jean-Paul Riopelle. Another highlight is the **Brousseau Inuit Art Collection**, a 2639-piece personal collection spanning 50 years.

Battlefields Park Historic Site

(Map p132; Parc des Champs de Bataille; ☑418-649-6157; www.ccbn-nbc.gc.ca; 835 Wilfrid-Laurier Ave; ☻8:30am-5:30pm; 🚼)
✐ One of Québec City's must-sees, this verdant clifftop park contains the **Plains of Abraham**, site of the infamous 1759 battle between British general James Wolfe and French general Louis-Joseph Montcalm that determined the fate of the North American continent. Packed with old cannons, monuments and commemorative plaques, it's a favorite local spot for picnicking, running, skating, skiing and snowshoeing, along with Winter Carnival festivities and open-air summer concerts. For information, visit the **Plains of Abraham Information & Reception Centre** (☑855-649-6157, 418-649-6157; www.ccbn-nbc.gc.ca; 835 Ave Wilfrid-Laurier; ☻8:30am-5:30pm Jul & Aug, 8:30am-5pm Mon-Fri, from 9am Sat & Sun Sep-Jun).

Fortifications of Québec National Historic Site Historic Site

(Map p132; ☑418-648-7016; www.pc.gc.ca/fortifications; western entrance 2 Rue d'Auteuil, eastern entrance Frontenac Kiosk, Terrasse Dufferin; ☻10am-5pm mid-May–mid-Oct, to 6pm Jul & Aug; 🚌3, 11) **FREE** These largely restored old walls are protected as a Canadian National Historic site and a Unesco World Heritage site. Walking the complete 4.6km circuit around the walls on your own is free of charge, and you'll enjoy fine vantage points on the city's historical buildings as you trace the perimeter of the Old Town.

In summer, 90-minute guided walks (adult/child $10/5) are also available, beginning at the **Frontenac kiosk** (the historic site's information center on Terrasse Dufferin) and ending at Artillery Park. Walks depart at 10:30am and 2:30pm.

🥾 Terrasse Dufferin

Perched on a clifftop 60m above the St Lawrence River, this 425m-long **boardwalk** (Map p132) is a marvelous setting for a stroll, with spectacular, sweeping views. In summer it's peppered with street performers; in winter it hosts a dramatic toboggan run. Near the statue of Samuel de Champlain, stairways descend to the recent excavations of Champlain's second fort, which stood here from 1620 to 1635. Nearby, you can take the funicular to the Old Lower Town.

NDRIY BLOKHIN / SHUTTERSTOCK ©

Musée de la Place-Royale Museum

(Map p132; ☑418-646-3167; www.mqc.org; 27 Rue Notre-Dame; adult/teen/child $7/2/free; ☻10am-5pm Tue-Sun; 🚼) This interpretive center touts the Place-Royale neighborhood as the cradle of French history. The exhibits focus on the individual people, houses and challenges of setting up on the shores of the St Lawrence River. It goes a bit heavy on random artifacts, but it still includes some worthwhile displays that help illuminate what local life was like from the 1600s to the 20th century. Children will have lots of fun dressing up in the historical costumes in the basement.

In summer, guides in period garb offer tours of the adjacent Place-Royale.

Musée de l'Amérique Francophone Museum

(Map p132; Museum of French-Speaking America; ☑418-643-2158; www.mcq.org; 2 Côte de la Fabrique; adult/teen/child $8/2/free; ☻10am-

Québec Old Town

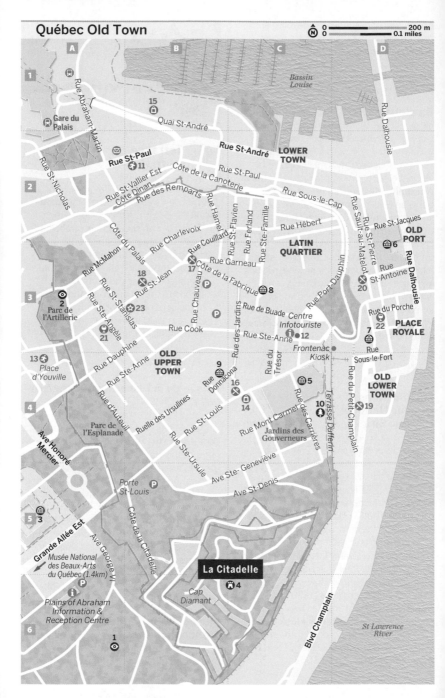

N

0 — 200 m
0 — 0.1 miles

Bassin Louise

Gare du Palais

Rue Abraham-Martin

Quai St-André

Rue St-André

LOWER TOWN

15

Rue St-Paul

Rue St-Vallier Est
Côte Dinan
Rue des Remparts

Côte de la Canoterie

Rue St-Paul

11

Rue Sous-le-Cap

Rue St-Nicholas

Côte du Palais

Rue McMahon

Rue Charlevoix

Rue Hamel

Rue Couillard

Rue St-Flavien
Rue Ferland
Rue Ste-Famille

Rue Hébert

LATIN QUARTIER

Rue Pierre
Rue Sault-au-Matelot

Rue St-Jacques

OLD PORT

6

18

17

Rue St-Jean

23

Côte de la Fabrique

Rue Garneau

8

Rue de Buade

Rue St-Antoine

20

Rue Dalhousie

2
Parc de l'Artillerie

Rue St-Stanislas

Rue Ste-Angèle

Rue Chauveau

Rue des Jardins

Centre Infotouriste

12

Rue du Porche

22

PLACE ROYALE

21

Rue Cook

Rue Ste-Anne

7

Rue Sous-le-Fort

13

Place d'Youville

Rue Dauphine

OLD UPPER TOWN

Rue Ste-Anne

9

Donnacona

Rue du Trésor

Frontenac Kiosk

Rue du Petit-Champlain

OLD LOWER TOWN

16

5

14

10

19

Rue d'Auteuil

Ruelle des Ursulines

Rue St-Louis

Rue Mont Carmel

Rue des Carrières

Terrasse Dufferin

Ave Honoré Mercier

Parc de l'Esplanade

Rue Ste-Ursule

Jardins des Gouverneurs

Ave Ste-Geneviève

Ave St-Denis

Porte St-Louis

5
3

Grande Allée Est

Côte de la Citadelle

← *Musée National des Beaux-Arts du Québec (1.4km)*

Ave George VI

Plains of Abraham Information & Reception Centre

La Citadelle

4

Cap Diamant

Blvd Champlain

St Lawrence River

1

Québec Old Town

5pm) On the grounds of the **Séminaire de Québec** (Québec Seminary), this museum is purported to be Canada's oldest. Permanent exhibits exploring seminary life during the colonial era are complemented by temporary exhibitions. The priests here were avid travelers and collectors, and there are some magnificent displays of the scientific objects they brought back with them from Europe, such as old Italian astronomical equipment. There's also a wonderful short film on New World history from a Québécois perspective.

Musée des Ursulines   Museum
(Map p132; ☎418-694-0694; www.ursulines-uc.com; 12 Rue Donnacona; adult/youth/child $8/3/free; ☺10am-5pm Tue-Sun May-Sep, 1-5pm Tue-Sun Oct-Apr; 🚌3, 7, 11) Housed in a historic convent, this thoughtful, well-laid-out and wheelchair-accessible museum tells the fascinating story of the Ursuline nuns' lives and their influence in the 17th and 18th centuries. The sisters established North America's first school for girls in 1641, educating both Aboriginal and French students. Displays on convent school life are enlivened by a vast array of historic artifacts, including examples of the Ursulines' expert embroidery. The adjoining chapel dates from 1902 but retains some interiors from 1723.

Hôtel du Parlement   Historic Building
(Map p132; Parliament Building; ☎418-643-7239; www.assnat.qc.ca; 1045 Rue des Parlementaires; ☺8:30am-4:30pm Mon-Fri, 9:30am-4:30pm Sat & Sun late Jun-Aug, 8am-5pm Mon-Fri Sep-late Jun) **FREE** Home to Québec's Provincial Legislature, the Parliament building is a Second Empire structure completed in 1886. Free 30-minute tours, offered in English and French year-round, get you into the **National Assembly Chamber**, the **Legislative Council Chamber** and the **Speakers' Gallery**. The facade is decorated with 23 bronze statues of significant provincial historical figures, including explorer Samuel de Champlain (1570–1635), early New France governor Louis de Buade Frontenac (1622–98) and the legendary generals James Wolfe (1727–59) and Louis-Joseph Montcalm (1712–59).

🟢 ACTIVITIES
Corridor du Littoral/Promenade Samuel-de-Champlain   Cycling
Starting southwest of Québec City at Cap-Rouge and extending northeast via the Old Lower Town to Montmorency Falls, the Corridor du Littoral is a 48km multipurpose recreation path along the St Lawrence River, popular with cyclists, walkers and

St-Roch & St-Jean-Baptiste

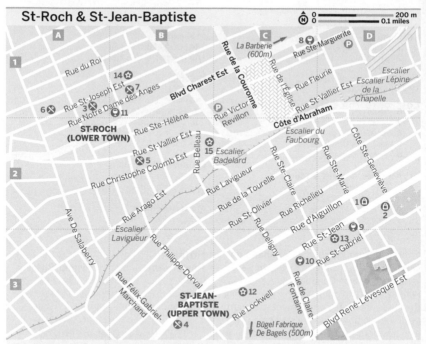

St-Roch & St-Jean-Baptiste

🎯 Shopping
1 Érico	D2
2 JA Moisan Épicier	D2

✴ Eating
3 Bati Bassak	A1
4 Chez Victor	B3
5 La Cuisine	B2
6 L'Affaire est Ketchup	A1
7 Le Croquembouche	B1

🍷 Drinking & Nightlife
8 La Revanche	C1
9 Le Moine Échanson	D2
10 Le Sacrilège	C3
11 Macfly Bar & Arcade	B1

🎭 Entertainment
12 Bateau de Nuit	C3
13 Fou-Bar	D3
14 Le Cercle	B1
15 Scanner	B2

in-line skaters. The heart of the path is the Promenade Samuel-de-Champlain, an especially beautiful 2.5km section.

Cyclo Services — Cycling

(Map p132; ☎877-692-4050, 418-692-4052; www.cycloservices.net; 289 Rue St-Paul; rental per 2/24hr from $15/35; ⊗9am-5:30pm Mon-Fri, 10am-5pm Sat & Sun, variable hours Nov-Apr; ⛷) This outfit rents a wide variety of bikes (hybrid, city, tandem, road and kids' bikes) and organizes excellent cycling tours of the city and outskirts to places such as Wendake

or Parc de la Chute Montmorency. The knowledgeable and fun guides frequently give tours in English. In winter, it rents snowshoes only, and hours are limited; call ahead.

Place d'Youville Skating Rink — Ice Skating

(Map p132; ☎418-641-6256; just outside Porte St-Jean; skating free, skate rentals $8; ⊗noon-10pm Mon-Thu, 10am-10pm Fri-Sun mid-Oct–mid-Mar; ⛷) In the shadow of the old town walls, this improvised outdoor rink is one of the most scenic and popular places for ice-skating once winter rolls around. It's a great place to mingle with locals, and you can also rent skates on-site.

⊕ TOURS

Les Tours Voir Québec   Walking

(Map p132; ☏418-694-2001, 866-694-2001; www.toursvoirquebec.com; 12 Rue Ste-Anne; tours from $23) This group offers excellent tours on the history, architecture and food of Québec City. The popular two-hour 'grand tour' takes in the Old City's highlights, while the food tour includes tastings of wines, cheeses, crêpes, chocolate, maple products and other Québécois specialties at a variety of shops and restaurants. Reserve ahead.

Les Promenades Fantômes   Walking

(Map p132; ☏418-692-0624; www.promenades fantomes.com; 12 Rue Ste-Anne; adult/child $18.50/15.75; ⊗8pm May-Oct) Take a nocturnal trip by the light of a swinging lantern and learn about bygone Québec City's shadowy side.

ⓕ SHOPPING

The best streets for window-shopping include Rue du Petit-Champlain and Rue St-Paul in the Old Lower Town, Ave Cartier in Montcalm, Rue St-Joseph in St-Roch, and Rue St-Jean (both inside and outside the walls). As a general rule, stores in Québec City keep later hours on Thursday and Friday nights.

JA Moisan Épicier   Food

(Map p134; ☏418-522-0685; www.jamoisan.com; 695 Rue St-Jean; ⊗8:30am-9pm Mon-Sat, 10am-7pm Sun) Established in 1871, this charming store bills itself as North America's oldest grocery. It's a browser's dream come true, packed with beautifully displayed edibles and kitchen and household items. Many products fall on the 'You've got to be kidding!' side of expensive, but you'll find

items here you've never seen before, along with heaps of local goods and gift ideas.

Marché du Vieux-Port   Food & Drinks

(Map p132; ☏418-692-2517; www.marchevieux port.com; 160 Quai St André; ⊗9am-6pm Mon-Fri, to 5pm Sat & Sun; ⸙) ⌔ At this heaving local food market, you can buy fresh fruits and vegetables as well as dozens of local specialties, from Île d'Orléans blackcurrant wine to ciders, honeys, cheeses, sausages, chocolates, herbal hand creams and, of course, maple-syrup products. Weekends see huge crowds and more wine tastings than can be considered sensible.

Art Inuit Brousseau   Arts & Crafts

(Map p132; ☏418-694-1828; www.artinuit.ca; 35 Rue St-Louis; ⊗9:30am-5:30pm) A stunning gallery selling soapstone, serpentine and basalt Inuit sculptures from Northern Québec. Prices range from $45 to several thousand dollars.

Érico   Chocolate

(Map p134; ☏418-524-2122; www.ericochoco latier.com; 634 Rue St-Jean; ⊗10:30am-6pm Mon-Wed & Sat, to 9pm Thu & Fri, 11am-6pm Sun, extended hours summer) The exotic smells and flavors here will send a chocolate lover into conniptions of joy. The main shop brims with truffles, chocolate-chip cookies, ice cream and seasonal chocolate treats, while the quirky museum next door has a dress made entirely of chocolate, old-fashioned gumball machines dispensing 25¢ samples, and a window where you can watch the chocolatiers at work.

⊗ EATING

Le Croquembouche   Bakery $

(Map p134; www.lecroquembouche.com; 225 Rue St-Joseph Est; pastries from $2; ⊗7am-6:30pm Tue-Sat, to 5pm Sun; ⸙) Widely hailed as Québec City's finest bakery, Croquembouche draws devoted locals from dawn to dusk. Among its seductive offerings are fluffy-as-a-cloud croissants, tantalizing cakes and éclairs, brioches brimming with raspberries, and gourmet sandwiches on fresh-baked bread. There's also a stellar array of *danoises* (Danish pastries), including orange and anise; cranberry, pistachio and chocolate; and lemon, ginger and poppy seed.

Bügel Fabrique De Bagels Canadian $

(418-523-7666; www.bugel-fabrique.ca; 164 Rue Crémazie Ouest; mains $7-15; 7am-7pm Sun & Mon, to 9pm Tue-Sat) Don't be fooled by the title: there's more than bagels at this cute neighborhood nook. More accurately, imagine bagels and then some: served with Brie and pesto, or au gratin with ham and asparagus, or topped with smoked salmon. Ingredients are locally sourced, and the coffee is strong as a mule.

La Cuisine Diner $

(Map p134; 418-523-3387; www.barlautrecuisine.com; 205 Rue St-Vallier Est; mains $10; 11am-1am Mon-Wed, 11am-3am Thu & Fri, 2pm-3am Sat, 2pm-1am Sun) Retro decor and comfort food served till the wee hours are the hallmarks of this trendy, low-lit local hangout midway between St-Jean Baptiste and St-Roch. Formica tables, mismatched china and silverware, light fixtures made from colanders, a vintage Wurlitzer jukebox, and board games give the place a fun, relaxed feel. On weekend nights, DJs spin everything from electronica to soul.

Bati Bassak Cambodian, Thai $

(Map p134; 418-522-4567; 125 Rue St-Joseph Est; mains $12-19; 11am-2pm Tue-Fri, 5-9:30pm Tue-Sun;) This bustling Thai-Cambodian eatery is a welcome change of pace, serving a menu full of tasty meat and fish dishes, along with several veggie offerings. Weekday lunch specials offer especially good value at $10 to $14 including appetizer, tea and dessert. No alcohol is served, but you're welcome to bring your own.

Chez Boulay Québécois $$

(Map p132; 418-380-8166; www.chezboulay.com; 1110 Rue St-Jean; lunch menus $17-26, dinner mains $20-34; 11:30am-10pm Mon-Fri, 10am-10pm Sat & Sun) Renowned chef Jean-Luc Boulay's

Québec City for Children

While much of the old city may initially feel geared toward adults, there are great things to do with younger ones. Around the edges of the center, you can find sights fully designed for kids' enjoyment.

In the historic area, walking the Fortifications (p131) suits all ages. La Citadelle ceremonies (p126), which include uniformed soldiers, are winners, too. Terrasse Dufferin (p131), with its river views and buskers, always delights children. Place d'Armes and Place-Royale are also good for street performers.

Choco-Musée Érico (p135) is a museum and store devoted to all things chocolate. Get a history lesson, see the kitchen, sample a chunk and try to resist the shop.

Aquarium du Québec (418-659-5264, 866-659-5264; www.sepaq.com/ct/paq; 1675 Ave des Hôtels; adult/child $18.50/9.25; 9am-5pm Jun-Oct, 10am-4pm Nov-May;) has walrus, seals, polar bears and thousands of smaller species.

Children enjoy the 'bee safari' and adults enjoy the mead at **Musée de l'Abeille** (418-824-4411; www.musee-abeille.com; 8862 Blvd St-Anne; 9am-5pm May, Jun, Sep & Oct, to 6pm Jul & Aug;) FREE, a beekeeping *économusée* (workshop) 30km northeast of the city on Hwy 138.

EMILY RIDDELL / GETTY IMAGES ©

latest venture serves an ever-evolving menu inspired by seasonal Québécois staples such as venison, goose, wild mushrooms and Gaspé Peninsula seafood. Lunch specials and charcuterie platters for two (served 2pm to 5pm) offer an affordable afternoon pick-me-up, while the sleek, low-lit dining area with views of the open kitchen makes a romantic setting for dinner.

Batinse   Québécois $$

(Map p132; ☑581-742-2555; www.batinse.com; 1200 Rue St-Jean; mains $18-27; ⊙11am-11:45pm Mon-Fri, from 9am Sat & Sun) ✔ The kitchen staff here have fun, and it's hard not to smile along with their eclectic menu, which jukes from steak with a tea sauce to salmon pie topped with quail-egg béchamel to a divine shrimp and chorizo salad. Hip, locally sourced and not to be missed.

Le Cochon Dingue   French $$

(Map p132; ☑418-692-2013; www.cochondingue.com; 46 Blvd Champlain; mains $15-34; ⊙7am-10pm Mon-Thu, to 11pm Fri, 8am-11pm Sat, to 10pm Sun; 👬) Since 1979, this ever-popular choice has been serving visitors and locals

straight-ahead French standbys, from café au lait *en bôl* (in a bowl) to croque monsieur, sandwiches, *steak frites* (steak and fries), salads, mussels or quiche. It's all good day-to-day food and a kid-friendly place to boot. There's outside seating in warm weather for crowd-watching.

L'Affaire est Ketchup   Bistro $$

(Map p134; ☑418-529-9020; 46 Rue St-Joseph Est; mains $17-34; ⊙6-11pm Tue-Sun) Book ahead for this quirky local favorite with only eight tables. Dressed in T-shirts and baseball caps, bantering relaxedly with one another as they cook on a pair of electric stoves, founders François and Olivier specialize in home cooking with a trendy modern twist. A good selection of wines and mixed drinks is available from the well-stocked bar.

1608   Cheese $$

(Map p132; ☑418-692-3861; www.1608bar-avin.com; 1 Rue des Carrières; mains $22-34; ⊙4pm-midnight Mon-Thu, 2pm-1am Fri-Sun) At this Frontenac-based wine-and-cheese bar you can either select some cheeses

JA Moisan Épicier (p135)

☆ Winter Carnival

Winter, the longest season, holds a special place in the hearts of Québec City residents. The annual 17-day **Carnaval de Québec** (Québec Winter Carnival; www.carnaval.qc.ca; ☉Jan or Feb) is perhaps Québec's best cultural event, presided over by Bonhomme de Neige, a giant snowman clad in a traditional Québécois hat and sash who has become one of the city's most beloved symbols. Local residents join Bonhomme in droves to celebrate the joys of the northern winter – staging ice canoe races across the St Lawrence River, horse-drawn sleigh competitions, colorful night parades, and rides for all ages on dog sleds, snow tubes and ice slides.

Bonhomme de Neige
SERKAN SENTURK / SHUTTERSTOCK ©

yourself or let the staff take you down a wine-and-cheese rabbit hole that's difficult to emerge from – without gaining a few kilos, anyway. Wine, *fromage* and a view of the St Lawrence by candlelight all make for a very romantic setting.

Chez Victor   Burgers $$

(Map p134; ☎418-529-7702; www.chezvictor burger.com; 145 Rue St-Jean; mains $13-18; ☉11:30am-9pm Sun-Wed, to 10pm Thu-Sat; ☎) One of Québec City's best-loved neighborhood eateries, Chez Victor specializes in juicy burgers, served with a hefty dash of creativity. Choose from deer, salmon, wild boar, straight-up beef or vegetarian, which you can then dress a number of ways (Brie, smoked bacon, cream cheese etc). You'll

find several other branches around town, including one down by the Vieux-Port.

Toast!   Bistro $$$

(Map p132; ☎418-692-1334; www.restaurant toast.com; 17 Rue Sault-au-Matelot; mains $25-38; ☉6-10:30pm Sun-Thu, to 11pm Fri & Sat) Under the direction of Christian Lemelin (voted Québec's best chef in 2014 by a jury of his peers), Toast! is among the city's finest. The house's signature foie gras appetizer is followed by a sumptuous array of dishes and a superb wine list, with fiery red decor setting a romantic mood. In summer, dine alfresco in the vine-covered back courtyard.

Aux Anciens Canadiens   Québécois $$$

(Map p132; ☎418-692-1627; www.auxanciens canadiens.qc.ca; 34 Rue St-Louis; mains $31-59, 3-course menu from $20; ☉noon-9:30pm) Housed in the historic Jacquet House, which dates from 1676, this place is a well-worn tourist destination, specializing in robust country cooking and typical Québécois specialties served by waitstaff in historic garb. The *menu du jour,* offered from noon to 6pm, is by far the best deal at around $20 for three courses, including a glass of wine or beer.

⊘ DRINKING & NIGHTLIFE

Le Sacrilège   Bar

(Map p134; ☎418-649-1985; www.lesacrilege. com; 447 Rue St-Jean; ☉noon-3am) With its unmistakable sign of a laughing, dancing monk saucily flaunting his knickers, this bar has long been the watering hole of choice for Québec's night owls, who start or end their weekend revelry here. Even on Monday, it's standing-room only. There's a popular terrace out back; get to it through the bar or the tiny brick alley next door.

Le Moine Échanson   Wine Bar

(Map p134; ☎418-524-7832; www.lemoine echanson.com; 585 Rue St-Jean; ☉7:30am-10pm Mon-Thu, to 11pm Fri, 10am-11pm Sat & Sun) A darling of the city's wine connoisseurs, this convivial brick-walled bistro pours an enticing and ever-changing array of wines from all over the Mediterranean, by the glass and by the bottle, accompanied by hearty and homespun snacks ($9 to $16) and main dishes ($18 to $24) such as blood sausage, cheese fondue or lentil soup. Reservations recommended.

Bar Ste-Angèle   Bar

(Map p132; ☑418-692-2171; 26 Rue Ste-Angèle; ◷8pm-3am) A low-lit, intimate hideaway, where the genial staff will help you navigate the list of cocktail pitchers and local and European bottled beers.

La Revanche   Bar

(Map p134; ☑418-263-5389; 585 Blvd Charest Est; ◷5pm-midnight Mon, 4pm-1am Tue-Thu, to 2am Fri, noon-2am Sat, to midnight Sun) This eclectic bar-cafe is dedicated to table-top and board gaming. Seriously, there's a wall at Revanche that looks like it could have been plucked from a toy store. Staff are on hand to help you learn the ropes of any game. Pro tip: several pints do not, in fact, improve your Jenga performance.

Macfly Bar & Arcade   Bar

(Map p134; ☑418-528-7000; 422 Rue Caron; ◷4pm-3am) This bar's *Back to the Future*-ish title isn't an accident: the entire interior evokes the 1980s, or at least a specific idea of what the '80s were about – old-school arcade consoles, bright counter tops, and rows of pinball machines that await your wizardry. Not that it's easy to top your highest score after a couple of well-pulled beers...

L'Oncle Antoine   Pub

(Map p132; ☑418-694-9176; 29 Rue St-Pierre; ◷11am-1am) Set clandestinely in the stone cave-cellar of one of the city's oldest surviving houses (dating from 1754), this great tavern pours out excellent Québec microbrews (try the Barberie Noir stout or the strong Belgian-style Fin du Monde), several drafts *(en tût)* and various European beers.

La Barberie   Brewery

(☑418-522-4373; www.labarberie.com; 310 Rue St-Roch; ◷noon-1am) This cooperative St-Roch microbrewery is beloved for its spacious tree-shaded deck, its ever-evolving

selection of eight home brews, and its unique BYO policy, which allows customers to bring snacks in from the outside. Seasonal offerings range from classic pale ales to quirkier options such as orange stout or hot pepper amber. Undecided? Sample 'em all in the popular eight-beer carousel!

⊗ ENTERTAINMENT

Le Cercle   Live Music

(Map p134; ☑ 418-948-8648; www.le-cercle.ca; 226½ Rue St-Joseph Est; ⊙11:30am-1:30am Mon-Wed, 11:30am-3am Thu & Fri, 3pm-3am Sat, 10am-1:30am Sun) This very cool art space and show venue draws a hip crowd for its international DJs and underground bands, ranging from indie rock to electronica, blues to Cajun. It hosts numerous other events, including film, fashion and comic-strip festivals, book- and album-release parties, wine tastings and more. Affordable tapas, weekend brunches and an atmospheric bar space sweeten the deal.

Fou-Bar   Live Music

(Map p134; ☑ 418-522-1987; www.foubar. ca; 525 Rue St-Jean; ⊙2:30pm-3am) Laid-back and with an eclectic mix of bands, this bar is one of the town's classics for good live music. It's also popular for its reasonably priced food menu and its free *pique-assiettes* (appetizers) on Thursday and Friday evenings.

Scanner   Live Music

(Map p134; ☑ 418-523-1916; www.scannerbistro. com; 291 Rue St-Vallier Est; ⊙3pm-3am Sat-Thu, 11:30am-3am Fri) Ask any local between the ages of 18 and 35 to suggest a cool place for a drink and this is where they might send you. DJs and live bands serve up a potent musical mix, from heavy metal to hard rock to punk to rockabilly. There's a terrace outside in summer, plus Foosball and pool inside year-round.

Les Yeux Bleus   Live Music

(Map p132; ☑ 418-694-9118; 1117 Rue St-Jean; ⊙9pm-3am Mon, Tue & Thu, 8pm-3am Wed, 4pm-3am Fri-Sun) One of the city's better *boîtes à*

chanson (live, informal singer-songwriter clubs), this is the place to catch newcomers, the occasional big-name Francophone concert and Québécois classics.

Bateau de Nuit   Live Music

(Map p134; ☑ 418-977-2626; 275 Rue St-Jean; ⊙7pm-3am Mon & Tue, from 5pm Wed-Fri, from 8pm Sat & Sun) We really appreciate it when our dive bars come with a heavy dose of live music, which is exactly the case at this sweet little venue. The in-the-know bar staff can tell you about local musicians, or whoever carved their initials into the wall – the crowd here has likely played both roles, to be fair.

ⓘ INFORMATION

Centre Infotouriste (☑ 418-649-2608, 877-266-5687; www.bonjourquebec.com; 12 Rue Ste-Anne; ⊙9am-5pm Nov-Jun, to 7pm Jul & Aug, to 6pm Sep & Oct) Québec City's main tourist office, in the heart of the Old Town, opposite Château Frontenac.

CLSC et Unité de Médecine Familiale de la Haute-Ville (☑ 418-641-2572; www.ciusss-capitale nationale.gouv.qc.ca/node/2023; 55 Chemin Ste-Foy; ⊙8am-8:30pm Mon-Fri, to 4pm Sat & Sun) Québec City's main health clinic for minor ailments.

Post Office The main post office is near the train station in the Old Lower Town.

Tourism Québec City (☑ 418-641-6290, 877-783-1608; www.quebecregion.com) Travel and tourism information.

ⓘ GETTING THERE & AWAY

AIR

Québec City's petite **Aéroport International Jean-Lesage de Québec** (YQB; ☑ 418-640-3300, 418-640-2600; www.aeroportdequebec. com; 505 Rue Principal) lies about 15km west of the center. It mostly has connections to Montréal, but there are also flights to Toronto, Ottawa, Chicago, Newark, New York City (JFK), and Caribbean resorts such as Cancún and Varadero. Check the website for additional destinations.

BUS

Orléans Express (www.orleansexpress.com) runs daily services from Montréal to Québec City's **Gare du Palais bus station** (☑418-525-3000; 320 Rue Abraham-Martin), adjacent to the train station. Prices for the journey (three to 3½ hours) start at $25/50 for a one-way/return ticket.

If you're coming from Montréal, your bus may first stop 10km west of the center at **Ste-Foy-Sillery Station** (☑418-650-0087; 3001 Chemin des Quatre Bourgeois), so ask before you get off.

CAR & MOTORCYCLE

Québec City lies about 260km northeast of Montréal (three hours by car). The most common routes are Autoroute 40 along the north shore of the St Lawrence River, and Autoroute 20, on the south shore.

TRAIN

VIA Rail (www.viarail.ca) has several trains daily between Montréal's Gare Centrale and Québec City's **Gare du Palais** (☑888-842-7245; www.viarail.ca; 450 Rue de la Gare du Palais). Normal prices for the 3½-hour journey start at $98/196 for a one-way/return ticket, but we've seen promotional offers as low as $38 for a one-way seat.

Service is also good along the so-called Québec City–Windsor corridor that connects Québec City with Montréal, Ottawa, Toronto and Niagara Falls.

ⓘ GETTING AROUND

TO/FROM THE AIRPORT

A taxi is your best option for travel between the airport and downtown Québec City, as there is no convenient public transportation along this route. A taxi costs a flat fee of $34.25 to go into the city. Returning to the airport, you'll pay the metered fare, which should be less than $30.

BICYCLE

Québec City has an extensive network of bike paths (some 70km in all), including a route along the St Lawrence that connects to paths along the Riviére St-Charles. Pick up a free map at the tourist office or at local bike shops.

ⓘ Ride in a Calèche

In Québec City, a *calèche* (horse-drawn carriage) costs $100 for a 40-minute tour for up to four passengers. You'll find them just inside the Porte St-Louis, in the Parc de l'Esplanade and near Le Château Frontenac.

BUS

RTC (www.rtcquebec.ca) offers efficient service all around town. Single rides on RTC buses cost $3.50; alternatively, purchase a day pass for $8.25, a five-day pass for $28.50 or unlimited weekend rides for $15. The most convenient hub for catching multiple buses is on Place d'Youville, just outside the Old Town walls.

CAR & MOTORCYCLE

Avis, Budget, Enterprise and Hertz have central offices and desks at the airport.

Parking garages in and around the Old Town typically charge a day rate of $16 to $20 Monday to Friday, and $8 to $12 on weekends. In the Old Upper Town, the most central garage, and one of the cheapest, is underneath the Hôtel de Ville, just a couple of blocks from the Château Frontenac. In the Old Lower Town, there are a couple of convenient lots along Rue Dalhousie. Metered street parking is also widely available, but expensive ($2 per hour). Many guesthouses provide discount vouchers for nearby parking garages.

In winter, nighttime snow removal is scheduled on many streets between 11pm and 6:30am. Don't park during these hours on any street with a '*déneigement*' (snow removal) sign and a flashing red light, or you'll wake up to a towed vehicle and a hefty fine.

TAXI

Flag fall is a standard $3.45 plus another $1.70 per kilometer and 63¢ per minute spent waiting in traffic. Prices are posted on the windows inside taxis. **Taxis Coop** (☑418-525-5191; www.taxiscoop-quebec.com) is a local operator.

OTTAWA

Ottawa at a Glance...

Descriptions of Ottawa read like an appealing dating profile: dynamic, gregarious, bilingual, and likes long walks along the river. In person, the attractive capital fits the bill. For architecture buffs, Canada's huge Gothic parliament buildings regally anchor the downtown core, and for those seeking culture and history, the city's world-class museums house a variety of intriguing collections. Of course, average temperatures sit well below 0°C (32°F) from December to March, but locals celebrate winter with outdoor pursuits and the Winterlude festival. When spring clicks to summer, auspicious tulips cheer downtown, while fall brings streets lined with trees in eye-popping shades of red and yellow.

One Day in Ottawa

Get yourself to **Parliament Hill** (p148) for happy snaps with the Peace Tower and a quick tour of the lavish, Harry Potter–esque interior. Next, visit the carefully curated collection at the **National Gallery of Canada** (p150). Pause for lunch at **ByWard Market Sq** (p154). Sample a fried dough beavertail and make tracks to the **Rideau Canal** (p153): in winter it becomes one of the world's largest ice-skating rinks (7.8km long).

Two Days in Ottawa

On day two, cover the major sights flanking the **Ottawa Locks** (p151), then gravitate toward the awe-inducing architecture, city views and fascinating exhibits of the **Canadian Museum of History** (p146). Stop by **Wilf & Ada's** (p154) for a diner-style lunch, then choose another museum or two before cocktails and tacos at **El Camino** (p154) or *plats du jour* at **Métropolitain Brasserie** (p155).

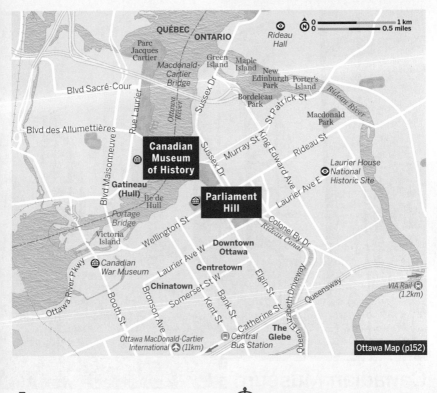

Ottawa Map (p152)

Arriving in Ottawa

Ottawa MacDonald-Cartier International Airport Take bus 97 from pillar 14 outside the arrivals area ($3.65, 40 minutes) or grab a taxi (around $30, 20 minutes).

VIA Rail Station Located 7km east of downtown; take a taxi or an OC Transpo bus (www.octranspo.com; $3.65).

Central Bus Station Located just off Queensway (Hwy 417), near Kent St.

Where to Stay

Ottawa has an impressive array of accommodations in all price ranges. Reservations are recommended during summer and over festival times, especially Winterlude. Downtown and Centretown offer numerous options, including boutique hotels, suite hotels, and hostels around ByWard Market. South of the market, the Sandy Hill district has pleasant B&Bs among its stately heritage homes and international embassies.

Canadian Museum of History

Through a range of spectacular exhibits, this high-tech, must-see museum recounts 20,000 years of human history.

Across the river, in Hull, Québec, the museum boasts incredible views back to Parliament Hill.

First Nations

The museum's smooth stone exterior honors the aboriginal belief that evil dwells in angled nooks. Inside, the Grand Hall is said to have the world's largest indoor collection of totem poles. Wander along a boardwalk, getting an up-close look at the towering poles and the recreated facades of six traditional Aboriginal houses.

Next door, the First People's Hall is a permanent exhibit of over 2000 incredible images, objects and documents that tell the story of the First Nations. This is where you'll find some of the museum's oldest artifacts; keep your eyes peeled for one of the oldest representations of the human face.

Great For...

☑ **Don't Miss**

Temporary events, hands-on exhibitions and big-screen films (check the website for details).

ⓘ Need to Know

☎819-776-7000; www.historymuseum.ca; 100 Rue Laurier, Gatineau; adult/child 3-12yr $15/9, with Canadian War Museum $23/13; ⊘9:30am-5pm Fri-Wed, to 8pm Thu; ♿

✕ Take a Break

The museum has two cafes and a bistro to keep you nourished.

★ Top Tip

Hop on an Aqua-Taxi ferry to get here from Ottawa Locks.

There's also a fascinating section on the relationship of Canada's Aboriginal people with the land and their ongoing contributions to Canadian society.

Canadian History Hall

Its no small feat to fill 40,000 sq ft of gallery space with authentic artifacts that stretch from objects recovered from Canada's very first inhabitants all the way to present-day images of the arrival of 25,000 Syrian refugees. Rather than focusing on historical bigwigs, the hall spotlights the lives and experiences of everyday people through some 1200 images and 1500 artifacts. As well as a re-creation of a 4000-year-old family who were found buried with 350,000 handmade beads, and the forensic facial reconstruction of 800-year-old 'kayak man,' you'll find stories of

Canada's 'dark chapters,' such as Japanese internment camps and residential schools, and current topics such as Canada's First Nations Idle No More Movement and the fight for LGBTQ rights.

Five years in the making, this brand-new gallery is due to open amid much fanfare on Canada Day (July 1) 2017, in celebration of Canada's 150th birthday.

Children's Museum

Fancy climbing aboard an extravagantly decorated Pakistani bus or a three-wheeled rickshaw from Thailand? Curious to step inside a Bedouin tent, and houses in India, Indonesia and Mexico? You can, in the Canadian Children's Museum, just around the corner from the History Museum. Over 30 exhibition spaces, based on a 'Great Adventure' theme, whisk kids off on a journey around the world. We're talking props, costumes, artifacts you can pick up and play with, and all sorts of toys and games. And the best part? Admission is free with your History Museum ticket.

OGNJEN1234 / SHUTTERSTOCK ©

Parliament Hill

Set on the banks of the Ottawa River, this is the political and cultural heart of the city.

Great For...

☑ Don't Miss

Joining up to a thousand people on the lawns for a free yoga session on summertime Wednesdays at noon.

Parliament Buildings

Vast, yawning archways, copper-topped turrets and Gothic revival gargoyles dominate the facade of the stunning lime and sandstone Parliament buildings. Completed in 1865, Canada's political core includes the main building, known as the Centre Block – home to the Senate, House of Commons and parliamentary library, and supporting the iconic 92.2m Peace Tower – and the East Block, the nerve center of Canada's government during its first century.

At noon on weekdays, listen out for the Peace Tower carillon bells ringing for 15 minutes; the recital runs from 11am to noon in July and August.

Note that these are not the first Parliament buildings to stand on the site. The original was built between 1859 and 1866

❶ Need to Know

📞613-992-4793; www.parl.gc.ca; 111 Wellington St; 🕑East Block tours 9:45am-4:45pm Jul-early Sep, Centre Block tours 9am-4:30pm Jul-early Sep, hours vary early Sep-Jun, sound-and-light show 10pm Jul, 9:30pm Aug, 9pm early Sep; `FREE`

✗ Take a Break

Head to nearby Métropolitain Brasserie (p155) for delicious Gallic dishes.

★ Top Tip

On summer evenings, enjoy the free bilingual sound-and-light show on the lawns.

in anticipation of the nation's birth, but all that remain are the East Block and the library. When a small fire broke out in the Centre Block's Commons Reading Room on February 3, 1916, it claimed seven lives and quickly consumed everything in its path. Thankfully, a quick-thinking employee closed the library's iron doors, saving the people inside and thousands of irreplaceable books.

Tours

Interesting from political and historical perspectives respectively, two free tours cover the Centre Block and the East Block.

Centre Block tours typically last 20 to 50 minutes, depending on parliamentary activity, and may be subject to rigorous security checks going in; East Block tours typically take 30 to 40 minutes. Tickets for the tours are administered on the same day only, and on a first-come, first-served basis, so arrive early at the ticket office.

You can climb the Peace Tower and visit the Memorial Hall, which commemorates Canadians who lost their lives in military service, under your own steam, either as part of your guided visit or on a separate ticket.

Free tours of the grounds are also offered.

Changing of the Guard

At 10am daily in summer, find a spot on the front lawns to witness the colorful changing of the guard. Originally a morning routine that began in 1959, it's now an iconic ceremony, complete with a regimental band and pipers. The Ceremonial Guard is comprised of two regiments – the Governor General's Foot Guards and the Canadian Grenadier Guards.

⊙ SIGHTS

Most of Ottawa's numerous world-class museums are within walking distance of each other. Some offer free general admissions on Thursday evenings, and many close a day or two weekly (normally Monday) in winter.

National Gallery of Canada — Museum

(☏613-990-1985, 800-319-2787; www.gallery. ca; 380 Sussex Dr; adult/child $12/6, 5pm-8pm Thu free; ⊗10am-6pm daily May-Sep, 10am-5pm Tue-Sun Oct-Apr, to 8pm Thu year-round) The National Gallery is a work of art in itself: its striking ensemble of pink granite and glass spires echoes the ornate copper-topped towers of nearby Parliament. Inside, vaulted galleries exhibit predominantly Canadian art, classic and contemporary, including an impressive collection of work by Inuit and other indigenous artists. It's the world's largest Canadian collection, although additional galleries of European and American treasures include several recognizable names and masterpieces. Interpretive panels guide visitors through the nation's history and cultural development.

Notre Dame Cathedral-Basilica — Church

(☏613-241-7496; www.notredameottawa. com; 385 Sussex Dr; ⊗9am-6pm) Built in the 1840s, this shimmering tin-topped house of worship is the oldest church in all of Ottawa and the seat of the city's Roman Catholic archbishop. Pick up the small pamphlet at the entrance outlining the church's many idiosyncratic features, including elaborate wooden carvings and the dazzling indigo ceiling peppered with gleaming stars.

Canadian War Museum — Museum

(☏819-776-8600; www.warmuseum.ca; 1 Vimy Pl; adult/child 3-12yr $15/9, with Canadian Museum of History $23/13; ⊗9:30am-5pm Fri-Wed, to 8pm Thu) Fascinating displays twist through the labyrinthine interior of this sculpture-like, modern museum, tracing Canada's military history with the nation's most comprehensive collection of war-related artifacts. Many of the touching and

Notre Dame Cathedral-Basilica

KARAMYSH / SHUTTERSTOCK ©

thought-provoking exhibits are larger than life, including a replica of a WWI trench. Take a look at the facade in the evening, if you can: flickering lights pulse on and off spelling 'Lest We Forget' and 'CWM' in both English and French Morse code.

Laurier House National Historic Site   Historic Site

(🖉613-992-8142; www.parkscanada.gc.ca; 335 Laurier Ave East; adult/child $4/2; ⏱10am-5pm daily Jul & Aug, Thu-Mon late May, Jun, Sep & early Oct) This copper-roofed Victorian home built in 1878 was the residence of two notable prime ministers: Wilfrid Laurier and the eccentric Mackenzie King. The home is elegantly furnished, displaying treasured mementos and possessions from both politicos. Don't miss the study on the top floor.

Canadian Museum of Nature   Museum

(🖉613-566-4700; www.nature.ca; 240 McLeod St; adult/child 3-12yr $13.50/9.50, 5-8pm Thu free; ⏱9am-5pm Wed & Fri-Sun, to 8pm Thu; 🚌1, 5, 6, 7, 14) This imposing baronial building houses one of the world's best natural history collections, which the vast museum brings to life with modern and interactive exhibits. There's an impressive collection of fossils, the full skeleton of a blue whale and an excellent stock of dinosaur skeletons and models. Everyone loves the realistic mammal and bird dioramas depicting Canadian wildlife – the taxidermic creatures are so lifelike, you'll be glad they're behind a sheet of glass.

Canada Aviation and Space Museum   Museum

(🖉613-991-3044; www.casmuseum.techno -science.ca; 11 Aviation Pkwy; adult/child 3-12yr $13/8; ⏱9am-5pm mid-May–Aug, from 10am Wed-Mon Sep–mid-May; 🚌129) With around 120 aircraft housed in this mammoth steel hangar situated about 5km northeast of downtown, you could be forgiven for thinking you were at the airport. Wander through the warehouse, try a flight simulator and

★ **Top Five for Kids**

Canadian Museum of Nature (p151)

Canada Science & Technology Museum (p151)

Canadian Children's Museum (p147)

Rideau Canal (p153)

Canadian Tire Centre (p157)

get up close and personal with colorful planes ranging from the Silver Dart of 1909 to the first turbo-powered Viscount passenger jet.

Canada Science & Technology Museum   Museum

(🖉613-991-3044; www.sciencetech.techno muses.ca; 1867 St Laurent Blvd; adult/child $12/8; ⏱9:30am-5pm) Currently closed for renovations, expect ambient squeaks and boinks to fill the air of this hands-on museum when it reopens in summer 2017 as contented visitors gingerly turn knobs and push buttons, exploring the physical laws governing things like optical illusions and time. A walk through the 'Crazy Kitchen' is a blast: the lopsided galley makes you stumble from start to finish. There are trains out back to enlighten you on the science of coal and steam propulsion and a large display of space technology. Popular with adults and kids alike, it's informative and fun!

Ottawa Locks   Historic Site

The series of steep, step-like locks between the Château Laurier and Parliament Hill marks the north end of the 200km Rideau Canal, which flows all the way down to Kingston. Colonel By, the canal's visionary engineer, set up headquarters here in 1826.

Bytown Museum   Museum

(🖉613-234-4570; www.bytownmuseum.ca; 1 Canal Lane; adult/child $6.50/3; ⏱10am-5pm Fri-Wed, 10am-8pm Thu Jun-Sep, 11am-4pm Thu-Mon Oct-May) Descend the stairs alongside the Ottawa Locks on Wellington St to find

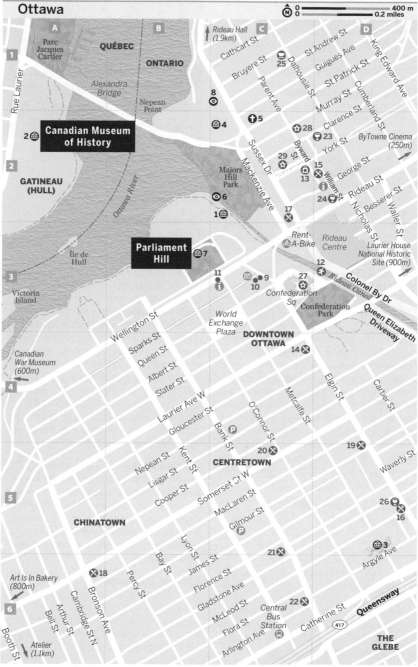

Ottawa

N 0   400 m
    0   0.2 miles

QUÉBEC

Parc Jacques Cartier

ONTARIO

Alexandra Bridge

Nepean Point

↑ Rideau Hall (1.9km)

Cathcart St

Bruyère St

Parent Ave

25

St Andrew St

Guigues Ave

Dalhousie St

St Patrick St

Murray St

Cumberland St

King Edward Ave

8

4

5

Sussex Dr

28

29

13

23

York St

George St

ByTowne Cinema (250m)

15

William St

24

Rideau St

Besserer St

Nicholas St

Waller St

Canadian Museum of History

2

GATINEAU (HULL)

Rue Laurier

Ottawa River

Île de Hull

Victoria Island

Majors Hill Park

Mackenzie Ave

6

1

17

Rent-A-Bike

Rideau Centre

Rideau Hall

12

Laurier House National Historic Site (900m)

Parliament Hill

7

11

10

9

27

Confederation Sq

Confederation Park

Colonel By Dr

Rideau Canal

Queen Elizabeth Driveway

Cartier St

Canadian War Museum (600m)

Wellington St

Sparks St

Queen St

Albert St

Slater St

World Exchange Plaza

DOWNTOWN OTTAWA

14

Laurier Ave W

Gloucester St

Nepean St

Lisgar St

Cooper St

Kent St

Bank St

Gloucester St

O'Connor St

Metcalfe St

Elgin St

20

CENTRETOWN

19

Waverly St

Somerset St W

MacLaren St

Gilmour St

CHINATOWN

26

16

Art Is In Bakery (800m)

18

Bronson Ave

Percy St

Lyon St

Bay St

James St

Florence St

Gladstone Ave

McLeod St

Flora St

21

3

Argyle Ave

Cambridge St N

Arthur St

Bell St

Booth St

Atelier (1.1km)

Arlington Ave

Central Bus Station

22

Catherine St

Queensway

417

THE GLEBE

Ottawa

the Bytown Museum, sitting at the last lock before the artificial canal plunges into the waters of the Ottawa River. This well-curated collection of artifacts and documents about Ottawa's colonial past is displayed in the city's oldest stone building.

Rideau Hall   Notable Building
(☎613-991-4422; www.gg.ca/rideauhall; 1 Sussex Dr; ⊙10am-4:30pm Jul-early Sep, noon-4pm Sat & Sun May, Jun, Sep & Oct) FREE Home of the Governor General, Rideau Hall was built in the 1830s with grand additions made by successive governors. There are free 45-minute walking tours of the fancy residence, featuring anecdotes about the various goings-on over the years. Otherwise, from 8am to one hour before sunset, the grounds are free to be enjoyed at your leisure (as is the building between 3pm and 4:30pm in July and August).

Royal Canadian Mint   Notable Building
(☎613-993-8990; www.mint.ca/tours; 320 Sussex Dr; guided tours adult/child $6/3, weekends $4.50/2.25; ⊙10am-5pm) Although Canada's circulation-coin mint is in Winnipeg, the royal mint holds its own by striking special pieces. The imposing stone building,

which looks a bit like the Tower of London, has been refining gold and minting since 1908. Weekday tours of the coin-making process are highly recommended: visitors can glimpse the transformation as sheets of metal are spun into loads of coins. This doesn't happen on weekends, so the tour price is discounted.

⊙ ACTIVITIES

Rideau Canal   Ice Skating
(www.ottawatourism.ca/ottawa-insider/rideau -canal-skateway) Ottawa's most famous outdoor attraction, the Rideau Canal, became Canada's 14th location to be named a National Historic site in 2007. It's ideal for boating, with parks, small towns, lakes and many places to stop en route, and in winter, it turns into one of the world's largest skating rinks.

The 7.8km artery of groomed ice between downtown and Dow's Lake features numerous heated rest stops and changing stations, but most importantly, skaters can pause to purchase scrumptious slabs of fried dough called beavertails. Huts all along the canal rent out skates for around $13 per hour (with a $50 deposit).

ByWard Market

The **ByWard Market** (🗷613-562-3325; www.byward-market.com; cnr York & ByWard Sts; ⏲6am-6pm) is the best place in town for one-stop shopping. Anchoring the market district, this sturdy maroon-brick building, which dates to 1926, is also the perfect place to stop when hunger strikes. Aside from the fresh produce and cheese, an array of international takeaway joints offers falafel, spicy curries, flaky pastries, sushi... the list goes on. Look for the stand selling beavertails, Ottawa's signature sizzling flat-dough dish.

Many merchants operate booths year-round, but the winter weather drastically reduces the number of businesses. In summer, over 260 stalls fill the streets, selling fresh produce from local farms, alongside flowers, seafood, cheese, baked goods, souvenirs and more.

The market is located between William, Byward, George and York Sts.

TOURS

Gray Line   Tours
(🗷613-562-9090; www.grayline.com/ottawa; cnr Sparks & Elgin Sts; ⏲Apr-Oct) Sightseeing tours including hop-on, hop-off bus services, bus-and-bike tours and Ottawa River cruises. Check the website or visit the sidewalk ticket booth for schedules and pricing. Bus tours depart from the booth, cruises from the Ottawa Locks.

Haunted Walk   Walking
(🗷613-232-0344; www.hauntedwalk.com; 46 Sparks St; walks $16-19) Has several ghoulish walking tours including visits to the old county jail, now the HI hostel.

Ottawa Walking Tours   Walking
(🗷613-799-1774; www.ottawawalkingtours.com; 90 Wellington St; adult/child under 11yr $15/free)

These informative and fun two-hour tours with professional guides depart from the Terry Fox statue in front of the tourist office. Cash only.

🍴 EATING

Wilf & Ada's   Diner $
(🗷613-231-7959; www.wilfandadas.com; 510 Bank St; mains $14; ⏲7am-3pm Mon-Fri, from 8am Sat & Sun) This 'scratch diner' is one of Ottawa's hippest breakfast and lunch spots, with its retro art and everything made from scratch. Breakfast is all home-cured bacon, buttermilk French toast, 'homies' (home fries) and maple syrup, while chunky sandwiches, soup, salads and poutine are served for lunch. If it's full, head round the back to the affiliated cafe Arlington Five.

Art Is In Bakery   Bakery $
(🗷613-695-1226; www.artisinbakery.com; 250 City Centre Ave; sandwiches $8-13; ⏲7am-6pm Mon-Fri, 8am-5pm Sat, 9am-4pm Sun; P🛜) Start the day with a breakfast sandwich or croissant and excellent cappuccino at this buzzy bakery cafe, occupying a warehouse space on an industrial estate. The gourmet sandwiches have fillings such as pickle melt and Thai chicken, with gluten-free options and salads available.

Saigon Boy
Noodle House   Vietnamese $
(🗷613-230-8080; 648 Somerset St W; mains $11; ⏲11am-9pm) Locals rate Saigon Boy as the city's best choice for *pho,* a Vietnamese soup containing rice noodles with beef or chicken. Other dishes, such as grilled pork and rice, are also available.

El Camino   Mexican $$
(🗷613-422-2800; eatelcamino.com; 380 Elgin St; tacos $6; ⏲5:30pm-late Tue-Sun, takeout noon-2:30pm Tue-Fri) With a hip industrial aesthetic underscored by Day of the Dead references, El Camino is either praised as Ottawa's taco joint of the hour or derided as overpriced. Come for chorizo and crispy fish tacos, eaten at benches or taken out,

ByWard Market

and cocktails ($13) such as the sweet and spicy El Fuego – and book ahead.

Union
Local 613
Modern American $$

(📞613-231-1010; www.union613.ca; 315 Somerset St W; mains $25; 🕐food served 11:30am-2pm Wed-Fri, from 10am Sat & Sun, 5:30-10pm Mon-Sat; 📶) Among low-lit decor of hummingbirds and hot-air balloons, drink the house beers and other local craft brews from screw-top jars. It's food with attitude, including Southern fried chicken and cornmeal-crusted catfish, and there's a 'speakeasy' behind a bookshelf in the basement (open 10:30pm to 2am Wednesday to Saturday).

Town
Italian $$

(📞613-695-8696; www.townlovesyou.ca; 296 Elgin St; mains $20; 🕐11:30am-2pm Wed-Fri, 5-10pm daily) Slick, smart and ineffably cool, this joint is always packed: arty-farty hipsters bump elbows with wealthy coiffured housewives. Ottawa foodies appreciate the use of local produce and northern Italian recipes, resulting in a short and seasonal

menu of small and large plates, such as the mainstay ricotta-stuffed meatballs, with an abundance of Niagara wines to accompany.

Métropolitain
Brasserie
French $$

(📞613-562-1160; www.metropolitainbrasserie. com; 700 Sussex Dr; snacks $5-16, mains $18-35; 🕐9am-midnight) Métropolitain puts a modern spin on the typical brasserie with its swirling zinc countertop, flamboyant fixtures and Gallic soundtrack: you will feel like you are dining on the set of *Moulin Rouge*. 'Hill Hour' (4pm to 7pm on weekdays, and from 9:30pm daily) buzzes with the spirited chatter of hot-blooded politicos as they down cheap *plats du jour*.

Beckta Dining &
Wine Bar
Canadian $$$

(📞613-238-7063; www.beckta.com; 150 Elgin St; lunch mains $17-25, dinner menu $68; 🕐11:30am-3pm Mon-Fri, 5:30-10pm daily) 🍴 Book in advance for one of the hottest tables in the capital, if not the whole country. Beckta offers an upmarket dining experience with

From left: Rideau Canal (p153); Gord Downie performs at the National Arts Centre; Canadian Tire Centre

an original spin on regional cuisine. Lunch is à la carte, while dinner is a three-course menu or inspired five-course tasting menu ($95) – a great way to experience the bigger picture at work here, with a wine pairing offered.

Atelier   Fusion $$$

(☏613-321-3537; www.atelierrestaurant.ca; 540 Rochester St; menu $110; ⏱5:30-8:30pm Tue-Sat) ✈ The brainchild of celebrated chef and molecular gastronomy enthusiast Marc Lépine, Atelier is a white-walled laboratory dedicated to tickling the taste buds. There's no oven or stove – just Bunsen burners, liquid nitrogen and hot plates to create the unique 12-course tasting menu.

Whalesbone
Oyster House   Seafood $$$

(☏613-231-8569; www.thewhalesbone.com; 430 Bank St; mains $25-40; ⏱11:30am-2pm Mon-Fri, 5-10pm daily) ✈ If the local chefs are purchasing their fish from Whalesbone's wholesale wing (or should we say 'fin'), then there's really no doubt that it's the best place in town for seafood. The on-site restaurant offers up a short list of fresh

faves such as oysters, lobster and scallops ceviche on small plates. Book ahead.

🍸 DRINKING & NIGHTLIFE

Clocktower Brew Pub   Bar

(☏613-241-8783; www.clocktower.ca; 89 Clarence St; ⏱11:30am-11:45pm) Enjoy homemade brews such as Raspberry Wheat and Bytown Brown amid exposed brick and ByWard bustle. There are bar snacks aplenty and four additional locations around town.

I Deal Coffee   Coffee

(☏613-562-1775; www.idealcoffees.com; 176 Dalhousie St; coffee $3; ⏱7am-7pm Mon-Fri, from 8:30am Sat, 9am-6pm Sun) Ideal indeed; handcrafted blends are produced and roasted on-site. The decor is thin, with bins and sacks of 'light organic blend' and 'prince of darkness' stacked next to the roaster; it's all about rich, flavorful cups of joe (hot or iced).

Highlander Pub   Pub

(☏613-562-5678; www.thehighlanderpub.com; 115 Rideau St; ⏱11am-1am) Kilted servers,

17 taps and 200 single malt Scotches all add to the wonderful Scottish appeal of this ByWard Market area pub. The food is good too!

Manx
Bar

(☎613-231-2070; www.manxpub.com; 370 Elgin St; mains $13-15; ⏰11:30am-1am Mon-Wed, to 2am Thu & Fri, 10am-2am Sat) 'Ottawa's original sinkhole,' as this basement bar has called itself since Rideau St collapsed in 2016, offers a great selection of Canadian microbrews (including the beloved Creemore), served on copper-top tables. There's food, too – brunch here is popular at weekends.

⊗ ENTERTAINMENT

National Arts Centre
Theater

(NAC; ☎613-947-7000; www.nac-cna.ca; 53 Elgin St) The capital's premier performing arts complex delivers opera, drama, Broadway shows, and performances by its resident symphony orchestra. Freshly renovated, the modish complex stretches along the canal in Confederation Sq.

Zaphod Beeblebrox
Live Music

(☎613-562-1010; www.zaphods.ca; 27 York St; ⏰8pm-late) Taking its name from the *Hitchhiker's Guide to the Galaxy* alien, this space-obsessed 'nightclub at the edge of the universe' serves exotic cocktails such as its trademark Pan Galactic Gargle Blaster. For earthlings looking to forget the cares of terra firma, it's a kick-ass music venue and club with punky attitude.

ByTowne Cinema
Cinema

(☎613-789-3456; www.bytowne.ca; 325 Rideau St) Ottawa's indie heart has been screening independent and international movies for 70 years.

Rainbow Bistro
Live Music

(☎613-241-5123; www.therainbow.ca; 76 Murray St) An oldie but a goodie: the best place in town to catch live blues. See live music here nightly in summer, with some sets starting as early as 3pm.

Canadian Tire Centre
Spectator Sport

(☎613-599-0100; www.canadiantirecentre.com; 1000 Palladium Dr, Kanata) Ottawa is a

🍴 Food Trucks

During weekday lunchtimes, food trucks across downtown sell everything from poutine to seafood to Ottawa's hungry workers. Plan your street-food odyssey around town by downloading the food-truck app from www.street foodapp.com/ottawa. You can also find a map on the City of Ottawa website (www.ottawa.ca).

hard-core hockey town. It's worth getting tickets to a game even if you're not into hockey – the ballistic fans put on a show of their own. NHL team the Ottawa Senators play here, at their home ground, about 25km southwest of the center in Ottawa's west end. Big-ticket concerts also take place here.

ℹ️ INFORMATION

ByWard Market Information Centre (📞613-244-4410; www.byward-market.com; ByWard & George Sts; ⏰7:30am-6pm Jul & Aug, 8am-5pm Sep-Jun) Covers the whole city.

Capital Information Kiosk (📞844-878-8333; www.canada.pch.gc.ca/eng/1446841663343; 90 Wellington St; ⏰9am-6pm mid-May–mid-Sep, to 5pm mid-Sep–mid-May) This helpful office is the city's hub for information and bookings.

Central Post Office (📞866-607-6301; www.canadapost.ca; 59 Sparks St; ⏰8:30am-5pm Mon-Fri) The main post office, occupying a historic building.

Ottawa Hospital (📞613-722-7000; www.ottawa hospital.on.ca; 501 Smyth Rd; ⏰emergency 24hr) Southeast of downtown in Alta Vista; has an emergency department.

Ottawa Tourism (www.ottawatourism.ca) Offers a comprehensive online look at the nation's capital, and can assist with planning itineraries and booking accommodations.

ℹ️ GETTING THERE & AWAY

AIR

The state-of-the-art **Ottawa MacDonald-Cartier International Airport** (YOW; 📞613-248-2125; www.yow.ca; 1000 Airport Pkwy) is 15km south of the city and, perhaps surprisingly, is very small. Almost all international flights require a transfer before arriving in the capital. Nonetheless, numerous North American carriers serve the airport, including Air Canada, WestJet, Porter Airlines, United Airlines, Delta and American Airlines.

BUS

The **central bus station** (📞613-238-6668; 265 Catherine St) is just off Queensway (Hwy 417), near Kent St. Several companies operate bus services from the station, including **Greyhound** (📞800-661-8747; www.greyhound.ca) with services to Toronto (from $71, 5½ hours, six daily).

CAR & MOTORCYCLE

Major car-rental chains are represented at the airport and offer several locations downtown, on Catherine St and at the train station (both just off Hwy 417). You will likely get a better deal hiring a car in Toronto.

TRAIN

The **VIA Rail Station** (📞888-842-7245; www.viarail.ca; 200 Tremblay Rd) is 7km east of downtown, near the Hwy 19/Riverside Dr exit of Hwy 417. Trains run to Toronto ($108, 4½ hours, eight daily) via Brockville and Kingston, and to Québec City via Montréal ($62, two hours, six daily).

ℹ️ GETTING AROUND

TO/FROM THE AIRPORT

The cheapest way to get to the airport is by city bus. Take bus 97 from Slater St between Elgin St and Bronson Ave (make sure you are heading in the 'South Keys & Airport' direction). The ride takes 40 minutes and costs $3.65.

Ottawa Shuttle Service (📞613-680-3313; www.ottawashuttleservice.com; 1 or 2 passengers $59; ⏰office 10am-10pm) offers private and shared shuttles from downtown hotels.

Blue Line Taxi (☎613-238-1111; www.blueline taxi.com) and **Capital Taxi** (☎613-744-3333; www.capitaltaxi.com) offer cab services; the fare to/from downtown is around $30.

BICYCLE

Right on the Rideau Canal bike path, the friendly staff at **Rent-A-Bike** (☎613-241-4140; www. rentabike.ca; East Arch Plaza Bridge, 2 Rideau St; rentals per hour from $10; ☺7am-7pm Apr-Oct) will set you up with a bike and offer tips about scenic trails. The Capital Information Kiosk (p158) has bike maps.

CAR & MOTORCYCLE

There is free parking in World Exchange Plaza on Albert St on weekends. Hourly metered parking can be found throughout downtown, and in parking lots charging around $20 a day. There are lots charging around $10 a day dotted around Centretown, including on Somerset St W east of Lyon St N.

During winter, overnight on-street parking is prohibited if there has been (or is likely to be) more than 7cm of snow – to allow the snowplows to come through.

PUBLIC TRANSPORTATION

OC Transpo (☎613-741-4390; www.octranspo. com) operates Ottawa's bus network and light-rail system known as the O-train. Bus rides cost $3.65 ($1.90 for children under 13) and you can pay on the bus with exact change. You can also purchase a day pass ($8.50) from the driver, and buy books of six tickets ($9.90) at convenience stores. Adults pay $5.15 on express routes. Your ticket allows you to transfer to other buses for a period of 90 minutes.

Ottawa and Hull/Gatineau operate separate bus systems. A transfer is valid from one system to the other, but may require an extra payment.

The O-train will become more useful when the Confederation Line is completed in 2018, providing a link between Parliament and the VIA Rail Station.

THE PRAIRIES

The Prairies at a Glance...

Comprising the wide-open provinces of Alberta, Saskatchewan and Manitoba, the magnitude of this land is only fully appreciated while standing on the edge of a vivid-yellow canola field counting three different storms on the horizon. Travel the Prairies' byways and expect surprises, whether it's a moose looming up on an otherwise empty road or the dinosaur-encrusted badlands around Drumheller. Calgary has become unexpectedly cool, with top museums and cocktail bars; Winnipeg will stun you with its arts scene; while Saskatoon will wow you with its music. There aren't so many people on the prairies – but those that are here will go out of their way to make your visit memorable.

Three Days in the Prairies

Spend the day in Calgary exploring the **Glenbow Museum** (p170) and the **National Music Centre** (p166), then grab a meal from **Market** (p171) on trendy 17th Ave. The next day, get into dino mode by taking a day trip to **Drumheller** (p164) and visiting the **Royal Tyrrell Museum of Palaeontology** (p164). Back in Calgary, head east to step back in time at the authentic **Ukrainian Cultural Heritage Village** (p168).

One Week in the Prairies

Head east to **Saskatoon** (p174) to enjoy the urban pleasures – especially the food and drink – of the Paris of the Prairies. Carry on across those endless golden fields to **Winnipeg** (p177). Take in the **Canadian Museum for Human Rights** (p177) and the eclectic **St-Boniface Museum** (p178). End your Prairies sojourn with live music at **Times Chang(d) High & Lonesome Club** (p180) and a drink with the locals at the **King's Head Pub** (p180).

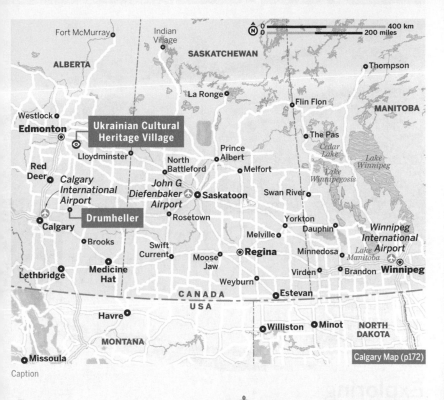

Caption

Arriving in the Prairies

Calgary International Airport Take
bus 300 ($3, 45 minutes) or a taxi ($35)
to the centre.

John G Diefenbaker Airport A taxi into
central Saskatoon costs around $20.

Winnipeg International Airport Take
bus 15 ($2.65) or grab a cab ($25).

Bus Greyhound plies the Prairies, linking all major cities.

Train VIA Rail scoots across the Prairies,
stopping in Winnipeg and Saskatoon.

Where to Stay

Calgary has recently found its independent spirit and established a range
of boutique hotels across different
price ranges. Hotels downtown in both
Calgary and Winnipeg can be expensive,
although many run frequent specials;
Saskatoon offers better deals. All three
have chain motels on the outskirts.
During events such as the Calgary
Stampede or music festivals, rates rise
and availability plummets; book ahead.

JEFF WHYTE / SHUTTERSTOCK ©

Exploring Drumheller

This community in the Red Deer River Valley was founded on coal but now thrives on another sub-terranean resource – dinosaur bones.

Great For...

☑ Don't Miss

Discovering your own dino treasures on a summertime dinosaur dig ($15) at the Royal Tyrrell Museum.

A small town set amid Alberta's enigmatic badlands, Drumheller is serious about its paleontology. Add in the museums in nearby East Coulee and the ghosts of Wayne, and you've got a full itinerary.

Palaeontology Museum

The fantastic **Royal Tyrrell Museum of Palaeontology** (☑403-823-7707; www.tyrrellmuseum.com; 1500 North Dinosaur Trail, Midlands Provincial Park; adult/child $18/10; ⊙9am-9pm mid-May–Aug, 10am-5pm Sep, 10am-5pm Tue-Sun Oct–mid-May; ⛨) is one of the preeminent dinosaur museums on the planet. Look for the skeleton of 'Hell-Boy,' a new dinosaur discovered in 2005, and 'Black Beauty,' a 67-million-year-old *Tyrannosaurus rex* rearing its head into the sky. Unlike some other dinosaur exhibits, there's nothing dusty or musty about this

❶ Need to Know

Tourist Information Center (📞403-823-1331; www.traveldrumheller.com; 60 1st Ave W; 🕒9am-9pm) At the foot of the *T rex*. The entrance to the body of the beast is in the same building.

✖ Take a Break

Stop by **Ivy's Awesome Kitchen & Bistro** (www.ivysawesomekitchen.com; 35 3rd Ave West; mains $8-12; 🕒8am-5pm; 📶) for home-style cooking.

> ### ★ Top Tip
> Go on a dinosaur hunt – there are over 30 colorful dino sculptures around town.

super-modern place. Children will love the interactive displays.

World's Largest Dinosaur

In a town filled with dinosaurs, this **T rex** (60 1st Ave W; $3; 🕒10am-6pm; 🚻) is the king of them all. Standing 26m high above a parking lot, it dominates the Drumheller skyline. You can climb the 106 steps to the top for great views.

Dinosaur Trail & Hoodoo Drive

The scenic 48km Dinosaur Trail loop runs northwest from Drumheller and includes Hwys 837 and 838.

The loop takes you past **Midland Provincial Park**, where you can take a self-guided hike, and past the vast **Horsethief Canyon** and its picturesque views. Glide peacefully across the Red Deer River on the free,

cable-operated **Bleriot Ferry**, which has been running since 1913. On the west side of the valley, pause at **Orkney Viewpoint**, which overlooks the area's impressive canyons.

The 25km Hoodoo Drive starts about 18km southeast of Drumheller on Hwy 10. Along this drive you'll find the best examples of hoodoos – weird, eroded, mushroom-like columns of sandstone rock – between Rosedale and Lehigh; there's also an interpretive trail.

This area was once the site of a prosperous coal-mining community; the historic **Atlas Coal Mine** (📞403-822-2220; www.atlascoalmine.ab.ca; East Coulee; $10, tours $20-25; 🕒9:45am-5pm Sep-Jun, to 7:30pm Jul-Aug) and **East Coulee School Museum** (📞403-822-3970; www.ecsmuseum.ca; 359 2nd Ave, East Coulee; 🕒10am-5pm) are both worth a stop. Take the side trip on Hwy 10X from Rosedale to the small community of **Wayne** (population 27) with its famous and supposedly haunted saloon.

National Music Centre

Looking like a whimsical copper castle, this fabulous new museum will take you on a ride through Canada's musical history.

Great For...

☑ Don't Miss

The guitar Guess Who used to record 'American Woman.'

With studio space and numerous theaters, the National Music Centre is all about getting Canadian artists heard. Check the website for who's playing.

Get Musical

Who wouldn't want to try out a drum kit, strum an electric guitar or step into a sound-recording room to sing your heart out? You can also create your own instruments here with rubber-bands string, pegs and other unlikely objects. And be sure to find your groove in the Body Phonic Room, where your moves control the tunes.

The Collection

With over 2000 musical artifacts, you're certain to find something to wow you. You'll find everything from Elton John's 'songwrit-

❶ Need to Know

📞403-543-5115; www.studiobell.ca; 850 4 St SE; adult/child $18/11; ⊙10am-5pm Wed-Sun

✕ Take a Break

You won't want to take a break – but if you do, there's an excellent cafe on-site.

★ Top Tip

If you're looking for cool and very-Canadian souvenirs, be sure to stop in at the gift shop.

ing' piano to Shania Twain's dresses and the Rolling Stone's mobile recording studio. Keep your eye's peeled for the Electronic Sackbut, a Canadian forerunner to 1970s synthesizers that is being restored and cloned for visitors to test out.

The Canadian Hall of Fame is especially impressive. From Leonard Cohen to Justin Bieber, Neil Young, Drake, Gordon Lightfoot, Diana Krall and Sarah McLachlan, Canadian's sure know how to hold a tune.

Sound Sculpture

As you wander into the Skywalk between the museum and the neighboring King Eddie building, you may wonder where the whistling and humming is coming from. Look up and you'll see 16 piano pieces hanging from the ceiling. These

are instruments that were destroyed in Calgary's 2013 flood, repurposed and solar powered to fill the air with music once again.

The Tragically Hip

If you're not Canadian, you're forgiven for not knowing the Tragically Hip – almost. Formed in the '80s in Kingston, Ontario, they sell out stadiums across the country. Their lyrics tell stories linked to Canada's geography and history and their unique sound is often quoted as being 'distinctly Canadian.' With 14 studio albums, two live albums and 54 singles under their belt, along with 14 Juno Awards and nine number-one albums, it's not surprising that they figure prominently in the National Music Centre.

When Gord Downie, the Hip's singer and songwriter, was diagnosed with brain cancer in 2016, the country went into mourning. One final tour across the country included a Canada Day performance at the then-brand-new Centre.

Ukrainian Cultural Heritage Village

With original buildings and authentic characters, experience firsthand what life was like for Ukrainian immigrants on the prairies.

Great For...

☑ **Don't Miss**

Hopping on a free horse-drawn-wagon ride from Thursday to Monday during summer.

The People

By visiting the Heritage Village, you are paying homage to the 250,000 Ukrainian immigrants who came to Canada between 1892 and 1930. Many settled in central Alberta, where the landscape reminded them of the snowy steppes of home.

The interpreters you encounter here aren't just staff in costume; they perform in roles of real-life immigrants from Ukraine and go about their day as if they really are the hotelier, the farmer, the schoolteacher or the blacksmith. Some speak only Ukrainian; others speak English with heavy accents. They know the history and family tree of the person they've assumed and won't – at any cost – break character. Expect to be asked if you'd like a hotel room or if your horse needs shoes. Be sure to visit the very new immigrants in their *burdei*

Dancers outside St Vladimir's Orthodox Church

PETER CARROLL / GETTY IMAGES ©

ℹ Need to Know

☑780-662-3640; www.history.alberta.
ca/ukrainianvillage; adult/child/family
$15/10/40; ⊙10am-5pm May-Sep

✖ Take a Break

Before you leave, visit the kiosk for
some of the best pierogi and cabbage
rolls this side of Lviv.

> ★ **Top Tip**
> Wear good walking shoes – these are
> turn-of-the-century dirt roads.

(sod house) to see what they've brought
with them and how they're beginning to
farm the land. If you don't speak Ukrainian,
be prepared for lots of charades!

The Buildings

The buildings are all original, moved here
from various towns in Alberta, refurbished
to their original state and filled with authentic furnishings. Around 35 are set out like a
genuine village, with more added each year.
Highlights include a sod house, three Byz-
antine churches, a hotel, a grain elevator
and a schoolhouse.

When the 1920s school was first renovated, students who had once attended
were invited to visit. Now in their 80s, these
students sat in their original seats and felt
the time-warp effect of the painstakingly
accurate renovation.

What's Nearby

Virtually across the road, **Elk Island
National Park** (www.pc.gc.ca/elkisland;
adult/6-16yr/senior $7.80/3.90/6.80, campsites
& RV sites $25.50, campfire permits $8.80;
⊙dawn-dusk) contains the highest density
of wild hoofed animals in the world after
the Serengeti; many come here to see the
resident wild bison. The wood bison live entirely in the quieter southern portion of the
park (which is cut in two by Hwy 16), while
the plains bison inhabit the north.

Most of the infrastructure lies in the
north, too, around Astotin Lake. Here you'll
find a campground, a nine-hole golf course
(its clubhouse has a restaurant), a beach
and a boat launch.

Four of the park's 11 hiking trails lead
away from the lakeshore through trademark northern Albertan aspen parkland – a
kind of natural intermingling of the prairies
and boreal forests.

Calgary

Calgary will surprise you with its beauty, cool eateries, nightlife beyond honky-tonk, and long, worthwhile to-do list. Calgarians aren't known for their modesty; it's their self-love and can-do attitude that got them through disastrous flooding in 2013 and, in 2016, saw them helping residents of wildfire-stricken Fort McMurray with unquestioning generosity. We mustn't forget – Calgary also hosted the highly successful 1988 Winter Olympics, elected North America's first Muslim mayor, and throws one of Canada's biggest parties, the Calgary Stampede.

◉ SIGHTS

Glenbow Museum — Museum
(📞403-777-5506; www.glenbow.org; 130 9th Ave SE; adult/child/family $16/10/40; ⏰9am-5pm Mon-Sat, noon-5pm Sun, closed Mon Oct-Jun) With an extensive permanent collection and an ever-changing array of traveling exhibitions, the impressive Glenbow has plenty for the history buff, art lover and pop-culture fiend to ponder. Temporary exhibits are often daring, covering contemporary art and culture. Permanent exhibits bring the past to life with strong historic personalities and lots of voice recordings. Hang out in a tipi, visit a trading post and walk through the railcar of a train.

Calgary Tower — Notable Building
(📞403-266-7171; www.calgarytower.com; 101 9th Ave SW; adult/youth $18/9, ⏰observation gallery 9am-9pm Sep-Jun, to 10pm Jul-Aug) This 1968 landmark tower is an iconic feature of the Calgary skyline, though it has now been usurped by numerous taller buildings and is in danger of being lost in a forest of skyscrapers. There is little doubt that the aesthetics of this once-proud concrete structure have passed into the realm of kitsch, but, love it or hate it, the slightly phallic 191m structure is a fixture of the downtown area.

Prince's Island Park — Park
For a little slice of Central Park in the heart of Cowtown, take the bridge over to this island, with grassy fields made for tossing Frisbees, bike paths and ample space to stretch out. During the summer months, you can catch a Shakespeare production in the park's natural grass amphitheater or check out the Folk Music Festival in July. You'll also find the upscale River Island restaurant here.

✪ ACTIVITIES

Rapid Rent — Cycling
(www.outlawsports.ca; Barclay Pde SW; bikes/rollerblades/helmet per day from $30/15/5; ⏰10am-7pm Mon-Fri, to 6pm Sat, to 5pm Sun) Rents bikes, junior bikes, child trailers and rollerblades.

Olympic Oval — Ice Skating
(📞403-220-7954; www.ucalgary.ca/oval; University of Calgary; adult/child/family $7/5/18.50; ⏰Jul–mid Mar) Get the Olympic spirit at the University of Calgary, where you can go for a skate on Olympic Oval. Used for the speed-skating events at the Olympics, it offers public skating on the long track and has skates available to rent, as well as mandatory helmets. See the website for current schedules.

✪ TOURS

Calgary Walking Tours — Cultural
(📞855-620-6520; www.calgarywalks.com; adult/youth/under 7yr $18/15/free) Join the two-hour Core City tour to learn about the architecture, history and culture of various buildings, sculptures, gardens and hidden nooks.

Hammerhead Tours — Cultural
(📞403-590-6930; www.hammerheadtours.com; half-day city tours $58) Join a half-day tour of the city or a very full day tour to destinations like Drumheller, Head-Smashed-In Buffalo Jump or Lake Louise. Multiday and 'create-your-own' tours are also available.

✖ EATING

Al Forno Cafe & Bakery — Cafe $

(📞403-454-0308; www.alforno.ca; 222 7th St SW; mains $8-15; ⊙7am-9pm Mon-Fri, 8am-9pm Sat & Sun) This ultra-modern, super-comfortable cafe is the kind of place you'll want to hang out in all day. Beer on tap, carafes of wine and excellent coffee won't discourage you from lingering, nor will magazines, comfy sofas or window seats. With pastas, flatbreads, salads, soups and panini, all homemade, it's difficult to leave room for the amazing cakes, tarts and biscuits.

1886 Buffalo Cafe — Breakfast $

(187 Barclay Pde SW; ⊙6am-3pm Mon-Fri, from 7am Sat & Sun) This is a true salt-of-the-earth diner in the high-rise-dominated city center. Built in 1911 and the only surviving building from the lumber yard once here, the interior feels fairly authentic with family photos and antique clocks. This is a ketchup on the table, unlimited coffee refills kind of place famous for its brunches and especially its huevos rancheros.

Market — Canadian $$

(📞403-474-4414; www.marketcalgary.ca; 718 17th Ave SW; mains lunch $12-17, dinner $8-20; ⊙11:30am-late) With an earthy yet futuristic feel, award-winning Market has gone a step further in the fresh-local trend. Not only does it bake its own bread, it butchers and cures meat, makes cheese and grows 16 varieties of heirloom seeds year-round. As if that weren't enough, it's then all whipped into meals that are scrumptious and entirely satisfying.

Catch — Seafood $$

(📞403-206-0000; www.catchrestaurant.ca; 100 8th Ave SW; mains $17-27; ⊙11:30am-2pm Mon-Fri, 5-10pm Mon-Sat) The problem for any saltwater fish restaurant in landlocked Calgary is that if you're calling it fresh, it can't be local. Overcoming the conundrum, the lively, ever-popular Catch, situated in an old bank building on Stephen Ave Walk, flies its 'fresh catch' in daily from both coasts (British Columbia and the Maritimes).

Ox and Angela — Tapas $$

(📞403-457-1432; www.oxandangela.com; 528 17th Ave SW; tapas $4-14; ⊙11:30am-late) Re-creating Spain in modern Calgary isn't an obvious go-to but Ox and Angela has somehow managed it with colorful tiles and delicious tapas. Order piecemeal from a menu of Manchego cheese, tortilla (Spanish omelette) and cured *jamón serrano*.

Model Milk — Canadian $$$

(📞403-265-7343; www.modelmilk.ca; 108 17th Ave SW; mains $19-32; ⊙5pm-1am) Model Milk's revolving menu changes before the ink's even dry, but your choices are always great at the former dairy turned hip restaurant. Look for favorites like grits and sausage or chicken with buttermilk waffles and peanut coleslaw. More certain is the excellent service and the cool ambience that comes with an open kitchen and communal seating.

🛍 Get Your Cowboy On

Ever wondered how a cowboy hat is made? Well, here is your chance to find out. **Smithbilt Hats** (📞403-244-9131; www.smithbilthats.com; 1103 12th St SE; ⊙9am-5pm Mon-Thu, 8am-4:30pm Fri) has been shaping hats in the traditional way since you parked your horse out front. You can pick up one made of straw or beaver felt and priced accordingly.

Visit the factory and store run by the province's only Western boot manufacturer, **Alberta Boot Co** (📞403-263-4605; www.albertaboot.com; 50 50th Ave SE; ⊙9am-6pm Mon-Sat), and pick up a pair of your choice. Over 200 hours of labor go into each boot, which can be custom-designed. Prices range from $375 to $2100.

Calgary

N

0   500 m
0   0.25 miles

Memorial Dr

Centre St

Edmonton Trail

Prince's Island Park

Eau Claire Ave SW

1st Ave SW

2nd Ave SW

3rd Ave SW

Riverfront Ave SW

Centre St Bridge

Memorial Dr

Bow River

Langevin Bridge

Riverfront Ave SE

7th St SW

6th St SW

3rd St SW

2nd St SW

1st St SW

Centre St S

1st St SE

4th Ave SW

4th Ave SE

5th Ave SW

5th Ave SE

DOWNTOWN

6th Ave SW

6th Ave SE

7th Ave SW

C-Train

7th Ave SE

8th St SW

5th St SW

4th St SW

National Music Centre

Greyhound (1.2km)

8th Ave SW

Stephen Ave Walk

8th Ave SE

9th Ave SW

9th Ave SE

4th St SE

Rocky Mountaineer Train Station

1st St SE

Macleod Trail

Smithbilt Hats (1.5km)

10th Ave SW

10th Ave SE

11th Ave SW

11th Ave SE

12th Ave SW

BELTLINE

12th Ave SE

6th St SW

Olympic Way

13th Ave SW

13th Ave SE

2nd St SW

1st St SE

Centre St S

14th Ave SW

14th Ave SE

8th St SW

7th St SW

5th St SW

4th St SW

15th Ave SW

15th Ave SE

UPTOWN 17TH AVE

17th Ave SW

17th Ave SE

Stampede Park

C-Train

18th Ave SW

19th Ave SW

20th Ave SW

21st Ave SW

Elbow River

22nd Ave SW

4TH ST - MISSION DISTRICT

23rd Ave SW

24th Ave SW

Hillcrest Ave

Calgary

🍷 DRINKING & NIGHTLIFE

Proof
Cocktail Bar

(☎403-246-2414; www.proofyyc.com; 1302 1st St SW; ☺4pm-1am) This place might be small but the bar is big enough to require a library ladder. Big leather chairs and lots of metal and wood highlight craftsmanship – as do the expertly created cocktails. The drinks look so stunning, you almost don't want to drink them. Almost.

Analog Coffee
Coffee

(www.fratellocoffee.com; 740 17th Ave SW; coffees $2-5; ☺7am-10pm) The third-wave coffee scene is stirring in Calgary, led by companies like Fratello, which runs this narrow, overflowing hipster-ish cafe, which displays the beans of the day on a clipboard and has rows of vinyl spread along the back wall.

Barley Mill
Pub

(☎403-290-1500; www.barleymillcalgary.com; 201 Barclay Pde SW; ☺11am-late) Built in a 1900s style, with an actual waterwheel churning outside, the Barley Mill draws crowds for its pub grub, long lineup of draught beers and a well-stocked bar. Two patios for when it's warm and a big stone fireplace for when it's not keeps it busy in every season.

⭐ ENTERTAINMENT

Broken City
Live Music

(☎403-262-9976; www.brokencity.ca; 613 11th Ave SW; ☺11am-2am) There's something on stage here most nights – everything from jazz jams to hip-hop, along with comedy and quiz nights. The rooftop patio is ace in the summer, and the small but well-curated menu keeps you happy whether you're after a steak sandwich or vegan cauliflower wings.

Epcor Centre for the Performing Arts
Theater

(www.epcorcentre.org; 205 8th Ave SE) This is the hub for live theater in Calgary. With four theaters and one of the best concert halls in North America, here you can see everything from ballet to Bollywood.

Calgary Flames
Spectator Sport

(☎403-777-0000; http://flames.nhl.com) Archrival of the Edmonton Oilers, the Calgary Flames play ice hockey from October to April at the **Saddledome** (Stampede Park). Make sure you wear red to the game and head down to 17th Ave afterwards, or the 'Red Mile,' as they call it during play-offs.

ℹ INFORMATION

Tourism Calgary (www.tourismcalgary.com; 101 9th Ave SW; ☺8am-5pm) Operates a visitor center in the base of the Calgary Tower. The staff will help you find accommodations. Information booths are also available at both the arrivals and departures levels of the airport.

❶ GETTING THERE & AWAY

AIR

Calgary International Airport (YYC; www.ycc.com) is about 15km northeast of the center off Barlow Trail, a 25-minute drive away.

BUS

Greyhound Canada (☑ bus station 403-263-1234, ticket purchase 800-661-8747; www.greyhound.ca; 850 16th St SW) has services to Banff ($29, 1¾ hours) and Drumheller ($38, 1¾ hours). Canmore and Banff ($65, 2¼ hours, eight daily) are served by **Brewster** (www.brewster.ca).

CAR & MOTORCYCLE

All the major car-rental firms are represented at the airport and downtown.

❶ GETTING AROUND

TO/FROM THE AIRPORT

Sundog Tours (☑ 403-291-9617; www.sundogtours.com; adult/child one-way $15/8) runs every half-hour from around 8:30am to 9:45pm between all the major downtown hotels and the airport. You can also take bus 300 from the city center all the way to the airport ($3, 45 minutes). A taxi to the airport costs about $35.

CAR & MOTORCYCLE

Parking in downtown Calgary is an expensive nightmare. Luckily, downtown hotels generally have garages. Outside the downtown core, parking is free and easy to find. Calgary has Canada's largest fleet of car2go (www.car2go.com) smart cars, making it a super-convenient way to get around town and even to the airport.

CALGARY TRANSIT

Calgary Transit (www.calgarytransit.com) is efficient and clean. Choose the Light Rapid Transit (LRT) rail system (C-Train) or ordinary buses. One fare ($3) entitles you to transfer to other buses or C-Trains. The C-Train is free in the downtown area along 7th Ave between 10th St SW and 3rd St SE. If you're going further or need a transfer, buy your ticket from a machine on the C-Train platform. Most buses run at 15- to 30-minute intervals daily. There is no late-night service.

TAXI

For a cab, call **Checker Cabs** (☑ 403-299-9999; www.thecheckergroup.com) or **Calgary Cabs** (☑ 403-777-1111). Fares are $3 for the first 150m, then 20¢ for each additional 150m.

Saskatoon

Saskatoon is full of hidden treasures. Don't be misled by first appearances – head into the downtown core and inner neighborhoods to get a sense of this vibrant city. The majestic South Saskatchewan River winds through downtown, offering beautiful, natural diversions.

Saskatoon knows how to heat up cold winter days and short summer nights with a proud heritage of local rock and country music and a vibrant live-music scene.

◉ SIGHTS

Western Development Museum   Museum

(WDM; ☑ 306-931-1910; www.wdm.ca; 2610 Lorne Ave S; adult/child $10/4; ☺ 9am-5pm; 🅿) The flagship Saskatoon branch of the province's Western Development Museum is a faithful re-creation of Saskatoon the boom town, c 1910. Inside Canada's longest indoor street, you can roam through the town's many buildings, from a dentist's office straight out of a horror film to the pharmacy, the walls of which are lined with hundreds of vintage concoctions. There are trains, tractors, buggies, sleighs and a jail. It's about 4km south of downtown.

Remai Modern   Gallery

(☑ 306-975-7610; www.remaimodern.org; Spadina Cres) A huge new attraction that anchors River Landing, Remai Modern will house the collection from the now-closed Mandel Art Gallery. The stunning building will also have regular rotating special exhibitions after it opens in 2017.

Meewasin Valley   Nature Reserve

(www.meewasin.com) The Meewasin Valley, formed by the South Saskatchewan's wide

Meewasin Valley, Saskatoon

swath through the center of town, is named for the Cree word for 'beautiful.' Mature trees populate the riverbanks, while sections of the 60km **Meewasin Trail** extend from downtown paths, winding through forests and along the riverbank. Popular with walkers, cyclists and wandering travelers, picnic areas line the trails. Further north, **Mendel Island** is home to abundant wildlife.

🜃 TOURS

Shearwater Boat Cruises   Boating
(☏888-747-7572; www.shearwatertours.com; Spadina Cres E; adult/child from $24/15; ⊙Tue-Sun May-Sep) Open-top boats cruise the river all summer long. Ponder the bridges while enjoying a cool drink from the bar; Friday sunset cruises are popular. The dock is near the University Bridge.

✖ EATING

Grazing Goat   Fusion $$
(☏306-952-1136; www.thegrazinggoatgood-eats.com; 210 20th St W; mains lunch $11-15,

dinner $18-28; ⊙11:30am-2pm & 5pm-midnight Tue-Sat) A funky bare-brick restaurant and lounge on the revitalized 20th St strip in Riversdale. The eclectic menu personifies a farm-to-table ethos. There are numerous small-plate and sharing choices that go well with the long (and superb) cocktail and beer list.

Truffles Bistro   Canadian $$$
(☏306-373-7779; www.trufflesbistro.ca; 230 21st St E; mains $24-32; ⊙5-10pm Mon-Fri, 10am-2:30pm & 5-10pm Sat, 10am-2pm Sun) Smooth jazz sets up the classic ambience of this modern bistro. Fine wines accompany beautifully presented, delightfully simple preparations of *steak frites* (steak and fries), pork tenderloin and local Lake Diefenbaker trout. The menu changes with the seasons. Excellent desserts.

Ayden Kitchen & Bar   Canadian $$$
(☏306-954-2590; www.aydenkitchenandbar. com; 265 3rd Ave S; mains $20-40; ⊙11:30am-2pm & 5:30-10pm Mon-Fri, 5:30-10pm Sat) 🍸 Saskatoon's restaurant of the moment works magic with local produce and other

Remai Arts Centre

SCOTT PROKOP / SHUTTERSTOCK ©

seasonal specialties. Chef Dale MacKay and his co-chef and butcher Natan Guggenheimer are stars on the Canadian food scene. You never know what surprises they have in store at this unpretentious downtown bistro. Book ahead.

🍷 DRINKING & NIGHTLIFE

Congress Beer House   Pub
(☎306-974-6717; www.congressbeerhouse.com; 215 2nd Ave S; ⊗11am-1am) This huge pub has a bit of a ski-lodge vibe. Seating is at tables and in comfy leather booths. As you'd surmise, the beer list is the best in the province, with numerous choices of hard-to-get brews. The food options are excellent, with creative takes on burgers and other pub faves (mains $10 to $20).

Hose and Hydrant   Pub
(☎306-477-3473; www.hoseandhydrant.com; 612 11th St E; ⊗11:30am-11pm) A fun pub in a converted fire station. Enjoy tables on a patio and deck with mellow side-street outlooks.

Drift Sidewalk Cafe & Vista Lounge   Lounge
(☎306-653-2256; www.driftcafe.ca; 339 Ave A S; ⊗8am-10pm Sun-Thu, to midnight Fri & Sat) Split personalities mark this hip Riversdale spot. The cafe serves crepes, sandwiches and a long list of varied snacks through the day; enjoy a coffee at a table outside. The lounge is sleeker and has a fun cocktail list, many with house-made libations. It also serves mid-priced international dishes.

🎭 ENTERTAINMENT

Persephone Theatre   Theater
(☎306-384-7727; www.persephonetheatre. org; 100 Spadina Cres E; ticket prices vary) This perennial theatrical standout has excellent new quarters in the **Remai Arts Centre** at River Landing. Comedy, drama and musicals are all regulars.

Gordon Tootoosis Nīkānīwin Theatre   Theater
(GTNT; ☎306-933-2262; www.gtnt.ca; 914 20th St W; ⊗Feb-Jun) Contemporary stage pro-

ductions by Canadian First Nations, Métis and Inuit artists highlight cultural issues through comedy and drama.

Buds on Broadway
Live Music

(⏹306-244-4155; http://buds.dudaone.com; 817 Broadway Ave; ⏲11:30am-late) Classic blues and old-time rock and roll are the standards here in this beer-swilling joint.

Broadway Theatre
Cinema

(⏹306-652-6556; www.broadwaytheatre.ca; 715 Broadway Ave; adult/child $10/5) This historic Nutana cinema shows cult classics, art-house films and occasional local live performances. Regularly screens *South Park: Bigger, Longer and Uncut;* sing along with 'Blame Canada'!

ℹ INFORMATION

Planet S (www.planetsmag.com) Irreverent and free biweekly newspaper with good entertainment listings.

Tourism Saskatoon (⏹306-242-1206, 800-567-2444; www.tourismsaskatoon.com; 202 4th Ave N; ⏲8:30am-5pm Mon-Fri) Has local and regional info.

ℹ GETTING THERE & AWAY

AIR

John G Diefenbaker International Airport (YXE; ⏹306-975-8900; www.yxe.ca; 2625 Airport Dr) is 5km northeast of the city, off Idylwyld Dr and Hwy 16. WestJet and Air Canada have services to major Canadian cities.

BUS

STC (www.stcbus.com) covers the province extensively from the **bus station** (⏹306-933-8000; 50 23rd St E); buses head to Winnipeg ($134, 12½ hours, one daily).

TRAIN

Saskatoon's **train station** (Chappell Dr) is 8km southwest from downtown; the thrice-weekly VIA Rail Canadian stops here on its Vancouver–Toronto run.

ℹ GETTING AROUND

A taxi to the airport or train station costs about $20. **Blueline Taxi** (⏹306-653-3333; www.unitedgroup.ca) is easily reached.

Bike Doctor (⏹306-664-8555; www.bikedoctor.ca; 623 Main St; rentals per day from $60) rents bikes.

Saskatoon Transit (⏹360-975-7500; www.transit.saskatoon.ca; adult/child $3/2.25) runs city buses, which converge on the transit hub of 23rd St E (between 2nd and 3rd Aves N).

Winnipeg

Winnipeg surprises. Rising above the prairie, it's a metropolis where you least expect it. Cultured, confident and captivating, it's more than just a pit stop on the Trans-Canada haul, but a destination in its own right, with a couple of world-class museums and a wonderfully diverse dining scene.

◎ SIGHTS

Canadian Museum for Human Rights
Museum

(⏹204-289-2000; www.humanrightsmuseum.ca; Waterfront Dr & Provencher Blvd; adult/7-17yr/student $18/9/14; ⏲10am-5pm Thu-Tue, to 9pm Wed) Housed in a stunning contemporary building designed by American architect Antoine Predock, this terrific museum explores human rights issues as they relate to Canada, its culture and the rest of the world through the medium of striking interactive displays, videos, art and more. Exhibits don't shy away from sensitive subjects, such as the internment of Canadian Japanese during WWII and Aboriginal children forced into residential schools as recently as the 1990s.

Forks National Historic Site
Historic Site

(⏹204-957-7618; www.theforks.com; ♿) In a beautiful riverside setting, modern amenities for performances and interpretive exhibits in this park outline the area's history as the meeting place of Aboriginal people for centuries.

Louis Riel

Born in 1844 on the Red River near today's Winnipeg, Louis Riel became a leader of the Métis – like him, people of mixed Aboriginal and European backgrounds. He battled for their rights, and helped lead the Red River Rebellion, which gave the Métis political power but led to his exile in the US. Riel eventually returned to Canada; in 1885 he was tried for treason and hanged.

The third Monday of February is a provincial holiday in Riel's honor. You can find numerous Riel legacies in Manitoba and Saskatchewan. **Riel House** (☏204-257-1783; www.parkscanada.ca/riel; 330 River Rd; adult/child $4/2; ☺10am-5pm Jul & Aug) is his birthplace and the family house where he was taken after his execution, and his grave is at **St-Boniface Basilica** (151 Ave de la Cathédrale).

Try to catch a performance of the seasonal play, **Trial of Louis Riel** (☏306-728-5728; www.rielcoproductions. com; 2445 Albert St, Royal Saskatchewan Museum; adult/child $20/10; ☺Jul & Aug), which dramatizes his trial for treason.

The rivers routinely overflow during spring runoff and flooded pathways are not uncommon, an event as exciting as it is dangerous. Follow the waterways with a canoe from **Splash Dash** (☏204-783-6633; www.splashdash.ca; adult/child $11/9; ☺10am-sunset May-Oct). Kids can go nuts in the heritage-themed playground, the **Variety Heritage Adventure Park.**

Winnipeg Art Gallery   Gallery
(WAG; ☏204-786-6641; www.wag.ca; 300 Memorial Blvd; adult/child $12/6; ☺11am-5pm Tue, Wed & Fri-Sun, to 9pm Thu) This ship-shaped gallery plots a course for contemporary Manitoban and Canadian artists, including the world's largest collection of Inuit work, alongside a permanent collection of European Renaissance art. Temporary

exhibits include artworks by Chagall and Karel Funk, and serpentinite carvings by internationally successful Inuit carver Oviloo Tunnillie.

St-Boniface Museum   Museum
(☏204-237-4500; http://msbm.mb.ca; 494 Ave Taché; adult/6-17yr/student $6/4.50/5.50; ☺10am-4pm Mon-Fri, noon-4pm Sat & Sun) A mid-19th-century convent is Winnipeg's oldest building and the largest oak-log construction on the continent. The museum inside focuses on the establishment of St-Boniface, the birth of the Métis nation, and the 3000km journey of the first of the Grey Nuns, who arrived here by canoe from Montréal. Artifacts include pioneer furniture and tools, First Nations' beadwork and weaponry, and the coffin used to transport the body of Louis Riel after his execution.

Manitoba Museum   Museum
(☏204-956-2830; www.manitobamuseum.ca; 190 Rupert Ave; adult/child from $11/9; ☺10am-5pm late May-Sep, reduced hours rest of year; ▣) Nature trips through the subarctic, history trips into 1920s Winnipeg, cultural journeys covering the past 12,000 years – if it happened in Manitoba, it's here. Amid the superb displays are a planetarium and an engaging science gallery. One exhibit shows what Churchill was like as a tropical jungle, a mere 450 million years ago, while a replica of the *Nonsuch,* the 17th-century ship that opened up the Canadian west to trade, is another highlight.

⊙ TOURS

Historic Exchange District Walking Tours   Walking
(☏204-942-6716; www.exchangedistrict.org; Old Market Sq; adult/child $10/free; ☺9am-4:30pm Mon-Sat early May-Aug) Entertaining themed and history tours departing from Old Market Sq. Book in advance.

SquarePeg Tours   Walking
(☏204-898-4678; www.squarepegtours.ca; adult/child from $12/8) Numerous entertaining and historically themed walking tours – includ-

ing the popular 'Murder, Mystery & Mayhem' and 'Pestilence, Shamans & Doctors' – depart on regular schedules all summer. 'Symbols, Secrets & Sacrifices Under the Golden Boy' is a much-acclaimed look at the hidden meanings in the capital, while the 'Naughty Bawdy Tour' of the Exchange District is for over-18s only.

Routes on the Red — Tours

(www.routesonthered.ca) Offers thorough, downloadable tours of Winnipeg for walkers, cyclists, drivers and skiers.

🍴 EATING

Forks Market — Market $

(www.theforks.com; 1 Forks Market Rd; mains $5-12; ⊘9:30am-6pm Mon-Thu & Sat, to 9pm Fri; 🅿🚻) Gourmet food specialists, vendors selling prepared foods and an array of ethnic food stalls, running the gamut from Japanese tapas, Caribbean and Chilean to hearty Polish and Sri Lankan, are the unbeatable draw here. Enjoy the bounty at tables scattered about inside or picnic by the river outside.

Marion Street Eatery — Canadian $

(📞204-233-2843; www.marionstreeteatery.com; 393 Marion St; mains $12-15; ⊘11am-8pm Mon & Tue, 7am-8pm Wed-Sat, 9am-2pm Sun; 🅿🛜🍴) With its industrial-chic decor and plenty of room around the horseshoe bar for solo diners, this bustling spot is all about eating well. It specialises in comfort food, from apple whiskey pancake stack for breakfast to the chunky extreme BLT and quite possibly the best mac 'n' cheese in Manitoba.

King + Bannatyne — Sandwiches $

(📞204-691-9757; www.kingandbannatyne. com; 100 King St; mains from $9; ⊘11am-9pm Mon-Sat) The hand-cut meat sandwiches at this brisk, casual spot verge on sublime. There are only five to choose from (brisket, smoked chicken, slow-roast pork...) with one sole delicious concession to the noncarnivorous: the roast portobello with melted provolone. Get yours with a house pickle, soup of the day or salt-roasted caramel corn. Perfect.

Winnipeg surprises. Rising above the prairie, it's an unexpected metropolis

Canadian Museum for Human Rights (p177)

Deer + Almond
Fusion $$

(☑204-504-8562; www.deerandalmond.com; 85 Princess St; mains $12-25; ⊙11am-3pm & 5-11pm Mon-Sat) At the most innovative restaurant in the Exchange District, with an ever-changing menu, chef Mandel's daring pairing of ingredients marks him as some kind of mad genius. And yet it all comes together: the wild sockeye and cherries, the Cornish hen and maple chutney... The cocktails and beers don't disappoint either, and you shouldn't leave without trying one of the unusual desserts.

😃 DRINKING & NIGHTLIFE

King's Head Pub
Pub

(☑204-957-7710; www.kingshead.ca; 120 King St; ⊙11am-2am; 🛜) Vaguely British, the gregarious sidewalk tables are the place to be in the Exchange District on a balmy evening. Inside, it's all rough and tumble wood and it can get seriously loud (hint: this is not the venue for a romantic date). Of the pub dishes, the Indian-Canadian crossover (Butter Chicken Poutine) stands out.

Tavern United
Bar

(☑204-944-0022; 345 Graham Ave; ⊙noon-late) The rooftop patio is massive, with views across to the MTS Centre. It bustles with a sports-bar vibe and rocks for Jets home games. Glacially slow service on game nights.

⭐ ENTERTAINMENT

Times Chang(d) High & Lonesome Club
Live Music

(☑204-957-0982; www.highandlonesomeclub. ca; 234 Main St; ⊙7pm-late) Honky-tonk/country/rock/blues weekend bands jam while beer and whiskey flow at this small, rough, raunchy and real throwback. Don't miss the Sunday-night jam.

Royal Winnipeg Ballet
Ballet

(☑204-956-2792; www.rwb.org; Centennial Concert Hall, 555 Main St) An excellent international reputation means performances at Centennial Concert Hall are popular.

Ice hockey match between the Winnipeg Jets and the Colorado Avalanche

JONATHAN KOZUB / GETTY IMAGES ©

Manitoba Opera
Opera

(☏204-942-7479; www.manitobaopera.mb.ca; Centennial Concert Hall, 555 Main St; tickets $35-115; ☺Nov-Apr) From classics, such as *The Marriage of Figaro,* to premieres, such as *Massenet Werther*.

Winnipeg Symphony Orchestra
Classical Music

(☏204-949-3999; www.wso.ca; Centennial Concert Hall, 555 Main St; tickets $20-60; ☺Sep-May) Classical-music performances, as well as appearances by the likes of Jann Arden and Sheena Easton.

Winnipeg Jets
Ice Hockey

(www.nhl.com/jets; ☺Sep-Apr) There's Manitoba mania for the Jets who play at the **MTS Centre** (☏204-987-7825; www.mtscentre.ca; 260 Hargrave St). The ice-hockey games are raucous and often sold out; ask around for tickets.

❶ INFORMATION

Explore Manitoba Centre (☏204-945-3777; 25 Forks Market Rd; ☺10am-6pm) Provincial information center at the Forks; has plenty of info on Winnipeg and the rest of Manitoba.

Millennium Library (☏204-986-6450; http://wpl.winnipeg.ca/library; 251 Donald St; ☺10am-9pm Mon-Thu, to 6pm Fri & Sat; ☎) Free wi-fi and internet computers.

Tourisme Riel (☏204-233-8343; www.tourismeriel.com; 219 Blvd Provencher; ☺9am-5pm) St-Boniface visitor information center that specializes in Francophone attractions.

❶ GETTING THERE & AWAY

AIR

Winnipeg International Airport (YWG; www.waa.ca; 2000 Wellington Ave) has a flash terminal a convenient 10km west of downtown. It has services to cities across Canada, and to major hubs in the US. Regional carriers handle remote destinations, including Churchill.

BUS

Greyhound buses stop at a **terminal** (☏204-949-7777; www.greyhound.ca; 2015 Wellington Ave) at Winnipeg International Airport.

TRAIN

VIA Rail's transcontinental Canadian departs **Union Station** (123 Main St) three times weekly in each direction. The painfully slow Hudson Bay service to Churchill runs twice a week via Thompson.

❶ GETTING AROUND

TO/FROM THE AIRPORT

A downtown taxi costs around $25; some hotels have free shuttles. Winnipeg Transit bus 15 runs between the airport and downtown every 20 minutes between 5:50am and 12:50am and takes 30 minutes.

BUS

Winnipeg Transit (☏204-986-5700; www.winnipegtransit.com; adult/child $2.65/2) runs extensive bus routes around the area, most converging on Fort St. Get a transfer and use exact change. Its free Downtown Spirit runs three daily routes, connecting the Forks with Portage Ave, the Exchange District and Chinatown.

CAR & MOTORCYCLE

Downtown street parking (free after 6pm) and parking lots are plentiful. Break-ins are common at Union Station, so enclosed lots downtown are a better option if you're taking the train.

WATER TAXI

See the city from a new perspective on the water bus run by **River Spirit** (☏204-783-6633; www.splashdash.ca; one-way/day pass $3.50/20; ☺noon-9pm Mon-Wed, to 11pm Thu-Sun Jul & Aug) between the Forks, the Legislature Building, Osborne Village, St-Boniface and the Exchange District.

THE ROCKIES

The Rockies at a Glance...

With the Rocky Mountains stretched across them, Banff and Jasper National Parks are filled with dramatic, untamed wilderness. Mountaintops scrape the skyline while enormous glaciers cling to their precipices. Glassy lakes flash emerald and sapphire and deep forests blanket wide valleys. Through it all wander bears, elk, moose, wolves and bighorn sheep. However you choose to experience the Rockies, be it through hiking, backcountry skiing, paddling or simply relaxing at a lake's edge, the intensity and scale of the region will bowl over even the most seasoned traveler.

Two Days in the Rockies

Spend a day exploring Banff Town, taking in the **Whyte Museum** (p190) and getting out on the river with **Banff Canoe Club** (p190), before warming up in the **hot springs** (p190). Join the locals at **Bear St Tavern** (p193) for dinner. The next day visit **Lake Louise** (p186), hiking to the **Lake Agnes Teahouse** (p186), and then riding the **gondola** (p187) and counting grizzly bears meandering beneath you.

Four Days in the Rockies

Spend day three driving the **Icefields Pkwy** (p188), taking in the gorgeous lakes and getting out onto the **Athabasca Glacier** (p189). Spend your final day in Jasper. Grab snacks from the **Other Paw Bakery** (p196), join a boat tour on **Maligne Lake** (p195) to set eyes on Spirit Island, soak away any aches at **Miette Hot Springs** (p194), then toast the adventure with the folks at **Jasper Brewing Co** (p197).

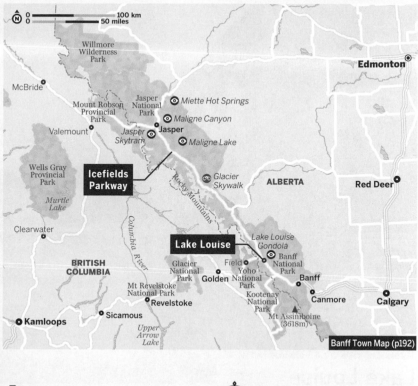

Arriving in the Rockies

Bus Greyhound operates daily buses from Banff and Jasper to Calgary and Vancouver. Brewster Transportation has services between Banff, Jasper, Calgary and Lake Louise. SunDog also has buses between Banff, Jasper and Lake Louise.

Car Major car rental companies have branches in both Banff Town and Jasper.

Train VIA Rail has thrice-weekly services between Jasper and Vancouver or east to Toronto.

Where to Stay

Staying in Banff and Jasper can be a pricey affair. There are plenty of upmarket cabins and lodges, along with plenty of mediocre ones charging top prices; shop around and book ahead. If you're willing to rough it a little, many campgrounds and hostels have million-dollar locations and let you experience the true magic of the parks.

YINYANG / GETTY IMAGES ©

Lake Louise

Phenomenal Lake Louise – one of the most spectacular sights in the Rockies – is impossible to describe without resorting to shameless clichés.

Serene and implausibly turquoise Lake Louise is surrounded by an amphitheater of finely chiseled mountains that hoist Victoria Glacier up for all to see. Famous for its teahouses, grizzly bears and hiking trails, the Lake Louise area is also well-known for its much-commented-on crowds. But, frankly, who cares? You don't come to Lake Louise to dodge other tourists. You come to share in a sight that has captured the imaginations of mountaineers, artists and visitors for more than a century.

Great For...

☑ Don't Miss

Hiring a canoe from the Lake Louise Boathouse to paddle across the icy waters.

Hiking & Skiing

From the towering concrete lump of Chateau Lake Louise, set out on the 3.4km grunt past Mirror Lake, up to the **Lake Agnes Teahouse** (lunch $7-13; ⊗9am-6pm Jun-Aug, 10am-5:30pm Sep & Oct) on its eponymous body of water. After tea made

❶ Need to Know

Lake Louise Visitors Centre (Samson Mall, Lake Louise village; ⊘9am-7pm mid-Jun–Aug, to 5pm May–mid-Jun & Sep–mid-Oct, 9am-4:30pm Thu-Sun mid-Oct–Apr)

✕ Take a Break

Stop in at the **Trailhead Café** (Samson Mall, Lake Louise village; sandwiches $6-10; ⊘8am-5:30pm) for a hearty, homemade packed lunch.

★ Top Tip

Get here via Bow Valley Pkwy rather than Hwy 1; Bow Valley isn't fenced, so it's great for wildlife sightings.

from glacier water and soup or thick-cut sandwiches (cash only), you can trek 1.6km further and higher to the view-embellished Big Beehive lookout and Canada's most unexpectedly sited gazebo. Be sure to bring along bug spray and a bear bell.

The **Lake Louise Ski Area** (www.skilouise. com; day pass adult/youth from $92/72; ♿) has plenty of beginner and intermediate terrain on four separate mountains. The front side is a good place to get your ski legs back while the far side offers some great challenges, from the knee-pulverizing moguls of Paradise Bowl to the high-speed cruising of the Larch area.

Lake Louise Gondola

For a bird's-eye view of the Lake Louise area – and a good chance of spotting grizzly bears on the avalanche slopes – climb aboard the **Lake Louise Gondola** (☎403-522-3555; www.lakelouisegondola.com; off Hwy 1A; adult/child $33/16; ⊘9am-4pm May-Jun & Sep-Oct, 8am-5:30pm Jul & Aug; ♿), which crawls up the side of Whitehorn Mountain to a dizzying viewpoint 2088m above the valley floor. Look out for the imposing fang of 3544m Mt Temple piercing the skyline on the opposite side of the valley. Take the gondola up for 360-degree views, and the chairlift down for an open-air thrill.

Moraine Lake

Thirteen kilometers to the southeast along a winding seasonal road is Moraine Lake, another spectacularly located body of water; it may not have the dazzling color of its famous sibling, but has an equally beguiling backdrop in the Valley of Ten Peaks and the jaw-dropping Tower of Babel, which ascends solidly skyward.

Glacier Skywalk

PETER UNGER / GETTY IMAGES ©

Icefields Parkway

As the highest and most spectacular road in North America, the Icefields Pkwy takes you about as close as you're going to get to the Rockies' craggy summits in your vehicle.

Great For...

☑ Don't Miss

The **Glacier Skywalk** (www.brewster. ca; adult/child skywalk $32/16, skywalk & glacier tour $85/43; ☺10am-5pm Apr-Oct) — a glass-floored, glass-sided, open-air walkway suspended high above the Sunwapta River.

Much of the route followed by the parkway was established in the 1800s by Aboriginal people and fur traders. An early road was built during the 1930s as part of a work project for the unemployed, and the present highway was opened in the early 1960s.

While you can cover the 230km route between Lake Louise and Jasper within a few hours, it's worth spending at least a day exploring the region to discover the parkway's brilliant glacial lakes, gushing waterfalls and exquisite viewpoints.

Athabasca Glacier

The tongue of the Athabasca Glacier runs from the Columbia Icefield to within walking distance of the **Icefield Discovery Centre** (www.brewster.ca; Icefields Pkwy; ☺10am-5pm May-Oct) **FREE**. It has retreated

❶ Need to Know

Parks Canada has a desk at the Discovery Centre. At the parkway entrances, you can purchase your park pass and pick up a map.

✘ Take a Break

Stop by rustic **Num-Ti-Jah Lodge** (☎403-522-2167; www.num-ti-jah.com; Icefields Pkwy; mains $32-45; ⊘5-10pm May-Oct) for a 1940s-hunting-lodge vibe.

★ Top Tip

It's possible to tackle the parkway by bike – the road is wide and there are plenty of strategically spaced campgrounds, hostels and hotels.

about 2km since 1844. To reach its bottom edge, walk from the Discovery Centre along the 1.8km Forefield Trail, then join the 1km Toe of the Athabasca Glacier Trail.

The more popular way to get on the glacier is via a Snocoach **ice tour** (www.columbiaicefield.com; Snocoach & Skywalk tour adult/child $85/43; ⊘9am-6pm Apr-Oct). The large hybrid bus-truck grinds a track onto the ice and gives you a 25-minute wander on the glacier. Dress warmly, wear good shoes and bring a water bottle to try some freshly melted glacial water.

Peyto Lake

You'll have already seen the indescribable blue of Peyto Lake in a thousand publicity shots, but there's nothing like gazing at the real thing – especially since the outlook for this lake is from a lofty vantage point several hundred feet above the water. From the bottom of the lake parking lot, follow a paved trail for 15 minutes up a steady gradual incline to the wooden lookout platform.

Sasquatch Sightings

In 1811 David Thompson, a young surveyor forging across the Rocky Mountains en route to Jasper, became the first European to encounter a 'Monster Bear.' He had stumbled upon tracks near the Athabasca River that measured a staggering 36cm by 20cm.

Around Saskatchewan River, the Stoney people had been catching glimpses of Monster Bears throughout the previous century. It was known to them as 'M-s-napeo' – today it's more commonly called Sasquatch or Bigfoot. Big, hairy and supposedly preceded by a foul smell, sightings continue to be reported by locals and visitors around Banff and Jasper National Parks right into the present decade.

Banff Town

A resort town with boutique shops, night-clubs and fancy restaurants is not something any national-park purist would want to claim credit for. But Banff is no ordinary town. It developed as a service center for the park that surrounds it. Today it brings busloads of tourists keen to convene with shops as much as nature, as well as artists and writers who are drawn to Banff.

Nevertheless, wander 15 minutes in any direction and you're in wild country. Banff civilized? It's just a rumor.

◎ SIGHTS

Whyte Museum of the Canadian Rockies   Museum

(www.whyte.org; 111 Bear St; adult/student/child $10/4/free; ◎10am-5pm) Founded by local artists Catharine and Peter Whyte, the century-old Whyte Museum is more than just a rainy-day option. It boasts a beautiful, ever-changing gallery displaying art from 1800 to present, by both regional, Canadian and international artists, many with a focus on the Rockies. Watch for work by the Group of Seven (aka the Algonquin School). There's also a permanent collection telling the story of Banff and the hardy men and women who forged a home among the mountains.

Upper Hot Springs Pool   Hot Springs

(www.hotsprings.ca; Mountain Ave; adult/child/family $7.30/6.30/22.50; ◎9am-11pm mid-May–mid-Oct, 10am-10pm Sun-Thu, to 11pm Fri & Sat mid-Oct–mid-May) Banff quite literally wouldn't be Banff if it weren't for its hot springs, which gush out from 2.5km beneath **Sulphur Mountain** at a constant temperature of between 32°C (90°F) and 46°C (116°F) – it was the springs that drew the first tourists to Banff. You can still sample the soothing mineral waters at the Upper Hot Springs Pool, near the Banff Gondola.

Banff Gondola   Cable Car

(☑403-762-2523; Mountain Ave; adult/child $45/23, after 6pm $37/16; ◎8am-6pm May, 9am-9pm Jun, 8am-10pm Jul-Oct) In summer or winter, you can summit a peak near Banff thanks to the Banff Gondola, with four-person enclosed cars that glide up to the top of Sulphur Mountain in less than 10 minutes. Named for the thermal springs that emanate from its base, this peak is a perfect viewing point and a tick-box Banff attraction.

Fairmont Banff Springs   Landmark

(www.fairmont.com/banffsprings; 405 Spray Ave) Looming up beside the Bow River, the Banff Springs is a local landmark in more ways than one. Originally built in 1888, and remodeled in 1928 to resemble a cross between a Scottish baronial castle and a European château, the turret-topped exterior conceals an eye-poppingly extravagant selection of ballrooms and balustraded staircases. Non-guests are welcome to wander around; splash out on a coffee or a cocktail in one of the four (count 'em!) lounges.

✪ ACTIVITIES

Banff Canoe Club   Canoeing, Kayaking

(☑403-762-5005; www.banffcanoeclub.com; cnr Wolf St & Bow Ave; canoe & kayak rental per first/additional hour $36/20; ◎10am-6pm mid-May–mid-Sep) Rent a canoe or kayak and slide up the Bow River or the narrower, lazier Forty Mile Creek to Vermilion Lakes. Both routes will take you past gorgeous scenery with lots of opportunities for wildlife-spotting (such as beavers). Paddleboards are also available. Last rental is 5pm. Note that you cannot leave your belongings in the office cabin.

Sunshine Village   Skiing

(www.skibanff.com; day ski pass adult/youth $95/73) If restricted time or funds mean that you can only ski one resort in Banff,

Fairmont Banff Springs

choose Sunshine. Its 13.6-sq-km ski area is divided between 107 runs and the 6-hectare **Rogers Terrain Park**. It boasts the country's first heated chairlifts, too.

Soul Ski & Bike Cycling, Skiing
(📞403-760-1650; www.soulskiandbike.com; 203a Bear St; bike rental per hour $12-14, per day $42-49; ⏰10am-7pm) This is a good snowboard-cycling crossover outfitter. Hire bikes are mostly Trance models. Some of the ski equipment is positively deluxe.

🎯 TOURS

White Mountain Adventures Adventure
(📞403-760-4403; www.whitemountainadventures. com; 120 Eagle Cres; ⏰8am-5pm Mon-Fri) From easy strolls to snowshoeing and heli-hiking, this well-regarded adventure tour service offers charter trips along popular Banff trails, covering nature spotting and local history, as well as points of interest.

the Banff Springs is a local landmark in more ways than one.

Hydra River Guides Rafting
(📞403-762-4554; www.raftbanff.com; 211 Bear St; ⏰9am-7pm) This well-regarded company has been running rafting trips for three decades. Hardier rafters can try the full-day trip ($179); for novices and families there's a sedate float trip ($55).

🛍 SHOPPING

All in the Wild Gallery & Gifts Art
(📞403-760-3141; www.bantlephoto.com; 105 Banff Ave; ⏰10am-8pm Mon-Wed, to 9pm Thu-Sun) Pop in to see the work of the superb wildlife photographer Jason Leo Bantle, with images taken in some of Canada's most remote regions. Pick up a print, a coffee-table book or a children's wildlife book.

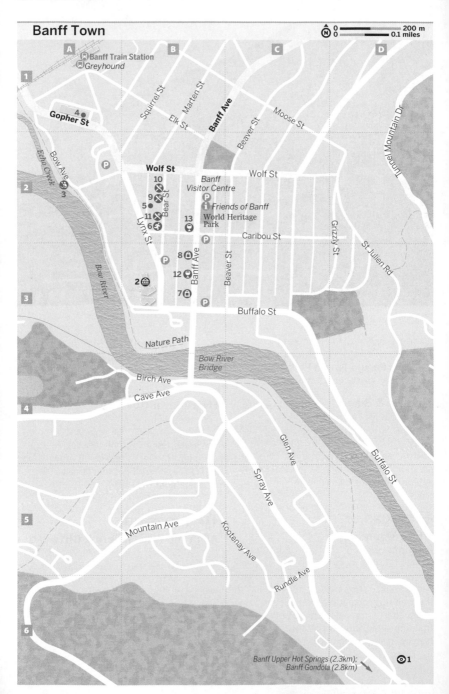

Banff Town

N 0 — 200 m
0 — 0.1 miles

Banff Train Station
Greyhound

Squirrel St
Marten St
Elk St
Gopher St
Banff Ave
Beaver St
Moose St
Bow Ave
Echo Creek

4

P

3

Wolf St

10
9
5
11
6
13

Bear St

Lynx St

Banff
Visitor Centre

Wolf St

Friends of Banff
World Heritage
Park

Caribou St

Grizzly St

St Julien Rd

Tunnel Mountain Dr

Bow River

P

8

2

12

7

Banff Ave

Beaver St

Buffalo St

P

Nature Path

Bow River
Bridge

Birch Ave

Cave Ave

Glen Ave

Spray Ave

Buffalo St

Mountain Ave

Kootenay Ave

Rundle Ave

Banff Upper Hot Springs (2.3km);
Banff Gondola (2.8km)

1

Banff Town

Monod Sports Sports & Outdoors
(www.monodsports.com; 129 Banff Ave; ◎10am-9pm) Banff's oldest outdoor-equipment supplier is still the best. Women's and men's clothing from big brands such as Patagonia, Arc'teryx, Icebreaker, Columbia and North Face feature, supplemented by dedicated sections for rucksacks, equipment and footwear. Staff is super-knowledgeable.

❌ EATING

Wild Flour Cafe $
(☑403-760-5074; www.wildflourbakery.ca; 211 Bear St; mains $5-10; ◎7am-7pm; ☕🍴) 🍴 If you're in need of a relatively guilt-free treat, come here for cheesecake, dark-chocolate torte or – well, 'and' really – macaroons. These, along with breakfasts, well-stuffed sandwiches on homemade bread, and soups, are all organic. Not surprisingly, it's busy; so much so that a smaller version with the bare necessities (coffee and pastries) is opening on Banff Ave.

Saltlik Steak $$
(☑403-762-2467; www.saltlik.com; 221 Bear St; mains $18-29; ◎11am-late Mon-Fri, 11:30am-late Sat & Sun) With rib eye in citrus-rosemary butter and peppercorn New York strip loin on the menu, Saltlik is clearly no plain-Jane steakhouse knocking out flavorless T-bones. No, this polished dining room abounds with rustic elegance and a list of steaks the length of many establishments'

entire menu. In a town not short on steak providers, this could be number one.

Bear St Tavern Pub Food $$
(www.bearstreettavern.ca; 211 Bear St; mains $15-19; ◎11:30am-late) This gastro-pub hits a double whammy: ingeniously flavored pizzas washed down with locally brewed pints. Banffites head here in droves for a plate of pulled-pork nachos or a bison-and-onion pizza, accompanied by pitchers of hoppy ale. The patio overlooking Bison Courtyard is the best place to linger if the weather cooperates.

Nourish Vegetarian $$
(☑403-760-3933; www.nourishbistro.com; 215 Bear St; mains $12-29; ◎11:30am-10pm; 🍴) Confronted by a huge and strangely beautiful papier-mâché tree when you walk in the door, you instantly know this vegetarian bistro is not average. With locally sourced dishes like bourbon-glazed stuffed mushrooms and gluten-free beer-batter onion rings, Nourish has carved out a gourmet following in Banff. Dinner is served as shareable platters (think giant tapas).

◎ DRINKING & NIGHTLIFE

Wild Bill's Legendary Saloon Bar
(☑403-762-0333; www.wildbillsbanff.com; 201 Banff Ave; ◎11am-late) Forget swanky wine bars and cafes – you haven't really been to Banff if you miss Wild Bill's. Hang out

with real live cowboys and get an eyeful of two-stepping, bull riding, karaoke and live music of the twangy Willie Nelson variety. The grub is exactly what you'd expect: big portions of barbecued pork rinds, crispy corn fritters, burgers and chili.

Elk & Oarsman   Pub

(www.elkandoarsman.com; 119 Banff Ave; ⊙11am-1am) Located upstairs with a crow's-nest view of Banff Ave, this is the town's most refined sports pub, with a decent lineup of beers on tap and live music; the kitchen will fix you up with some good food if you so desire. The rooftop patio is prime real estate in the summer.

❶ INFORMATION

Banff Visitor Centre (☑403-762-1550; www. pc.gc.ca/banff; 224 Banff Ave; ⊙9am-7pm mid-Jun–Aug, to 5pm Sep–mid-Jun) The Parks Canada office doles out info and maps. This is where you can find current trail conditions and weather forecasts, and register for backcountry hiking and camping.

Friends of Banff (☑403-760-5331; www.friends ofbanff.com; 224 Banff Ave) Charitable organization that runs educational programs, including walking tours and junior naturalist workshops. It also runs Park Radio 101.1FM, offering weather and trail reports, local history and info. It runs a gift shop and has an info booth inside the Banff Visitor Centre.

❶ GETTING THERE & AWAY

BUS

Greyhound Canada (☑800-661-8747; www. greyhound.ca; 327 Railway Ave) Operates buses to Calgary ($28, 1¾ hours, four daily), Vancouver ($104, 13 hours, four daily) and points in between.

Brewster Transportation (☑403-762-6750; www.brewster.ca; 100 Gopher St) Will pick you up from your hotel. It services Calgary ($65, 1¼ hours), Jasper ($100, five hours, daily) and Lake Louise ($30, one hour, several daily).

SunDog (www.sundogtours.com) Also runs transport between Banff and Jasper (adult/child $69/39, five hours, daily) and Lake Louise ($20, one hour, daily).

CAR & MOTORCYCLE

All of the major car-rental companies have branches in Banff Town. During summer, reserve ahead. If you're flying into Calgary, reserving a car at the airport may yield a better deal.

❶ GETTING AROUND

Four hybrid 'Roam' buses on two main routes are run by **Banff Transit** (☑403-762-1215; www. banff.ca). Route maps are printed on all bus stops. Buses start running at 6:30am and finish at 11pm; the fare is $2/1 per adult/child (or $5 for a day pass).

Metered taxis can easily be hailed on the street, especially on Banff Ave. Otherwise call **Banff Taxi** (☑403-762-4444).

Jasper

Jasper is a larger, less trammeled, more wildlife-rich version of Banff. Its rugged backcountry wins admiring plaudits for its deep river canyons, rampart-like mountain ranges and delicate ecosystems. Jasper scores high marks for its hiking, pioneering history and easy-to-view wildlife.

◉ SIGHTS

Miette Hot Springs   Hot Springs

(www.pc.gc.ca/hotsprings; Miette Rd; adult/child/family $6/5/18.50; ⊙8:30am-10:30pm) More remote than Banff's historic springs, Miette Hot Springs ('discovered' in 1909) are 61km northeast of Jasper off Hwy 16, near the park boundary. The soothing waters, kept at a pleasant 40°C (104°F), are surrounded by peaks and are especially enjoyable when the fall snow is drifting down and steam envelops the crowd. Raining summer evenings also make for stunning, misty conditions.

Maligne Lake   Lake

Almost 50km from Jasper at the end of a stunning road that bears its name, 22km-long Maligne Lake is the recipient of a lot of hype. The baby-blue water and a craning circle of rocky, photogenic peaks are a feast for the eyes. Spirit Island is the lake's most classic view; reach by boat with **Maligne Tours** (780-852-3370; www.malignelake.com; 616 Patricia St, Jasper Town; adult/child $65/33; May-Sep).

Maligne Canyon   Canyon

A steep, narrow gorge shaped by a river flowing at its base, this canyon at its narrowest is only a few meters wide and drops a stomach-turning 50m beneath your feet. Crossed by six bridges, it has various **trails** leading out from the parking area on Maligne Lake Rd, where there's also a quaint, basic teahouse. In the winter, waterfalls freeze solid into sheets of white ice and are popular with ice climbers.

Jasper Skytram   Cable Car

(780-852-3093; www.jaspertramway.com; Whistlers Mountain Rd; adult/child/family $40/20/100; 9am-8pm Apr-Oct) If the average, boring views from Jasper just aren't blowing your hair back, go for a ride on this sightseeing gondola. The journey zips up through various mountain life zones to the high barren slopes of the Whistlers, where there's a small, pricey cafe. From the top of the gondola you can take the steep 1.5km hike to the mountain's true summit, where views stretch for 75km.

🌀 ACTIVITIES

Freewheel Cycle   Cycling

(www.freewheeljasper.com; 618 Patricia St; bike rental per day $40; 9am-10pm;) Rents and sells cycling gear; this is a good place for families, with kids' bikes and chariots ($24 per day) available.

Vicious Cycle   Cycling

(780-852-1111; www.viciouscanada.com; 630 Connaught Dr; bike rental per hour/day from

🔁 Jasper Town to Maligne Lake

The inspiring 46km drive between Jasper and Maligne Lake is almost obligatory for anyone with a day to spare in Jasper. The road twists and turns and it seems like at every corner there's an opportunity to see some wildlife. This is one of the best places in Jasper to look for deer, elk, moose and, if you're lucky, bear. The ideal time to see wildlife is early in the morning or at dusk.

American black bear and cubs
WESTEND61 PREMIUM / SHUTTERSTOCK ©

$8/32; 9am-6pm) Super-cool cycling shop rents bikes in summer and snowboards in winter. You can also pick up a helmet, trail map and lock. Reserve ahead online.

Gravity Gear   Adventure Sports

(780-852-3155; www.gravitygearjasper.com; 618 Patricia St) If you're after outdoor gear, these guys likely have it for rent, from ice-climbing crampons to backcountry skis. They're also fountains of knowledge on local activities.

Jasper Riding Stables   Horseback Riding

(780-852-7433; www.jasperstables.com; Pyramid Lake Rd; 1-/2-/3-hour rides $47/79/115; May-Oct;) For gentle trail rides through local backcountry, call in at these stables. With over 50 horses, they'll match you to a suitable four-legged friend. Riders must be six years of age.

Spirit Island, Maligne Lake (p195)

The baby-blue water and a craning circle of photogenic peaks are a feast for the eyes.

TOURS

Jasper Adventure Centre
Outdoors

(780-852-5595; www.jasperadventurecentre. com; 611 Patricia St; 8am-9pm May-Oct, to 5pm Nov-Apr) The veteran on the guiding scene runs numerous local tours, as well as some further afield to the Icefields and Lake Louise. One of their most popular trips is the three-hour Wildlife Discover Tour (adult/child $65/35). In winter their office relocates to the train station, from where they organize dog-sledding and ice walks.

Jasper Walks & Talks
Hiking

(780-852-4994; www.walksntalks.com; 626 Connaught Dr; adult/child $90/50; Jun-Oct) A local resident and former Parks Canada guide leads small groups on breathtaking five- to six-hour tours that can take in Mt Edith Cavell Meadows, Maligne Canyon or the Valley of Five Lakes.

EATING

Other Paw Bakery
Cafe, Bakery $

(610 Connaught Dr; snacks $2-6; 7am-6pm) An offshoot of the Bear's Paw, a larger cafe around the corner, the Other Paw offers the same insanely addictive mix of breads, pastries, muffins and coffee, along with tasty soups and well-stuffed wraps. This one stays open later, too.

Olive Bistro
Mediterranean $$

(780-852-5222; www.olivebistro.ca; 401 Patricia St; mains $16-25; 5-11pm;) This casual restaurant with big booths has a classy menu. Choose from main dishes like whiskey barbecue ribs, bison lasagna or wild-mushroom risotto, or opt for sharing plates like white-truffle scallops or a charcuterie plate of local smoked meats. The cocktails are excellent and there's often mellow live music.

Fiddle River Seafood Co
Seafood **$$$**

(🖉780-852-3032; 620 Connaught Dr; mains $23-29; ⏰5-10pm) Being almost 1600km from the sea makes some customers understandably leery, but Jasper's premier seafood joint is no slouch. Pull up a seat near the window and tuck into innovative creations such as Earl Grey–smoked candy salmon or crispy coconut prawns. Whenever possible, the river fish and meat is Alberta-sourced. Try butter chicken or braised elk Stroganoff.

🍺 DRINKING & NIGHTLIFE

Jasper Brewing Co
Brewery

(🖉780-852-4111; www.jasperbrewingco.ca; 624 Connaught Dr; ⏰11:30am-1am) 🍴 This brewpub was the first of its type in a Canadian national park, using glacial water to make its fine ales, including the signature Rockhopper IPA and the slightly more adventurous Rocket Ridge Raspberry Ale. It's a sit-down affair, with TVs and a good food menu.

Downstream Bar
Bar

(620 Connaught Dr; ⏰4pm-late) This is likely the most well-stocked bar in town, with a wide array of whiskeys, vodkas and other alcoholic indulgences – and a bar staff who know how to use them. There's some awesome food to keep your head above water and, often, live music.

ℹ️ INFORMATION

Friends of Jasper (🖉780-852-4767; www.friends ofjasper.com; 500 Connaught Dr; ♿) **FREE**

Jasper Information Centre (🖉780-852-6176; www.pc.gc.ca/jasper; 500 Connaught Dr; ⏰9am-7pm May-Oct, 10am-5pm Nov-Apr) This wonderful information center is housed in Jasper's oldest building, dating from 1913. You'll find Parks Canada and the local tourist information stand plus an excellent gift shop.

Park Wardens' Offices (🖉Banff 403-762-1470, Jasper 780-852-6167)

ℹ️ GETTING THERE & AWAY

BUS

The **bus station** (607 Connaught Dr) is at the train station. Greyhound buses have daily services to Edmonton ($70, from five hours) and Vancouver ($148, from 12 hours).

Departing from the same station, **Brewster Transportation** (🖉403-762-6700; www.brewster .ca) operates express buses to Lake Louise village ($75, four hours, at least one daily) and Banff Town ($100, five hours, at least one daily). **SunDog** (www.sundogtours.com; 414 Connaught Dr; ⏰8am-8pm) also has daily services from May to October to Lake Louise ($59), Banff ($69) and Calgary airport ($119).

CAR & MOTORCYCLE

International car-rental agencies have offices in Jasper Town.

TRAIN

VIA Rail (🖉888-842-7245; www.viarail.ca) offers thrice-weekly train services west to Vancouver ($242, 20 hours) and east to Toronto ($516, 62 hours).

ℹ️ GETTING AROUND

Maligne Valley Shuttle (🖉780-852-3331; www. maligneadventures.com; one-way/round-trip adult $30/60, youth $14/30) Runs a 9am daily shuttle from outside the Jasper Information Centre to Maligne Lake, with stops at trailheads along the way. Shuttles return from the lake at 10:15am, 2pm and 5pm.

Jasper Taxi (🖉780-852-3600) Metered cabs.

Skiing at Whistler

Named for the furry marmots that populate the area and whistle like deflating balloons, this gabled alpine village is one of the world's most popular ski resorts.

Great For...

☑ Don't Miss

Skiing the Saddle run, for top views and the feeling of soaring down the mountain.

Skiing & Snowboarding

Comprising 37 lifts and crisscrossed with over 200 runs, the Whistler-Blackcomb sister mountains are also physically linked by the resort's mammoth 4.4km **Peak 2 Peak Gondola** (📞604-967-8950; www.whistlerblackcomb.com/discover/360-experience; 4545 Blackcomb Way; adult/teen/child $57/50/29; ⏰10am-4:45pm). It takes just 11 minutes to shuttle wide-eyed powder hogs between the two high-alpine areas, so you can hit the slopes on both mountains on the same day.

More than half the resort's runs are aimed at intermediate-level skiers, and the season typically runs from late November to April on Whistler and from November to June on Blackcomb – December to February is the peak for both.

❶ Need to Know

☑604-967-8950; www.whistlerblackcomb. com; 2-day winter lift ticket adult/child $258/129

✕ Take a Break

Purebread (☑604-962-1182; www. purebread.ca; 4338 Main St; baked goods $3-6; ⊗8:30am-5:30pm) will satisfy your cravings, from salted caramel bars to homity pie.

★ Top Tip

Beat the crowds with an early-morning Fresh Tracks ticket ($20) for an extra hour on the slopes and breakfast at the Roundhouse Lodge.

Snowboard fans should also check out the freestyle terrain parks, mostly located on Blackcomb, including the Snow Cross and the Big Easy Terrain Garden. There's also the popular Habitat Terrain Park on Whistler.

Cross-Country Skiing & Snowshoeing

A pleasant stroll or free shuttle bus away from Whistler village, **Lost Lake** (☑604-905-0071; www.crosscountryconnection.ca; day pass adult/child $20/10; ⊗8am-8pm mid-Dec–Mar) is the hub for 25km of wooded cross-country ski trails, suitable for novices and experts alike. Around 4km of the trail is lit for additional nighttime skiing and there's a handy 'warming hut' providing lessons and equipment rentals. Snowshoers are also well served in this area: you can stomp off on your own on 15km of trails or rent equipment and guides.

Southwest of the village via Hwy 99, **Whistler Olympic Park** (☑604-964-0060; www.whistlersportlegacies.com; 5 Callaghan Valley Rd, Callaghan Valley; park access per vehicle weekdays/weekends $10/15) is a pristine, snow-swathed venue that hosted several 2010 Olympic Nordic events. Now perfect for visiting (and local) snowshoers and cross-country skiers, it has more than 130km of marked trails.

Getting There & Away

While most visitors arrive by car from Vancouver via Hwy 99, Greyhound Canada ($26, 2½ hours, four daily) and Pacific Coach Lines ($55, two hours, six daily) also service the route. **Snowbus** (☑604-451-1130; www.snowbus.com) operates a wintertime service from Vancouver (adult $38, up to three hours, up to three daily).

View over Vancouver from Grouse Mountain

VANCOUVER

In this Chapter

Vancouver at a Glance...

Tucked in between snowy peaks and the wild Pacific Ocean, Vancouver boasts forest trails, sandy beaches, kayaking routes, seawall bike lanes and the mighty green jewel of Stanley Park. Downtown is thus just the start of Vancouver – walk or hop public transit and within minutes you'll be in one of the city's many diverse and distinctive 'hoods. Whether discovering the coffee shops of Commercial Dr, the hipster haunts of Main St, the indie bars and restaurants of Gastown, the heritage-house beachfronts and browsable stores of Kitsilano, or the great natural landscapes beyond, you'll find plenty to fall in love with.

One Day in Vancouver

Get to **Stanley Park** before the crowds to stroll the seawall and explore the Lost Lagoon. Stump up for a sustainable lunch at **Forage** (p219), then head to **English Bay Beach** (p208). Give your credit card a workout along **Robson St** and stop in at **Vancouver Art Gallery** (p208). Head to **Tacofino** (p218) in Gastown for nachos and tequila flights and end the day with a live show at the **Commodore Ballroom** (p223).

Two Days in Vancouver

Start your wander at **Granville Island** (p206). Peruse the cool shops and fill your belly in the market before heading to **Chinatown** to spend some time exploring the aromatic grocery and apothecary stores on Keefer St. End your afternoon at the **Dr Sun Yat-Sen Classical Chinese Garden** (p209). Continue east to Commercial Drive for burgers at **Cannibal Café** (p217) and brews at **Callister Brewing Company** (p220).

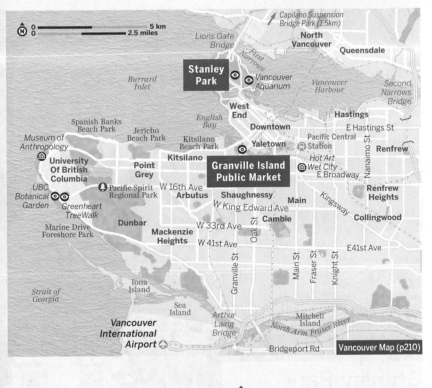

Arriving in Vancouver

Vancouver International Airport Take a Canada Line train downtown ($7.75 to $10.50, 25 minutes) or grab a cab (up to $45).

Pacific Central Train Station SkyTrain it from the Main St-Science World Station downtown ($2.75, five minutes).

BC Ferries services arrive at Tsawwassen, an hour south of Vancouver, and at Horseshoe Bay. Both are accessible by regular transit bus services.

Where to Stay

Metro Vancouver is home to more than 25,000 hotel, B&B and hostel rooms – many in or around the downtown core. The city is packed with visitors in summer, so book ahead. Rates peak in July and August, but there are good spring and fall deals, when you can also expect some accompanying 'Wet Coast' rainfall. See p227 for more information.

ALISON RIDGWAY / LONELY PLANET ©

Stanley Park

One of North America's largest urban green spaces, Stanley Park is revered for its dramatic forest-and-mountain oceanfront views.

Great For...

☑ **Don't Miss**

The family of beavers who currently reside on Beaver Lake; you'll likely spot them swimming around their large den.

This 400-hectare woodland is studded with nature-hugging trails, family-friendly attractions and tasty places to eat.

Seawall

Built in stages between 1917 and 1980, the park's 8.8km seawall trail is Vancouver's favorite outdoor hangout. Encircling the park, it offers spectacular waterfront vistas on one side and dense forest on the other.

The seawall some of the park's top highlights. You'll pass alongside the **HMCS Discovery** (1200 Stanley Park Dr; 🚌19) naval station and, about 1.5km from the W Georgia St entrance, you'll come to the ever-popular **Totem Poles**. Remnants of an abandoned 1930s plan to create a First Nations 'theme village,' the bright-painted poles were joined by the addition of three exquisitely carved Coast Salish welcome arches.

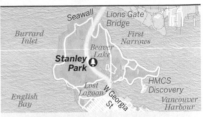

❶ Need to Know

It typically takes around three hours to walk the 8.8km seawall, but bike rentals are also available on nearby Denman St.

✕ Take a Break

The park's **Stanley's Bar & Grill** (☎604-602-3088; www.stanleyparkpavilion. com; 610 Pipeline Rd; �),9am-8pm Jul & Aug, 9am-5pm Sep-Jun; ☐19) is a great spot for a patio beer among the trees.

★ Top Tip

Head to Ceperley Meadows in the summer for wildly popular free outdoor movie screenings by Fresh Air Cinema (www.freshaircinema.ca).

Lost Lagoon

A few steps from the park's W Georgia St entrance lies Lost Lagoon, which was originally part of Coal Harbour. After a causeway was built in 1916, the new body of water was renamed, transforming itself into a freshwater lake. Today it's a bird-beloved nature sanctuary – keep your eyes peeled for blue herons – and its perimeter pathway is a favored stroll for wildlife nuts. The **Stanley Park Nature House** (☎604-257-8544; www.stanleyparkecology.ca; north end of Alberni St, Lost Lagoon; �),10am-5pm Tue-Sun Jul & Aug, 10am-4pm Sat & Sun Sep-Jun; ☀; ☐19) **FREE** here has exhibits on the park's wildlife, history and ecology – ask about the fascinating and well-priced guided walks.

Beaches & Views

Second Beach is a family-friendly area on the park's western side, with a playground, an ice-cream stand and a huge outdoor **swimming pool** (☎604-257-8371; www.vancouverparks.ca; cnr N Lagoon Dr & Stanley Park Dr, Stanley Park; adult/child $5.86/2.95; �),10am-8:45pm mid-Jun–Aug, reduced hours low-season; ☀; ☐19). For a little more tranquillity, try Third Beach, a favored summer-evening destination for Vancouverites.

Perhaps the most popular vista is at Prospect Point. One of Vancouver's best lookouts, this lofty spot is located at the park's northern tip. In summer, you'll be jostling for elbow room with tour parties; heading down the steep stairs to the viewing platform usually shakes them off. Also look out for scavenging raccoons here (don't pet them).

Granville Island Public Market

A multisensory smorgasbord of fish, cheese, fruit and bakery treats, this is one of North America's finest public markets.

Great For...

☑ Don't Miss

The alfresco farmers market (June to September) with BC cherries, peaches and blueberries.

Forgotten Past

The Public Market is the centerpiece of one of Canada's most impressive urban regeneration projects. Built as a district for small factories in the early part of the last century, Granville Island – which has also been called Mud Island and Industrial Island over the years – had declined into a paint-peeled, no-go area by the 1960s. But the abandoned sheds began attracting artists and theater groups by the 1970s, and the old buildings slowly started springing back to life with some much-needed repairs and upgrades. Within a few years, new theaters, restaurants and studios had been built and the Public Market quickly became an instantly popular anchor tenant. One reason for the island's popularity? Only independent, one-of-a-kind businesses operate here.

Need to Know

604-666-6655; www.granvilleisland.com/public-market; Johnston St; 9am-7pm; 50, miniferries

Take a Break

Dine at Bistro 101 (p219), the reasonably priced training restaurant of the Pacific Institute of Culinary Arts.

★ Top Tip

If you're an incurable foodie, the delicious market tour organized by Vancouver Foodie Tours (p215) is the way to go.

Taste-Tripping

Come hungry: there are dozens of food stands to weave your way around at the market. Among the must-see stands are **Oyama Sausage Company**, replete with hundreds of smoked sausages and cured meats; **Benton Brothers Fine Cheese**, with its full complement of amazing curdy goodies from British Columbia (BC) and around the world (look for anything by Farm House Natural Cheese from Agassiz, BC); and **Granville Island Tea Company** (Hawaiian rooibos recommended), with its tasting bar and more than 150 steep-tastic varieties to choose from. Baked goodies also abound: abandon your diet at **Lee's Donuts**, and **Siegel's Bagels**, where the naughty cheese-stuffed baked bagels are not to be missed. And don't worry: there's

always room for a wafer-thin album-sized 'cinnamon record' from **Stuart's Baked Goods**. French-themed **L'Epicerie Rotisserie and Gourmet Shop** has also been a popular addition to the market in recent years. It sells vinegars, olive oils and Babapapa pop bottles with delicious, fresh-cooked picnic-friendly takeout chicken and sausages.

In the unlikely event you're still hungry, there's also a small international food court: avoid off-peak dining if you want to snag a table and indulge in a good-value selection that runs from Indian curries to German sausages. And if you want to dive into some regional, seasonal produce, there's even a **farmers market** just outside the market building between June and October where you can, due to a recent law change, also sample BC-made booze (look out for brews by Four Winds, Brassneck, Powell Street, Central City and Main Street).

⊙ SIGHTS

◉ Downtown & West End

Vancouver Art Gallery — Gallery

(VAG; ☎604-662-4700; www.vanartgallery. bc.ca; 750 Hornby St; adult/child $20/6; ⊙10am-5pm Wed-Mon, to 9pm Tue; ☒5) The VAG has dramatically transformed since 2000, becoming a vital part of the city's cultural scene. Contemporary exhibitions – often showcasing Vancouver's renowned photoconceptualists – are now combined with blockbuster international traveling shows. Check out **FUSE** (☎604-662-4700; www.vanartgallery.bc.ca/fuse; Vancouver Art Gallery; $24; ⊙8pm-midnight; ☒5), a quarterly late-night party where you can hang out with the city's young arties over wine and live music.

English Bay Beach — Beach

(cnr Denman St & Beach Ave; ☒5) Wandering south on Denman St, you'll spot a clutch of palm trees ahead announcing one of Canada's best urban beaches. Then you'll see Vancouver's most popular public artwork: a series of oversized laughing figures that makes everyone smile. There's a party atmosphere here in summer as locals catch rays and panoramic ocean views...or just ogle the volleyballers prancing around on the sand.

Bill Reid Gallery of Northwest Coast Art — Gallery

(☎604-682-3455; www.billreidgallery.ca; 639 Hornby St; adult/child $10/5; ⊙11am-5pm mid-May–Sep, 11am-5pm Wed-Sun Oct–mid-May; ⑤Burrard) Showcasing carvings, paintings and jewelry from Canada's most revered Haida artists and many others, this tranquil gallery is lined with fascinating and exquisite works – plus handy touch-screens to tell you all about them. The space centers on the Great Hall, where there's often a carver at work. Be sure to also hit the mezzanine level: you'll come face to face with an 8.5m-long bronze of intertwined magical creatures, complete with impressively long tongues.

FlyOver Canada — Theater

(☎604-620-8455; www.flyovercanada.com; 999 Canada Pl; adult/child $22/14; ⊙10am-

Vancouver Art Gallery

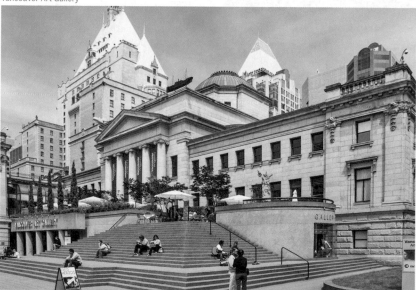

DEYMOSHR / SHUTTERSTOCK ©

9pm, reduced hours in winter; 🚻; Ⓢ Waterfront) Canada Place's newest attraction, this breathtaking movie-screen simulator ride makes you feel like you're swooping across the entire country, waggling your legs over grand landscapes and city landmarks from coast to coast. En route, your seat will lurch, your face will be sprayed and you'll likely have a big smile on your face. And once the short ride is over, you'll want to do it all again.

◎ Yaletown

Engine 374 Pavilion Museum

(www.roundhouse.ca; Roundhouse Community Arts & Recreation Centre, 181 Roundhouse Mews; ⊙10am-4pm, reduced hours off-season; 🚻; Ⓢ Yaletown-Roundhouse) **FREE** May 23, 1887, was an auspicious date for Vancouver. That's when Engine 374 pulled the very first transcontinental passenger train into the fledgling city, symbolically linking the country and kick-starting the eventual metropolis. Retired in 1945, the engine was, after many years of neglect, restored and placed in this splendid pavilion. The friendly volunteers here will show you the best angle for snapping the perfect photo of the engine.

Roundhouse Community Arts & Recreation Centre Arts Center

(📞604-713-1800; www.roundhouse.ca; 181 Roundhouse Mews, cnr Davie St & Pacific Blvd; ⊙9am-10pm Mon-Fri, to 5pm Sat & Sun; Ⓢ Yaletown-Roundhouse) Home of the Engine 374 Pavilion, Yaletown's main community gathering space colonizes a handsomely restored heritage railway roundhouse. It offers a full roster of events and courses for locals and visitors, including popular drop-in running classes and Philosopher's Cafe debating events. Check the website calendar to see what's on.

◎ Gastown & Chinatown

Dr Sun Yat-Sen Classical Chinese Garden & Park Gardens

(📞604-662-3207; www.vancouverchinese-garden.com; 578 Carrall St; adult/child $14/10;

👪 Vancouver for Children

Family-friendly Vancouver is stuffed with activities and attractions for children.

In summer, Vancouver's biggest and best water park, Granville Island (p213), is conveniently located near the ever-popular Kids Market (p213). For more water (and sand!) play, head to family-friendly **Kitsilano Beach** (cnr Cornwall Ave & Arbutus St; 🚌22).

If it's not quite beach weather, inch over a canyon on the (deliberately) wobbly wooden bridge at **Capilano Suspension Bridge Park** (📞604-985-7474; www.capbridge.com; 3735 Capilano Rd, North Vancouver; adult/child $40/12; ⊙8:30am-8pm Jun-Aug, reduced hours off-season; 🅿🚻; 🚌236), then take some short trails through the forest to learn about the towering trees and local critters.

Capilano Suspension Bridge
ALEXANDER HOWARD / LONELY PLANET ©

⊙9:30am-7pm mid-Jun–Aug, 10am-6pm Sep & May–mid-Jun, 10am-4:30pm Oct-Apr; Ⓢ Stadium-Chinatown) A tranquil break from clamorous Chinatown, this intimate 'garden of ease' reflects Taoist principles of balance and harmony. Entry includes a 45-minute guided tour, where you'll learn about the symbolism behind the placement of the gnarled pine trees, winding covered pathways and ancient limestone formations. Look out for the lazy turtles bobbing in the jade-colored water.

Vancouver

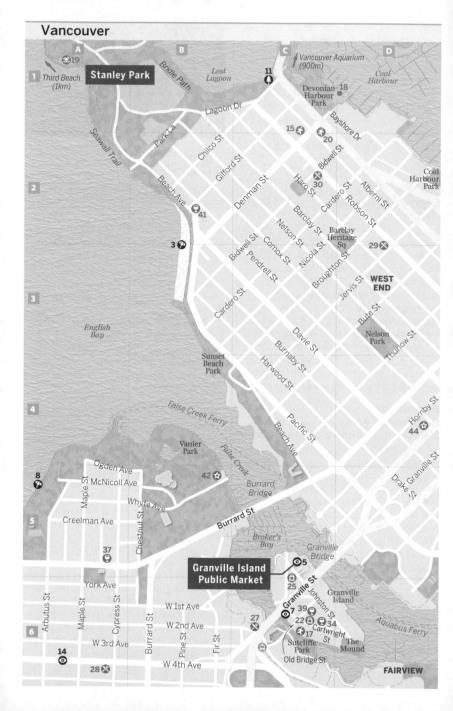

A **B** **C** **D**

Vancouver Aquarium
(900m)

1 Third Beach
(1km)

Stanley Park

Bridle Path

Lost
Lagoon

11

Devonian
Harbour
Park

18

Coal
Harbour

19

Lagoon Dr

Bayshore Dr

Park La

Chilco St

Gifford St

15 20

Bidwell St

Coal
Harbour
Park

Seawall Trail

Beach Ave

2

Denman St

Haro St

30

Cardero St

Robson St

Alberni St

41

Barclay St

Nelson St

Nicola St

Barclay
Heritage
Sq

Broughton St

29

**WEST
END**

3

Bidwell St

Comox St

Pendrell St

Cardero St

Jervis St

Bute St

Nelson
Park

Thurlow St

3

English
Bay

Davie St

Burnaby St

Harwood St

Sunset
Beach
Park

Pacific St

Hornby St

4

False Creek Ferry

Beach Ave

44

8

Vanier
Park

False Creek

42

Burrard
Bridge

Ogden Ave

McNicoll Ave

Maple St

Whyte Ave

Granville St

Drake St

5

Creelman Ave

Chestnut St

Burrard St

Broker's
Bay

Granville
Bridge

**Granville Island
Public Market**

5

37

York Ave

Granville St

25

Granville
Island

Johnston St

7 39

22 34

Cartwright
St

17

Aquabus Ferry

6

14

Arbutus St

Maple St

Cypress St

Burrard St

Pine St

Fir St

W 1st Ave

W 2nd Ave

W 3rd Ave

W 4th Ave

27

Sutcliffe
Park

The
Mound

Old Bridge St

28

FAIRVIEW

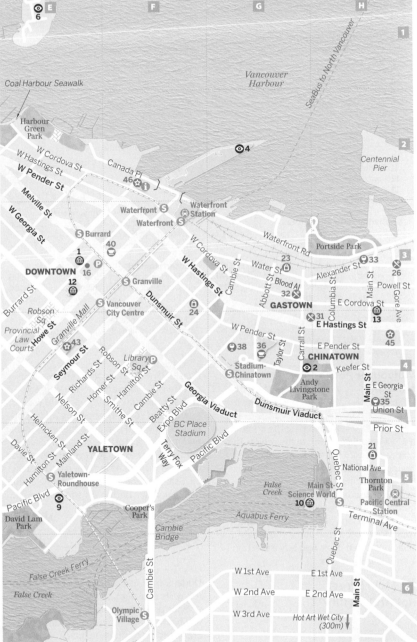

Vancouver

Vancouver Police Museum
Museum

(📞604-665-3346; www.vancouverpolicemuseum.ca; 240 E Cordova St; adult/child $12/8; ◎9am-5pm Tue-Sat; 🚌4) Illuminating the crime-and-vice-addled history of the region, this quirky museum is lined with confiscated weapons and counterfeit currency. It also has a former mortuary room where the walls are studded with preserved slivers of human tissue – spot the bullet-damaged brain slices. Consider adding a **walking tour** ($20) to learn all about the area's salacious olden days. And buy a toe-tag T-shirt in the gift shop.

◎ Main Street

Hot Art Wet City
Gallery

(📞604-764-2266; www.hotartwetcity.com; 2206 Main St; ◎noon-5pm Wed-Sat; 🚌3) **FREE**

Possibly the most fun you can have at a private gallery in Vancouver, trip up the stairs at this funky little space and you're guaranteed some eye-popping art to look at. Lowbrow and pop art is the usual focus, and mostly local artists are showcased. There's a new exhibition every month or so and past themes have ranged from art on bike saddles and beer bottles to the annual, highly popular, button-art show.

Science World
Museum

(📞604-443-7440; www.scienceworld.ca; 1455 Quebec St; adult/child $25.75/17.75; ◎10am-6pm, to 8pm Thu Jul & Aug, reduced hours off-season; P 🚻; S Main St-Science World) Under Vancouver's favorite geodesic dome (okay, its only one), this ever-popular science and nature showcase has tons of exhibition space and a cool outdoor park crammed with hands-on fun (yes, you *can* lift 2028kg). Inside, there are two floors of educational play, from a walk-in hamster wheel to an air-driven ball maze.

◎ Kitsilano & UBC

Museum of Anthropology Museum

(☑604-822-5087; www.moa.ubc.ca; 6393 NW Marine Dr; adult/child $18/16; ⏰10am-5pm Wed-Sun, to 9pm Tue; **P**; ☒99B-Line) Vancouver's best museum is studded with spectacular First Nations totem poles and breathtaking carvings – but it's also teeming with artifacts from cultures around the world, from Polynesian instruments to Cantonese opera costumes. Take one of the free daily **tours** (check ahead for times) for some context, but give yourself at least a couple of hours to explore on your own. It's easy to immerse yourself here.

UBC Botanical Garden Gardens

(www.botanicalgarden.ubc.ca; 6804 SW Marine Dr; adult/child $9/5; ⏰9:30am-4:30pm, to 8pm Thu mid-Mar–Oct, 9:30am-4pm Nov–mid-Mar; ☒99 B-Line, then C20) You'll find a giant collection of rhododendrons, a fascinating apothecary plot and a winter green space of off-season bloomers in this 28-hectare complex of themed gardens. Save time for the attraction's **Greenheart TreeWalk** (☑604-822-4208; www.botanicalgarden.ubc.ca; UBC Botanical Garden, 6804 SW Marine Dr; adult/child $20/10; ⏰10am-4:30pm daily, to 7:30pm Thu Apr-Oct; **P**♿), which lifts visitors 17m above the forest floor on a 308m guided ecotour. A combined botanical garden and walkway ticket costs $20.

Pacific Spirit Regional Park Park

(www.pacificspiritparksociety.org; cnr Blanca St & W 16th Ave; **P**; ☒99 B-Line) This stunning 763-hectare park stretches from Burrard Inlet to the North Arm of the Fraser River, a green buffer zone between the UBC campus and the city. A smashing spot to explore with 70km of walking, jogging and cycling trails, you'll also find **Camosun Bog wetland** (accessed by a boardwalk at 19th Ave and Camosun St), a bird and plant haven.

West 4th Avenue Area

(www.shopwest4th.com; ☒4) This strollable smorgasbord of stores and restaurants may have your credit cards whimpering for mercy after a couple of hours. Since Kits is now a bit of a middle-class utopia, shops that once sold cheap groceries are now more likely to be hawking designer yoga gear, hundred-dollar hiking socks and exotic (and unfamiliar) fruits from around the world.

✪ ACTIVITIES

Bayshore Rentals Cycling

(☑604-688-2453; www.bayshorebikerentals.ca; 745 Denman St; per 1/8hr $6/23.80; ⏰9am-dusk; ☒5) One of several rival businesses taking advantage of their Stanley Park proximity, Bayshore will rent you just about anything to get you rolling around the nearby seawall. The mountain bikes are its bread and butter, but it also rents in-line skates, tandems (you know you want one) and rugged toddler bike trailers so you can tow your kids like the royalty they are.

Spokes Bicycle Rentals Cycling

(☑604-688-5141; www.spokesbicyclerentals. com; 1798 W Georgia St; adult bicycle rental per hour/day from $6.67/26.67; ⏰8am-9pm, reduced hours off-season; ☒5) On the corner of W Georgia and Denman Sts, this is the biggest of the bike shops servicing the Stanley Park cycling trade. It can kit you and your family out with all manner of bikes, from cruisers to kiddie one-speeds. Ask for tips on riding the Seawall; it extends far beyond Stanley Park.

**Granville Island
Water Park** Water Park

(⏰summer; ♿; ☒50) **FREE** Vancouver's biggest and best water park is conveniently located near Granville Island's **Kids Market** (☑604-689-8447; www.kidsmarket.ca; 1496 Cartwright St; ⏰10am-6pm; ♿; ☒50), which means you'll have the perfect lure for enticing your sprogs away from the toy shops. There's also a large pond nearby that's

Science World (p212)

often filled with friendly ducks and geese; in May and June, you'll often spot fuzzy babies of the feathered variety here.

Ecomarine Paddlesport Centres — Kayaking

(☎604-689-7575; www.ecomarine.com; 1300 Discovery St, Jericho Sailing Centre; 2hr kayak/paddleboard rentals $39/29; ⊙10am-dusk Mon-Fri, 9am-dusk Jun-Aug; ☐4) The friendly folk at Ecomarine offer gear rentals plus a wide range of guided kayak and stand-up paddleboard (SUP) tours from their seasonal Jericho Beach spot. Also run courses and even SUP yoga classes – check ahead before you arrive in town.

◷ TOURS

Sins of the City Walking Tour — Walking

(☎604-665-3346; www.sinsofthecity.ca; 240 E Cordova St, Vancouver Police Museum; adult/student $20/16; ☐14) If your criminal interests are triggered by the Vancouver Police Museum, take one of their excellent Sins of the City walking tours, which weave through Gastown and Chinatown in search of former brothels, opium dens and gambling houses. The tours last around two hours and are a great way to see the far less salubrious side of the shiny, glass-towered metropolis.

Cycle City Tours — Tours

(☎604-618-8626; www.cyclevancouver.com; 648 Hornby St; tours from $59, bicycle rental per hour/day $8.50/34; ⊙9am-6pm, reduced hours in winter; ⑤Burrard) Striped with an ever-increasing number of dedicated bike lanes, Vancouver is a good city for two-wheeled exploring. But if you're not great at navigating, consider a guided tour with this friendly operator. If you're a beer fan, aim for the Craft Beer Tour ($90), with nine tasty samples included. Alternatively, go it alone with a rental; there's a bike lane right outside.

Harbour Cruises — Boating

(☎604-688-7246; www.boatcruises.com; 501 Denman St; adult/child from $35/12; ⊙May–mid-Oct; ☐19) View the city – and some unexpected wildlife – from the water on a

75-minute narrated harbor tour, weaving past Stanley Park, Lions Gate Bridge and the North Shore mountains. There's also a lovely 2½-hour sunset dinner cruise (adult/child $83/69) plus a long, languid lunch trek to lovely Indian Arm ($72) that makes you feel like you're a million miles from the city.

Vancouver Foodie Tours   Tours

(604-295-8844; www.foodietours.ca; tours from $50) Of several culinary-themed city stroll operators that have emerged here in recent years, Vancouver Foodie Tours is one of the most popular. Engaging hosts lead diverse, sample-heavy strolls around Gastown, Granville Island or local finger-licking food trucks: the trick is not to eat before you arrive. And don't worry, the walking will burn off every single calorie you consume (perhaps).

🛍 SHOPPING

Vancouver's retail scene has developed dramatically in recent years. Hit Robson St's mainstream chains, then discover the hip, independent shops of Gastown, Main St and Commercial Dr. Granville Island is stuffed with artsy stores and studios, while South Granville and Kitsilano's 4th Ave serve up a wide range of ever-tempting boutiques.

Paper Hound   Books

(604-428-1344; www.paperhound.ca; 344 W Pender St; ☺10am-7pm Sun-Thu, to 8pm Fri & Sat; 🚊14) Proving the printed word is alive and kicking, this small but perfectly curated secondhand-book store opened a couple of years ago and has already become a dog-eared favorite among locals. It is a perfect spot for browsing your day away. You'll find tempting tomes (mostly used but some new) on everything from nature to poetry to chaos theory. Ask for recommendations: they really know their stuff here.

John Fluevog Shoes   Shoes

(604-688-6228; www.fluevog.com; 65 Water St; ☺10am-7pm Mon-Wed & Sat, to 8pm Thu &

🛍 Shop the Museums

The city's museums and galleries offer some unexpected buying opportunities. You don't have to see an exhibition to visit these shops, and keep in mind that you're helping to fund the institutions you're buying from.

Museum of Anthropology shop (p213) Perhaps the best of all the city's museum stores, this one has a fantastic array of First Nations and international indigenous artworks, ranging from elegant silver jewelry to fascinating masks.

Vancouver Art Gallery gift shop (p208) Back downtown, this is like a lifestyle store for artsy types, with clever contemporary knickknacks and large art books to leave on your coffee table.

Science World gift shop (p212) And if you need to buy something cool for a kid back home, hit the Science World gift shop for all manner of intriguing educational goodies.

Fri, noon-6pm Sun; Ⓢ Waterfront) Like an art gallery for shoes, this alluringly cavernous store showcases the famed footwear of local designer Fluevog, whose men's and women's boots and brogues are what Doc Martens would have become if they'd stayed interesting and cutting-edge. Pick up that pair of thigh-hugging dominatrix boots you've always wanted or settle on some designer loafers that would make anyone walk tall.

Eastside Flea   Market

(www.eastsideflea.com; Ellis Bldg, 1014 Main St; $3; ☺6-10pm Fri, 11am-5pm Sat & Sun 3rd weekend of the month; 🚊3) Running for years at halls around the city, the monthly flea's new Ellis Building location means 50 new and vintage vendors, plus food trucks, live music and a highly inviting atmosphere.

Neptoon Records — Music

(📞604-324-1229; www.neptoon.com; 3561 Main St; ⏰11am-6:30pm Mon-Sat, noon-5pm Sun; 🚌3) Vancouver's oldest independent record store is still a major lure for music fans, with its *High Fidelity* ambience and time-capsule feel. But it's not resting on its laurels here: you'll find a well-priced array of new and used vinyl and CD recordings, plus some serious help with finding that obscure Sigue Sigue Sputnik recording you've been looking for.

Gallery of BC Ceramics — Arts & Crafts

(📞604-669-3606; www.bcpotters.com; 1359 Cartwright St; ⏰10:30am-5:30pm; 🚌50) The star of Granville Island's arts-and-crafts shops and the public face of the Potters Guild of BC, this excellent spot exhibits and sells the striking works of its member artists. You can pick up one-of-a-kind ceramic tankards or swirly-painted soup bowls; the hot items are the cool ramen-noodle cups, complete with holes for chopsticks. It's well-priced art for everyone.

Paper-Ya — Arts & Crafts

(📞604-684-2534; www.paper-ya.com; 1666 Johnston St, Net Loft; ⏰10am-7pm; 🚌50) A magnet for slavering stationery fetishists (you know who you are), the treasure trove of trinkets here ranges from natty pens to traditional washi paper. It's not all writing-related ephemera, though. Whoever does the buying also curates an eclectic, ever-changing roster of hard-to-resist treats including cool watches, adult coloring books and well-priced animal-themed earrings (we like the bats and cat heads).

Mountain Equipment Co-Op — Sports & Outdoors

(MEC; 📞604-872-7858; www.mec.ca; 130 W Broadway; ⏰10am-9pm Mon-Fri, 9am-6pm Sat, 10am-6pm Sun, reduced hours off-season; 🚌9) Grown hikers weep at the amazing selection of clothing, kayaks, sleeping bags and clever camping gadgets at this cavernous outdoors store: MEC has been encouraging fully fledged outdoor enthusiasts for years. You'll have to be a member to buy, but that's easy to arrange for just $5.

From left: Beetroot fries; Second Beach swimming pool (p205); Seawall trail (p204); Dr Sun Yat-Sen Classical Chinese Garden & Park (p209)

Equipment – canoes, kayaks, camping gear etc – can be rented here.

Regional Assembly of Text
Arts & Crafts

(☏604-877-2247; www.assemblyoftext.com; 3934 Main St; ☺11am-6pm Mon-Sat, noon-5pm Sun; ☐3) This ironic antidote to the digital age lures ink-stained locals with its journals, handmade pencil boxes and T-shirts printed with typewriter motifs. Check out the tiny under-the-stairs gallery showcasing zines from around the world.

Kidsbooks
Books

(www.kidsbooks.ca; 2557 W Broadway; ☺9:30am-6pm Mon-Thu & Sat, 9:30am-9pm Fri, 11am-6pm Sun; ☐; ☐9) From *Squishy McFluff* to *The Great Big Dinosaur,* this huge child-friendly store – reputedly Canada's biggest kids' bookshop – has thousands of novels, picture books and anything else you can think of to keep your bookish sprogs quiet. There are also regular readings by visiting authors and a selection of quality toys and games if they need a break from all that strenuous page-turning.

⊗ EATING

Don't tell Toronto or Montrèal, but Vancouver is the real culinary capital of Canada. Loosen your belt and dive right into North America's best Asian dining scene, a smorgasbord of fresh-caught seafood, and a farm-to-table movement that's revitalized the notion of West Coast cuisine. Then there's the nation-leading craft-beer scene, plus the city's emerging craft liquor producers.

Cannibal Café
Burgers $

(☏604-558-4199; www.cannibalcafe.ca; 1818 Commercial Dr; mains $11-16; ☺11:30am-10pm Mon-Thu, 11:30am-midnight Fri, 10am-midnight Sat, 10am-10pm Sun; ☐20) This is a punk-tastic diner for fans of seriously real burgers made with love. You'll find an inventive array from classics to the recommended Korean-BBQ burger. Top-notch ingredients will ensure you never slink into a fast-food chain again. Check the board outside for daily specials and keep in mind there are happy-hour deals from 3pm to 6pm weekdays.

Commercial Drive

Coffee is a way of life on the Drive, where generations of Italian families have been serving the city's best java since arriving in the 1950s. You'll find elderly Italian grandparents rubbing shoulders with cool-ass hipsters here; they're all after the same thing – that perfect cup of coffee to see them through the day.

Tacofino   Mexican $

(☑604-899-7907; www.tacofino.com; 15 W Cordova St; tacos $6-12; 🚇14) Food-truck favorite Tacofino made an instant splash with this huge, handsome dining room (think stylish geometric-patterned floors and hive-like lampshades). The simple menu focuses on a handful of taco options (six at lunch, more at dinner), plus nachos, soups and a boozy selection of beer, agave and naughty tequila flights. Fish tacos are the top seller, but we love the super-tender lamb *birria* (stew).

There are additional menu options at dinner time but consider dropping by for happy hour, from 3pm to 6pm daily when you can scoff two tacos for $10.

Jamjar   Lebanese $

(☑604-252-3957; www.jamjaronthedrive.com; 2280 Commercial Dr; small plates $6-12, mains $17-22; ⊗11:30am-10pm; ☏; 🚇20) This super-friendly, cafe-style joint has a rustic-chic interior and a folky Lebanese menu of ethically sourced ingredients and lots of vegetarian options. You don't have to be a veggie to love the crispy falafel balls or the

utterly irresistible deep-fried cauliflower stalks – which will have you fighting for the last morsel if you made the mistake of ordering to share.

Purebread   Bakery $

(☑604-563-8060; www.purebread.ca; 159 W Hastings St; baked goods $3-6; ⊗8:30am-5:30pm; ☏; 🚇14) When Whistler's favorite bakery opened here, salivating Vancouver-ites began flocking in en masse. Expect to stand slack-jawed in front of the glass panels as you try to choose from a cornucopia of cakes, pastries and bars. Cake-wise, we love the coconut buttermilk loaf, but make sure you also pick up a crack bar or salted caramel bar to go (or preferably both).

And if you think power bars taste like the soles of old running shoes, sink your teeth into Purebread's velvet-soft go go bar, then walk it all off with a 50km stroll.

Mr Red Cafe   Vietnamese $

(☑604-559-6878; 2680 W Broadway; mains $6-14; ⊗11am-9pm; ☏; 🚇9) Serving authentic northern Vietnamese homestyle dishes that look and taste like there's a lovely old lady making them out back. Reservations are not accepted; dine off-peak to avoid waiting for the handful of tables, then dive into shareable gems like pork baguette sandwiches, *cha ca han oi* (spicy grilled fish) and the ravishing pyramidical rice dumpling, stuffed with pork and a boiled quail's egg.

Fable   Canadian $$

(☑604-732-1322; www.fablekitchen.ca; 1944 W 4th Ave; mains $19-31; ⊗11:30am-2pm Mon-Fri, 5:30-10pm Mon-Sat, brunch 10:30am-2pm Sat & Sun; 🚇4) One of Vancouver's favorite farm-to-table restaurants is a lovely rustic-chic room of exposed brick, wood beams and prominently displayed red rooster logos. But looks are just part of the appeal. Expect perfectly prepared bistro dishes show-casing local seasonal ingredients, such as duck, lamb and halibut. It's great gourmet comfort food with little pretension – hence the packed room most nights. Reservations recommended.

Dock Lunch International $$

(☑604-879-3625; 152 E 11th Ave; mains $10-14; ☺11:30am-5pm Mon-Fri, 11am-3pm Sat & Sun) Like dining in a cool hippie's home, this utterly charming room in a side-street house serves a daily-changing menu of one or two soul-food mains (think spicy tacos or heaping weekend brunches). Arrive early and aim for one of the two window seats and you'll soon be chatting with the locals or browsing the cookbooks and Huxley novels on the shelves.

Bistro 101 Canadian $$

(☑604-724-4488; www.picachef.com; 1505 W 2nd Ave; ☺11:30am-2pm & 6-9pm Mon-Fri; ☑50) Vancouver's best-value gourmet dining option, the training restaurant of the **Pacific Institute of Culinary Arts** is popular with in-the-know locals, especially at lunchtime, when $22 gets you a delicious three-course meal (typically three options for each course) plus service that's earnestly solicitous. The dinner option costs $8 more and there's a buffet offering on the first Friday of the month. Reservations recommended.

Forage Canadian $$

(☑604-661-1400; www.foragevancouver.com; 1300 Robson St; mains $16-29; ☺6:30-10am & 5pm-midnight Mon-Fri, 7am-2pm & 5pm-midnight Sat & Sun; ☑5) ✐ A champion of the local farm-to-table scene, this sustainability-friendly restaurant is the perfect way to sample the flavors of the region. Brunch has become a firm local favorite (turkey-sausage hash recommended), and for dinner the idea is to sample an array of tasting plates. The menu is innovative and highly seasonal, but look out for the seafood chowder with quail's egg. Reservations recommended.

Guu with Garlic Japanese $$

(☑604-685-8678; www.guu-izakaya.com; 1698 Robson St; small plates $4-9, mains $8-16; ☺11:30am-2:30pm & 5:30pm-12:30am Mon-Sat, 11:30am-2:30pm & 5:30pm till midnight Sun; ☑5) One of Vancouver's best *izakayas* (Japanese pubs), this welcoming, wood-lined joint is a cultural immersion. Hotpots and noodle bowls are available but it's best to experiment with some Japanese bar tapas, including black cod with miso mayo,

Gastown

deep-fried egg and pumpkin balls or fin-ger-lickin' *tori-karaage* fried chicken. Garlic is liberally used in most dishes. It's best to arrive before opening time for a seat.

Ask for Luigi   Italian $$$

(☏604-428-2544; www.askforluigi.com; 305 Alexander St; mains $22-24; ⏱11:30am-2:30pm & 5:30-10:30pm Tue-Fri, to 11pm Sat, to 9:30pm Sun; 🚌4) Consider an off-peak lunch if you don't want to wait too long for a table at this white-clapboard, shack-look little charmer (reservations are not accepted). Inside, you'll find a checkerboard floor and teak-lined interior crammed with tables and delighted diners tucking into (and sharing) plates of scratch-made pasta that mama never used to make; think bison tagliatelle and borage-and-ricotta ravioli.

Vij's   Indian $$$

(☏604-736-6664; www.vijsrestaurant.ca; 3106 Cambie St, Cambie Village; mains $19-27; ⏱5:30-10pm; ✍; 🚌15) A sparkling (and far larger) new location for Canada's favorite East Indian chef delivers a warmly sump-tuous lounge coupled with a cavernous dining area and cool rooftop patio. The menu, a high-water mark of contempo-rary Indian cuisine, fuses BC ingredients, global flourishes and classic ethnic flavors to produce many inventive dishes. Results range from signature 'lamb pop-sicles' to flavorful meals like sablefish in yogurt-tomato broth.

🍺 DRINKING & NIGHTLIFE

Callister Brewing
Company   Microbrewery

(☏604-569-2739; www.callisterbrewing.com; 1338 Franklin St; ⏱2-9pm Mon-Thu, 2-10pm Fri, 1-10pm Sat, 1-8pm Sun; 🚌14) One of the most exciting of East Van's beer district microbreweries, Callister's red-painted former industrial space exterior houses a Spartan tasting room with beer-barrel tables on a bare concrete floor. But there's nothing austere about the booze selection: four on-site nano-breweries share the same equipment to produce a wide array of differing brews. Order a selection of small-glass samples and dive right in.

'Lamb popsicles', Vij's

Storm Crow Tavern   Pub

(☏604-566-9669; www.stormcrowtavern.com; 1305 Commercial Dr; ☺11am-1am Mon-Sat, 11am-midnight Sun; 🛜; 🚌20) Knowing the difference between Narnia and *Neverwhere* is not a prerequisite at this smashing Commercial Dr nerd pub. But if you do, you'll certainly make new friends. With displays of Dr Who figures and steampunk ray-guns – plus a TV that always seems to be screening *Game of Thrones* – dive into the craft beer and settle in for a fun evening.

Mario's Coffee Express   Coffee

(595 Howe St; mains $4-8; ☺6:30am-4pm Mon-Fri; Ⓢ Burrard) A java-lover's favorite that only downtown office workers seem to know about. You'll wake up and smell the coffee long before you make it through the door here. The rich aromatic brews served up by the man himself are the kind of ambrosia that makes Starbucks drinkers weep. You might even forgive the 1980s Italian pop percolating through the shop.

Devil's Elbow Ale & Smoke House   Pub

(☏604-559-0611; www.devilselbowalehouse.com; 562 Beatty St; ☺11:30am-midnight Mon-Thu, 11:30am-1am Fri, 10am-1am Sat, 10am-midnight Sun; Ⓢ Stadium-Chinatown) A cave-like brick-and-art-lined pub that feels like a local secret, this is the place to combine barbecued grub with brews from one of BC's best microbreweries. Owned by the team behind Squamish's Howe Sound Brewing, you'll find great ales to try, from Hopraiser IPA to Father John's Winter Ale. The weekday $15 beer-included lunch deal is recommended.

Sylvia's Lounge   Bar

(☏604-681-9321; www.sylviahotel.com; 1154 Gilford St; ☺7am-11pm Sun-Thu, to midnight Fri & Sat; 🚌5) Part of the permanently popular Sylvia Hotel, this was Vancouver's first cocktail bar when it opened in the mid-1950s. Now a comfy, wood-lined neighborhood bar favored by in-the-know locals (they're the ones hogging the window seats as the sun sets dramatically over English Bay), it's a great spot for an end-of-day

---

🍴◯🍴 Vancouver's Street-Food-A-Palooza

A late starter to the North American street-food movement, Vancouver now has the tastiest scene in Canada. The downtown core has the highest concentration of trucks. You'll find everything from Korean sliders to salmon tacos, Thai green curry to barbecued brisket sandwiches. A visit that doesn't include at least one street-food meal isn't really a visit at all.

There are now more than 125 trucks on streets around the city. See www.streetfoodapp.com/vancouver for the latest locations and lineups. Catch as many trucks as you can at the annual summertime YVR Food Fest (www.yvrfoodfest.com).

---

wind down. There's live music here on Wednesdays and Thursdays.

Brickhouse   Pub

(730 Main St; ☺8pm-2am Mon-Sat, 8pm-midnight Sun; 🚌3) Possibly Vancouver's most original pub, this old-school hidden gem is a welcoming, windowless tavern lined with Christmas lights, fish tanks and junk-shop couches. It's like hanging out in someone's den, and is popular with artsy locals and in-the-know young hipsters. Grab an ale at the bar, slide onto a chair and start chatting: you're bound to meet someone interesting.

Alibi Room   Pub

(☏604-623-3383; www.alibi.ca; 157 Alexander St; ☺5-11:30pm Mon-Thu, 5pm-12:30am Fri, 10am-12:30am Sat, 10am-11:30pm Sun; 🛜; 🚌4) Vancouver's best craft-beer tavern has an exposed brick bar that stocks an ever-changing roster of around 50 drafts, mostly from celebrated BC breweries such as Driftwood, Four Winds and Yellow Dog. Adventurous taste-trippers – hipsters and veteran beer fans alike – enjoy the $11.50 'frat bat' of four samples: choose your own

From left: Commodore Ballroom; Alibi Room (p221); Kitsilano Beach (p209)

or ask to be surprised. Check the board for ever-changing guest casks.

Brassneck Brewery — Microbrewery

(☎604-259-7686; 2184 Main St; ☺2-11pm Mon-Fri, noon-11pm Sat & Sun; ☐3) Vancouver's favorite microbrewery concocted more than 50 different beers in its first six months of operating and continues to win new fans with an ever-changing chalkboard of intriguing libations with names like Bivouac Bitter, Stockholm Syndrome and Magician's Assistant. Our recommendation? The delicious Passive Aggressive dry-hopped pale ale. Arrive early for a seat in the small tasting bar, especially on weekends.

Shameful Tiki Room — Bar

(www.shamefultikiroom.com; 4362 Main St; ☺5pm-midnight Sun-Thu, to 1am Fri & Sat; ☐3) This windowless snug instantly transports you to a Polynesian beach. The lighting – including glowing puffer-fish lampshades – is permanently set to dusk and the walls are lined with tiki masks and rattan coverings under a straw-shrouded ceiling. But it's the drinks that rock: seriously well-crafted

classics from Zombies to Mai Tais to a four-person Volcano Bowl (don't forget to share it).

Catfe — Cafe

(☎778-379-0060; www.catfe.ca; International Village Mall, 88 Pender St; with/without cafe purchase $5/8; ☺11am-9pm Fri-Wed; ⓐ; ⓢStadium-Chinatown) Vancouver's only cat cafe; book online for your time slot (walk-ins may also be available), buy a coffee and then meet the moggies in the large feline play room, where at least a dozen whiskered wonders await. All the cats come from the SPCA (Society for the Prevention of Cruelty to Animals) and are available for adoption via their usual procedures.

Corduroy — Bar

(☎604-733-0162; www.corduroyrestaurant. com; 1943 Cornwall Ave; ☺4pm-2am Mon-Sat, 4pm-midnight Sun; ☐22) Handily located near the first bus stop after the Burrard Bridge (coming from downtown), this tiny spot is arguably Kitsilano's best haunt. Slide onto a bench seat and peruse the oddball artworks – junk-shop pictures and carved masks – then order a house beer from the

ASIF ISLAM / SHUTTERSTOCK ©

shingle-covered bar: if you're lucky, it'll be served in a boot-shaped glass.

Artisan Sake Maker
Brewery

(🕿604-685-7253; www.artisansakemaker.com; 1339 Railspur Alley; ⊙11:30am-6pm; 🚍50) This tiny sake producer uses locally grown rice – making it the first of its kind in Canada – and should be on everyone's Granville Island to-do list. Twinkle-eyed sake maker Masa Shiroki produces several tipples and you can dive in for a bargain $5 three-sake tasting. It's an eye-opening revelation to many drinkers who think sake is a harsh beverage. Takeout bottles are available.

Liberty Distillery
Distillery

(🕿604-558-1998; www.thelibertydistillery. com; 1494 Old Bridge St; ⊙11am-8pm; 🚍50) Vancouver's most attractive craft distillery has a handsome, saloon-like tasting room where you can gaze through windows at the shiny, steampunk-like booze-making equipment beyond. It's not all about looks, though. During happy hour (Monday to Thursday, 3pm to 6pm), sample house-made gin, vodka and white whiskey plus

great cocktails for just $6 a pop. Tours are available ($10; Saturdays and Sundays, 11:30am and 1:30pm).

❀ ENTERTAINMENT

Half-price day-of-performance tickets for shows around the city are available from **Tickets Tonight** (🕿604-684-2787; www. ticketstonight.ca; 200 Burrard St).

Commodore Ballroom
Live Music

(🕿604-739-4550; www.commodoreballroom. com; 868 Granville St; 🚍10) Local bands know they've made it when they play Vancouver's best mid-sized venue, a restored art-deco ballroom that still has the city's bounciest dance floor – courtesy of tires placed under its floorboards. If you need a break from your moshing, collapse at one of the tables lining the perimeter, catch your breath with a bottled Stella and then plunge back in.

Bard on the Beach
Performing Arts

(🕿604-739-0559; www.bardonthebeach.org; Vanier Park, 1695 Whyte Ave; tickets $20-57; ⊙Jun-Sep; 🚍22) Watching Shakespeare

Paddleboarding near Burrard Bridge

performed while the sun sets against the mountains beyond the tented stage is a Vancouver summertime highlight. There are usually three of Shakespeare's plays, plus one Bard-related work (*Rosencrantz and Guildenstern are Dead,* for example), to choose from during the run. Q&A talks are staged after Tuesday-night performances, along with regular opera, fireworks and wine-tasting nights throughout the season.

Fox Cabaret   Live Music

(www.foxcabaret.com; 2321 Main St; ☐3) New owners have transformed (and fully pressure-washed) this independent nightlife venue, formerly one of North America's last-remaining porn cinemas, ditching the dodgy flicks in favour of live music, DJ nights and regular events like Saturday's Alternative Dance Party and Sunday's popular comedy night. Check the online calendar before you arrive in town; there's always something eclectic on stage in this narrow, high-ceilinged venue.

Pacific Cinémathèque   Cinema

(☑604-688-3456; www.thecinematheque.ca; 1131 Howe St; tickets $11, double bills $16; ☐10) This beloved cinema operates like an ongoing film festival with a daily-changing program of movies. A $3 annual membership is required – organize it at the door – before you can skulk in the dark with other chin-stroking movie buffs who probably named their children (or pets) after Fellini and Bergman.

Rickshaw Theatre   Live Music

(☑604-681-8915; www.liveatrickshaw.com; 254 E Hastings St; ☐14) Revamped from its grungy 1970s incarnation, the funky Rickshaw shows that Eastside gentrification can be positive. The stage of choice for many punk and indie acts, it's an excellent place to see a band. There's a huge mosh area near the stage and rows of theater-style seats at the back.

Vancouver Poetry Slam   Performing Arts

(www.cafedeuxsoleils.com; Cafe Deux Soleils, 2096 Commercial Dr; tickets $6-10; ☉7pm

Mon; ⑤Commercial-Broadway) If you thought poetry was a tweedy, soporific experience, check out the events organized by the Vancouver Poetry House at Cafe Deux Soleils for a taste of high-speed, high-stakes slamming. The expert performers will blow your socks off with their verbal dexterity, which often bears more than a passing resemblance to rap. Every fourth Monday is also Youth Slam.

ⓘ INFORMATION

INTERNET ACCESS

Most Vancouver hotels provide in-room wi-fi or (less-often) high-speed cable internet services for guests. It's usually free but check with your hotel when booking.

Coffee-shop chains Blenz (www.blenz. com), Take 5 (www.take5cafe.ca) and Waves (www.wavescoffee.com) have free wi-fi. The **Vancouver Public Library** (☑604-331-3603; www.vpl.ca; 350 W Georgia St; ⊘10am-9pm Mon-Thu, 10am-6pm Fri & Sat, 11am-6pm Sun; 🛜; ⑤Stadium-Chinatown) also offers free wi-fi and internet-enabled computers.

TOURIST INFORMATION

Tourism Vancouver Visitor Centre (☑604-683-2000; www.tourismvancouver.com; 200 Burrard St; ⊘8:30am-5pm; ⑤Waterfront) Large repository of resources for visitors; services and info available include free maps, visitor guides, half-price theater tickets, and accommodation and tour bookings.

ⓘ GETTING THERE & AWAY

AIR

Canada's second-busiest airport, **Vancouver International** (YVR; ☑604-207-7077; www.yvr. ca; 🛜) lies 13km south of downtown in the city of Richmond.

BUS

Most intercity nontransit buses trundle to a halt at Vancouver's neon-signed Pacific Central train station. It's the main arrival point for cross-Canada and transborder Greyhound buses

Canadian Dance Hub

Vancouver is a major center for Canadian dance, offering an esoteric array of classical ballet and edgy contemporary fare. The city is home to more than 30 professional companies as well as many internationally recognized choreographers. To touch base with the region's hotfoot crowd, pirouette over to downtown's **Dance Centre** (☑604-606-6400; www.thedancecentre.ca; 677 Davie St; ☐10). Also, plan your visit to coincide with July's **Dancing on the Edge festival** (www.dancingonthe edge.org).

(www.greyhound.com, www.greyhound.ca); cross-border budget bus services on Bolt Bus (www.boltbus.com); and services from Seattle and Seattle's Sea-Tac International Airport on Quick Shuttle (www.quickcoach.com).

BOAT

Main services to Tsawwassen arrive from Vancouver Island's Swartz Bay, near Victoria, and Duke Point, near Nanaimo. Services also arrive from the Southern Gulf Islands. From Horseshoe Bay to downtown, take bus 257 (adult/child $4/2.75, 45 minutes), which is faster than bus 250. It takes about 35 minutes.

TRAIN

Pacific Central Station (1150 Station St; ⑤Main St-Science World) is the city's main terminus for long-distance trains from across Canada on VIA Rail (www.viarail.com), and from Seattle (just south of the border) and beyond on Amtrak (www. amtrak.com). The Main St-Science World SkyTrain station is just across the street for connections to downtown and beyond.

ⓘ GETTING AROUND

TO/FROM THE AIRPORT

SkyTrain's Canada Line operates a rapid-transit train service from the airport to downtown.

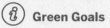 **Green Goals**

Vancouver has an active plan to be the world's greenest city by 2020. Among its raft of goals, the city aims to drastically cut waste and carbon emissions, as well as improve regional ecosystems.

Trains run every few minutes from early morning until after midnight and take around 25 minutes to reach downtown's Waterfront Station. A taxi downtown (around 30 minutes) will usually cost between $35 and $45, plus tip (15% is the norm).

BICYCLE

○ Vancouver is a relatively good cycling city, with more than 300km of designated routes crisscrossing the region. In 2016, a new public bike-share scheme called **Mobi** (www.mobibikes.ca) was introduced.

○ Cyclists can take their bikes for free on SkyTrains, SeaBuses and transit buses, which are all now fitted with bike racks. Cyclists are required by law to wear helmets.

BOAT

○ The iconic SeaBus shuttle is part of the TransLink transit system (regular transit fares apply) and it operates throughout the day, taking 12 minutes to cross Burrard Inlet between Waterfront Station and Lonsdale Quay in North Vancouver.

○ Tickets must be purchased from vending machines on either side of the route before boarding.

BUS

○ Vancouver's TransLink (www.translink.ca) bus network is extensive. Exact change is required; buses use fare machines and change is not given. Fares cost $2.75/1.75 per adult/child and are valid for up to 90 minutes of transfer travel.

○ Bus services operate from early morning to after midnight in central areas. There is also a handy night-bus system that runs every 30 minutes between 1:30am and 4am.

CAR & MOTORCYCLE

For sightseeing in the city, you'll be fine without a car. For visits that incorporate the wider region's mountains and communities, however, a vehicle makes life much simpler.

Most major car-rental agencies have desks at the airport and around the city.

TRAIN

○ TransLink's SkyTrain rapid-transit network (www.translink.bc.ca) currently consists of three routes. A fourth route, the Evergreen Line, is scheduled to begin operations in 2017.

○ Compass tickets for SkyTrain trips can be purchased from station vending machines prior to boarding.

○ SkyTrain journeys cost $2.75 to $5.50 (plus $5 more if you're traveling from the airport), depending on how far you are going.

TAXI

Vancouver currently does not allow Uber-type services. Taxis include:

Black Top & Checker Cabs (☏604-731-1111; www.btccabs.ca; 🖃)

Vancouver Taxi (☏604-871-1111; www.vancouvertaxi.cab)

Yellow Cab (☏604-681-1111; www.yellowcabonline.com; 🖃).

Where to Stay

Be aware that there will be some significant additions to most quoted room rates. You'll pay an extra 8% Provincial Sales Tax (PST) plus 5% Goods and Services Tax (GST) and an additional 3% Hotel Room Tax.

Neighborhood	Atmosphere
Downtown	Walking distance to stores, restaurants, nightlife and some attractions; great transit links to wider region; good range of hotels. Can be pricey; some accommodations overlook noisy traffic areas.
West End	Walking distance to Stanley Park; many midrange restaurants nearby; heart of the gay district; quiet residential streets; mostly high-end B&Bs with a couple of additional chain hotels. Can be a bit of a hike to the city center.
Yaletown & Granville Island	Close to shops and many restaurants; good transport links to other areas. Few accommodation options to choose from.
Fairview & South Granville	Quiet residential streets; well-priced heritage B&B sleepovers; good bus and SkyTrain access to downtown. Few local nightlife options.
Kitsilano & UBC	Comfy heritage houses and good UBC budget options; direct transit to downtown; on the doorstep of several beaches. Scant nightlife options; can feel a bit too quiet and laid-back.
North Shore	Better hotel rates than city center; handy access to downtown via SeaBus; close to popular attractions such as Grouse Mountain and Capilano Suspension Bridge. Takes time to get to other major attractions.

Craigdarroch Castle (p236), Victoria

VANCOUVER ISLAND

Vancouver Island at a Glance...

Comparable in size to Taiwan or the Netherlands, Vancouver Island is just a short ferry hop from the mainland, but feels worlds away. Victoria, the charming provincial capital, has a distinctive English feel with double-decker buses and high tea, while the rest of the island is studded with colorful communities and a lot of rugged wilderness. Witness a salmon run, surf Tofino's endless Long Beach, sample local wine and cheese, and see the biggest trees of your life. Vancouver Island is not shy of wowing visitors.

Two Days on Vancouver Island

Spend a day exploring **Victoria** (p236), taking in **Craigdarroch Castle** (p236) and the **Royal BC Museum** (p236) before wandering through **Chinatown** (p232). In summer or early autumn, head to **Fisherman's Wharf** (p236) for ice cream, and hop aboard a whale-watching **tour** (p236). On day two, head to **Goldstream Provincial Park** (p237) to get a taste of the forest. End the day with a live show at the **Royal Theatre** (p240).

Four Days on Vancouver Island

Head up island to **Parksville** (p240) for a day spent on long stretches of warm sand. Visit **Morningstar Farm** (p240) and shop for things you didn't know you needed at **Coombs** (p241). On day three, cross the island to **Tofino** (p234), stopping at Cathedral Grove en route. Take a long walk on Long Beach or test your surfing skills. Visit **Eagle Aerie Gallery** (p235) and then chill like the locals.

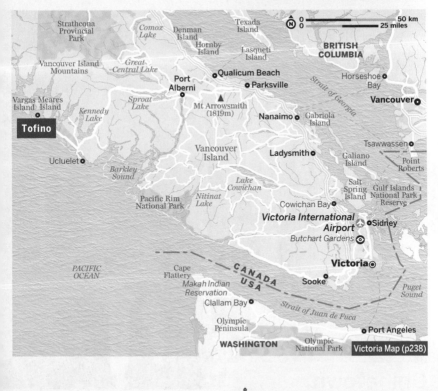

Arriving on Vancouver Island

Victoria International Airport YYJ Airport Shuttle (www.yyjairportshuttle.com) buses run to downtown Victoria ($25, 30 minutes). A taxi costs around $50.

BC Ferries (www.bcferries.com) Arrive from mainland Tsawwassen at Swartz Bay, 27km north of Victoria (take bus 70 or 72).

Harbour Air (www.harbourair.com) Floatplane services arrive into Victoria's Inner Harbour.

Where to Stay

The island is lined with accommodation options, from the swank hotels of Victoria to the luxe boutique resorts of the west coast. Tofino is notoriously pricey, but Ucluelet up the road offers better deals. Elsewhere, you'll find campgrounds, boutique spa hotels and some of BC's best hostels.

Fan Tan Alley

Chinatown

Canada's oldest – and perhaps smallest – Chinatown welcomes visitors with a bright traditional gate, vintage shops and cozy cafes.

Great For...

☑ Don't Miss

Chinatown's fabulous New Year's celebration and Dragon Dance parade if you're visiting in January/February.

History

Established in 1858, Victoria's Chinatown had a population of 3283 by the turn of the century, with 189 Chinese companies. A major entry port for Asian immigration to Canada, Victoria's Chinatown was the springboard for several thousand Chinese miners hit with gold rush fever and for 15,000 Chinese builders hired to build the Canadian Pacific Railway. Once the largest Chinese settlement in Canada, it had a fully functioning school, a newspaper and a community organization that served as an advocate for Chinese immigrants' rights. Today the community is still home to a Chinese school, a local Chinese newspaper, acupuncture clinics and Chinese charities.

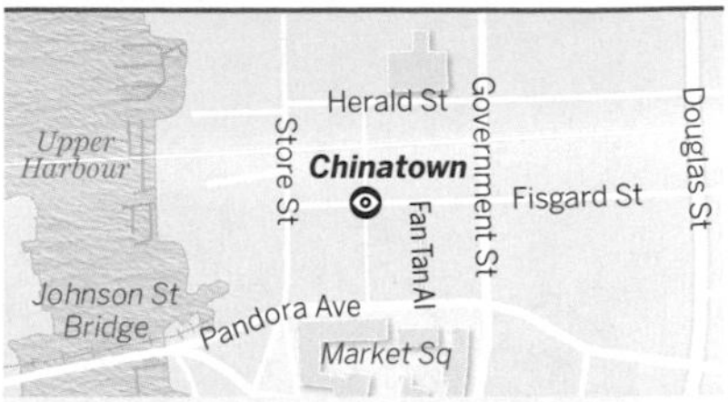

Need to Know

Check out www.chinatown.library.uvic.ca for history, shops and events.

Take a Break

Stop for a spot of tea, thin-sliced sandwiches and something sweet at Venus Sophia (p237).

★ Top Tip

If you want to dig deeper, join a guided Chinatown amble with Discover the Past (p236).

Fan Tan Alley

The atmospheric and very narrow Fan Tan Alley was once the site of opium factories and gambling dens and named after a popular betting game. Running the block between Fisgard St and Pandora Ave, it's believed to be the narrowest street in North America – ranging from 6ft to just 3ft wide.

By the 1960s, with opium and gambling gone, the alley was all but boarded up and the city, considering it a fire hazard, slated it for the wrecking ball. Chinatown itself was not in top form, with many closed or condemned buildings. Few knew of the cultural life that continued behind the scenes.

The local Chinese charities and some residents took action. To restore the alley, artists were offered cheap studio and living space in the alley in exchange for renovations. Slowly, Chinatown was revitalized to where it is now. Wander down Fan Tan Alley today and discover a warren of cool boutiques, yoga studios and a used record store. Keep your eyes peeled near the Fisgard end of the alley for a doorkeeper's peephole that would once have been used to alert locals of a police raid.

Shopping

It's a good thing Chinatown isn't any bigger; you'd never finish shopping. But a couple of must-sees include **Fantan Trading Ltd** (250-381-8882; 551 Fisgard St; 10am-5:30pm Mon-Sat, 11:30am-5:30pm Sun), a labyrinthine Chinatown fixture hawking everything from paper lanterns to fake bonsai trees, and **Fan Tan Home & Style** (250-382-4424; www.fantanvictoria.com; 541 Fisgard St; 10am-5:30pm Mon-Sat, noon-5pm Sun; 70), in a vintage Chinatown building for must-have furnishings, accessories and bath products – plus locally made artisan jewelry.

BRUCE POLLOCK / EYEEM / GETTY IMAGES ©

Tofino

From resource outpost to hippie enclave to resort town, Tofino remains Vancouver Island's favorite outdoorsy retreat.

Great For...

☑ Don't Miss

Cathedral Grove, en route to Tofino, with an easy trail winding through a forest of hulking 800-year-old trees.

Surfing

Picture-perfect Long Beach is perfect for walks, sandcastle building and sunbathing. It's also a favorite haunt of surfers. Standing on the ocean's edge and watching the Pacific pound in, there's a good chance you'll want to join them. Check out **Pacific Surf School** (www.pacificsurfschool.com; 430 Campbell St; board rental 6/24hr $15/20) or **Surf Sister** (☑250-725-4456; www.surfsister. com; 625 Campbell St; lessons $79) for lessons and equipment.

On the Water

Join **Remote Passages** (☑250-725-3380; www.remotepassages.com; 51 Wharf St; tours from $64) or **Tofino Sea Kayaking** (☑250-725-4222; www.tofinoseakayaking.com; 320 Main St; tours from $64) to kayak through Clayoquot Sound, or paddle the waves in

❶ Need to Know

Tourism Tofino Visitor Centre (☑250-725-3414; www.tourismtofino.com; 1426 Pacific Rim Hwy; ◷9am-8pm Jun-Aug, reduced hours off-season)

✕ Take a Break

Woodsy **Shelter** (☑250-725-3353; www.shelterrestaurant.com; 601 Campbell St; mains $12-32; ◷11am-midnight) serves gourmet comfort grub.

★ Top Tip

The drive here is spectacular, but if you're short on time, Orca Airways (www.flyorcaair.com) flies from Vancouver.

---

man Beach, Long Beach, Second Bay and Wickaninnish Beach.

Meares Island

Visible through the mist and accessible via kayak or tour boat from the Tofino waterfront, Meares Island is home to the Big Tree Trail, a 400m boardwalk through old-growth forest that includes a stunning 1500-year-old red cedar. The island was the site of the key 1984 Clayoquot Sound anti-logging protest that kicked off the region's latter-day environmental movement.

Eagle Aerie Gallery

Showcasing the work of world-renowned First Nations artist Roy Henry Vickers, this dramatic, longhouse-style **gallery** (☑250-725-3235; www.royhenryvickers.com; 350 Campbell St; ◷10am-5pm) is a downtown landmark. Inside you'll find beautifully presented paintings and carvings as well as occasional opportunities to meet the man himself.

a canoe with a First Nations guide with **T'ashii Paddle School** (☑250-266-3787; www.tofinopaddle.com; 1258 Pacific Rim Hwy; tours from $65). The waters around Tofino are also a great place to experience those graceful giants of the sea – **Jamie's Whaling Station** (☑250-725-3919; www.jamies.com; 606 Campbell St; adult/child $109/79) will take you out in search of orcas.

Storm-Watching

Started as a clever marketing ploy to lure off-season visitors, storm-watching has become a popular reason to visit the island's wild west coast between November and March. View spectacularly crashing winter waves, then scamper back inside for hot chocolate with a face freckled by sea salt. The best spots to catch a few crashing spectacles are Cox Bay, Chester-

Victoria

This picture-postcard provincial capital is fueled by an increasingly younger demographic, with hip shops, coffee bars and innovative restaurants that would make any city proud. Activity fans should also hop on their bikes: Victoria has more cycle routes than any other Canadian city. There's also BC's best museum, a park fringed by a windswept seafront and outdoor activities from kayaking to whale-watching.

◎ SIGHTS

Royal BC Museum　　　　Museum
(☑250-356-7226; www.royalbcmuseum.bc.ca; 675 Belleville St; adult/child from $16/11; ☺10am-5pm daily, to 10pm Fri & Sat mid-May–Sep; ♿; 🚌70) This is not your average museum. With a hulking woolly mammoth, Captain Vancouver's ship to climb through and a longhouse to relax in and an Old Town from the 1890s, complete with a cinema and train station – it's far from dull. There are also changing exhibits that might explore anything from gold panning to dinosaurs. The on-site IMAX shows related films.

Craigdarroch Castle　　　　Museum
(☑250-592-5323; www.thecastle.ca; 1050 Joan Cres; adult/child $14/5; ☺9am-7pm mid-Jun–Aug, 10am-4:30pm Sep–mid-Jun; 🅿; 🚌14) One of Canada's finest stately home attractions, this elegant turreted mansion illuminates the lives of the city's Victorian-era super-rich. Lined with sumptuous wood paneling and stained-glass windows, the rooms are teeming with period antiques, giving the impression the residents have just stepped away from their chairs. Climb the tower's 87 steps for distant views of the Olympic Mountains. Save time to read up on the often-tragic story behind the family that lived here.

Beacon Hill Park　　　　Park
(www.beaconhillpark.ca; Douglas St; 🅿♿; 🚌3) Fringed by crashing ocean, this waterfront park is ideal for feeling the breeze in your hair – check out the windswept trees along the clifftop. You'll also find a gigantic totem

pole, a Victorian cricket pitch and a marker for Mile 0 of Hwy 1, alongside a statue of Canadian legend Terry Fox. If you're here with kids, consider the popular **children's farm** (www.beaconhillchildrensfarm.ca) as well.

Fisherman's Wharf　　　　Landmark
(www.fishermanswharfvictoria.com; Just off Fisherman's Wharf Park; 🅿; 🚌30) A waterfront walk from the Inner Harbour (or, even better, a short hop by mini ferry) delivers you to this floating, boardwalk-linked clutch of houseboats, shops and eateries (including fish-and-chips). A fun and easy excursion for an hour or so.

☞ TOURS

Eagle Wing Tours　　　　Whale-Watching
(☑250-999-0502; www.eaglewingtours.ca; 12 Erie St, Fisherman's Wharf; adult/child $125/95; ☺Mar-Oct) Popular and long-established whale-watching boat tour operator.

Architectural Institute of BC　　　　Walking
(☑604-683-8588, ext 325; www.aibc.ca; tours $10; ☺10am & 1pm Tue-Sun Jul & Aug) Five great-value, history and building-themed walking tours, covering angles from ecclesiastical to Canada's oldest Chinatown. All tours start at the downtown visitor center.

Pedaler　　　　Cycling
(☑778-265-7433; www.thepedaler.ca; 719 Douglas St; tours from $49, rentals from $10; ☺9am-6pm, reduced hours off-season) Offering bike rentals and several guided two-wheeled tours around the city, including the Hoppy Hour Ride with its craft-beer-sampling focus.

Ocean River Sports　　　　Kayaking
(☑250-381-4233; www.oceanriver.com; 1824 Store St; rental per 2hr $40, tours from $75; ☺9:30am-6pm Mon-Fri, to 6pm Sat, 10am-5pm Sun) Rentals and kayak day tours in the area (including evening options). Stand up paddleboarding and multiday tours also available.

Discover the Past　　　　Walking
(☑250-384-6698; www.discoverthepast.com; adult/child $15/13; ☺10:30am Sat year-round,

plus Tue & Thu Jun-Aug) Offers ghost walks and history walks; its Chinatown Walks option is the best way to explore the stories behind one of the city's oldest neighborhoods.

🄰 SHOPPING

Ditch Records   Music
(📞250-386-5874; 784 Fort St; ⊘10am-6pm Mon-Sat, 11am-5pm Sun; 🚌14) A fave record store among the locals, Ditch is lined with tempting vinyl, plenty of CDs and many furtive musos perusing releases by acts like Frazey Ford and Nightmares on Wax. An ideal rainy-day hangout, but if it suddenly feels like time to socialize, you can book gig tickets here, too.

Rogers' Chocolates   Food
(📞250-881-8771; www.rogerschocolates.com; 913 Government St; ⊘9:30am-7pm; 🚌70) This charming, museum-like confectioner serves the best ice-cream bars, but repeat offenders usually spend their time hitting the menu of rich Victoria Creams, one of which is usually enough to substitute for lunch. Varieties range from peppermint to seasonal specialties and they're good souvenirs, so long as you don't scoff them all before you get home (which you will).

✖ EATING

Pagliacci's   Italian $$
(📞250-386-1662; www.pagliaccis.ca; 110 Broad St; mains $12-25; ⊘11:30am-3pm & 5:30-10pm, to 11pm Fri & Sat; 🚌70) A local legend that's often elbow-to-elbow packed on busy evenings, this New York–style Italian restaurant serves great pasta dishes often with a West Coast or regional seafood twist. Save room for a hulking slice of cheesecake but make sure you share it with everyone at your table (and any tables nearby).

Pink Bicycle   Burgers $$
(📞250-384-1008; www.pinkbicycleburger.com; 1008 Blanshard St; mains $13-16; ⊘11:30am-9pm Mon-Sat; 🛜; 🚌14) The city's best gourmet burger joint – nip inside and you'll be

⤵ Goldstream Provincial Park

You don't have to go far to experience that great big wilderness. Just 16km from Victoria, **Goldstream Provincial Park** (📞250-478-9414; www.goldstreampark.com; 2930 Trans-Canada Hwy; 🅿) offers an easy wander through woods that are home to the occasional bear or cougar and 600-year-old trees. Come in late October to experience the phenomenal salmon run. Head to the park's visitor center for area info and natural-history exhibits.

Aside from nature watching, you'll also find great hiking: marked trails range from tough to easy and some are wheelchair accessible. Recommended treks include the hike to 47.5m-high Niagara Falls (not that one) and the steep, strenuous route to the top of Mt Finlayson, one of the region's highest promontories.

Goldstream River
WINDCOAST / SHUTTERSTOCK ©

joining chatty locals who'll never go back to regular fast food. Spend time perusing the menu of more than a dozen made-with-love varieties, then dive into a blue-cheese lamb burger or maple salmon burger. Feeling naughty? Go for a side of truffle fries.

Venus Sophia   Vegetarian $$
(📞250-590-3953; www.venussophia.com; 540 Fisgard St; mains $10-19; ⊘10am-6pm Jul & Aug, 11am-6pm Wed-Sun Sep-Jun; 🍴; 🚌70) A delightful tearoom combining traditional tea service (including a lovely afternoon tea) with beautifully presented vegetarian lunches, this is a uniquely tranquil respite from Chinatown's sometimes busy streets.

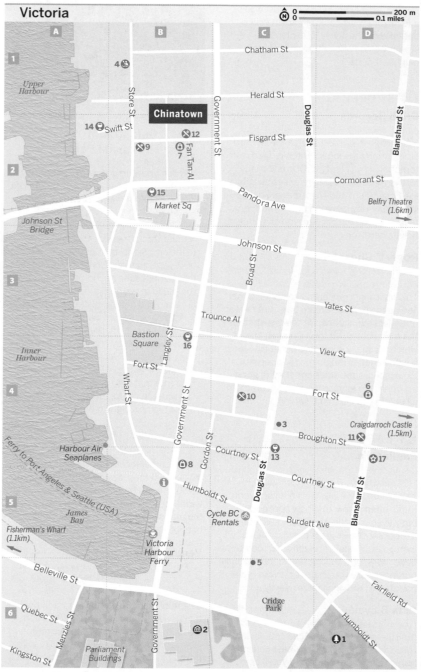

Victoria

Chinatown

Upper Harbour

Store St

Chatham St

Herald St

Government St

Fisgard St

Douglas St

Blanshard St

Cormorant St

Belfry Theatre
(1.6km)

14 Swift St

4

12

9

7 Fan Tan Al

15

Market Sq

Pandora Ave

Johnson St
Bridge

Johnson St

Broad St

Yates St

Trounce Al

Inner
Harbour

Bastion
Square

Langley St

16

View St

Fort St

Fort St

6

Wharf St

10

Craigdarroch Castle
(1.5km)

Government St

Gordon St

3

Broughton St

11

Ferry to Port Angeles & Seattle (USA)

Harbour Air
Seaplanes

Courtney St

13

17

8

Courtney St

Humboldt St

Douglas St

Blanshard St

James
Bay

Cycle BC
Rentals

Burdett Ave

Fisherman's Wharf
(1.1km)

Victoria
Harbour
Ferry

5

Belleville St

Fairfield Rd

Quebec St

Menzies St

Cridge
Park

Humboldt St

Government St

Kingston St

Parliament
Buildings

2

1

Victoria

Try the blue-cheese-and-pear panino and an organic tea (served in mismatched vintage cups) from the wide selection.

Olo   Canadian $$$
(☑250-590-8795; www.olorestaurant.com; 509 Fisgard St; mains $24-30; ☺5pm-midnight Sun-Thu, to 1am Fri & Sat; ✐) Slightly confusingly re-invented from the Ulla restaurant that used to be here, version 2.0 ploughs the farm-to-table furrow even deeper. The sophisticated seasonal menu can include anything from Quadra Island scallops to local smoked duck breast, but the multicourse, family-style tasting menu is the way to go if you're feeling flush (from $45 per person).

⊙ DRINKING & NIGHTLIFE

Canoe Brewpub   Pub
(☑250-361-1940; www.canoebrewpub.com; 450 Swift St; ☺11:30am-11pm Sun-Wed, to midnight Thu, to 1am Fri & Sat; ☑70) The cavernous brick-lined interior is great on rainy days, but the patio is also the best in the city with its usually sunny views over the harbor. Indulge in on-site-brewed treats, like the hoppy lager and the summer-friendly honey wheat ale. Grub is also high on the menu, with the mussels recommended.

Drake   Bar
(☑250-590-9075; www.drakeeatery.com; 517 Pandora Ave; ☺11:30am-midnight; ☎; ☑70) Victoria's best taphouse, this redbrick hangout has more than 30 amazing craft drafts, in-cluding revered BC producers like Townsite, Driftwood and Four Winds. Arrive on a rainy afternoon and you'll find yourself still here several hours later. Food-wise, the smoked tuna club is a top-seller but the cheese and charcuterie plates are ideal for grazing.

Garrick's Head Pub   Pub
(☑250-384-6835; www.garrickshead.com; 66 Bastion Sq; ☺11am-late; ☑70) Great spot to dive into BC's brilliant craft-beer scene. Pull up a perch at the long bar and you'll be faced with 55-plus taps serving a comprehensive menu of beers from Driftwood, Phillips, Hoyne and beyond. There are always 10 rotating lines with intriguing tipples (ask for samples) plus a comfort-grub menu of burgers et al to line your boozy stomach.

Big Bad John's   Pub
(☑250-383-7137; www.strathconahotel.com; 919 Douglas St; ☺noon-2am; ☑70) Easily missed from the outside, this dark little hillbilly-themed bar feels like you've stepped into the backwoods. But rather than some dodgy banjo players with mismatched ears, you'll find good-time locals enjoying the cave-like ambience of peanut-shell-covered floors and a ceiling dotted with old bras.

⊙ ENTERTAINMENT

Belfry Theatre   Theater
(☑250-385-6815; www.belfry.bc.ca; 1291 Gladstone Ave; ☑22) A 20-minute stroll from downtown, the celebrated Belfry Theatre

showcases contemporary plays in its lovely former-church-building venue.

Royal Theatre   Theater

(📞888-717-6121; www.rmts.bc.ca; 805 Brought-on St; 🚌70) With a rococo interior, the Royal Theatre hosts mainstream theater productions, and is home to the Victoria Symphony and Pacific Opera Victoria.

🛈 INFORMATION

Tourism Victoria Visitor Centre (📞250-953-2033; www.tourismvictoria.com; 812 Wharf St; ⊙8:30am-8:30pm mid-May–Aug, 9am-5pm Sep–mid-May; 🚌70) Busy, flyer-lined visitor center overlooking the Inner Harbour.

🛈 GETTING THERE & AWAY

AIR

Harbour Air (📞250-384-2215; www.harbourair.com) flies into the Inner Harbour from downtown Vancouver ($205, 30 minutes).

Victoria International Airport (📞250-953-7500; www.victoriaairport.com) is 26km north of the city via Hwy 17. Frequent Air Canada (www.aircanada.com) services arrive from Vancouver ($169, 25 minutes), while Westjet (www.westjet.com) flights arrive from Calgary ($265, 1½ hours). Both offer cross-Canada connections.

BOAT

BC Ferries (📞250-386-3431; www.bcferries.com) arrive from mainland Tsawwassen (adult/vehicle $17/56, 1½ hours) at Swartz Bay, 27km north of Victoria via Hwy 17.

Victoria Clipper (📞250-382-8100; www.clippervacations.com) runs from Victoria's Inner Harbour to Seattle (adult/child US$109/54, three hours, up to twice daily). **Black Ball Transport** (📞250-386-2202; www.ferrytovictoria.com) serves Port Angeles (adult/child/vehicle US$18.50/9.25/64, 1½ hours, up to four daily).

BUS

Buses rolling into the city include Greyhound Canada (www.greyhound.ca) services from Nanaimo ($26, two hours, up to six daily) and **Tofino Bus** (📞250-725-2871; www.tofinobus.com) services

from points across the rest of the island. Frequent **BC Ferries Connector** (📞778-265-9474; www.bcfconnector.com) services, via the ferry, arrive from Vancouver (from $45, 3½ hours) and Vancouver International Airport ($50, four hours).

🛈 GETTING AROUND

BICYCLE

Victoria is a great cycling capital, with routes crisscrossing the city and beyond. Check the website of the Greater Victoria Cycling Coalition (www.gvcc.bc.ca) for local resources. Bike rentals are offered by **Cycle BC Rentals** (📞250-380-2453; www.cyclebc.ca; 685 Humboldt St; 🚌1).

BOAT

Victoria Harbour Ferry (📞250-708-0201; www.victoriaharbourferry.com; fares from $6) covers the Inner Harbour and beyond with its colorful armada of little boats.

BUS

Victoria Regional Transit (www.bctransit.com/victoria) buses (fare/day pass $2.50/5) cover a wide area from Sidney to Sooke, with some routes served by modern-day double-deckers. Children under five travel free.

TAXI

Call **Yellow Cab** (📞250-381-2222; www.yellowcabvictoria.com) or **BlueBird Cabs** (📞250-382-2222; www.taxicab.com).

Parksville & Qualicum

This popular mid-island seaside region, which also includes rustic Coombs, has been a traditional destination for vacationing families for decades. Look past the water parks and miniature-golf attractions and you'll see why. The beaches here are huge and sandy with calmer water than on the island's west coast.

◎ SIGHTS

Morningstar Farm   Farm

(📞250-954-3931; www.morningstarfarm.ca; 403 Lowry's Rd, Parksville; ⊙9am-5pm; 👶)

JENNY T / SHUTTERSTOCK ©

Fisherman's Wharf (p236), Victoria

FREE Check out the region's 'locavore' credentials at this delightful and highly welcoming working farmstead. Let your kids run wild – most will quickly fall in love with the rabbits – then hunt down some samples from the on-site Little Qualicum Cheeseworks and Mooberry Winery: Bleu Claire cheese is recommended, along with a bottle of velvety blueberry wine to go.

Coombs Old
Country Market   Market

(☏250-248-6272; www.oldcountrymarket. com; 2326 Alberni Hwy, Coombs; ☺9am-7pm) The mother of all pit stops, this sprawling, ever-expanding indoor food and crafts menagerie is stuffed with bakery and produce delectables. It attracts huge numbers of visitors on summer days, when cameras are pointed at the grassy roof, where a herd of goats spend the season. Nip inside for giant ice-cream cones, heaping pizzas and the deli makings of a great picnic. Souvenir required? Grab a Billy Gruff chocolate bar.

🍴 EATING

Bistro 694   Canadian $$

(☏250-752-0301; www.bistro694.com; 694 Memorial Ave, Qualicum Beach; mains $21-30; ☺4pm-9pm Wed-Sun) Ask the locals and they'll tell you to cancel your dinner plans and head straight here. You'll find an intimate, candlelit dining room little bigger than a train carriage and a big-city menu fusing top-notch regional ingredients with knowing international nods. We favor the seafood route, especially if the Balinese prawn curry or highly addictive seafood crepes are available. Reserve ahead.

ℹ INFORMATION

For more information on the area visit www. parksvillequalicumbeach.com.

ℹ GETTING THERE & AWAY

Tofino Bus services arrive in Parksville from Victoria ($35, two to three hours, three daily) and Nanaimo ($17, 30 minutes, three daily) among others.

HAIDA GWAII

Haida Gwaii at a Glance...

The bewitching Haida Gwaii is a lush archipelago of some 450 islands lying 80km west of the British Columbia coast. The number-one attraction is remote Gwaii Haanas National Park, nicknamed 'Canada's Galápagos' and brimming with unique species of flora and fauna. The real soul of the islands, however, is the Haida culture itself. Haida reverence for the environment is protecting the last stands of superb old-growth rainforests, where the spruce and cedars are some of the world's largest. Amid this sparsely populated, wild and rainy place are bald eagles and bears, while off-shore, sea lions, whales and orcas abound.

One Day in Haida Gwaii

Get your culture fix at **Haida Heritage Centre** (p246) at Kay Llnagaay in Skidegate. Head north through the dense forest toward Masset, exploring the small towns of Tlell and Port Clements en route and visiting the **Port Clements Museum** (p250). In Masset, explore the **Dixon Entrance Maritime Museum** (p250) and check out local artwork. Treat yourself to dinner at **Charters Restaurant** (p251).

Two Days in Haida Gwaii

Join a one-day boat tour with **Haida Style Expeditions** (p249) to see the highlights of **Gwaii Haanas National Park Reserve** (p248), including cultural sites and a midday traditional Haida feast.

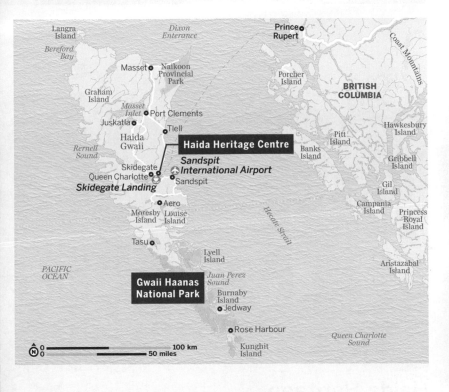

Map labels:
Langra Island
Dixon Enterance
Prince Rupert
Coast Mountains
Bereford Bay
Masset
Naikoon Provincial Park
Porcher Island
BRITISH COLUMBIA
Graham Island
Masset Inlet Port Clements
Juskatla
Tlell
Hawkesbury Island
Haida Gwaii
Haida Heritage Centre
Pitt Island
Rernell Sound
Sandspit International Airport
Banks Island
Gribbell Island
Skidegate
Queen Charlotte
Sandspit
Gil Island
Skidegate Landing
Aero
Campania Island
Princess Royal Island
Moresby Island
Louise Island
Hecate Strait
Tasu
Lyell Island
Aristazabal Island
PACIFIC OCEAN
Juan Perez Sound
Gwaii Haanas National Park
Burnaby Island
Jedway
Rose Harbour
Queen Charlotte Sound
Kunghit Island
N 0 — 100 km
0 — 50 miles

Arriving in Haida Gwaii

Sandspit International Airport Located on Moresby Island, 12km east of the ferry landing at Aliford Bay. There are daily Air Canada flights from Vancouver.

Skidegate Landing BC Ferries from Prince Rupert dock here on Graham Island.

Where to Stay

Small inns and B&Bs are mostly found on Graham Island. There are numerous choices in Queen Charlotte (QCC) and Masset, with many in between and along the spectacular north coast. Naikoon Provincial Park has two campgrounds, including a dramatic, windswept one on deserted Agate Beach, 23km east of Masset.

Haida Heritage Centre

One of the top attractions in the north, this marvelous cultural center celebrates the rich traditions of the Haida.

A visit to the Heritage Centre at Kay Llnagaay gives visitors a glimpse into the Haida's traditions and living culture.

Totem Poles

Even if you're not lucky enough to see one being carved, a tour of the center's iconic totem poles will fill you in on the animals, crests and stories that they tell.

Endangered Language

The Haida language, X̱aayda Kil, is both tricky and beautiful. One of the 52 First Nations languages in Canada, it is unique in both its sound and construction and not closely related to any other language. Originally it was spoken only by the Haida on Haida Gwaii, but spread with those who moved north to Prince of Wales Island in southeast Alaska.

Great For...

☑ Don't Miss

The remarkable model of Skidegate before colonial times.

Totem pole detail

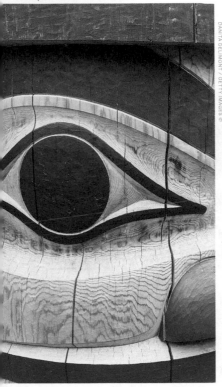

DANITA DELIMONT / GETTY IMAGES ©

ℹ Need to Know

☏250-559-7885; www.haidaheritagecentre. com; Hwy 16, Skidegate; adult/child $16/5; ⊙10am-6pm Mon-Wed, to 8pm Thu-Sun Jun-Aug, 10am-5pm Tue-Sat Sep-May

✗ Take a Break

Stop for lunch at the center's Kay Bistro, where the food rivals the sea views.

★ Top Tip

In summer, join worthwhile free tours of the collection, and talks and walks by Parks Canada rangers.

A century ago, virtually all Haida were fluent in X̱aayda Kil. These days, it is believed that there are fewer than 50 fluent speakers left, the majority of whom are 70 years of age or older. Recently, there has been a resurgence of interest by younger Haidas to learn their language, with classes, camps and dictionaries being created. The Heritage Centre works hard to both preserve, use and share the language and you'll have ample opportunity to encounter it in the displays and on tours.

Canoe-Building

For the Haida, creating a canoe is more than just boat-building. It reflects their connection with the sea and is a revered art. The giant cedars of Haida Gwaii make excellent vessels and the Haida were known up and down the coast for their seafaring

canoes. The tree would need to be large enough to fit numerous men and selection was incredibly important. The outside was first carved, then the inside burned away. Hot water was used to make the wood more malleable for shaping. The beauty of the canoes made them prized possessions sought after by chiefs of other tribes. For the Haida, the canoes brought great strength for transportation, trade, fishing and war.

With the catastrophic arrival of smallpox to Haida Gwaii in 1862, up to 70% of the Haida population was obliterated. With them went much of the cultural knowledge. The revival of canoe-building in the 1990s was done through knowledge passed down through oral storytelling, through photographs and with the discovery of a partially dug out canoe deep in the Haida Gwaii rainforest. Today you can witness the creation of canoes at the Heritage Centre and join a Canoe Chat to learn about the cultural significance of these stunning vessels.

Totem poles, SGang Gwaay

Gwaii Haanas National Park Reserve

This huge Unesco World Heritage site encompasses Moresby and 137 smaller islands at its southern end.

Great For...

☑ Don't Miss

Gandll K'in Gwaayaay (Hot-Water Island) with its stunning hot springs along the coast.

The park combines a time-capsule look at abandoned Haida villages alongside hot springs, amazing natural beauty and some of the continent's best kayaking

Cultural Heritage

Archaeological finds have documented more than 500 ancient Haida sites, including villages and burial caves throughout the islands. The most famous village is SGang Gwaay (Ninstints) on Anthony Island, where rows of weathered totem poles stare eerily out to sea. Other major sights include the ancient village of Skedans, on Louise Island, and Hotspring Island, the natural hot springs of which are back on after being disrupted by earthquakes in 2012. The sites are protected by Haida Gwaii caretakers, who live on the islands in summer.

Legacy Pole

In 2013 the magnificent Gwaii Haanas Legacy Pole was raised at Windy Bay, the first new pole in the protected area in 130 years.

Visiting

Access to the park is by boat or plane only. A visit demands a decent amount of advance planning and usually requires several days. From May to September, you must obtain a reservation, unless you're with a tour operator. All visitors must register with the park, and any visitor not on a guided tour must attend a free orientation at the park office. The number of daily reservations is limited, and user fees apply (adult/child $20/10 per day). A few much-coveted standby spaces are made available daily via Parks Canada.

Joining a Tour

Many people visit the park with a guide. Tours last from one day to two weeks. Many operators can also set you up with rental kayaks (average per day/week $60/300) and gear for independent travel.

Haida Style Expeditions (☎250-637-1151; www.haidastyle.com; tours $275-375; ☺May–mid-Sep) lets you buzz through the reserve in a large inflatable boat. This Haida-run outfit offers four different one-day tours (eight to 12 hours) that together take in the most important sights in the park.

Archipelago Ventures (☎250-652-4913, 888-559-8317; www.tourhaidagwaii.com; 6-day tours from $2350) runs multiday kayak trips that fully explore the reserve. Guests are housed on the mothership MV *Island Bay*, which is run like a small community. Itineraries are flexible.

Queen Charlotte, Skidegate & Masset

Haida Gwaii lies 80km west of the BC coast, and about 50km from the southern tip of Alaska. The principal town is Graham Island's Queen Charlotte (previously Queen Charlotte City and still known by its old QCC acronym), 6km west of the ferry dock at Skidegate Landing. Graham Island is linked to Moresby Island to the south by ferry from Skidegate Landing.

Haida Gwaii was formerly known as the Queen Charlotte Islands, the name of which was officially dropped in 2010.

◎ SIGHTS

The Haida Gwaii portion of the Yellowhead Hwy (Hwy 16) heads 110km north from Queen Charlotte past Skidegate, **Tlell** and **Port Clements**. The last was where a golden spruce tree, famous for its colour, that stood on the banks of the Yakoun River was cut down by a demented forester in 1997. The incident is detailed in the best-selling *The Golden Spruce* by John Vaillant, an excellent book on the islands and Haida culture.

All along the road to Masset, look for little seaside pullouts, oddball boutiques and funky cafes that are typical of the islands' character.

Naikoon Provincial Park　　　Park

(☏250-626-5115; www.bcparks.ca; off Hwy 16) Much of the island's northeastern side is devoted to the beautiful 726-sq-km Naikoon Provincial Park, which combines sand dunes and low sphagnum bogs, surrounded by stunted and gnarled lodgepole pine, and red and yellow cedar. The starkly beautiful **beaches** on the north coast feature strong winds, pounding surf and flotsam from across the Pacific. They can be reached via the stunning 26km-long Tow Hill Rd, east of Masset.

Wooden steps and a boardwalk make visiting the **Tow Hill Lookout** and **Blow Hole** near the end of Tow Hill Rd easy. Allow about one hour for a looping walk with

many steps. A 21km loop trail traverses a good bit of the park to/from **Fife Beach** at the end of the road. The park also has campsites ($16).

Dixon Entrance Maritime Museum　　　Museum

(☏250-626-6066; 2182 Collinson Ave; adult/child $3/free; ◷1-6pm daily Jun-Aug, 2-4pm Sat & Sun Sep-May) Housed in what was once the local hospital, the museum features exhibits on the history of this seafaring community, with displays on shipbuilding, medical pioneers, military history and nearby clam and crab canneries. Local artists also exhibit work here.

Port Clements Museum　　　Museum

(☏250-557-4576; www.portclementsmuseum.ca; 45 Bayview Dr; adult/child $3/free; ◷10am-4pm Jun–mid-Sep, 2-4pm Sat & Sun mid-Sep–May) Learn about early logging practices and check out toys and tools from pioneering days. Nearby is the fenced-in cutting of the famous but felled **Golden Spruce**. It's alive but rather shrub-like.

❸ ACTIVITIES

Yakoun Lake　　　Hiking

(☏250-557-6810) Hike 20 minutes through ancient stands of spruce and cedar to pristine Yakoun Lake, a large wilderness lake towards the west side of Graham Island. A small beach near the trail is shaded by gnarly Sitka alders. Dare to take a dip in the bracing waters, or just enjoy the sweeping views.

❻ TOURS

Moresby Explorers　　　Adventure

(☏800-806-7633, 250-637-2215; www.moresby explorers.com; Sandspit; 1-day tours from $215) Offers one-day Zodiac tours, including the Louise Island trip that takes in the town of Skedans and its important totem poles, as well as much longer trips (the four-day trip is highly recommended). Also rents kayak and gear, and provides logistics.

❽ EATING

The best selection of restaurants is in Queen Charlotte (QCC), and there are also a few good options in Skidegate and Masset. Ask at the visitor centers about local Haida feasts, where you'll enjoy the best salmon and blueberries you've ever had. Good supermarkets are found in QCC and Masset.

Moon Over Naikoon   Bakery **$**
(☏250-626-5064; 16443 Tow Hill Rd, Masset; snacks from $3; ⊙8am-5pm Jun-Aug) Embodying the spirit of its location, on a road to the end of everything, this tiny community center cum bakery is housed in an old school bus in a clearing about 6km from Masset. The baked goods and coffee are brilliant.

Charters Restaurant   Seafood **$$**
(☏250-626-3377; 1650 Delkatla Rd, Masset; mains $15-30; ⊙5-9pm Wed-Sun) The numbers are small: six tables, three mains. But the pleasure is great: simply delicious food, such as seafood fettuccine and fresh local halibut. The changing menu also features burgers, ribs, salads and more. The attention to detail is extraordinary: the greens used to ornament plates are grown under lights in the kitchen. Reserve ahead.

❶ INFORMATION

Download, browse online or pick up a free copy of the encyclopedic annual *Haida Gwaii Visitors Guide* (www.gohaidagwaii.ca).

Parks Canada (☏250-559-8818, reservations 877-559-8818; www.parkscanada.ca/gwaii haanas; Haida Heritage Centre at Kay Llnagaay, Skidegate; ⊙office 8:30am-noon & 1-4:30pm Mon-Fri) Has a lot of information online.

QCC Visitor Centre (☏250-559-8316; www. queencharlottevisitorcentre.com; 3220 Wharf St, QCC; ⊙9am-8pm Mon-Sat, noon-8pm Sun May-Sep, shorter hours Oct-Apr) Handy visitor center that can make advance excursion bookings by phone.

Sandspit Airport Visitor Center (☏250-637-5362; ⊙9:30-11:30am & 1-4pm) Useful visitor center.

❶ GETTING THERE & AWAY

AIR

The main airport for Haida Gwaii is at Sandspit on Moresby Island, 12km east of the ferry landing at Aliford Bay. Note that reaching the airport from Graham Island is time-consuming – make sure you give yourself plenty of time. There's also a small airport at Masset. Air Canada (www. aircanada.com) flies daily between Sandspit and Vancouver.

Eagle Transit (☏250-559-4461, 877-747-4461; www.eagletransit.net; airport shuttle adult/child $30/22) buses meet Sandspit flights and serve Skidegate and QCC.

FERRY

The **BC Ferries** (☏250-386-3431; www.bcferries. com) service is the most popular way to reach the islands. Mainland ferries dock at Skidegate Landing on Graham Island. Services run between Prince Rupert and Skidegate Landing five times a week in summer and three times a week in winter on the *Northern Adventure*. Travel time is six to seven hours; fares cost adults $39 to $48, children half-price, and cars $139 to $169. Cabins are useful for overnight schedules (from $90).

❶ GETTING AROUND

The main road on Graham Island is Hwy 16, which is fully paved. Off paved Hwy 16, most roads are gravel or worse. There is no public transit.

Renting a car can cost roughly the same ($60 to $100 per day) as bringing one over on the ferry. Rental companies include **Budget** (☏250-637-5688; www.budget.com; Sandspit Airport), as well as several small, locally owned firms.

You can rent bikes at the small Sandspit Airport Visitor Center for $30 per day and take them across to Graham Island on the ferry.

THE YUKON

The Yukon at a Glance...

This vast and thinly populated wilderness, where most four-legged species far outnumber humans, has a grandeur and beauty only appreciated by experience. Few places in the world today have been so unchanged over the course of time.

Any visit to the Yukon will mean spending plenty of time outdoors: Canada's five tallest mountains and the world's largest ice fields below the Arctic are all within Kluane National Park. Get set to appreciate the bustle of Whitehorse and the offbeat vibe of Dawson City before you head off into the wilds beyond.

Two Days in the Yukon

Spend a day exploring **Whitehorse** (p260), taking in the museums and galleries, then indulge in some fantastic, locally sourced and creatively prepared food at **Antoinette's** (p260). On day two, get a taste of adventure and join a paddling excursion out onto the **Yukon River** (p258). You'll feel like you've earned that pizza and beer at the **Dirty Northern Public House** (p261), and you may catch a live act there as well.

Four Days in the Yukon

Head north to Dawson City and take in the **Klondike sites** (p256). Join a **Gold-bottom Tour** (p263) to try your hand at gold panning. Stop by the **Drunken Goat Taverna** (p263) for a delicious Greek feast and spend a little time at **Diamond Tooth Gertie's Gambling Hall** (p257) for some honky-tonk piano and dancing.

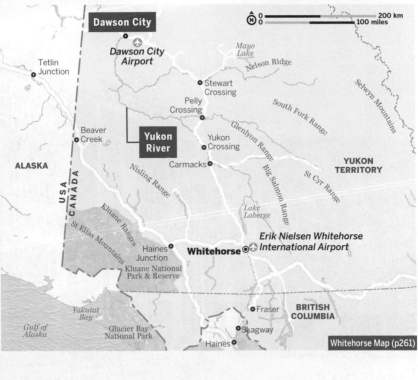

200 km
100 miles

Dawson City

Dawson City
Airport

Tetlin
Junction

Mayo
Lake

Nelson Ridge

Stewart
Crossing

Pelly
Crossing

South Fork Range

Selwyn Mountains

Beaver
Creek

Yukon
River

Yukon
Crossing

Glenlyon Range

ALASKA

Nisling Range

Carmacks

Big Salmon Range

St Cyr Range

**YUKON
TERRITORY**

USA
CANADA

Kluane Ranges

St Elias Mountains

Lake
Laberge

Haines
Junction

Whitehorse

Kluane National
Park & Reserve

Erik Nielsen Whitehorse
International Airport

Yakutat
Bay

Gulf of
Alaska

Glacier Bay
National Park

Fraser

Skagway

Haines

**BRITISH
COLUMBIA**

Whitehorse Map (p261)

Arriving in the Yukon

Erik Nielsen Whitehorse International Airport Services to Vancouver and Calgary; a taxi to the center (10 minutes) will cost around $22.

Dawson City Airport Air North serves Whitehorse and Old Crow, and Inuvik in the NWT.

Bus Greyhound Canada buses from Whitehorse connect with the rest of BC and Canada. Husky Bus runs from Whitehorse to Dawson City thrice-weekly.

Where to Stay

Basic sleeping accommodations can be found at strategic points along the Alaska Hwy and other major roads. Whitehorse and Dawson have a range of good choices, but both can get almost full during the peak of summer – book ahead. Many places in Dawson City will pick you up at the airport; ask in advance.

Downtown Hotel, Dawson City (p262)

MILES ERTMAN / GETTY IMAGES ©

Dawson's Klondike History

Not only one of Canada's most historic and evocative towns, atmospheric Dawson City also boasts a seductive, funky vibe.

Great For...

☑ Don't Miss

Stopping in at **Harrington's Store** (cnr 3rd Ave & Princess St; ◷9:30am-8:30pm) to see photos from Dawson's heyday.

The Gold Rush

The Klondike Gold Rush continues to be the defining moment for the Yukon. Certainly it was the population high point, Around 40,000 gold seekers washed ashore in Skagway, hoping to strike it rich in the gold fields of Dawson City, some 700km north.

To say that most were ill-prepared for the enterprise is an understatement. Although some were veterans of other gold rushes, a high percentage were American men who thought they'd just pop up North and get rich. The reality was different. They had to contend with scammers, trips over the frozen Chilkoot Pass with their 1000lb of gear, and building their own boats to cross the lakes and Yukon River to Dawson. Scores died trying.

The Klondike gold-rush mobs were mostly too late to the action by at least a year.

Need to Know

Unless noted otherwise, Dawson City sights, attractions and many businesses are closed outside of the summer high season.

✕ Take a Break

Stop in at Klondike Kate's (p263) for home-cooking.

★ Top Tip

Join a Goldbottom Tour (p263) to try your hand at gold panning.

historic site is roughly where gold was first found in 1896. A fascinating 500m-long walk passes interpretive displays. Pick up a guide ($2.50) at the Visitor Information Centre (p263).

Diamond Tooth Gertie's Gambling Hall

This popular re-creation of an 1898 saloon, **Gertie's** (☑867-993-5575; cnr Queen St & 4th Ave; $10; ☉7pm-2am Mon-Fri, 2pm-2am Sat & Sun May-Sep) is complete with small-time gambling, a honky-tonk piano and dancing girls. The casino helps promote the town and fund culture. Each night there are three different floor shows with singing and dancing.

Dawson City Museum

Make your own discoveries among the 25,000 gold-rush artifacts at this **museum** (☑867-993-5291; 5th Ave; adult/child $9/7; ☉10am-6pm May-Aug). Engaging exhibits walk you through the grim lives of the miners. The museum is housed in the landmark 1901 Old Territorial Administration building.

By they time they got there, the best sites had all been claimed. Sick and broke, the survivors glumly made their way home.

Klondike National Historic Sites

It's easy to relive the gold rush at myriad preserved and restored **National Historic Sites** (☑867-993-7210; www.pc.gc.ca/dawson; Parks Canada passes adult $7-31). Parks Canada runs walking tours (p263) that allow access into various examples of the 26 restored buildings. Take several tours so you can see a wide variety. Outside of tours, various buildings such as the Palace Grand Theatre are open for free on a rotating basis, usually 4:30pm to 5:30pm.

Bonanza Creek Discovery Site

Up the valley from Dredge No 4, the **Bonanza Creek** (Bonanza Rd) **FREE** national

The Yukon River

Paddle the Yukon River

Canoe expeditions down the Yukon River are epic. Paddle past Klondike-era cabins, gold dredges on the banks, bears fishing and moose lapping up the cold water.

Great For...

☑ Don't Miss

Trying your luck with a fishing rod – perhaps you'll hook an Arctic grayling or a great northern pike.

Most canoeing and kayaking trips begin in Whitehorse and head to Carmacks or on to Dawson City, ranging from eight to 16 days of wilderness camping. Outfitters offer gear of all kinds (canoes and kayaks are about $40 to $50 per day), guides, tours, lessons and planning services, and can arrange transportation back to Whitehorse.

Thirty-Mile Section

A Canadian Heritage site, this narrow river channel flows from Lake Laberge, 96km north of Whitehorse, to the confluence of the Teslin River. With clear, blue-green waters and perpendicular bluffs stretching 100m up from the river, its one of the most scenic stretches of the Yukon River. An important salmon migration area, this region

Klondike Kate's (p263)

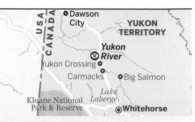

ⓘ Need to Know

See outfitters' websites for details.

✕ Take a Break

Other than fish straight from the river, you or your guide will need to bring all supplies.

★ Top Tip

Most paddlers use the map *The Yukon River: Marsh Lake to Dawson City*; available at www.yukonbooks.com.

Big Salmon

Further north, Big Salmon River meets the Yukon River, widening the course. At the confluence is an abandoned turn-of-the-century First Nations village and a trading post on the riverbanks.

is also home to bald and golden eagles, trumpeter swans, wolverines and grizzly bears that prowl the riverside.

While paddling may seem easy in this stretch, with the current pulling your canoe on an almost effortless journey, this stretch was the most difficult part of the run for gold seekers traveling to Dawson City. The strong currents and shifting shoals claimed more ships than any other stretch of the Yukon River. Along the way, you'll see simple graves and pass locations named after wrecked boats, such as Tanana Reef and Domville Creek. Also watch for abandoned cabins, a dilapidated shipyard and the abandoned village of Hootalinqua.

Outfitters

Kanoe People (📞867-668-4899; www.kanoe people.com; cnr 1st Ave & Strickland St; 1-day Yukon River paddle tour $95) At the river's edge. Can arrange any type of trip including paddles down Teslin and Big Salmon Rivers. Gear, maps and guidebooks for sale.

Klondike Canoeing Rentals (📞867-334-2889; www.klondikecanoe.yk.ca; canoe/kayak rental per day $40/50) Can supply all canoeing and kayaking needs plus arrange transportation to/ from river locations.

Up North Adventures (📞867-667-7035; www. upnorthadventures.com; 103 Strickland St; 19-day Yukon River canoe trip for beginners $3000; ⏰9am-7pm) Offers guided tours, rentals and transportation on the major rivers. Also paddling lessons to get you started.

Whitehorse

The capital city of the Yukon Territory, Whitehorse is not immediately appealing, but rewards the curious. It has a well-funded arts community and good restaurants, and exploring the waterfront and sights within earshot of the rushing Yukon River can easily take a day or more.

◎ SIGHTS

MacBride Museum
Museum

(☎867-667-2709; www.macbridemuseum.com; cnr 1st Ave & Wood St; adult/child $10/5; ☺9:30am-5pm) The Yukon's attic covers the gold rush, First Nations, intrepid Mounties and more. Old photos vie with old stuffed critters, and daily demonstrations, such as gold-panning, are good fun. Various buildings colorfully re-create the Yukon's past; don't miss the stuffed albino moose.

SS Klondike
Historic Site

(☎867-667-4511; www.parkscanada.ca; cnr South Access Rd & 2nd Ave; ☺9:30am-5pm May-Aug) FREE Carefully restored, this was one of the largest stern-wheelers used on the Yukon River. Built in 1937, it made its final run upriver to Dawson in 1955 and is now a national historic site.

Yukon Beringia Interpretive Centre
Museum

(☎867-667-8855; www.beringia.com; Km 1473 Alaska Hwy; adult/child $6/4; ☺9am-6pm) This place focuses on Beringia, a mostly ice-free area that encompassed the Yukon, Alaska and eastern Siberia during the last ice age. Engaging exhibits re-create the era, right down to the actual skeleton of a 3m-long giant ground sloth – although some prefer the giant beaver.

Arts Underground
Gallery

(☎867-667-4080; 305 Main St, Hougen Centre lower level; ☺10am-5pm Tue-Sat) Operated by the Yukon Arts Society. There are carefully selected and well-curated rotating exhibits.

⊕ SHOPPING

Mac's Fireweed Books
Books

(☎867-668-2434; www.macsbooks.ca; 203 Main St; ☺8am-8pm Mon-Sat, to 6pm Sun) Mac's has an unrivaled selection of Yukon titles. It also stocks topographical maps, road maps and periodicals.

North End Gallery
Arts & Crafts

(☎867-393-3590; www.yukonart.ca; 1116 1st Ave; ☺9am-7pm Mon-Sat, to 5pm Sun) High-end Canadian art gallery featuring top Yukon artists.

⊗ EATING

Klondike Rib & Salmon
Canadian $$

(☎867-667-7554; www.klondikerib.com; 2116 2nd Ave; mains $12-25; ☺11am-9pm May-Sep) It looks touristy and it seems touristy and it *is* touristy, but the food is excellent at this sprawling casual place with two decks. Besides the namesakes (the salmon kabobs are tops), there are other local faves.

Burnt Toast
Bistro $$

(☎867-393-2605; www.burnttoastcafe.ca; 2112 2nd Ave; mains $8-25; ☺8am-9pm Mon-Sat, 9:30am-2pm Sun) The food is far better than the coy name suggests! Brunch is excellent at this inviting bistro (try the French toast) and lunch and dinner specials abound. Food is local and seasonal; consult the blackboard. Good salads, sandwiches and Yukon meats.

Antoinette's
Fusion $$$

(☎867-668-3505; www.antoinettesfoodcache.ca; 4121 4th Ave; dinner mains $20-35; ☺11am-2pm & 4:30-9pm Mon-Fri, 4:30-9pm Sat) Antoinette Oliphant runs one of the most creative kitchens in the Yukon. Her eponymous restaurant has an ever-changing, locally sourced menu. Many dishes have a Caribbean flair. There is often live bluesy, loungey music on weekends.

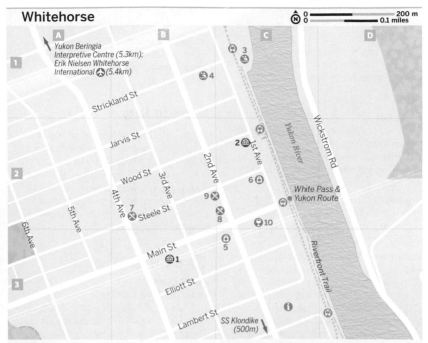

Whitehorse

🍷 DRINKING & NIGHTLIFE

**Dirty Northern
Public House**   Pub

(📞867-633-3305; www.facebook.com/dirty
northernpublichouse; 103 Main St; ⊘3pm-late)
There are hints of style at this upscale
pub, which has a great draft-beer selection
and makes excellent mixed drinks. Grab a
booth and chase the booze with a wood-
ed pizza. Top local acts perform many
ts.

ℹ INFORMATION

VIC (📞867-667-3084; www.travelyukon.com;
100 Hanson St; ⊘8am-8pm) An essential stop
with vast amounts of territory-wide information.

ℹ GETTING THERE & AWAY

AIR

Erik Nielsen Whitehorse International Airport
(YXY; 📞867-667-8440; www.gov.yk.ca/yxy; off
Alaska Hwy; 📶) is five minutes west of downtown.

Air Canada and Westjet serve Vancouver. Locally owned Air North (www.flyairnorth.com) serves Dawson City (with flights on to Inuvik, NWT, and Old Crow), plus Vancouver, Kelowna, Edmonton and Calgary. Condor (www.condor.com) has weekly summer flights to/from Frankfurt.

BUS

Husky Bus (✆867-993-3821; www.huskybus. ca) Serves Dawson City ($110, thrice weekly) and makes all stops along the Klondike Hwy. Departures are from the VIC. It will do pickups of paddlers and canoes along the Klondike Hwy with advance arrangement.

Greyhound Canada (✆867-667-2223, 800-661-8747; www.greyhound.ca; 2191 2nd Ave) Runs south along the Alaska Hwy to Dawson Creek ($285, 20 hours, thrice-weekly).

White Pass & Yukon Route (✆867-633-5710; www.wpyr.com; 1109 1st Ave; adult/child one-way $130/65; ⊙ticket office 9am-5pm Mon-Sat mid-May–mid-Sep) Offers a jaw-droppingly scenic daily 10-hour rail and bus connection to/from Skagway, AK, via Fraser, BC, in season. On some days the bus meets the train in Carcross, which maximizes the beautiful train ride (this is the preferred option).

🛈 GETTING AROUND

BUS

Whitehorse Transit System (✆867-668-7433; $2.50; ⊙Mon-Sat) runs through the center. Route 3 serves the airport, route 5 passes the Robert Service Campground.

CAR & RV

Check your rental rate very carefully as it's common for a mileage charge to be added after the first 100km, which will not get you far in the Yukon. Also understand your insurance coverage and ask whether damage from Yukon's rugged roads is included.

Budget (✆867-667-6200; www.budget.com; Erik Nielsen Whitehorse International Airport)

Fraserway RV Rentals (✆800-661-2441, 867-668-3438; www.fraserwayrvrentals.com; 9039 Quartz Rd) Rents all shapes and sizes of RV from

$200 per day depending on size (it matters) and season. Mileage extra; rates can quickly add up.

Whitehorse Subaru (✆867-393-6550; www. whitehorsesubaru.com; 17 Chilkoot Way) Has good rates; most cars have manual transmissions.

Dawson City

Set on a narrow shelf at the confluence of the Yukon and Klondike Rivers, a mere 240km south of the Arctic Circle, Dawson was the center of the Klondike Gold Rush. Today, you can wander the dirt streets of town, passing old buildings with dubious permafrost foundations, and discover Dawson's rich cultural life.

◎ SIGHTS

Jack London Interpretive Centre　　　Museum
(✆867-993-5575; Firth St; adult/child $5/free; ⊙11am-6pm May-Aug) In 1898 Jack London lived in the Yukon, the setting for his most popular stories, including *Call of the Wild* and *White Fang*. At the writer's cabin there are excellent daily interpretive talks. A labor of love by the late historian Dick North, Dawne Mitchell and others, this place is a treasure trove of stories – including the search for the original cabin.

SS Keno　　　Historic Site
(cnr Front & Queen Sts; Parks Canada admission $7; ⊙noon-4pm May-Aug) The SS *Keno* was one of a fleet of paddle wheelers that worked the Yukon's rivers for more than half a century. Grounded along the waterfront, the boat re-creates a time before any highways.

🏃 ACTIVITIES

Dawson City River Hostel　　　Canoeing, Cycling
(www.yukonhostels.com; bike rental per day from $25; ⊙May-Sep) Arranges all manner of canoe rentals, trips and transportation from

Whitehorse and points further downstream to Dawson and from Dawson to the Alaskan towns of Eagle and Circle.

TOURS

Goldbottom Tours History
(☎867-993-5750; www.goldbottom.com; tours with/without transport from Dawson $55/45; ⊙May-Sep) Run by the legendary Millar mining family. Tour their placer mine 15km up Hunker Creek Rd, which meets Hwy 2 just north of the airport. The three-hour tours include a gold-panning lesson; you get to keep what you find. You can also just pan for gold on their site for $20. The ticket office is on Front St.

Parks Canada Walking Tours Walking
(single tour $7, unlimited tours $31; ⊙May-Aug) Parks Canada docents, often in period garb, lead excellent walking tours. On each tour, learn about a few of the 26 restored buildings and the many characters that walked the streets (many of whom could be called 'streetwalkers'). There are also self-guided 90-minute audio tours (adult $7, 9am to 5pm).

EATING

Drunken Goat Taverna Greek $$
(☎867-993-5800; www.drunkengoattaverna.com; 2nd Ave; mains $14-28; ⊙noon-9pm) Follow your eyes to the flowers, your ears to the Aegean music and your nose to the excellent Greek food, run year-round by the legendary Tony Dovas. A new terrace out back is a fine place to while away an evening.

Klondike Kate's Canadian $$
(☎867-993-6527; www.klondikekates.ca; cnr King St & 3rd Ave; mains $8-25; ⊙4-9pm Mon-Sat, 8am-3pm & 4-9pm Sun Apr-Oct) Two ways to know spring has arrived: the river cracks up and Kate's reopens. Locals in the know prefer the latter. The long and inventive menu has fine sandwiches, pastas and fresh Yukon fish. Look for great specials. Excellent list of Canadian craft brews.

DRINKING & NIGHTLIFE

Bombay Peggy's Pub
(☎867-993-6969; www.bombaypeggys.com; cnr 2nd Ave & Princess St; ⊙11am-11pm Mar-Nov) There's always a hint of pleasures to come swirling around the tables of Dawson's most inviting bar. Enjoy good beers, wines and mixed drinks inside or out.

INFORMATION

Northwest Territories Information Centre
(☎867-993-6167; www.spectacularnwt.com; Front St; ⊙9am-7pm May-Sep) Maps and information on the NWT and the Dempster Hwy.

VIC (☎867-993-5566; www.travelyukon.com; cnr Front & King Sts; ⊙8am-8pm May-Sep) Combines tourist and Parks Canada information (buy activity tickets and passes here).

GETTING THERE & AWAY

Dawson City is 527km from Whitehorse. Public transportation to/from Whitehorse is often in flux. Dawson City Airport is 19km east of Dawson, although should you fly in, there are no rental cars. **Air North** (☎800-661-0407; www.flyairnorth.com) serves Whitehorse.

Husky Bus (☎867-993-3821; www.huskybus.ca) serves Whitehorse ($110, thrice-weekly) and makes all stops along the Klondike Hwy. Departures are from the VIC. Husky will do pickups of paddlers and canoes along the Klondike Hwy with advance arrangement. The company uses the **Klondike Experience** (☎867-993-3821; www.klondikeexperience.com; 954 2nd Ave; tours $25-120; ⊙May-Aug) office.

Moraine Lake (p187), the Rocky Mountains

In Focus

Peace Bridge, Calgary (p170)

Canada Today

In 2015 Canada got a major facelift with Liberal prime minister Justin Trudeau. Suddenly the world saw photographs of a young leader surfing, hiking, marching in gay pride parades and championing women's rights. There was a collective sigh of relief as Canada became cool again. But with oil prices plummeting and the not-too-quiet whisper of recession in the air, the future isn't looking rose-tinted for everyone; tension between natural resources and a carbon-free economy runs high.

Economy

Compared to its international brethren, Canada weathered the global financial crisis pretty well. Yes, the economy dropped into a recession, and Ottawa posted its first fiscal deficit in 2009 after 12 years of surplus. But six years later, Canada clawed its way out and was the only one of the seven major industrialized democracies to return to surplus in 2015. The Conservative government of the time focused on federal job cuts that impacted many departments, including Parks Canada and Aboriginal Affairs. In their first full year back in office, the Liberals planned for a $30 billion deficit in 2016–17, claiming investment in job creation, support for the middle class and infrastructure would build a brighter, more sustainable future.

belief systems
(% of population)

43
Roman Catholic

28
Other

23
Protestant

4
Christian

2
Muslim

if Canada were 100 people

28 would be of British Isles origin

23 would be of French origin

15 would be of European origin

34 would be of Other origin

population per sq km

⬆ ≈ 4 people

Canada

USA

France

Oil Between Neighbors

Voltaire may have written off Canada as 'a few acres of snow' back in the mid-18th century, but those few acres have yielded vast amounts of oil, timber and other natural resources, and propelled Canada to an enviable standard of living.

Extracting and developing the resources have, however, come with an ecological price. Oil, in particular, is a conundrum. Northern Alberta's Athabasca Oil Sands are the world's second-biggest oil reserves, and they've done an excellent job boosting the economy. They also produce 5% of Canada's greenhouse gas emissions, according to Environment Canada. The pro-industry camp says improvements are being made and, when compared to other oil producers such as Saudi Arabia and Venezuela, the oil sands measure up, especially when human-rights issues and decreased transportation distances are factored in (most of Canada's oil goes to the USA).

The controversial Keystone XL pipeline played into these themes. Aimed to funnel Alberta's crude oil to refineries on the Texas and Louisiana coast, much of it was already built when the US State Department refused approval for the pipeline's completion in late 2015, saying Canada could be doing more to curb carbon emissions. The project was also contentious within Canada, with environmentalists and Aboriginal communities vocal about their concerns regarding damage to sacred sites and water contamination. Interestingly, the US rejection did little to antagonize relations between the new Canadian Liberal government and the US Democrats, but instead brought strong disapproval of the Liberals from oil-industry communities in Canada. Many believe the pipeline could return to the table.

Politics

After being under Conservative rule for almost 10 years, Canada went to the polls in record numbers in 2015 in an election that strongly divided the population. Resource-based communities backed the Conservatives, while many others felt the party had sold out to big business and was being short-sighted in supporting industry over the environment. Many also feared that a split in votes between the leftist New Democratic Party (NDP) and the Liberals would return the Conservatives to power.

The Liberals took back the reigns with a majority leadership headed by the young Justin Trudeau. Son of Pierre Trudeau, the country's 15th prime minister, Justin is a media magnet much like his father, and Canada is witnessing a return to the Trudeau-mania of the 1970s and '80s. Just 43 when he took office, Justin's forthright support of women, children, immigrants, same-sex marriage, marijuana legalization and environmentalism has been welcomed by many Canadians disheartened by Conservative rule. For them, Trudeau embodies much of what it means to be Canadian. Meanwhile, industry-based communities are less than enamored.

Inuit child in an igloo

TON KOENE PHOTOGRAPHY / GETTY IMAGES ©

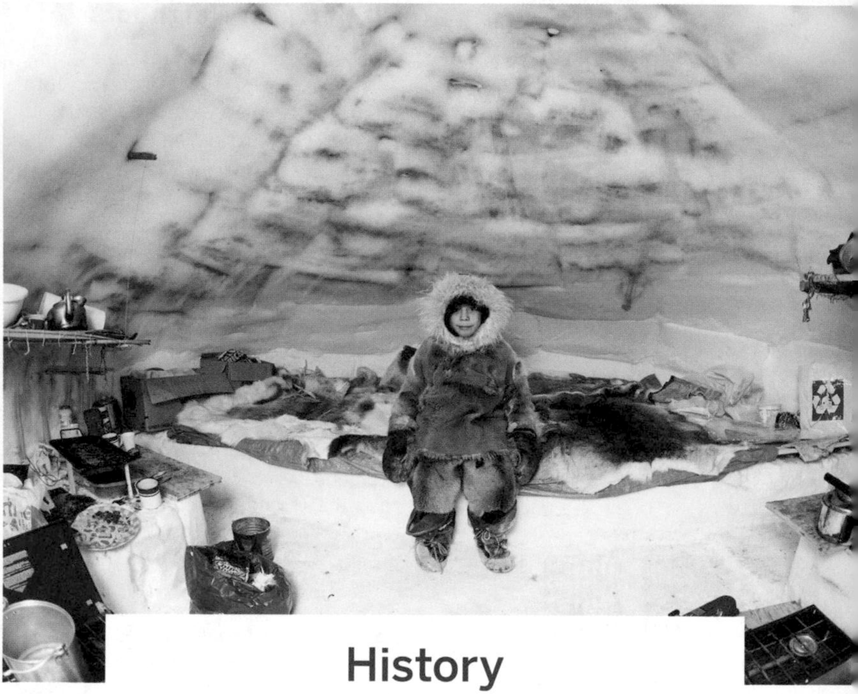

History

The human story of Canada begins around 15,000 years ago, when Aboriginal locals began carving communities from the abundant wilderness. Everything changed, though, when the Europeans rolled in from the late 15th century onward, staking claims that triggered rumbling conflicts and eventually shaped a vast new nation. Much of this colorful heritage is accessible to visitors, with Canada boasting more than 950 national historic sites.

c 25,000 BC
The first humans arrive in Canada by crossing the land bridge that once connected Siberia to North America.

AD 1000
Viking Leif Eriksson and crew wash up at L'Anse aux Meadows, becoming the first Europeans in North America.

1497
John Cabot sails from Britain and finds Newfoundland instead of China.

Baffin Island

MICHAEL NOLAN / ROBERTHARDING / GETTY IMAGES ©

Early Locals & Viking Visitors

The first Canadians most likely came from Asia, chasing down caribou and bison across the one-time land link between Siberia and Alaska and eventually settling throughout the Americas. The north proved particularly popular for its abundance of tasty fish and seal dinners, and these early Aboriginal communities eventually spread to four main regions in what would become Canada: the Pacific, the Plains, southern Ontario/St Lawrence River, and the northeast woodlands.

About 2500 BC, a second major wave of migration from Siberia brought the ancestors of the Inuit to Canada. These early Inuit were members of the Dorset Culture, named after Cape Dorset on Baffin Island, where its remains were first unearthed. Around AD 1000, a separate Inuit cultural group – the whale-hunting Thule of northern Alaska – began making its way east through the Canadian Arctic. As these people spread, they overtook the Dorset Culture. The Thule are the direct ancestors of Canada's modern-day Inuit.

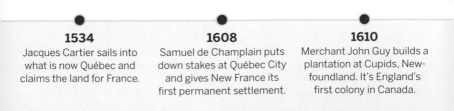

1534	1608	1610
Jacques Cartier sails into what is now Québec and claims the land for France.	Samuel de Champlain puts down stakes at Québec City and gives New France its first permanent settlement.	Merchant John Guy builds a plantation at Cupids, Newfoundland. It's England's first colony in Canada.

★ **Best Historic Neighborhoods**

Gastown, Vancouver
Québec City, Québec
Old Montréal, Montréal
Downtown Halifax, Nova Scotia

Apartments in Gastown, Vancouver

These original communities lived and thrived for thousands of years before anyone else turned up and stayed. Around AD 1000, Viking explorer Leif Eriksson and his hairy posse poked ashore on the east coast, sticking around long enough to establish winter settlements and a few hardy outposts. Life was tough for these interlopers and the hostile reception from the locals eventually sent them back where they came from. Without a glowing recommendation from these first European visitors, it was several centuries before anyone else bothered to make the epic journey across the Atlantic.

Return of the Europeans

After Christopher Columbus made heading west from Europe across the ocean fashionable again with his 1492 journey in search of Asia, avaricious European monarchs began queuing up to sponsor expeditions. In 1497 Giovanni Caboto – better known as John Cabot – sailed under a British flag as far west as Newfoundland and Cape Breton. His great discovery turned out to be a surfeit of cod stocks, triggering a hungry rush of boats from Europe, including Spanish whaling vessels.

King François I of France looked over the fence at his neighbors, stroked his beard, and ordered Jacques Cartier to appear before him. By this time, the hunt was on not only for the fabled Northwest Passage route but also for gold, given the shiny discoveries made by Spanish conquistadors among the Aztec and Inca civilizations.

But upon arrival in Labrador, Cartier found only 'stones and horrible rugged rocks.' He kept exploring, though, and soon went ashore on Québec's Gaspé Peninsula to claim the land for France. The local Iroquois thought he was a good neighbor at first, until he kidnapped two of the chief's sons and took them to Europe. Rather surprisingly, Cartier returned them a year later when sailing up the St Lawrence River.

1670
King Charles II creates the Hudson's Bay Company to shore up the local fur trade for the British.

1755
The English deport some 14,000 French Acadians from the Bay of Fundy region during the Great Expulsion.

1759
The French and English come to blows on the Plains of Abraham at Québec City. The battle lasts less than an hour; France loses.

Fur: The New Gold

While these early explorers were always looking for gold to please their royal sponsors back home, it eventually become clear that the riches of the new land were not quite so sparkly. With fur the latest fashion of the French court, the New World's lustrous and abundant pelts were suddenly in huge demand across Europe.

In 1588 the French crown granted the first trading monopoly in Canada, only to have other merchants promptly challenge the claim. And so the race for control of the fur trade was officially on. The economic value of this enterprise and, by extension, its role in shaping Canadian history, cannot be underestimated. It was the main reason behind the country's European settlement, at the root of the struggle for dominance between the French and the British, and the source of strife and division between various Aboriginal groups.

To support their claims, French pioneers established a tentative foothold on Île Ste-Croix (a tiny islet in the river on the present US border with Maine) in 1604. They soon moved to Port Royal (today's Annapolis Royal) in Nova Scotia. Exposed and difficult to defend, neither site was ideal for controlling the inland fur trade. As the would-be colonists moved up the St Lawrence River, they came upon a spot their leader, Samuel de Champlain, considered prime real estate – where today's Québec City now stands. It was 1608 and 'New France' had landed.

Pirates

Atlantic Canada had a notorious history of pirates. Peter Easton was the first in 1602, plundering around Newfoundland. Black Bart, aka Bartholomew Roberts, was another, c 1720. He disliked booze and gambling and encouraged prayer among his employees. In Halifax, pirates were called 'privateers' and were sanctioned by the government.

Brits Take Over

While the French enjoyed their plush fur monopoly for several decades, the Brits mounted a challenge in 1670 when King Charles II formed the Hudson's Bay Company. He granted it a trade monopoly over a vast northern area that would today encompass about 40% of Canada.

As both countries reaffirmed and expanded their claims, skirmishes broke out between groups of colonizers, mirroring the wars that were engulfing Europe in the first half of the 18th century. Things came to a head with the Treaty of Utrecht, which forced the French to recognize British claims in the region.

But the enmity and military skirmishes between the two continued for several decades, culminating in a 1759 battle on Québec's Plains of Abraham that is remembered today as one of Canada's most important military events. Besieging the city in a surprise

1763
The Treaty of Paris expels France from Canada after France loses the Seven Years' War.

1775
American rebels invade Canada and try to entice Québec to join the revolt against the British in the American Revolution.

1793
Explorer Alexander Mackenzie makes the first transcontinental journey across the land.

Canadian War Museum

★ **Best History Museums**

Maritime Museum of the Atlantic (p84), Halifax

Canadian War Museum (p150), Ottawa

Musée d'Archéologie et d'Histoire Pointe-à-Callière (p109), Montréal

Royal BC Museum (p236), Victoria

and bloody attack that left both commanding generals dead, the Brits eventually won the day and the French were forced to hand over control of Canada in the resulting 1763 Treaty of Paris.

Managing their newly acquired territory was a tricky challenge for the Brits, who had to contend with aboriginal uprisings as well as resentment from French Canadians. Next, the restless American colonies started rumbling from the south. To keep the French Canadians on side, the Québec Act of 1774 confirmed the French Canadians' right to their religion, allowed them to assume political office and restored the use of French civil law. It worked: during the American Revolution (1775–83), when most French Canadians refused to take up arms in support of the American cause.

After the revolution, the English-speaking population exploded when some 50,000 settlers from the newly independent USA migrated north. Called United Empire Loyalists due to their presumed allegiance to Britain, the majority ended up living in Nova Scotia and New Brunswick, while a smaller group settled along the northern shore of Lake Ontario and in the Ottawa River Valley (forming the nucleus of what became Ontario). About 8000 settlers moved to Québec, creating the first sizeable Anglophone community in the French-speaking bastion.

Canada Splits... Then Unites

Accommodating the interests of Loyalist settlers, the British government passed the Constitutional Act of 1791, which divided the colony into Upper Canada (today's southern Ontario) and Lower Canada (now southern Québec). Lower Canada retained French civil laws, but both provinces were governed by the British criminal code. These divisions didn't help matters, with rising tensions and arguments caused by the clear dominance of the British over the French in administrative matters across the two regions. Two French rebellions kicked off in the 1830s and although each was swiftly quelled, it was an indication that the ill-conceived division was unsustainable. The Brits then tried a different approach.

1858	**1867**	**1885**
Prospectors discover gold along the Fraser River in BC, spurring thousands of hopefuls to move north and start panning.	The British North America Act unites the colonies under the Dominion of Canada, a card-carrying member of the British Empire.	Canada's first national park opens in Banff, Alberta; meanwhile, in Craigellachie, BC, the Canadian Pacific Railway is completed.

The Union Act of 1840 sought to crush French nationalism by legislating that British laws, language and institutions were superior across both regions, now joined together as the Province of Canada. If anything, the union's clear underlying objective of destroying French identity made Francophones cling together even more tenaciously – the wounds can still be seen in Canada today.

With the rise of the USA after the American Civil War (1861–65), fragile Canada, whose border with the USA was established on the 49th parallel in 1818, sought to further solidify its status and prevent annexation. In 1864 Charlottetown, on Prince Edward Island, became the birthing room for modern Canada when the 'Fathers of Confederation' – a group of representatives from Nova Scotia, New Brunswick, Prince Edward Island, Ontario and Québec – got together and hammered out the framework for a new nation. The British North America Act was passed in 1867, creating a modern, self-governing nation originally known as the Dominion of Canada. The day the act became official, July 1, is now celebrated across the country as Canada's national holiday.

The Maple Leaf Symbol

It's on the penny, on Air Canada planes, on Toronto hockey-team jerseys – you can't escape the maple leaf. The leaf has been considered a national symbol for almost two centuries. In 1836, *Le Canadien* newspaper, published in Lower Canada, wrote about it as a suitable emblem for the nation. Ontario and Québec both were using it on their coat of arms by 1868. The Canadian Armed Forces used it during the world wars. And finally, after much wrangling over the design (one leaf? three leaves? 13 points?), the current 11-point leaf was granted national-symbol status and went on the flag in 1965.

Creating Confederation

Under Canada's first prime minister, John A Macdonald, land and colonies were slowly added to the confederation. The government acquired a vast northern swathe, now called the Northwest Territories (NWT), in 1869 for the paltry sum of £300,000 – about $11.5 million in today's money – from the Hudson's Bay Company. The land was sparsely populated, mostly by Plains First Nations and several thousand Métis, a racial blend of Cree, Ojibwe or Saulteaux and French Canadian or Scottish fur traders, who spoke French as their main language. Their biggest settlement was the Red River Colony around Fort Garry (today's Winnipeg).

The Canadian government immediately clashed with the Métis people over land-use rights, causing the latter to form a provisional government led by the charismatic Louis Riel. He sent the Ottawa-appointed governor packing and, in November 1869, seized control of Upper Fort Garry, thereby forcing Ottawa to the negotiating table. However, with his

1896
Prospectors find more gold, this time in the Yukon. The Klondike Gold Rush is on, with 40,000 aspirants heading to Dawson City.

1913
Immigration to Canada crests, with more than 400,000 people embracing the maple leaf.

1931
Aboriginal, Inuit and Métis children are removed from their communities and forced to attend schools to 'assimilate.'

Basketball team

★ **Canadian Inventions**

Foghorns (1854)

Basketball (1892)

Egg cartons (1911)

Insulin (1922)

IMAX (1967)

delegation already en route, Riel impulsively executed a Canadian prisoner he was holding at the fort.

Although the murder caused widespread uproar in Canada, the government was so keen to bring the west into the fold it agreed to most of Riel's demands, including special language and religious protections for the Métis. As a result, the then-pint-sized province of Manitoba was carved out of the NWT and entered the dominion in July 1870. Macdonald sent troops after Riel but he narrowly managed to escape to the USA. He was formally exiled for five years in 1875.

Rail Link to the West

Despite the progress toward confederation, the west coast remained a distant and forbidding frontier. British Columbia (BC), created in 1866 by merging the colonies of New Caledonia and Vancouver Island, finally joined in 1871 in exchange for the Canadian government assuming all its debt and promising to link it with the east within 10 years via a vast transcontinental railroad.

The Canadian Pacific Railway's construction is one of the most impressive and decisive chapters in Canada's history. Though essential in uniting the nation, it was a costly proposition, made even more challenging by the rough and rugged terrain the tracks had to traverse. To entice investors, the government offered major benefits, including massive land grants in western Canada. Workers drove the final spike into the track at Craigellachie, BC, on November 7, 1885.

Canada rang in the 20th century on a high note. Industrialization was in full swing, prospectors had discovered gold in the Yukon, and Canadian resources – from wheat to lumber – were increasingly in demand. In addition, the new railroad opened the floodgates to immigration. Between 1885 and 1914 about 4.5 million people arrived in Canada. This included large groups of Americans and Eastern Europeans, especially Ukrainians, who went to work cultivating the prairies.

1961
Saskatchewan introduces the country's first universal health-care plan, an idea that soon spreads to the rest of Canada.

1967
The Great Canadian Oil Sands plant opens at Fort McMurray, Alberta, and starts pumping out black gold.

1982
Queen Elizabeth II signs the Canada Act, giving Canada complete sovereignty.

By the time the guns of WWI fell silent in 1918, most Canadians were fed up with sending their sons and husbands to fight in distant wars for Britain. Under the government of William Lyon Mackenzie King, Canada made it clear that Britain could no longer automatically draw upon the Canadian military and even sent its own ambassador to Washington. This forcefulness led to the Statute of Westminster, passed by the British Parliament in 1931. It formalized the independence of Canada and other Commonwealth nations, although Britain retained the right to pass amendments to those countries' constitutions – a right only removed with the 1982 Canada Act. The British monarch remains Canada's head of state, although this is predominantly a ceremonial role and does not diminish the country's sovereignty.

In Remembrance

More than one million Canadians served in the armed forces during WWII from a population of approximately 11.5 million; 42,000 died. Over 3000 of those who volunteered and went to war for Canada were Aboriginal.

Modern-Day Canada

The period after WWII brought another wave of economic expansion and immigration, especially from Europe. The one province left behind during the 1950s boom years was Québec, caught in the grip of ultraconservative leader Maurice Duplessis. Only after his death did the province finally start getting up to speed during the 'Quiet Revolution' of the 1960s. Still, progress wasn't swift enough for radical nationalists who claimed independence was the only way to ensure Francophone rights. Québec has spent the ensuing years flirting with separatism, culminating in a cliffhanger 1994 referendum when a majority of less than 1% voted that the province should remain a part of Canada.

In 1960 Canada's Aboriginal peoples were finally granted Canadian citizenship. Issues involving land rights and discrimination played out in the decades that followed. In 1985 Canada became the first country in the world to pass a national multicultural act. Today, more than 20% of Canada's population is foreign-born. British Columbia has a long history of welcoming Japanese, Chinese and South Asian immigrants. The prairie provinces have traditionally been the destination of large numbers of Ukrainians, and Ontario, which has sizable Caribbean and Russian populations, is also home to 60% of Canada's Muslims.

The new millennium has been kind to Canada. The Canadian dollar took off around 2003 – thanks to oil, diamonds and other natural resources fueling the economy – and tolerance marches onward, with medical marijuana and gay marriage both legalized. The country showed off its abundant assets to the world when it successfully hosted the 2010 Winter Olympics in Vancouver. The nation shines again for its 150th birthday in 2017, with royal visits and its arms of tourism open wide.

1999
Nunavut, Canada's newest province, is chiseled from the icy eastern Arctic.

2013
Calgary is hit by epic floods; four people die and 100,000 others are forced from their homes.

2016
Fort McMurray and the surrounding area succumbs to wildfires, with 80,000 evacuated and an area larger than PEI razed.

National Gallery of Canada (p150), Ottawa

Arts & Culture

*Looking specifically at artistic output, overseas visitors
might be forgiven for thinking that culture in Canada
simply means Celine Dion, William Shatner, Margaret
Atwood and a few totem poles. But while Canadians
rarely shout about it, the country's creative and artistic
scenes are rich and vibrant across the nation, offering
a deep well of creativity for visiting culture vultures to
sink their beaks into.*

Literature

Canada's earliest inhabitants built their cultures on storytelling, passing important tales from generation to generation. Later authors created a written body of Canadian literature – the phrase 'Canlit' is still used here – that defined the struggles of creating a new life in a vast, sometimes barren wilderness. These often deeply affecting novels are the ideal accompaniment for an epic train ride across the prairies. Recommended authors for the long haul include Margaret Laurence and Robertson Davies, while many will also enjoy Lucy Maud Montgomery's *Anne of Green Gables*.

But if you want to hit an adult page turner during your travels, there are three main authors to focus on. If you read Mordecai Richler's *The Apprenticeship of Duddy Kravitz* while hanging around in Montréal's Plateau district, you'll almost feel the story on the streets around you (his later epic, *Barney's Version,* was made into a 2010 movie). Short-story writer Alice Munro won the 2013 Nobel Prize for Literature. Her work often focuses on small-town life in western Ontario. *The View from Castle Rock* provides a good sampler. And a trip to Canada that doesn't include a Margaret Atwood novel is like visiting a bar without having a drink. Consider top titles such as *Oryx and Crake, The Blind Assassin* or *The Handmaid's Tale* or dive into *Surfacing,* an enigmatic story where the Canadian wilderness is a character in itself.

Other Canadian authors to look out for in the local bookstore include Carol Shields, Douglas Coupland, William Gibson and Michael Ondaatje. If you time your visit well, you can join the local bookworms at literary events including the Vancouver Writers Fest (www.writersfest.bc.ca), Toronto's International Festival of Authors (www.ifoa.org) and the annual five-city Word on the Street (www.thewordonthestreet.ca).

Aboriginal Artists

There was little outside recognition of the art produced by local Aboriginal communities until the 20th century. But over the last 50 years or so, there's been a strong and growing appreciation of this body of work, led initially by the paintings, sculptures and carvings of revered Haida artist Bill Reid (1920–98), whose work appears on the back of the $20 bill. Also look out for colorful paintings by Norval Morrisseau; mixed-media works by Saskatchewan-born Edward Poitras; and challenging younger artists such as Marianne Nicolson and Brian Jungen, who explore political and environmental themes in their art.

Visual Arts

Canada's artistic bent was founded thousands of years ago when early Aboriginal inhabitants began adorning their homes with visual representations of the natural world. Later, European painters continued to use nature as their muse, often adding images of the mysterious Aboriginal locals to their canvases.

But the most famous artistic school in Canadian cultural history is the Group of Seven, a clutch of painters who banded loosely together in the early 1920s, creating bold, stylized representations of the striking Canadian landscape that still seem fresh and vibrant today. Members of the group – which included famed luminaries such as Tom Thomson, Lawren Harris and Arthur Lismer, and which later expanded beyond the original seven – would often disappear into the wilderness for months on end. It's during one of these trips that Thomson met his demise, drowning in a lake in 1917, just as he was at the height of his creative powers.

While Group of Seven paintings still attract huge prices and exhibitions of their work typically lure large crowds, Canada also has an energetic contemporary art scene. Internationally renowned latter-day stars include photo conceptualist Jeff Wall, painter and sculptor Betty Goodwin, and painter and avant-garde filmmaker Michael Snow – look out for their works at galleries across the country. And don't forget to check out the celebrated public-art scenes on the streets of Vancouver, Toronto and Montréal.

Music

Ask visitors to name a few Canadian musicians and they'll stutter to a halt after Justin Bieber, Celine Dion, Bryan Adams and Leonard Cohen. But ask the locals to do the same and they'll hit you with a roster of performers you've probably never heard of as well as a few that you always assumed were US-born. For the record, this is the homeland of classic

Art Gallery of Ontario

MIKECPHOTO / SHUTTERSTOCK ©

legends such as Neil Young and Joni Mitchell as well as modern superstars such as Rush, Arcade Fire, Drake, Michael Bublé and Diana Krall.

Working their list into a lather, it won't be long before most Canadians also mention the Tragically Hip, Barenaked Ladies, Blue Rodeo, Guess Who, Feist, New Pornographers, Sarah McLachlan, Oscar Peterson, Great Big Sea, Gordon Lightfoot and Bruce Cockburn: seminal Canadian musicians past and present that define the country's musical soundscape, yet often have little profile outside the country. The Hip, for example, can easily pack stadiums in Canada while they'd struggle to fill a midsized venue in most other countries.

To tap into the scene on your visit, drop into a local independent record store and ask for some recommendations. They'll likely point you to the area's best live-music venues and offer you some tips on who to look out for. And if you're a true die-hard traveling muso, consider timing your visit for a music festival. The Montréal Jazz Festival (www.montreal jazzfest.com) is one of the biggest in the world, while Toronto's North by Northeast (www. nxne.com) draws music industry executives hoping to find the rock stars of tomorrow. If you make it to Calgary, don't miss the brand new National Music Centre, which takes you on a musical journey across the country.

Film

There are two distinct sides to Canada's burgeoning movie industry. As a production hot spot, it's often used as a visual stand-in for US cities, which means you usually don't know you're watching a Canadian-made flick when you sit down to *X-Men* or *Twilight: New Moon*. But aside from being a busy back-lot for Hollywood – the nickname Hollywood North is frequently used here – there's a healthy independent Canadian movie-making scene with a flavor all its own.

Celebrated films made here over the years (and which are about as far from Hollywood blockbusters as you can imagine) include *Incendies* (2010, directed by Denis Villeneuve), *Away from Her* (2006, directed by Sarah Polley), *The Sweet Hereafter* (1997, directed by Atom Egoyan), *Thirty Two Short Films About Glenn Gould* (1993, directed by Francois Girard) and *The Red Violin* (1998), co-written by Don McKellar, who has often seemed like a one-man movie industry unto himself. Guy Maddin is another well-known local filmmaker. He typically films around his hometown of Winnipeg; see *Keyhole* (2011) for an example of his offbeat style.

You can dip into both sides of the Canadian film industry at the country's two main movie festivals. The Toronto International Film Festival (www.tiff.net) is a glitzy affair where Hollywood megastars drop by to promote their new offerings. In contrast, the Vancouver International Film Festival (www.viff.org) showcases art-house and independent flicks from Canada and around the world.

Lobster, Nova Scotia

Canadian Cuisine

Canadian cuisine has moved well beyond the doughnut, and cities such as Montréal, Toronto and Vancouver now offer world-leading dining scenes. Regions across the country have rediscovered distinctive local ingredients produced on their doorsteps, and chefs transform these into an impressive plateful.

Local Flavors

If you're starting from the east, the main dish of the Atlantic provinces is lobster – boiled in the pot and served with a little butter – and the best place to sample it is a community hall 'kitchen party' on Prince Edward Island. Dip into some chunky potato salad and hearty seafood chowder while waiting for your crustacean to arrive, but don't eat too much: you'll need room for the mountainous fruit pie coming your way afterwards.

Next door, Nova Scotia visitors should save their appetites for butter-soft Digby scallops and rustic Lunenberg sausage, while the favored food of nearby Newfoundland and Labrador often combines rib-sticking dishes of cod cheeks and sweet snow crab. If you're feeling really ravenous, gnaw on a slice of seal flipper pie – a dish you're unlikely to forget in a hurry.

★ **Best Restaurants**

Liverpool House (p116), Montréal

Beckta Dining & Wine Bar (p155), Ottawa

Lee (p53), Toronto

Toast! (p138), Québec city

Forage (p219), Vancouver

Restaurants lining Place Jacques-Cartier (p108), Montréal

ROLF HICKER / GETTY IMAGES ©

Québec is the world's largest maple syrup producer, processing around 6.5 million gallons of the sweet pancake accompaniment every year. In this French-influenced province, fine food seems to be a lifeblood for the locals, who will happily sit down for four-hour dinners where accompanying wine and conversation flow in equal measures.

The province's cosmopolitan Montréal has long claimed to be the nation's fine-dining capital, but there's an appreciation of food here at all levels that also includes hearty pea soups, exquisite cheeses and tasty pâtés sold at bustling markets. In addition, there's also that national dish, poutine, waiting to clog your arteries, plus smoked-meat deli sandwiches so large you'll have to dislocate your jaw to fit them in your mouth.

Ontario – especially Toronto – is a microcosm of Canada's melting pot of cuisines. Like Québec, maple syrup is a super-sweet flavoring of choice here, and it's found in decadent desserts such as beavertails (fried, sugared dough) and on breakfast pancakes the size of Frisbees. Head south to the Niagara Peninsula wine region and you'll also discover restaurants fusing contemporary approaches and traditional local ingredients, such as fish from the Great Lakes.

Far north from here, Nunavut in the Arctic Circle is Canada's newest territory, but it has a long history of Inuit food, offering a real culinary adventure for extreme-cuisine travelers. Served in some restaurants (but more often in family homes – make friends with locals and they may invite you in for a feast), regional specialties include boiled seal, raw frozen char and *maktaaq* – whale skin cut into small pieces and swallowed whole.

In contrast, the central provinces of Manitoba, Saskatchewan and Alberta have their own deep-seated culinary ways. The latter, Canada's cowboy country, is the nation's beef capital – you'll find top-notch Alberta steak on menus at leading restaurants across the country. If you're offered 'prairie oysters' here, though, you might want to know (or maybe you'd prefer not to) that they're bull's testicles prepared in a variety of ways designed to take your mind off their origin. In the Rockies things get wilder – try elk, bison and even moose.

There's an old Eastern European influence over the border in Manitoba, where immigrant Ukrainians have added comfort-food staples such as pierogi and thick, spicy sausages. Head next door to prairie-land Saskatchewan for dessert. The province's heaping fruit pies are its most striking culinary contribution, especially when prepared with tart Saskatoon berries.

In the far west, British Columbians have traditionally fed themselves from the sea and the fertile farmlands of the interior. Okanagan Valley peaches, cherries and blueberries – best purchased from seasonal roadside stands throughout the region – are the staple of many summer diets. But it's the seafood that attracts the lion's share of culinary fans. Tuc into succulent wild salmon, juicy Fanny Bay oysters and velvet-soft scallops and you may decide you've stumbled on foodie nirvana.

Top Dining Neighborhoods

Ask anyone in Toronto, Montréal or Vancouver to name Canada's leading foodie city and they'll likely inform you that you've just found it. But while each of the big three claims to be at the top table when it comes to dining, their strengths are so diverse they're more accurately defined as complementary courses in one great meal.

First dish on the table is Montréal, which was Canada's sole dine-out capital long before the upstarts threw off their fried-meat-and-mashed-potato shackles. Renowned for bringing North America's finest French-influenced cuisine to local palates, it hasn't given up its crown lightly. Chefs here are often treated like rock stars as they challenge old-world conventions with daring, even artistic, approaches – expect clever, fusion-esque gastronomy. You should also expect a great restaurant experience: Montréalers have a bacchanalian love for eating out, with lively rooms ranging from cozy old-town restaurants to the animated patios of Rue Prince Arthur and the sophisticated, often funky eateries of the Plateau.

If Montréal serves as an ideal starter, that makes Toronto the main course – although that's a reflection of its recent elevation rather than its prominence. Fusion is also the default approach in Canada's largest city, although it's been taken even further here with a wave of contemporary immigration adding modern influences from Asia to a foundation of European cuisines. With a bewildering 7000 restaurants to choose from, though, it can be a tough choice figuring out where to unleash your top-end dining budget. The best approach is to hit the neighborhoods: both the Financial District and Old York areas are studded with classy, high-end joints.

And while that appears to make Vancouver the dessert, it could be argued this glass-towered, West Coast metropolis is the best of the bunch. In recent years, some of the country's most innovative chefs have set up shop here, inspired by the twin influences of an abundant local larder and Canada's most cosmopolitan population. Fusion is the starting point here in fine-dining districts such as Yaletown and Kitsilano. But there's also a high level of authenticity in top-notch Asian dining: the best sushi bars and *izakayas* outside Japan jostle for attention with superb Vietnamese and Korean eateries.

Tasty Blogs

- National Nosh (www.thenational nosh.blogspot.com)

- Dinner with Julie (www.dinnerwith julie.com)

- Seasonal Ontario Food (www.seasonal ontariofood.blogspot.com)

- Vancouver Foodster (www.vancouver foodster.com)

The Basics

It's worth booking ahead for popular places, especially from Thursday to Sunday. Most cafes or budget restaurants don't accept reservations.

Restaurants Range from steakhouses to vegan raw food joints and everything in between. Many are family-friendly and casual; some are not.

Cafes Not just for coffee; you can often get sandwiches, soups and baked goods.

Bistros Small and often classy, with home-cooked food.

Delis Choose your food, have it wrapped and take it with you; usually have sandwiches and wraps.

Diners Brunches and lunches; often very family-friendly.

Pubs Home-cooked fish and chips, burgers and salads.

Wine

While many international visitors – especially those who think Canadians live under a permanent blanket of snow – are surprised to learn that wine is produced here, their suspicion is always tempered after a drink or two. Canada's wines have gained ever-greater kudos in recent years and while their small-scale production and the industry dominance of other wine regions mean they will never be global market leaders, these wines could definitely hold their own in an international taste-off.

Depending on how thirsty you are, you're rarely too far from a wine region in Canada. Which means that most visitors can easily add a mini taste-tripping tour to their visit if they'd like to meet a few producers and sample some intriguing local flavors.

Wine Festivals

Canada is dripping with palate-pleasing wine events, which makes it especially important to check the dates of your trip: raising a few glasses with celebratory locals is one of the best ways to encounter the country.

If you're in BC, it's hard to miss one of the Okanagan's three main festivals – see www.thewinefestivals.com for dates. If you prefer not to leave the big city, check out March's Vancouver International Wine Festival (www.vanwinefest.ca).

Across the country in Ontario, Niagara also stages more than one annual event to celebrate its winey wealth, including June's New Vintage Festival and September's giant Niagara Wine Festival. For information, visit www.niagarawinefestival.com.

Québec-bound oenophiles should drop into the annual Montréal Passion Vin (www.montrealpassionvin.ca), a swish two-day charity fundraiser focused on unique and rare vintages. For regional food as well as wine, the Eastern Townships' Magog-Orford area hosts the multiday Fête des Vendanges (www.fetedesvendanges.com) in September.

Visitors to the East Coast are not left out. Nova Scotia hosts a 50-event Fall Wine Festival (www.mynslc.com) in mid-September.

Canoeing, Québec

Outdoor Activities

*Canada's endless variety of landscapes makes for
a fantastic playground. Whether it's snowboarding
Whistler's mountains, surfing Nova Scotia's swells or
paddling the Yukon River, adventures abound.*

Skiing & Snowboarding

It seems like almost everyone in Canada was born to ski. Visitors will find some of the
world's most renowned resorts here – British Columbia (BC), Alberta and Québec host
the premier ones – but it's also worth asking the locals where they like to hit the slopes:
for every big-time swanky resort, there are several smaller spots where the terrain and the
welcome can be even better.

Québec boasts some big slopes – Le Massif, near Québec City, has a vertical drop of
770m (2526ft) – located handily close to the cities. Most of these lower-elevation resorts,
such as Mont-Tremblant, are a day's drive from Toronto and less than an hour from Québec
City and Montréal. Ski areas in Québec's Eastern Townships offer renowned gladed runs
that weave through a thinned forest.

Head west and you'll hit the big mountains and vast alpine terrains. Glide down gargan-
tuan slopes at Whistler-Blackcomb, which has North America's highest vertical drop and

Hiking on the Cape Breton coast, Nova Scotia

ALEXANDER HOWARD / LONELY PLANET ©

★ **Outdoors Resources**

Parks Canada (www.pc.gc.ca) National park action.

Canada Trails (www.canadatrails. ca) Hiking, biking and cross-country skiing.

Paddling Canada (www.paddling canada.com) Kayaking and canoeing.

most impressive terrain variation. You'll also slide through stunning postcard landscapes in the Canadian Rockies, especially at Sunshine in Banff National Park.

In BC's Okanagan Valley, resorts such as Apex and Big White boast good snow every year. Snowpack ranges from 2m to 6m-plus, depending on how close the resort is to the Pacific Ocean. The deepest, driest snow in the world piles up in BC's Kootenay region. Ski it at Nelson's Whitewater, Rossland's Red Mountain or Fernie's Alpine Resort.

For cross-country skiing, Canmore (www.canmorenordic.com) in Alberta offers popular trails that were part of that other Canadian Winter Olympics, Calgary in 1988. For further information and resources covering the national scene, check the website of the Canadian Ski Council (www.skicanada.org).

Hiking

You don't have to be a hiker to hike in Canada. While there are plenty of multiday jaunts for those who like tramping through the wilderness equipped only with a Swiss Army knife, there are also innumerable opportunities for those who prefer a gentle stroll around a lake with a pub visit at the end.

The country's hiking capital is Banff National Park, crisscrossed with stupefying vistas accessible to both hard and soft eco-adventurers. At Lake Louise, for example, you can march through dense spruce and pine forests, then ascend into alpine meadows carpeted with wildflowers and surrounded by rugged glaciers and azure lakes. Also in the Rockies region, Wilcox Ridge and Parker Ridge offer breathtaking glacier views.

In BC's provincial parks system (www.bcparks.ca), you'll have a choice of more than 100 parks: check out Garibaldi Park's landscape of ancient volcanoes (not far from Whistler) and Mt Robson Park's popular Berg Lake alpine trail. Vancouver's North Shore is home to the Grouse Grind, a steep forest hike that's also known as 'Mother Nature's Stairmaster.' Across the water in Vancouver Island's Pacific Rim Park, the lush 75km West Coast Trail (www.west coasttrail.com) is undoubtedly one of the country's most breathtaking, combining traditional First Nations trails and life-saving routes used by shipwreck survivors.

Out east, awe-inspiring trails pattern the landscape. In southern Ontario, the Bruce Trail (www.brucetrail.org) tracks from Niagara Falls to Tobermory. It's the oldest and longest continuous footpath in Canada and spans more than 850km. Though portions are near cities such as Hamilton and Toronto, it's surprisingly serene. Cape Breton Highlands National Park offers exquisite hiking over stark, dramatic coastline. Newfoundland's trails make for fantastic shoreline hiking and often provide whale views. The East Coast Trail (www.eastcoasttrail.ca) on the Avalon Peninsula is particularly renowned for its vistas.

And don't forget the cities. Canada's major metropolises offer some great urban hikes, an ideal way to get to know the communities you're visiting. Slip into your runners for a stroll (or a jog) with the locals in Montréal's Parc du Mont-Royal or in Vancouver's gemlike Stanley Park, where the idyllic seawall winds alongside towering trees and lapping ocean.

Kayaking & Canoeing

The Canadian Arctic, kayaking's motherland, still remains one of its special places: cruise the polar fjords of Ellesmere Island and watch narwhals and walruses during the fuse-short summer. Further south, slide silently past ancient forests and totem poles in BC's Gwaii Haanas National Park Reserve, or in the province's Johnstone Strait and watch orcas breaching. The East Coast has sea kayaking galore. Paddlers in Witless Bay or Gros Morne, Newfoundland, often glide alongside whales.

Fishing

Built on its aboriginal and pioneer past, Canada has a strong tradition of fishing, and you can expect to come across plenty of opportunities to hook walleye, pike, rainbow or lake trout on your travels. Among the best fishing holes to head for are Lunenburg in Nova Scotia and the Miramichi River in New Brunswick. And while salmon are the usual draw on the Pacific coastline, hopping aboard a local vessel for some sea fishing off Haida Gwaii can deliver the kind of giant catches you'll be bragging about for years to come.

If you're on a tight schedule and don't have time for multiday odysseys, there are plenty of more accessible ways to get your kayaking fix. Big cities like BC's Vancouver and Victoria offer tours and lessons near town, while the province's Sunshine Coast and Salt Spring Island offer crenulated coastlines combined with tranquil sea inlets.

As old as kayaking, and equally as Canadian, is the canoe. Experienced paddlers can strike out on one of 33 Canadian Heritage Rivers (www.chrs.ca). Some of the best include the Northwest Territories' South Nahanni River (near Fort Simpson) and Ontario's French River (near Sudbury).

Mountain Biking & Cycling

Mountain biking is a big deal in Canada. While cycling enthusiasts in Europe might be into trundling around town or along a gentle riverside trail, in Canada you're more likely to find them hurtling down a mountainside covered in mud. Given the landscape, of course, it was just a matter of time before the wheels went off-road here.

If you need to ease yourself in, start gently with BC's Kettle Valley Rail Trail (www.kettle valleyrailway.ca), near Kelowna. This dramatic segment of converted railway barrels across picturesque wooden trestle bridges and through canyon tunnels.

Looking for more of an adrenaline rush? In Vancouver's North Shore area, you'll be riding on much narrower and steeper trestles. Birthplace of freeride mountain biking (which combines downhill and dirt jumping), this area offers some unique innovations: elevated bridges, log rides and skinny planks that loft over the wet undergrowth. It's a similar story up at Whistler where the melted ski slopes are transformed into a summertime bike park that draws thousands every year – especially during the annual Crankworx Mountain Bike Festival (www.crankworx.com/whistler) in July.

For road touring, Canada's East Coast, with more small towns and less emptiness, is a fantastic place to pedal, either as a single-day road ride or a multiday trip. Circle Québec's Lac St-Jean; try any part of the 4000km Route Verte (www.routeverte.com), the longest network of bicycle paths in the Americas; or follow Prince Edward Island's bucolic red roads and its Confederation Trail (www.tourismpei.com/pei-cycling).

Hockey: The National Pastime

Canadians aren't fooling around when it comes to hockey. They play hard and well and if they're not playing, they cheer and catcall like they mean it.

Grassroots hockey, aka pond hockey, takes place in communities across the country every night on a frozen surface. All you need is a puck, a hockey stick and a few friends to live the dream.

If you'd rather watch than play, Vancouver, Edmonton, Calgary, Toronto, Ottawa, Winnipeg and Montréal all have NHL (www.nhl.com) teams who skate tough and lose the odd tooth. Minor pro teams and junior hockey clubs fill many more arenas with rabid fans; check the Canadian Hockey League (www.chl.ca) and American Hockey League (www.theahl.com) for local stick wielders.

Rock Climbing & Mountaineering

All those inviting crags you've spotted on your trip are an indication that Canada is a major climbing capital, ideal for both short sport climbs or epic big-wall ascents.

British Columbia's Squamish region, located between Vancouver and Whistler, is a climbing center, with dozens of accessible (and not so accessible) cracks, faces, arêtes and overhangs. Tap into the scene via Squamish Rock Guides (www.squamishrockguides.com). Canmore, near Banff, is another ideal destination for rock climbers, no matter what your skill level. For the adventure of a lifetime, the Northwest Territories' Cirque of the Unclimbables is certainly near the top of the list. If your trip takes you out east instead, Ontario's favorite climbing havens dot the Bruce Peninsula.

If mountaineering is more your thing, the Rockies are the recommended first stop. Yamnuska (www.yamnuska.com) is one company that offers ice climbing, ski mountaineering and avalanche training in the region. The Matterhorn of Canada is BC's Mt Assiniboine, located between the Kootenay and Banff National Parks. Other western classics include Alberta's Mt Edith Cavell, in Jasper; BC's Mt Robson and Sir Donald in the Rockies; and Garibaldi Peak, in Garibaldi Provincial Park, near Whistler. If you need a guide, check in with the excellent Alpine Club of Canada (www.alpineclubofcanada.ca).

Surfing & Windsurfing

If you're aiming to become a temporary beach bum on your Canada trip, head to the wild west coast of BC's Vancouver Island and hang out on the beaches around Tofino. Surfing schools and gear rental operations stud this region and you'll have an awesome time riding the swells (or just watching everyone else as you stretch out on the sand). Backed by verdant rainforest, it's an idyllic spot to spend some time.

June to September is the height of the season here, but serious surfers also like to drop by in winter to face down the lashing waves. Check Surfing Vancouver Island (www.surfingvancouverisland.com) for a taste of what to expect.

Some 6000km away, the east coast of Nova Scotia can also dish out some formidable swells. The US south coast's hurricane season (August to November) brings Canadians steep fast breaks, snappy right and left point breaks, and offshore reef and shoal breaks in areas like Lawrencetown, just outside Halifax, as well as across the entire South Shore region. There are also a couple of surf schools here. Scotia Surfer (www.scotiasurfer.com) has the lowdown.

Windsurfers set their sails for Howe Sound in Squamish, BC, and for Québec's Magdalen Islands, a small chain in the Gulf of St Lawrence.

Grizzly bear

Wildlife

On land, in the water and in the air, Canada is teeming with the kind of camera-worthy critters that make visitors wonder if they haven't stepped into a safari park by mistake. And when we say 'critters,' we're not talking small fry: this is the home of grizzlies, polar bears, moose and bald eagles, and offers perfect coastal viewing spots for a roll call of huge whales. Extra camera batteries are heartily recommended.

Grizzly Bears & Black Bears

Grizzly bears – *Ursus arctos horribilis* to all you Latin scholars out there – are most commonly found in the Rocky Mountain regions of British Columbia (BC) and Alberta. Standing up to 3m tall, they're recognizable by their distinctive shoulder hump and labrador-like snout. Solitary animals with no natural enemies (except humans), they enjoy crunching on elk, moose and caribou, but they're usually content to fill their bellies with berries and, if available, fresh salmon. Keep in mind that you should never approach any bear. And in remote areas, be sure to travel in groups.

In 1994, coastal BC's Khutzeymateen Grizzly Bear Sanctuary (near the northern town of Prince Rupert) was officially designated with protected status. Over 50 grizzlies

★ **Best Moose-Viewing**

Northern Peninsula, Newfoundland

Cape Breton Highlands National Park, Nova Scotia

Algonquin Provincial Park, Ontario

Maligne Lake, Jasper National Park, Alberta

currently live on this 45,000-hectare refuge. A few ecotour operators have permits for viewing the animals.

Just to confuse you, grizzlies can be brown or black, while their smaller, more prevalent relative, the black bear, is commonly brown. Canada is home to around half a million black bears and they're spread out across the country, except for Prince Edward Island, southern Alberta and southern Saskatchewan. In regions such as northern BC, as well as in Banff and Jasper National Parks, seeing black bears feasting on berries or dandelions as you drive past on the highway is surprisingly common.

The world's only white-colored black bears roam in northern BC. Born with a recessive gene, there are approximately 400 of these 'spirit bears' living in mostly coastal areas.

Polar Bears

Weighing less than a kilogram at birth, the fiercest member of the bear clan is not quite so cute when it grows up to be a hulking 600kg. But these mesmerizing animals still pack a huge visual punch for visitors. If your visit to Canada won't be complete until you've seen one, there's really only one place to go: Churchill, Manitoba, on the shores of Hudson Bay (late September to early November is the viewing season). About 900 of the planet's roughly 20,000 white-furred beasts prowl the tundra here.

Just remember: the carnivorous, ever-watchful predators are not cuddly cartoon critters. Unlike grizzlies and black bears, polar bears actively prey on people.

Moose

Canada's iconic shrub-nibbler, the moose is a massive member of the deer family that owes its popularity to its distinctively odd appearance: skinny legs supporting a humongous body and a cartoonish face that looks permanently inquisitive and clueless at the same time. And then there are the antlers: males grow a spectacular rack every summer, only to discard them come November.

Adding to their *Rocky and Bullwinkle Show* appeal, a moose can move at more than 50km/h and easily outswim two adults paddling a canoe – all on a vegetarian diet comprised mostly of tasty leaves and twigs.

You'll spot moose foraging for food near lakes, muskegs and streams, as well as in the forests of the western mountain ranges in the Rockies and the Yukon. Newfoundland is perhaps the moosiest place of all. In 1904, the province imported and released four beasts into the wild. They enjoyed the good life of shrub-eating and hot sex, ultimately spawning the 120,000 inhabitants that now roam the woods.

During mating season (September), the males can become belligerent, as can a mother with her calves, so keep your distance.

Elk, Deer & Caribou

Moose are not the only animals that can exhibit a Mr Hyde personality change during rutting season. Usually placid, male elk have been known to charge vehicles in Jasper National Park, believing their reflection in the shiny paintwork to be a rival for their harem of eligible females. It's rare, though, and Jasper is generally one of the best places in Canada to see this large deer species wandering around attracting camera-toting travelers on the edge of town.

White-tailed deer can be found anywhere from Nova Scotia's Cape Breton to the Northwest Territories' Great Slave Lake. Its bigger relative, the caribou, is unusual in that both males and females sport enormous antlers. Barren-ground caribou feed on lichen and spend most of the year on the tundra from Baffin Island to Alaska. Woodland caribou roam further south, with some of the biggest herds trekking across northern Québec and Labrador. These beasts, which have a reputation for not being especially smart, also show up in the mountain parks of BC, Alberta and Newfoundland, which is where many visitors see them. In 2009, the small herd in Banff National Park set off an avalanche that ultimately wiped out the population. Also known as reindeer, the caribou is on the Canadian 25-cent quarter.

Whales

More than 22 species of whale and porpoise lurk offshore in Atlantic Canada, including superstars like the humpback whale, which averages 15m and 36 tons; the North Atlantic right whale, the world's most endangered leviathan, with an estimated population of just 350; and the mighty blue whale, the largest animal on earth at 25m and around 100 tons. Then there's the little guy, the minke, which grows to 10m and often approaches boats, delighting passengers with acrobatics as it shows off. Whale-watching tours are very popular throughout the region.

You can also spot humpbacks and gray whales off the West Coast. But it's the orca that dominates viewing here. Their aerodynamic bodies, signature black-and-white coloration and incredible speed (up to 40km/h) make them the Ferraris of the aquatic world, and their diet includes seals, belugas and other whales (hence the 'killer whale' nickname). The waters around Vancouver Island, particularly in the Strait of Juan de Fuca, teem with orcas every summer. Whale-watching tours depart from points throughout the region; Tofino and Victoria are particular hot spots for operators. It's also not uncommon to see them from the decks of the BC ferries.

Belugas glide in Arctic waters to the north. These ghostly white whales are one of the smallest members of the whale family, typically measuring no more than 4m and weighing about 1 ton. They are chatty fellows who squeak, groan and peep while traveling in closely knit family pods. Churchill, Manitoba, is a good place to view them, as is Tadoussac, Québec (the only population outside the Arctic resides here).

Birds

Canada's wide skies are home to 462 bird species, with BC and Ontario boasting the greatest diversity. The most famous feathered resident is the common loon, Canada's national bird – if you don't spot one in the wild, you'll see it on the back of the $1 coin. Rivaling it in the ubiquity stakes are Canada geese, a hardy fowl that can fly up to 1000km per day and seems to have successfully colonized parks throughout the world.

The most visually arresting of Canada's birds are its eagles, especially the bald variety, whose wingspan can reach up to 2m. Good viewing sites include Brackendale, between

★ **Whale Hot Spots**
Witless Bay, Newfoundland
Digby Neck, Nova Scotia
Victoria, BC
Tofino, BC
Cabot Trail, Nova Scotia

Vancouver and Whistler in BC, where up to 4000 eagles nest in winter. Also train your binoculars on Bras d'Or Lake on Cape Breton Island, Nova Scotia, and on Vancouver Island's southern and western shorelines.

Seabirds flock to Atlantic Canada to breed. Think razorbills, kittiwakes, Arctic terns, common murres and, yes, puffins. Everyone loves these cute little guys, a sort of waddling penguin-meets-parrot, with black-and-white feathers and an orange beak. They nest around Newfoundland in particular. The preeminent places to get feathered are New Brunswick's Grand Manan Island and Newfoundland's Witless Bay and Cape St Mary's (both on the Avalon Peninsula near St John's). The best time is May through August, before the birds fly away for the winter.

Watching Wildlife

Seeing a bear foraging alongside the road or happening upon a moose swimming in a remote lake are the highlights of many visitors' trips to the parks. Keep in mind, however, that you're a guest in their home. A number of guidelines and laws exist to protect both you and the animals. Approaching or interfering with wildlife is a crime taken very seriously in this corner of the world – penalties are steep.

- Keep your distance – at least 10 bus lengths from bears, cougars and wolves and three bus lengths from elk, deer, sheep, goats and moose. If a bedded animal gets up or a feeding animal stops chewing, you're too close. Animals don't like the spotlight and those that feel threatened can (and do!) charge.

- If you see a female elk on her own, there's a calf nearby. If there's a bear cub, a mama bear is not far. *Never* get between a wild animal and her young. You will be viewed as a threat and treated likewise.

- Wildlife-watching is a spectator sport only: do not approach, entice or in any way disturb wildlife. Many people move closer and closer in an attempt to get a photo, frightening the animal and putting the photographer in a dangerous position.

- Never feed wildlife. Park rangers are almost always forced to put down animals that become accustomed to people, as the animals generally turn aggressive over time.

- If you see an animal from your car, slow down – it could dart in front of you at any moment. If you decide to stop, stay inside your car.

- Be particularly wary of animals that appear indifferent to your presence; they may appear cuddly and even docile, but they're not.

Ice hockey match

Spectator Sports

While Canadians have a solid reputation for being mild-mannered, that all changes when it comes to watching sports. Meek and peace-loving most of the time, locals will paint their faces, down a few too many Molsons and chant, scream and sing at the top of their lungs at hockey games that somehow seem to define their existence. For visitors, watching sports with these passionate locals is an eye-opening cultural experience.

Hockey

While Canada is a multi-faith country, there's one religion that rises above all others. Hockey – don't even bother calling it ice hockey here – rouses rabid emotions in die-hard fans and can trigger group hugging and uncontrollable sobbing at the drop of a puck, especially when the local team has just lost (like they have always done lately) in the annual Stanley Cup play-offs.

Canada has seven teams in the elite, US-dominated National Hockey League (NHL): the Vancouver Canucks, Calgary Flames, Edmonton Oilers, Ottawa Senators, Montréal Canadiens, Winnipeg Jets and Toronto Maple Leafs (don't make the mistake of calling them 'the Leaves'). The CBC Television website (www.cbc.ca/sports/hockey/nhl) has the details.

Women's National Soccer Team

With two Olympic bronze medals from 2012 and 2016, Canada's Women's National Soccer Team has gained a huge following. In 2002, Canada hosted FIFA's first U-19 Championship where the team won silver and thousands of fans woke up to the fact that Canada is good at sports other than hockey. The 2015 FIFA Women's World Cup was held in Vancouver. While the national team was disqualified, the tournament drew in 1,353,506 fans – setting a new record.

While tickets for games in some areas can be hard to come by – Vancouver Canucks games routinely sell out, for example, and booking as far ahead as possible for the September to June season is essential – you don't have to hit a stadium to catch a game. For a glimpse at what it feels like to be unreservedly in love with a Canadian hockey side, head to any local pub on game night and you'll be swept up in the emotion. And the beer will be better than the overpriced plastic cups of fizz on offer at the games themselves.

Minor pro teams and junior hockey clubs also fill arenas with fans. Check the Canadian Hockey League (www.chl.ca) and American Hockey League (www.theahl.com) for local stick wielders.

Football

We're not talking about soccer and we're not even talking about American Football here. With eight major teams across the country, the Canadian Football League (CFL) is second only to hockey in the hearts and minds of many north-of-the-border sports nuts. And while it's similar to American Football – think hefty padding, an egg-shaped ball and the kind of crunching tackles that would stop a grizzly bear – the Canadian version involves teams of 12 players and is fought out on a larger pitch.

Like hockey, the main annual aim of the Hamilton Tiger-Cats, Montréal Alouettes, Toronto Argonauts, Ottawa Redblacks, Winnipeg Blue Bombers, Saskatchewan Roughriders, Calgary Stampeders, Edmonton Eskimos and BC Lions is to win that elusive trophy, this one called the Grey Cup. Play-off games trigger raucous street celebrations in host cities, with fans from visiting teams parading around in team shirts hollering their undying love for their side.

Soccer

Canada's most popular participation sport, soccer – you won't get very far calling it football here – has traditionally mirrored the US experience by never quite reaching the heights of the continent's more established professional sports. But you can't keep a good pastime down, and while they struggled with early attempts at building support here (by importing fading stars from Europe and South America), recent leagues are on a much more solid footing.

The three biggest Canadian professional teams are Toronto FC, the Montréal Impact and the Vancouver Whitecaps. All have entered the sport's US-based top level Major League Soccer (MLS) class. The Canadian Soccer League (www.canadiansoccerleague.com) occupies a lower rung on the sport's ladder. It's dominated by teams from Ontario, including the North York Astros and Windsor Stars. Soccer is growing in popularity as a spectator sport in Canada, but tickets for top-level games are still relatively easy to buy – book ahead via club websites, though, if you have a particular date in mind.

Baseball

Following the 2004 relocation of the Montréal Expos to Washington (they're now called the Washington Nationals), Canada's only Major League Baseball (MLB) team is the Toronto Blue Jays, a member of the American League's Eastern Division. Founded in 1977 and playing in the city's cavernous downtown Sky Dome – now known as the Rogers Centre – they are the only non-US team to win the World Series (in 1993). Follow the team and check out ticket options for the April to early October season at www.bluejays.com.

There is also one professional minor league side in Canada: the Vancouver Canadians (www.milb.com), affiliated with the Blue Jays and playing in the Northwest League. Their recently refurbished outdoor stadium with mountain views is one of the best diamonds in Canada, so hit the bleachers and feel the nostalgic ambience of old-school summertime baseball.

Additional lower level teams across the country – including the Edmonton Capitals (www.capsbaseball.ca) and Winnipeg Goldeyes (www.goldeyes.com) – offer a similar family-friendly feel, while college teams are also popular if you want to catch the atmosphere of a game without paying Blue Jay prices.

Rocky Mountaineer train (p309), Banff National Park

Survival Guide

Directory A–Z

Accommodations

In popular destinations, such as Ottawa or Jasper, book ahead in summer, during major festivals and for ski season.

B&Bs From purpose-built villas to heritage homes or someone's spare room, these are often the most atmospheric lodgings.

Motels Dotting the highways into town, these are often family-run affairs that offer the most bang for your buck.

Hotels From standard to luxurious with a burgeoning number of boutique options.

Hostels Young backpacker hangouts, but favored by outdoor adventurers in remoter regions.

Camping Campgrounds are plentiful; private grounds often have fancier facilities.

Seasons

○ Peak season is summer (June–August), when prices are highest.

○ It's best to book ahead during summer, as well as during ski season at winter resorts, and during holidays and major events.

○ Some properties close down altogether in the off-season.

Amenities

○ At many budget properties (campgrounds, hostels, simple B&Bs) bathrooms are shared.

○ Midrange accommodations, such as most B&Bs, inns (*auberges* in French), motels and some hotels, generally offer the best value for money. Expect a private bathroom, cable TV and, in some cases, free breakfast.

○ Top-end accommodations offer an international standard of amenities.

○ Most properties offer in-room wi-fi. It's typically free in budget and midrange lodgings, while top-end hotels often charge a fee.

○ Air-conditioning is not a standard amenity at most budget and midrange places; ask before you book.

Price Ranges

The following price ranges refer to a double room that has a private bathroom in high season, unless stated otherwise. Tax (which can be up to 17%) is not included in prices listed.

$	less than $100
$$	$100–250
$$$	more than $250

Book Your Stay Online

For more accommodation reviews by Lonely Planet writers, check out http://hotels.lonely planet.com/canada. You'll find independent reviews, as well as recommendations on the best places to stay. Best of all, you can book online.

Customs Regulations

The Canada Border Services Agency (www. cbsa.gc.ca) website has the customs lowdown. A few regulations to note:

Alcohol You can bring in 1.5L of wine, 1.14L of liquor or 24 355mL beers duty-free.

Money You can bring in/take out up to $10,000; larger amounts must be reported to customs.

Pets You must carry a signed and dated certificate from a veterinarian to prove your dog or cat has had a rabies shot in the past 36 months.

Prescription drugs You can bring in/take out a 90-day supply for personal use (though if you're taking it to the USA, know it's technically illegal, but overlooked for individuals).

Tobacco You can bring in 200 cigarettes, 50 cigars, 200g of tobacco and 200 tobacco sticks duty-free.

Climate

Halifax

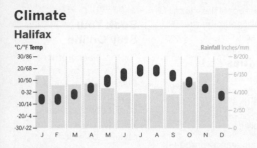

Toronto

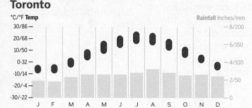

Vancouver

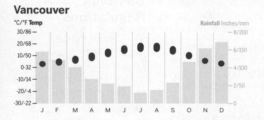

Electricity

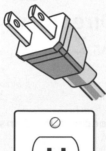

120V/60Hz

120V/60Hz

Discount Cards

Discounts are commonly offered for seniors, children, families and people with disabilities, though no special cards are issued (you get the savings on-site when you pay). Members of AAA and other automobile associations can also receive various travel-related discounts.

International Student Identity Card (www.isic. org) Provides students with discounts on travel insurance and admission to museums and other sights. There are also cards for those who are under 26 but not students, and for full-time teachers.

Parks Canada Discovery Pass (www.pc.gc.ca; adult/child/family $68/33/136) Provides access to more than 100 national parks and historic sites for a year. Can pay for itself in as few as seven visits over daily entry fees; also provides quicker entry into sites. Note that in 2017, all Parks Canada sites will be free in celebration of the country's 150th birthday.

Food

The following price ranges are for main dishes:

$	less than $15
$$	$15–25
$$$	more than $25

Health

Availability & Cost of Health Care

Medical services are widely available. For emergencies, the best bet is to find the nearest hospital and go to its emergency room. If the problem isn't urgent, call a nearby hospital and ask for a referral to a local physician, which is usually much cheaper than a trip to the emergency room.

Pharmacies are abundant, but prescriptions can be expensive without insurance.

Environmental Hazards

Cold exposure This can be a significant problem, especially in the northern regions. Keep all body surfaces covered, including the head and neck. Watch out for the 'Umbles' – stumbles, mumbles, fumbles and grumbles – which are signs of impending hypothermia.

Heat exhaustion Dehydration is the main contributor. Symptoms include weakness, headache, nausea and sweaty skin. Lay the victim flat with their legs raised; apply cool, wet cloths to the skin; and rehydrate.

Infectious Diseases

Giardiasis Intestinal infection. Avoid drinking directly from lakes, ponds, streams and rivers.

Lyme Disease Occurs mostly in southern Canada. Transmitted by deer ticks in late spring and summer. Perform a tick check after you've been outdoors.

West Nile Virus Mosquito-transmitted in late summer and early fall. Prevent by keeping covered (wear long sleeves, long pants, hats, and shoes rather than sandals) and apply a good insect repellent, preferably one containing DEET, to exposed skin and clothing.

Medical Checklist

Bring medications you may need clearly labeled in their original containers. A signed, dated letter from your physician that describes your medical conditions and medications, including generic names, is also a good idea.

Also consider packing: insect repellent; permethrin-containing insect spray for clothing, tents and bed nets; sunblock; and motion-sickness medication.

Recommended Vaccinations

No special vaccines are required or recommended for travel to Canada. All travelers should be up to date on routine immunizations.

Useful Websites

MD Travel Health (www.mdtravelhealth.com) General health resources.

Public Health Agency of Canada (www.phac-aspc.gc.ca) Canadian health resources.

World Health Organization (www.who.int) General health resources.

Insurance

Make sure you have adequate travel insurance, whatever the length of your trip. At a minimum, you need coverage for medical emergencies and treatment, including hospital stays and an emergency flight home. Medical treatment for non-Canadians is hugely expensive.

Also consider insurance for luggage theft or loss. If you already have a home-owners or renters policy, check what it will cover and get only supplemental insurance to protect against the rest. If you have prepaid a large portion of your vacation, trip cancellation insurance is worthwhile.

Worldwide travel insurance is available at www.lonelyplanet.com/travel-insurance. You can buy, extend and claim online at anytime – even if you're already on the road.

Internet Access

o It's easy to find internet access. Libraries and community agencies in practically every town provide free wi-fi and computers for public use. Note that usage time is often restricted (usually 30 minutes) and some facilities have erratic hours.

○ Internet cafes are limited to the main tourist areas; access generally starts around $2 per hour.

○ Wi-fi is widely available. Most lodgings offer access, as do many cafes, restaurants and bars.

○ For a list of wi-fi hot spots around Canada, visit Wi-Fi Free Spot (www.wififreespot.com).

Legal Matters

○ If you are arrested or charged with an offense, you have the right to keep your mouth shut and to hire any lawyer you wish (contact your embassy for a referral, if necessary). If you cannot afford one, ask to be represented by public counsel. There is a presumption of innocence.

○ Travelers should note that they can be prosecuted under the law of their home country regarding age of consent, even when abroad.

○ The blood-alcohol limit is 0.08% and driving cars, motorcycles, boats and snowmobiles while drunk is a criminal offense. If you are caught, you may face stiff fines, license suspension and other nasty consequences.

○ Consuming alcohol anywhere other than at a residence or licensed premises is also a no-no, which puts parks, beaches and the rest of the great outdoors off-limits.

○ Avoid illegal drugs, as penalties may entail heavy fines, possible jail time and a criminal record. The only exception is the use of marijuana for medical purposes, which became legal in 2001. Meanwhile, the decriminalization of pot possession for personal use remains a subject of ongoing debate among the general public and in Parliament.

LGBTI Travelers

Canada is tolerant when it comes to gays and lesbians, though this outlook is more common in the big cities than in rural areas. Same-sex marriage is legal throughout the country.

Montréal, Toronto and Vancouver are by far Canada's 'gayest' cities, each with a humming nightlife scene, publications and lots of associations and support groups. All have sizeable Pride celebrations, too, which attract big crowds.

Attitudes remain more conservative in the northern regions. Throughout Nunavut, and to a lesser extent in the Aboriginal communities of the Northwest Territories, there are some retrogressive attitudes toward homosexuality. The Yukon, in contrast, is more like British Columbia, with a live-and-let-live West Coast attitude.

The following are good resources for LGBTI travel in Canada:

Gay Canada (www.gaycanada.com) Search by province or city for queer-friendly businesses and resources.

Queer Canada (www.queercanada.ca) A general resource.

Xtra (www.xtra.ca) Source for gay and lesbian news nationwide.

Maps

○ Most tourist offices distribute free provincial road maps.

○ For extended hikes or multiday backcountry treks, it's a good idea to carry a topographic map. The best are the series of 1:50,000 scale maps published by the government's Centre for Topographic Information. These are sold by bookstores and parks around the country.

○ You can also download and print maps from Geo Base (www.geogratis.gc.ca).

Money

○ All prices are quoted in Canadian dollars ($), unless stated otherwise.

○ Canadian coins come in 5¢ (nickel), 10¢ (dime), 25¢

(quarter), $1 (loonie) and $2 (toonie or twoonie) denominations. The gold-colored loonie features the loon, a common Canadian waterbird, while the two-toned toonie is decorated with a polar bear.

o Paper currency comes in $5, $10, $20 and $50 denominations. The $100 and larger bills are less common.

o For changing money in the larger cities, currency exchange offices may offer better conditions than banks.

ATMs

o Many grocery and convenience stores, airports, and bus, train and ferry stations have ATMs. Most are linked to international networks, the most common being Cirrus, Plus, Star and Maestro.

o Most ATMs also spit out cash if you use a major credit card; note that you will be charged interest immediately for cash withdrawals. For exact fees, check with your own bank or credit card company.

o Visitors heading to Canada's more remote regions won't find an abundance of ATMs; it is wise to cash up beforehand.

Cash

Most Canadians don't carry large amounts of cash around for everyday use, relying instead on credit and debit cards. Still, carrying some cash,

Practicalities

o **Newspapers** The most widely available newspaper is the Toronto-based *Globe and Mail*. Other principal dailies are the *Montréal Gazette, Ottawa Citizen, Toronto Star* and *Vancouver Sun*. *Maclean's* is Canada's weekly news magazine.

o **Radio & TV** The Canadian Broadcasting Corporation (CBC) is the dominant nationwide network for both radio and TV. The CTV Television Network is its major competition.

o **Smoking** Banned in all restaurants, bars and other public venues nationwide.

o **Weights & Measures** Canada officially uses the metric system, but imperial measurements are used for many day-to-day purposes.

say $100 or less, comes in handy when making small purchases. In some cases, cash is necessary to pay for rural B&Bs and shuttle vans; inquire in advance to avoid surprises.

Credit Cards

Major credit cards such as MasterCard, Visa and American Express are widely accepted throughout Canada, except in remote, rural communities, where cash is king. You'll find it difficult or impossible to rent a car, book a room or order tickets over the phone without having a piece of plastic. Note that some credit card companies charge a 'transaction fee' (around 3% of the purchase price); check with your provider to avoid surprises.

Taxes & Refunds

Canada's federal goods and services tax (GST) adds

on 5% to just about every transaction. Most provinces also charge a provincial sales tax (PST) on top of the GST. Several provinces have combined the GST and PST into a harmonized sales tax (HST). Whatever the methodology, expect to pay between 10% to 15% in most cases. Unless otherwise stated, taxes are not included in the prices that are given.

Tipping

Tipping is a standard practice. Generally you can expect to tip:

Bar staff $1 per drink

Hotel bellhop $1 to $2 per bag

Hotel room cleaners From $2 per day (depending on room size and messiness)

Restaurant waitstaff 15% to 20%

Taxis 10% to 15%

Opening Hours

Opening hours vary throughout the year. We've provided high-season opening hours; hours will generally decrease in the shoulder and low seasons.

Banks 10am–5pm Monday to Friday; some open 9am–noon Saturday

Bars 5pm–2am daily

Clubs 9pm–2am Wednesday to Saturday

Restaurants breakfast 8–11am and lunch 11:30am–2:30pm Monday to Friday, dinner 5–9:30pm daily; some open for brunch 8am to 1pm Saturday and Sunday

Shops 10am–6pm Monday to Saturday, noon–5pm Sunday; some open to 8pm or 9pm Thursday and/or Friday

Supermarkets 9am–8pm; some open 24 hours

Uniquely Canadian Celebrations

National Flag Day (February 15) Commemorates the first time the maple leaf flag was raised above Parliament Hill in Ottawa, at the stroke of noon on February 15, 1965.

Victoria Day (late May) This day was established in 1845 to observe the birthday of Queen Victoria and now celebrates the birthday of the British sovereign, who's still Canada's titular head of state. Victoria Day marks the official beginning of the summer season (which ends with Labour Day on the first Monday of September). Some communities hold fireworks.

National Aboriginal Day (June 21) Created in 1996, it celebrates the contributions of Aboriginal peoples to Canada. Coinciding with the summer solstice, festivities are organized locally and may include traditional dancing, singing and drumming; storytelling; arts and crafts shows; canoe races; and lots more.

Canada Day (July 1) Known as Dominion Day until 1982, Canada Day was created in 1869 to commemorate the creation of Canada two years earlier. All over the country, people celebrate with barbecues, parades, concerts and fireworks.

Thanksgiving Day (mid-October) First celebrated in 1578 in what is now Newfoundland by explorer Martin Frobisher to give thanks for surviving his Atlantic crossing, Thanksgiving became an official Canadian holiday in 1872 to celebrate the recovery of the Prince of Wales from a long illness. These days, it's essentially a harvest festival involving a special family dinner of roast turkey and pumpkin, very much as it is practiced in the US.

Public Holidays

Canada has 10 national public holidays and more at the provincial level. Banks, schools and government offices close on these days.

Kids break for summer holidays in late June and don't return to school until early September. University students get even more time off, usually from May to early or mid-September. Most people take their big annual vacation during these months.

New Year's Day January 1

Good Friday March or April

Easter Monday March or April

Victoria Day Monday before May 25

Canada Day July 1; called Memorial Day in Newfoundland

Labour Day First Monday of September

Thanksgiving Second Monday of October

Remembrance Day November 11

Christmas Day December 25

Boxing Day December 26

Provincial holidays include the following:

Family Day Third Monday of February in Alberta, Ontario, Saskatchewan and Manitoba (second Monday in British Columbia); known as Louis Riel Day in Manitoba

St Patrick's Day Monday nearest to March 17

St George's Day Monday nearest to April 23

National Day Monday nearest to June 24 in Newfoundland;

June 24 in Québec (aka St-Jean-Baptiste Day)

Orangemen's Day Monday nearest to July 12 in Newfoundland

Civic Holiday First Monday of August everywhere except Newfoundland, Québec and the Yukon

Discovery Day Third Monday of August in the Yukon

Safe Travel

○ Canada is one of the safest countries in the world. Pickpocketing and muggings are rare, especially if you take obvious precautions. Resource cities feeling the economic crunch have a slightly higher crime risk.

○ Drink spiking is not common but definitely happens, and sexual assault around bar and club scenes means women in particular should be vigilant.

○ Drug use in Canada is illegal, including marijuana and magic mushrooms. The government is proposing marijuana legalization in 2017 *with* restrictions. In Canada, ignorance of the law is not accepted as a legitimate excuse for breaking it.

Telephone

Canada's phone system is almost identical to the USA's system.

Domestic & International Dialing

○ Canadian phone numbers consist of a three-digit area code followed by a seven-digit local number. In many parts of Canada, you must dial all 10 digits preceded by 📞1, even if you're calling across the street. In other parts of the country, when you're calling within the same area code, you can dial the seven-digit number only, but this is slowly changing.

○ For direct international calls, dial 📞011 + country code + area code + local phone number. The country code for Canada is 📞1 (the same as for the USA, although international rates still apply for all calls made between the two countries).

○ Toll-free numbers begin with 📞800, 📞877, 📞866 or 📞855 and must be preceded by 📞1. Some of these numbers are good throughout Canada and the USA, others only work within Canada, and some work in one province.

Emergency Numbers

Dial 📞911. This is *not* the emergency number in the Yukon, Northwest Territories or Nunavut.

Mobile Phones

Local SIM cards can be used in unlocked GSM 850/1900 compatible phones. Other phones must be set to roaming.

○ If you have an unlocked GSM phone, you should be able to buy a SIM card from local providers such as Telus (www.telus.com), Rogers (www.rogers.com) or Bell (www.bell.ca). Bell has the best data coverage.

○ US residents can often upgrade their domestic cell phone plan to extend to Canada. Verizon (www.verizonwireless.com) provides good results.

○ Reception is poor and often nonexistent in rural areas no matter who your service provider is.

Phonecards

○ Prepaid phonecards usually offer the best per-minute rates for long-distance and international calling. They come in denominations of $5, $10 or $20 and are widely sold in drugstores, supermarkets and convenience stores. Beware of cards with hidden charges, such as 'activation fees' or a per-call connection fee.

○ A surcharge ranging from 30¢ to 85¢ for calls made from public pay phones is common.

Public Phones

Coin-operated public pay phones are fairly plentiful. Local calls cost 50¢; many phones also accept prepaid phonecards and credit cards. Dialing the operator (📞0) or directory assistance (📞411 for local calls; 📞1 + area code + 555-1212 for long-distance calls) is free of charge from public phones; it may incur a charge from private phones.

Time

o Canada spans six of the world's 24 time zones. The Eastern zone in Newfoundland is unusual in that it's only 30 minutes different from the adjacent zone. The time difference from coast to coast is 4½ hours.

o Canada observes daylight-saving time, which comes into effect on the second Sunday in March, when clocks are put forward one hour, and ends on the first Sunday in November. Saskatchewan and small pockets of Québec, Ontario and BC are the only areas that do not switch to daylight-saving time.

o In Québec especially, times for shop hours, train schedules, film screenings etc are usually indicated by the 24-hour clock.

Tourist Information

o The Canadian Tourism Commission (www.canada.travel) is loaded with general information, packages and links.

o All provincial tourist offices maintain comprehensive websites packed with information helpful in planning your trip. Staff also field telephone inquiries and, on request, will mail out free maps and directories about accommodations, attractions and events. Some offices can also help with making hotel, tour or other reservations.

o For detailed information about a specific area, contact the local tourist office, aka visitor center. Just about every city and town has at least a seasonal branch with helpful staff, racks of free pamphlets and books and maps for sale.

Travelers with Disabilities

Canada is making progress when it comes to easing the everyday challenges facing people with disabilities, especially the mobility-impaired.

o Many public buildings, including museums, tourist offices, train stations, shopping malls and cinemas, have access ramps and/or lifts. Most public restrooms feature extra-wide stalls equipped with hand rails. Many pedestrian crossings have sloping curbs.

o Newer and recently remodeled hotels, especially chain hotels, have rooms with extra-wide doors and spacious bathrooms.

o Interpretive centers at national and provincial parks are usually accessible, and many parks have trails that can be navigated in wheelchairs.

Accessible Travel Online Resource

Download Lonely Planet's free Accessible Travel guide from http://lptravel.to/AccessibleTravel.

o Car rental agencies offer hand-controlled vehicles and vans with wheelchair lifts at no additional charge, but you must reserve them well in advance.

o For accessible air, bus, rail and ferry transportation check Access to Travel (www.accesstotravel.gc.ca), the federal government's website. In general, most transportation agencies can accommodate people with disabilities if you make your needs known when booking.

Visas

o Visitors from certain countries require a visa to enter Canada. Those who are exempt – including most EU members, Australians and New Zealanders (for visits of up to six months) – require an Electronic Travel Authorization (eTA; $7), with the exception of Americans. This must be applied for prior to traveling and can be completed online. It usually takes minutes but can take days. See www.cic.gc.ca/english/visit/eta-start.asp.

○ To find out if you need an eTA or are required to apply for a formal visa, go to www.cic.gc.ca/english/visit/visas.asp.

○ Visitor visas – aka Temporary Resident Visas (TRVs) – can now be applied for online at: www.cic.gc.ca/english/information/applications/visa.asp. Single-entry TRVs ($100) are usually valid for a maximum stay of six months from the date of arrival in Canada.

○ A separate visa is required for all nationalities if you plan to study or work in Canada.

○ Visa extensions ($100) need to be filed with the CIC Visitor Case Processing Centre in Alberta at least one month before your current visa expires.

Visiting the USA

○ Admission requirements are subject to rapid change. The US State Department (www.travel.state.gov) has the latest information; you can also check with a US consulate in your home country.

○ Under the US visa-waiver program, visas are not required for citizens of 38 countries – including most EU members, Australia and New Zealand – for visits of up to 90 days (no extensions allowed), as long as you can present a machine-readable passport and are approved under the Electronic System for Travel Authorization (www.cbp.gov/esta). Note that

you must register at least 72 hours before arrival with an e-passport, and there's a $14 fee for processing and authorization.

○ Canadians do not need visas to enter the USA, though they do need a passport or document approved by the Western Hemisphere Travel Initiative (www.getyouhome.gov). Citizens of all other countries need to apply for a US visa in their home country before arriving in Canada.

○ All foreign visitors (except Canadians) must pay a US$6 processing fee when entering at land borders. Note that you don't need a Canadian multiple-entry TRV for repeated entries into Canada from the USA, unless you have visited a third country.

Women Travelers

Canada is generally a safe place for women to travel – use the same common sense as you would at home.

In bars and nightclubs, solo women are likely to attract a lot of attention, but if you don't want company, most men will respect a firm 'no, thank you.' If you feel threatened, protesting loudly will often make the offender slink away – or will at least spur other people to come to your defense. Note that carrying mace or pepper spray is illegal in Canada.

Physical attacks are unlikely, but if you are assaulted, call the police immediately (911 except in the Yukon, Northwest Territories and Nunavut) or contact a rape crisis center. A complete list is available from the **Canadian Association of Sexual Assault Centres** (🕿 800-726-2743; www.casac.ca).

Resources for women travelers:

Her Own Way (www.travel.gc.ca/travelling/publications/her-own-way) Published by the Canadian government for Canadian travelers, but contains a great deal of general advice.

Journeywoman (www.journeywoman.com) Travel links and tips for women, with a section on Canada.

Transport

Getting There & Away

Flights, cars and tours can be booked online at www.lonelyplanet.com/bookings.

Entering the Country

Visitors to Canada must hold a valid passport with at least six months remaining before its expiration. Visitors from visa-exempt countries (with the exception of the US) are required to purchase an

Climate Change & Travel

Every form of transportation that relies on carbon-based fuel generates CO_2, the main cause of human-induced climate change. Modern travel is dependent on aeroplanes, which might use less fuel per kilometre per person than most cars but travel much greater distances. The altitude at which aircraft emit gases (including CO_2) and particles also contributes to their climate change impact. Many websites offer 'carbon calculators' that allow people to estimate the carbon emissions generated by their journey and, for those who wish to do so, to offset the impact of the greenhouse gases emitted with contributions to portfolios of climate-friendly initiatives throughout the world. Lonely Planet offsets the carbon footprint of all staff and author travel.

electronic travel authorization (eTA, $7), similar to the USA's ESTA visa waiver, before departing their home country. Visitors from non-visa-waiver countries must apply for the appropriate visa prior to arriving in Canada.

Note that questioning may be more intense at land border crossings and your car may be searched.

For updates (particularly regarding land-border crossing rules), check the websites for the US State Department (www.travel.state.gov) and Citizenship & Immigration Canada (www.cic.gc.ca).

Passports

Most international visitors require a passport to enter Canada. US citizens at land and sea borders have other options, such as an enhanced driver's license, permanent resident card or NEXUS card. See Canada Border Services (www.cbsa-asfc.gc.ca) for approved identification documents.

Air

Airports & Airlines

Toronto is far and away Canada's busiest airport, followed by Vancouver. Air Canada (www.aircanada.com), the national flagship carrier, is considered one of the world's safest airlines. All major global airlines fly to Canada. Other companies based in the country and serving international destinations:

WestJet (www.westjet.com) Calgary-based low-cost carrier serving destinations throughout Canada as well as across the US and Caribbean.

Porter Airlines (www.flyporter.com) Flies around eastern Canada and to US cities, including Boston, Chicago, Washington, DC, and New York.

Air Transat (www.airtransat.com) Charter airline from major Canadian cities to holiday destinations (ie southern USA and Caribbean in winter, Europe in summer).

Land

Border Crossings

There are around 25 official border crossings along the US–Canada border, from New Brunswick to British Columbia.

The website of the Canadian Border Services Agency (www.cbsa-asfc.gc.ca) shows current wait times at each. You can also access it via Twitter (@CBSA_BWT).

In general, waits rarely exceed 30 minutes, except during the peak summer season, and on Friday and Sunday afternoons, especially on holiday weekends. Some entry points are especially busy:

- Windsor, Ontario, to Detroit, Michigan

- Fort Erie, Ontario, to Buffalo, New York

- Niagara Falls, Ontario, to Niagara Falls, New York

- Québec to Rouse's Point/Champlain, New York

- Surrey, British Columbia, to Blaine, Washington

When returning to the USA, check the website for the US Department for Homeland Security (http://apps.cbp.gov/bwt) for border wait times.

All foreign visitors (except Canadians) must pay a $6 processing fee when entering the USA by land; credit cards are not accepted.

Bus

Greyhound (www.grey hound.com) and its Canadian equivalent, Greyhound Canada (www.greyhound. ca), operate the largest bus network in North America. There are direct connections between main cities in the USA and Canada, but you usually have to transfer to a different bus at the border (where it takes a good hour for all passengers to clear customs/immigration). Most international buses have free wi-fi on board.

Other notable international bus companies (with free wi-fi) include:

Megabus (www.megabus.com) Runs between Toronto and US cities, including New York City, Philadelphia and Washington, DC; usually cheaper than Greyhound. Tickets can only be purchased online.

Quick Coach (www.quickcoach. com) Runs between Seattle and Vancouver; typically a bit quicker than Greyhound.

Car & Motorcycle

The highway system of the continental USA connects directly with the Canadian highway system at numerous points located along the border. These Canadian highways then meet up with the east–west Trans-Canada Hwy further north. Between the Yukon and Alaska, the main routes available are the Alaska, Klondike and Haines Hwys.

If you are driving into Canada, you will need the vehicle's registration papers, proof of liability insurance and your home driver's license. Cars that are rented in the USA can usually be driven into Canada and back, but make sure your rental agreement says so. If you are driving a car that is registered in someone else's name, then you should bring a letter from the owner authorizing use of the vehicle in Canada.

Train

Amtrak (www.amtrak.com) and VIA Rail Canada (www. viarail.ca) run three routes between the USA and Canada: two in the east and one in the west. Customs inspections happen at the Canada–USA border, not upon boarding.

Sea

Various ferry services on the coasts connect the USA and Canada:

○ Bar Harbor, Maine, to Yarmouth, Nova Scotia: Bay Ferries Limited (www. ferries.ca/thecat)

○ Eastport, Maine, to Deer Island, New Brunswick: East Coast Ferries (www. eastcoastferries.nb.ca).

○ Seattle to Victoria, BC: Victoria Clipper (www. clippervacations.com).

○ Alaska to Port Hardy, BC: Alaska Marine Highway System (www.ferryalaska.com).

○ Bella Bella, Alaska, to Prince Rupert, BC: BC Ferries (www.bcferries.com).

Getting Around

Air

Air Canada operates the largest domestic-flight network in the country, serving some 150 destinations.

The Canadian aviation arena also includes many independent regional and local airlines, which tend to focus on small, remote regions, mostly in the North. Depending on the destination, fares in such noncompetitive markets can be high.

Air Passes

Star Alliance (www.star alliance.com) members Air Canada, United Airlines and US Airways have teamed up to offer the North American Airpass, which is available to anyone not residing in the USA, Canada, Mexico, Bermuda or the Caribbean. It's sold only in conjunction with an international flight operated by any Star Alliance member airline. You can buy as few as three coupons (from US$399) or as many as 10.

Air North (www.flyair north.com) has an Arctic Circle Air Pass for those traveling around the Yukon and Northwest Territories.

Bicycle

Much of Canada is great for cycling. Long-distance trips can be done entirely on quiet back roads, and many cities (including Edmonton, Montréal, Ottawa, Toronto and Vancouver) have designated bike routes.

○ Cyclists must follow the same rules of the road as vehicles, but don't expect drivers to always respect your right of way.

○ Helmets are mandatory for all cyclists in British Columbia, New Brunswick, Prince Edward Island and Nova Scotia, as well as for anyone under 18 in Alberta and Ontario.

○ The Better World Club (www.betterworldclub. com) provides emergency roadside assistance. Membership costs $40 per year, plus a $12 enrollment fee, and entitles you to two free pickups, and transport to the nearest repair shop, or home, within a 50km radius of where you're picked up.

Transportation

By air Most airlines will carry bikes as checked luggage without charge on international flights, as long as they're in a box. On domestic flights they usually charge between $30 and $65. Always check details before you buy the ticket.

By bus You must ship your bike as freight on Greyhound Canada. In addition to a bike box ($10), you'll be charged an oversize charge and GST. Bikes only travel on the same bus as the passenger if there's enough space. To ensure that yours arrives at the same time as (or before) you do, ship it a day early.

By train VIA Rail will transport your bicycle for $25, but only on trains offering checked-baggage service (which includes all long-distance and many regional trains).

Rental

○ Outfitters renting bicycles exist in most tourist towns.

○ Rentals cost around $15 per day for touring bikes and $25 per day for mountain bikes. The price usually includes a helmet and lock.

○ Most companies require a security deposit of $20 to $200.

Boat

Ferry services are extensive, especially throughout the Atlantic provinces and in British Columbia.

Walk-ons and cyclists should be able to get aboard at any time, but call ahead for vehicle reservations or if you require a cabin berth. This is especially important during summer peak season and holidays. Main operators:

Bay Ferries (☑888-249-7245; www.ferries.ca) Year-round service between St John, New Brunswick, and Digby's, Nova Scotia.

BC Ferries (☑250-386-3431, 888-223-3779; www.bcferries. com) Huge passenger-ferry systems with 25 routes and 47 ports of call, including Vancouver Island, the Gulf Islands, the Sechelt Peninsula along the Sunshine Coast and the islands of Haida Gwaii – all in British Columbia.

CTMA Ferries (☑418-986-3278, 888-986-3278; www. ctma.ca) Daily ferries to Québec's Îles de la Madeleine from Souris, Prince Edward Island (PEI).

Labrador Marine (☑866-535-2567, 709-535-0810; www. labradormarine.com) Connects Newfoundland to Labrador.

Marine Atlantic (☑800-341-7981; www.marine-atlantic.ca) Connects Port aux Basques and Argentia in Newfoundland with North Sydney, Nova Scotia.

Northumberland Ferries (☑902-566-3838, 888-249-7245; www.ferries.ca) Connects Wood Islands (PEI) and Caribou, Nova Scotia.

Provincial Ferry Services (www.gov.nl.ca/ferryservices) Operates coastal ferry services throughout Newfoundland.

Bus

Greyhound Canada (☑800-661-8747; www.greyhound.ca) Is the king, plowing along an extensive network in central and western Canada, as well as to/from the USA. Regional carriers pick up the slack, especially in the east.

Buses are generally clean, comfortable and reliable. Amenities may include on-board toilets, air-conditioning (bring a sweater), reclining seats, free wi-fi and on-board movies. Smoking is not permitted. On long journeys, buses make meal stops every few hours, usually at highway service stations.

Car & Motorcycle

Automobile Associations

Autoclub membership is a handy thing to have in Canada. The Canadian Automobile Association (www.caa.ca) offers services, including 24-hour emergency roadside assistance, to members of international affiliates, such as AAA in the USA, AA in the UK and ADAC in Germany. The club also offers trip-planning advice, free maps, travel-agency services and a range of discounts on hotels, car rentals etc.

The Better World Club (www.betterworldclub.com), which donates 1% of its annual revenue to environmental cleanup efforts, has emerged as an alternative. It offers service throughout the USA and Canada, and has a roadside-assistance program for bicycles.

Bring Your Own Vehicle

There's minimal hassle driving into Canada from the USA as long as you have your vehicle's registration papers, proof of liability insurance and your home driver's license.

Fuel

Gas is sold in liters. Prices are higher in remote areas, with Yellowknife usually setting the national record; drivers in Calgary typically pay the least for gas.

Fuel prices are usually lower in the USA, so fill up south of the border.

Insurance

Canadian law requires liability insurance for all vehicles, to cover you for damage caused to property and people.

○ The minimum requirement is $200,000 in all provinces except Québec, where it is $50,000.

○ Americans traveling to Canada in their own car should ask their insurance company for a Nonresident Interprovince Motor Vehicle Liability Insurance Card (commonly known as a 'yellow card'), which is accepted as evidence of financial responsibility anywhere in Canada. Although not mandatory, it may come in handy in an accident.

○ Car-rental agencies offer liability insurance. Collision Damage Waivers (CDW) reduce or eliminate the amount you'll have to reimburse the rental company if there's damage to the car. Some credit cards cover CDW for a certain rental period if you use the card to pay for the rental and decline the policy offered by the rental company. Always check with your card issuer to see what coverage it offers in Canada.

○ Personal accident insurance (PAI) covers you and any passengers for medical costs incurred as a result of an accident. If your travel insurance or your health insurance policy at home does this (and most do, but check), then this is one expense you can do without.

Rental

Car

To rent a car in Canada you generally need to:

○ be at least 25 years old (some companies will rent to drivers between the ages of 21 and 24 for an additional charge);

○ hold a valid driver's license (an international one may be required if you're not from an English- or French-speaking country);

○ have a major credit card.

You should be able to get an economy-size vehicle for about $35 to $70 per day. Child safety seats are compulsory (reserve them when you book) and cost about $15 per day.

Major international car-rental companies usually have branches at airports, at train stations and in city centers.

In Canada, on-the-spot rentals often are more expensive than pre-booked packages (ie cars booked with a flight).

Motorcycle

Several companies offer motorcycle rentals and tours. A Harley Heritage Softail Classic costs about $210 per day, including liability insurance and 200km mileage. Some companies have minimum rental periods, which can be as much as seven days. Riding a hog is especially popular in British Columbia.

Car2Go

Car2Go (www.car2go. com) operates in Vancouver, Calgary, Montreal and Toronto. It costs $35 to join and then 41¢ per minute or $15 per hour to use a vehicle. You locate the cars with a smartphone app and then can park and leave them anywhere within the designated downtown zone.

Coastline Motorcycle (☑250-335-1837, 866-338-0344; www.coastlinemc.com) Tours and rentals out of Victoria and Vancouver in British Columbia.
McScoots Motorcycle & Scooter Rentals (☑250-763-4668; www.mcscoots.com) Big selection of Harleys; also operates motorcycle tours. It's based in Kelowna, British Columbia.

Recreational Vehicle

The RV market is biggest in the west, with specialized agencies in Calgary, Edmonton, Whitehorse and Vancouver. For summer travel, book as early as possible. The base cost is roughly $175 to $280 per day in high season for midsize vehicles, although insurance, fees and taxes add a hefty chunk to that. Diesel-fueled RVs have considerably lower running costs.
Canadream Campers (☑403-291-1000, 800-461-7368; www.canadream.com) Based in Calgary, with rentals (including one-way rentals) in eight cities,

including Vancouver, Whitehorse, Toronto and Halifax.
Cruise Canada (☑800-671-8042; www.cruisecanada.com) Offers three sizes of RVs. Locations in Halifax, and in central and western Canada; offers one-way rentals.

Road Rules

○ Canadians drive on the right-hand side of the road.

○ Seat belt use is compulsory in Canada. Children who weigh under 18kg must be strapped into child-booster seats, except infants, who must be in a rear-facing safety seat.

○ Motorcyclists must wear helmets and drive with their headlights on.

○ Distances and speed limits are posted in kilometers. The speed limit is generally 40km/h to 50km/h in cities and 90km/h to 110km/h outside town.

○ Slow down to 60km/h when passing emergency vehicles (such as police cars and ambulances) stopped on the roadside with their lights flashing.

○ Turning right at red lights after coming to a full stop is permitted in all provinces (except where road signs prohibit it, and on the island of Montréal, where it's always a no-no). There's a national propensity for running red lights, however, so don't assume 'right of way' at intersections.

○ Driving while using a hand-held cell phone is illegal in Canada. Fines are hefty.

○ Radar detectors are not allowed in most of Canada (Alberta, British Columbia and Saskatchewan are the exceptions). If you're caught driving with a radar detector, even one that isn't being operated, you could receive a fine of $1000 and your device may be confiscated.

○ The blood-alcohol limit for drivers is 0.08%. Driving while drunk is a criminal offense.

Local Transportation

Bicycle

Cycling is a popular means of getting around during the warmer months, and many cities have hundreds of kilometers of dedicated bike paths. Bicycles typically can be taken on public transportation (although some cities have restrictions during peak travel times). All the major cities have shops renting bikes. Vancouver, Toronto and Montréal have bike-share programs.

Bus

Buses are the most common form of public transportation, and practically all towns have their own systems. Most are commuter-oriented, and offer only limited or no services in the evenings and on weekends.

Train

Toronto and Montréal are the two Canadian cities with subway systems. Vancouver's version is mostly an above-ground monorail. Calgary and Ottawa have efficient light-rail systems. Route maps are posted in all stations.

Taxi

Most of the main cities have taxis and smaller towns have one or two. They are usually metered, with a flag-fall fee of roughly $2.70 and a per-kilometer charge of around $1.75. Drivers expect a tip of between 10% and 15%. Taxis can be flagged down or ordered by phone.

Train

VIA Rail (☑888-842-7245; www.viarail.ca) operates most of Canada's intercity and transcontinental passenger trains, chugging over 14,000km of track. In some remote parts of the country, such as Churchill, Manitoba, trains provide the only overland access.

● Rail service is most efficient in the corridor between Québec City and Windsor, Ontario – particularly between Montréal and Toronto, the two major hubs.

● The rail network does not extend to Newfoundland, Prince Edward Island or the Northwest Territories.

● Free wi-fi is available on most trains.

● Smoking is prohibited on all trains.

Classes

There are four main classes:

● Economy class buys you a fairly basic, if indeed quite comfortable, reclining seat with a headrest. Blankets and pillows are provided for overnight travel.

● Business class operates in the southern Ontario/Québec corridor. Seats are more spacious and have outlets for plugging in laptops. You also get a meal and priority boarding.

● Sleeper class is available on shorter overnight routes. You can choose from compartments with upper or lower pullout berths, and private single, double or triple roomettes, all with a bathroom.

● Touring class is available on long-distance routes and includes sleeper class accommodations plus meals, access to the sightseeing car and sometimes a tour guide.

Costs

Taking the train is more expensive than the bus, but most people find it more comfortable. June to mid-October is peak season, when prices are about 40% higher. Buying tickets in advance (even just five days before) can yield big savings.

Long-Distance Routes

VIA Rail has several classic trains:
Canadian A 1950s stainless-steel beauty between Toronto and Vancouver, zipping through the northern Ontario lake country, the western plains via Winnipeg and Saskatoon, and Jasper in the Rockies over three days.

Hudson Bay From the prairie (slowly) to the subarctic: Winnipeg to polar-bear hangout Churchill.

Ocean Chugs from Montréal along the St Lawrence River through New Brunswick and Nova Scotia.

Jasper to Prince Rupert An all-daylight route from Jasper, Alberta, to coastal Prince Rupert, British Columbia; there's an overnight stop in Prince George (you make your own hotel reservations).

Privately run regional train companies offer additional rail-touring opportunities:
Algoma Central Railway (www. agawatrain.com) Access to northern Ontario wilderness areas.

Ontario Northland (www. ontarionorthland.ca) Operates the seasonal Polar Bear Express from Cochrane to Moosonee on Hudson Bay (round-trip $112).

Royal Canadian Pacific (☑877-665-3044; www. royalcanadianpacific.com) A cruise-ship-like luxury line running between and around the Rockies via Calgary.

Rocky Mountaineer Railtours (www.rockymountaineer.com) Gape at Canadian Rockies scenery on swanky trains between Vancouver, Kamloops and Calgary (two days from $1000).

White Pass & Yukon Route (www.wpyr.com) Gorgeous route paralleling the original White Pass trail from Whitehorse, Yukon, to Fraser, British Columbia (round-trip $160).

Reservations

Seat reservations are highly recommended, especially in summer, on weekends and around holidays. During peak season (June to mid-October), some of the most popular sleeping arrangements are sold out months in advance, especially on long-distance trains such as the *Canadian*. The *Hudson Bay* often books solid during polar-bear season (around late September to early November).

Train Passes

VIA Rail offers a couple of passes that provide good savings:

○ The 'System' Canrailpass (from $699) is good for seven trips on any train during a 21-day period. All seats are in economy class; upgrades are not permitted. You must book each leg at least three days in advance (which you can do online).

○ The 'Corridor' Canrailpass (from $299) is good for seven trips during a 10-day period on trains in the Québec City–Windsor corridor (which includes Montréal, Toronto and Niagara).

Language

English and French are the official languages of Canada. You'll see both on highway signs, maps, tourist brochures, packaging etc. In Québec the preservation of French is a major concern. Here, road signs and visitor information is often in French only.

New Brunswick is the only officially bilingual province but French is widely spoken, particularly in the north and east. Nova Scotia also has a significant French-speaking population, and there are pockets in most other provinces.

The French spoken in Canada is essentially the same as in France. Although many English-speaking (and most French-speaking) students in Québec are still taught the French of France, the local tongue is known as 'Québecois' or joual.

French sounds can almost all be found in English. The exceptions are nasal vowels (represented in our pronunciation guides by o or u followed by an almost inaudible nasal consonant sound m, n or ng), the 'funny' *u* (ew in our guides) and the deep-in-the-throat *r*. Bearing this in mind and reading the pronunciation guides here as if they were English, you'll be understood just fine.

Basics

Hello.	Bonjour.	bon·zhoor
Goodbye.	Au revoir.	o·rer·vwa
Excuse me.	Excusez-moi.	ek·skew·zay·mwa
Sorry.	Pardon.	par·don
Yes./No.	Oui./Non.	wee/non
Please.	S'il vous plaît.	seel voo play
Thank you.	Merci.	mair·see

How are you?
Comment allez-vous? ko·mon ta·lay·voo

Fine, and you?
Bien, merci. Et vous? byun mair·see ay voo

My name is ...
Je m'appelle ... zher ma·pel ...

What's your name?
Comment vous appelez-vous? ko·mon voo·za·play voo

Do you speak English?
Parlez-vous anglais? par·lay·voo ong·glay

I don't understand.
Je ne comprends pas. zher ner kom·pron pa

Directions

Where's ...?
Où est ...? oo ay ...

What's the address?
Quelle est l'adresse? kel ay la·dres

Could you write the address, please?
Est-ce que vous pourriez écrire l'adresse, s'il vous plaît? es·ker voo poo·ryay ay·kreer la·dres seel voo play

Can you show me (on the map)?
Pouvez-vous m'indiquer (sur la carte)? poo·vay·voo mun·dee·kay (sewr la kart)

Eating & Drinking

A table for (two), please.
Une table pour (deux), s'il vous plaît. ewn ta·bler poor (der) seel voo play

What would you recommend?
Qu'est-ce que vous conseillez? kes·ker voo kon·say·yay

What's in that dish?
Quels sont les ingrédients? kel son lay zun·gray·dyon

I'm a vegetarian.
Je suis végétarien/ végétarienne. zher swee vay·zhay·ta·ryun/ vay·zhay·ta·ryen (m/f)

I don't eat ...
Je ne mange pas ... zher ner monzh pa ...

That was delicious.
C'était délicieux! say·tay day·lee·syer

Please bring the bill.
Apportez-moi l'addition, s'il vous plaît. a·por·tay·mwa la·dee·syon seel voo play

Behind the Scenes

Acknowledgements

Climate map data adapted from Peel MC, Finlayson BL & McMahon TA (2007) 'Updated World Map of the Koppen-Geiger Climate Classification', Hydrology and Earth System Sciences, 11, pp1633–44.

This Book

This book was curated by Korina Miller and researched and written by Kate Armstrong, James Bainbridge, Adam Karlin, John Lee, Carolyn McCarthy, Korina Miller, Phillip Tang, Ryan Ver Berkmoes and Benedict Walker. This guidebook was produced by the following:

Destination Editor Alexander Howard

Product Editor Alison Ridgway

Senior Cartographer Corey Hutchison

Book Designer Mazzy Prinsep

Assisting Editors Kate Chapman, Kate Kiely, Kate Mathews, Susan Paterson, Gabrielle Stefanos, Saralinda Turner

Assisting Cartographers Alison Lyall, Anthony Phelan

Assisting Book Designers Cam Ashley, Clara Monito

Cover Researcher Naomi Parker

Thanks to Liz Heynes, Andi Jones, Jenna Myers, Tony Wheeler, Amanda Williamson

Send Us Your Feedback

We love to hear from travelers – your comments keep us on our toes and help make our books better. Our well-traveled team reads every word on what you loved or loathed about this book. Although we cannot reply individually to postal submissions, we always guarantee that your feedback goes straight to the appropriate authors, in time for the next edition. Each person who sends us information is thanked in the next edition, the most useful submissions are rewarded with a selection of digital PDF chapters.

Visit lonelyplanet.com/contact to submit your updates and suggestions or to ask for help. Our award-winning website also features inspirational travel stories, news and discussions.

Note: We may edit, reproduce and incorporate your comments in Lonely Planet products such as guidebooks, websites and digital products, so let us know if you don't want your comments reproduced or your name acknowledged. For a copy of our privacy policy visit lonelyplanet.com/privacy.

A — Z
Index

Symbols & Map Key

Look for these symbols to quickly identify listings:

- ◉ Sights
- ✪ Activities
- ◎ Courses
- ◉ Tours
- ✪ Festivals & Events
- ✪ Eating
- ◎ Drinking
- ✪ Entertainment
- ◎ Shopping
- ❶ Information & Transport

These symbols and abbreviations give vital information for each listing:

- 🌱 Sustainable or green recommendation
- **FREE** No payment required

- ☎ Telephone number
- ◷ Opening hours
- Ⓟ Parking
- ☻ Nonsmoking
- ❄ Air-conditioning
- @ Internet access
- ☎ Wi-fi access
- ☒ Swimming pool

- ▣ Bus
- ☒ Ferry
- ▣ Tram
- ▣ Train
- ◙ English-language menu
- ✎ Vegetarian selection
- ⚢ Family-friendly

Find your best experiences with these Great For... icons.

- Art & Culture
- Beaches
- Budget
- Cafe/Coffee
- Cycling
- Detour
- Drinking
- Entertainment
- Events
- Family Travel
- Food & Drink
- History
- Local Life
- Nature & Wildlife
- Photo Op
- Scenery
- Shopping
- Short Trip
- Sport
- Walking
- Winter Travel

Sights

- Beach
- Bird Sanctuary
- Buddhist
- Castle/Palace
- Christian
- Confucian
- Hindu
- Islamic
- Jain
- Jewish
- Monument
- Museum/Gallery/ Historic Building
- Ruin
- Shinto
- Sikh
- Taoist
- Winery/Vineyard
- Zoo/Wildlife Sanctuary
- Other Sight

Points of Interest

- Bodysurfing
- Camping
- Cafe
- Canoeing/Kayaking
- Course/Tour
- Diving
- Drinking & Nightlife
- Eating
- Entertainment
- Sento Hot Baths/ Onsen
- Shopping
- Skiing
- Sleeping
- Snorkelling
- Surfing
- Swimming/Pool
- Walking
- Windsurfing
- Other Activity

Information

- Bank
- Embassy/Consulate
- Hospital/Medical
- Internet
- Police
- Post Office
- Telephone
- Toilet
- Tourist Information
- Other Information

Geographic

- Beach
- Gate
- Hut/Shelter
- Lighthouse
- Lookout
- Mountain/Volcano
- Oasis
- Park
- Pass
- Picnic Area
- Waterfall

Transport

- Airport
- BART station
- Border crossing
- Boston T station
- Bus
- Cable car/Funicular
- Cycling
- Ferry
- Metro/MRT station
- Monorail
- Parking
- Petrol station
- Subway/S-Bahn/ Skytrain station
- Taxi
- Train station/Railway
- Tram
- Tube Station
- Underground/ U-Bahn station
- Other Transport

written articles on travel, culture and investment that have appeared in the likes of *BBC Travel,* the UK *Guardian* and *Independent, Condé Nast Traveller* and *Lonely Planet Traveller.*

Adam Karlin

Born in Washington, DC and raised in the rural Maryland tidewater, Adam has been exploring the world and writing about it since he was 17, and considers it a blessedly interesting way to live one's life – and also good fun.

John Lee

Originally from the UK, John moved to British Columbia to study at the University of Victoria in the 1990s. Eventually staying and moving to Vancouver, he started a freelance travel-writing career in 1999. Since then, he's been covering the region and beyond for Lonely Planet and other magazines, newspapers and online outlets around the world. He is a winner of numerous writing awards, a weekly columnist for Canada's *The Globe & Mail* national newspaper and very active on Twitter; catch up with him at www.johnleewriter.com and @johnleewriter.

Carolyn McCarthy

Carolyn specializes in travel, culture and adventure in the Americas. She has written for *National Geographic, Outside, BBC Magazine, Boston Globe* and other publications. A former Fulbright fellow and Banff Mountain Grant recipient, she has documented life in the most remote corners of Latin America. Carolyn gained her expertise by researching guidebooks in diverse destinations. She has contributed to more than 30 guidebooks for Lonely Planet, including Colorado, USA, Argentina, Chile, Panama, Peru and the USA National Parks guides. She is also the author of Lonely Planet's *Trekking in the Patagonian Andes.*

Phillip Tang

Phillip grew up on typically Australian *pho* and fish'n'chips. A degree in Chinese and Latin-American cultures launched him into travel and writing about it for Lonely Planet's *Canada, China, Japan, Korea, Mexico, Peru* and *Vietnam* guides. Phillip has made his home in Sydney, Melbourne, London and Mexico City. His travels include most countries in Europe, much of Asia and Latin America, as well as the greatest hits of North America. More pics and words: philliptang.co.uk.

Ryan Ver Berkmoes

Ryan has written more than 110 guidebooks for Lonely Planet. He grew up in Santa Cruz, California, which he left at age 17 for college in the Midwest, where he first discovered snow. All joy of this novelty soon wore off. Since then he has been traveling the world, both for pleasure and for work – which are often indistinguishable. He has covered everything from wars to bars. He definitely prefers the latter. Ryan calls New York City home. Read more at ryanverberkmoes.com and at @ryanvb.

Benedict Walker

Born in Newcastle, Australia, Ben holds notions of the beach as core to his idea of self, though he's traveled hundreds of thousands of kilometers from the sandy shores of home. Ben was given his first Lonely Planet guide (*Japan*) when he was 12. Two decades later, he'd write chapters for the same publication: a dream come true. A communications graduate and travel agent by trade, Ben whittled away his twenties gallivanting around the globe. He thinks the best thing about travel isn't as much about where you go as who you meet: living vicariously through the stories of kind strangers enriches one's own experience. Ben has also written and directed a play, and toured Australia managing the travel logistics for top-billing music festivals.

Our Story

A beat-up old car, a few dollars in the pocket and a sense of adventure. In 1972 that's all Tony and Maureen Wheeler needed for the trip of a lifetime – across Europe and Asia overland to Australia. It took several months, and at the end – broke but inspired – they sat at their kitchen table writing and stapling together their first travel guide, *Across Asia on the Cheap*. Within a week they'd sold 1500 copies. Lonely Planet was born.

Today, Lonely Planet has offices in Franklin, London, Melbourne, Oakland, Dublin, Beijing, and Delhi, with more than 600 staff and writers. We share Tony's belief that 'a great guidebook should do three things: inform, educate and amuse'.

Our Writers

Korina Miller

Korina grew up on Vancouver Island and has been exploring the globe independently since she was 16, visiting or living in 36 countries and picking up a degree in Communications and Canadian Studies, an MA in Migration Studies and a diploma in Visual Arts en route. As a writer and editor, Korina has worked on nearly 60 titles for Lonely Planet and has also worked with the BBC, the *Independent,* the *Guardian,* BBC5 and CBC, plus many independent magazines, covering travel, art and culture. She has recently set up camp back in Victoria, soaking up the mountain views and the pounding surf. Korina curated this guidebook, and also wrote the Plan, In Focus and Survival Guide.

Kate Armstrong

Kate has spent much of her adult life traveling and living around the world. A full-time freelance travel journalist, she has contributed to around 40 Lonely Planet guides and trade publications and is regularly published in Australia and worldwide. She is the author of several books and children's educational titles.

James Bainbridge

James is a British travel writer and journalist based in Cape Town, South Africa, from where he roams the globe and contributes to publications worldwide. He has been working on Lonely Planet projects for more than a decade, updating dozens of guidebooks and hosting TV productions everywhere from the African bush to the Great Lakes. The coordinating author of several editions of Lonely Planet's *South Africa, Lesotho & Swaziland, Turkey* and *Morocco* guides, he has

More Writers

STAY IN TOUCH LONELYPLANET.COM/CONTACT

AUSTRALIA The Malt Store, Level 3, 551 Swanston St, Carlton, Victoria 3053 ☑ 03 8379 8000, fax 03 8379 8111

IRELAND Unit E, Digital Court. The Digital Hub, Rainsford St, Dublin 8, Ireland

USA 124 Linden Street, Oakland, CA 94607 ☑ 510 250 6400, toll free 800 275 8555, fax 510 893 8572

UK 240 Blackfriars Road, London SE1 8NW ☑ 020 3771 5100, fax 020 3771 5101

 twitter.com/ lonelyplanet

facebook.com/ lonelyplanet

instagram.com/ lonelyplanet

youtube.com/ lonelyplanet

lonelyplanet.com/ newsletter